CASS LIBRARY OF AFRICAN STUDIES

GENERAL STUDIES

No. 90

Editorial Adviser : JOHN RALPH WILLIS
Department of History, University of California, Berkeley

I.—Ready for a *Bori* Spirit. II.—Possessed.

Bori is self-induced hysteria. During possession by the spirits, the patients imitate certain persons or animals, and often ill-treat themselves. The spirit is usually expelled by sneezing. *Vide* page 145 and Note III.

Hausa Superstitions and Customs

An Introduction to the Folk-Lore and the Folk

BY

A. J. N. TREMEARNE

With a new introductory note by
MERVYN HISKETT

*With forty-one illustrations, over two hundred
figures in the text, and a map*

Routledge
Taylor & Francis Group

LONDON AND NEW YORK

First published 1913 by
FRANK CASS AND COMPANY LIMITED

Published 2013 by Routledge
2 Park Square, Milton Park, Abingdon, Oxfordshire OX14 4RN
711 Third Avenue, New York, NY, 10017

First issued in paperback 2014

Routledge is an imprint of the Taylor & Francis Group, an informa business

New Introductory Note Copyright © 1970 M. Hiskett

ISBN 13: 978-0-714-61729-9 (hbk)
ISBN 13: 978-1-138-01094-9 (pbk)

INTRODUCTORY NOTE TO
THE NEW EDITION

The general background to Hausa folklore has been
admirably dealt with by M. G. Smith and Neil Skinner
in the *Foreword* and *Introduction* to the latter's translation of Edgar's *Tatsuniyoyi.** In this present *Introduction* I shall therefore confine myself, briefly, to
discussing the importance of Tremeane's collection in
relation to African Islamic Studies.

It is possible to categorize Hausa folkore in a
number of different ways. Tremeane himself did so
largely by subject matter, as the titles of his chapters
make clear. But it may be that an attempt to classify
the tales culturally will lead in the end to a deeper
understanding of the cultural history of the society in
which they arose.

There are two broad cultural periods in pre-colonial
Hausa history — the pre-Islamic period and the period
of Islam. The folklore reflects this division; but it also
raises many questions.

Hausa folklore is rich in the world-wide motifs
found in one form or the other in such widely dif-
fering cultures as those of India, Scandinavia, America,
Ireland and so on. For instance, as Tremeane points
out, Cinderella appears among the Hausa; so does Jack
the Giant Killer; the child-eating witch and many
other familiar characters of European folklore. But in
the midst of this mass of "world-wide" material, the
ultimate provenance of which it is almost certainly
impossible to trace, there appear a number of motifs
that seem, clearly enough to be Indian. These I have

*Volume One, in which the *Foreword* and *Introduction* appear,
was published by Frank Cass in 1969. Volumes Two and
Three will appear in 1970.

discussed in some detail elsewhere.* Particular examples which will be familiar to those even casually acquainted with Hausa stories are "Auta, the youngest son" the story of the clever francolin and that of the grateful fish. To assume that these stories came directly from India would be rash. But that they have a common motif with the Indian stories seems beyond question and their presence in Hausaland is chronologically and culturally puzzling. Is it to be explained by some remote link with the Indian sub-continent; or did the stories originate in Africa and spread from there to other parts of the world?

But there are other stories in Hausa folklore which can be more readily traced back to their origins. For instance the well-known Arabic collection of stories *Kalila wa Dhimna* has certainly contributed to Hausa folklore. So also has the famous early medieval Arabic 'Book of Songs' (Kitab *al-aghani*). Another most important source of Hausa stories is the Muslim 'Tales of the Prophets' (*Qisas al-anbiya*) of al-Thalabi. This important work of the eleventh century records the Old Testament stories of the prophets in their Islamized forms, together with certain stories arising from the purely Muslim tradition. Thus the presence of the *Qisas* in West African Muslim communities accounts at once for the currency of stories about Abraham, Solomon, the Alexander cycle and numerous Biblical and Hebraic motifs which are reflected in Tremeane's collection as well as in other compilations of Hausa folklore. This is of great historical importance, for many romantic theories have been erected linking West Africa with the Mediterranean world of antiquity on the strength of these Biblical echoes in West African mythology. Yet most of them are readily to be explained by the presence of the *Qisas* in the hands of literate West African Muslims in the course of the last two or three hundred years.

*'Historical and Islamic influences in Hausa folklore', Journal of the Folklore Institute, Indiana University, Vol. IV, Nos. 2/3.

Equally important as a source for Hausa stories is the great Islamic Saga of Saif b. Dhi Yazan, the legendary hero of the Arabs' wars against the Ethiopians. Versions of this story in which an Islamic cult hero wages war against the pagan negroes circulate widely in the Muslim Sudanic belt of West Africa and they are also to be associated with the common myth of Yemenite origin. One of the most interesting avenues of research now open to students of West African Islam seems to me to be to discover what part the Saif legend has played in West African folklore and to what extent it has been naturalized to conform to the history of the Hausas and other Islamic groups and to reflect their own confrontation with indigenous African animism.

The place of the Arabian Nights in the folklore of any Muslim or partially islamized society hardly needs emphasizing. But the Nights themselves are a complex body of folklore and they have their own chronology and history. Islamic scholars have indicated the existence of an early Persian and Indian stratum, much of it bawdy stuff that found its way by many routes into the Decameron cycle; then a later Baghdad stratum which seems to portray the mores and the rather institutionalized morality of medieval Islamic society and finally a late Cairene stratum, full of fantastic tales of genii, miraculous treasures, talismanic service and other wonders. In studying the local folklores of peoples on the fringes of the Islamic world, one would like to know not only that the Nights had contributed their share – a fact which can almost be taken for granted – but also from which strata of the Arabian stories they had drawn and what changes the stories had undergone in the process of naturalization. For instance, it would be reasonable to expect that the late Cairene stories would predominate in Hausa folklore, and this may indeed turn out to be the case; but it certainly seems to me that the earlier Indian and Persia cycle has been equally important while the Baghdad cycle does not seem to be so conspicuous.

But these are merely first impressions and much more research is needed either to confirm or disprove them.

The publication of this second impression of Tremeane's work, together with the publication of Skinner's translation of Edgar's *Tatsuniyoyi* are important events in the history of Hausa studies and they are particularly welcome at a time when there is a growing interest among students in the background of ideas that inform African cultures as well as in the phenomena of African languages and the structures of African societies. But this material should not be seen as exclusively African. It is also part of the general Islamic heritage and contains a wealth of evidence to enable us to explain and understand the nature of the Islamic presence in Africa.

July 1969   M. HISKETT

Foreword.

In offering this volume on the Hausas, who are interesting, not only on account of their beliefs and habits, but also because of the services of their soldiers to the Empire, I wish to express my best thanks to Messrs. Hartland and Crooke (ex-President and President respectively of the Folk-lore Society) for supplying many parallels to the tales—marked (H) or (C) *ad hoc;* to Professors Frazer and Westermarck for reading Part I; to Lieut. G. R. K. Evatt for several photographs, and for comparing my material with his own notes; to Mrs. Mary Gaunt, Colonel Elliot, Major Searight, the Royal Geographical Society, and the Royal Anthropological Institute for five photographs; and, lastly, to my wife for correcting the proofs, and to her friend, Miss E. M. Clarke, for most of the figures—some of which were drawn at the British Museum through the courtesy of the authorities there.

A. J. N. T.

Blackheath,
    September 27, 1912.

Abbreviations and References.

In Part I, figures in parentheses, *e.g.* (40), refer to the tales in Part II, while the Roman numerals, *e.g.,* XL, refer to the notes in Part III.

In Part II, a figure in parentheses refers to the number of a note in Part III under a Roman numeral corresponding to the number of the tale; thus (2) in Story 41 refers to Note XLI, 2. An asterisk after a word (*e.g.,* spit* in Stories 14 and 83) means that it has been purposely mistranslated. The correct rendering will be sent with pleasure to anyone who requires it for scientific purposes.

For the meanings of T.H.H., &c., see pages 9 and 10.

CONTENTS

Contents.

CONTENTS

CONTENTS

Illustrations.

PLATES.

ILLUSTRATIONS

FIGURES IN THE TEXT.

FIG. I.—Leather pillow. Most of the designs are made with black or red stain upon yellow leather, but the round spots are of green plush upon brown leather, and the arcs are of purple plush upon light green leather. The back of the pillow—which has an opening for the reception of the cotton stuffing—is of red leather of the same shade as the binding of this book. L., 36¼ in.

PART I.

Folk-lore and Folk-law.

CHAPTER I.

INTRODUCTION.

The People—Value of Folk-Lore—The Narrators—Difficulties of Collecting — Authorities — Commencement and Ending of Stories.

THE principal habitat of the Hausawa—or, as we call them, the Hausas—comprises the Hausa States, forming the greater part of what is now Northern Nigeria, which is British territory, a good deal of the French Possessions to the west, and also the hinterland of the Gold Coast. But the people, being great travellers and traders, are met with all over the Sudan, and many colonies have been established between Tripoli and Tunis in the north and the Bight of Benin in the south. Whether they came originally from the east or north-east, or whether they are indigenous, is still a moot question which is argued elsewhere.* At any rate, probably everyone will admit that they are a mixture of mixtures, and so it should not be surprising that we can recognize many familiar anecdotes in the tales collected in the West Sudan.

VALUE OF FOLK-LORE.—Many people regard folk-lore as being nothing but "a collection of silly stories," a kind of "serious foolishness"; and it must be admitted that legends and myths are likely to descend to such a level amongst civilized peoples, who neglect to study them, and retain them merely as nursery rhymes. But in their original form they contain much wisdom, or "lore," and they throw so much light upon the religious and legal systems of the inhabitants of the district in which they arise, that, in this early stage of its existence, a certain class of folk-lore is to a great extent an enunciation of folk-law. It will become more evident that this is so when we remember that ancient customs have often been brought to light in trials (*e.g.*, of witchcraft) before English courts—what, indeed was the Common Law?—and this continues here even in the present time, especially where land is concerned. In Northern Nigeria, a Resident has a book for "Informal Cases" in addition to the ordinary "Court Minute Book," and in it are entered accounts of trials —particularly marriage disputes—which, in the judge's opinion, should not be conducted in the ordinary man-

---

* *The Niger and the West Sudan* (Hodder and Stoughton), pages 51-64. I maintain that they came from the neighbourhood of Meroë, and that—although they have but little more connection with the Abyssinians than the Kafirs of South Africa have with the Kafirs of India—the words *Ba-haushe* (the Hausa's name for himself) and *Babushe* (a mythical ancestor) came from *Ba* (descendant) and *Habbeshi* (mixture). The fact that they still pay tribute to the Gwandara (who once owned most of the country) at certain festivals, points to a non-indigenous origin.

ner, because, being governed by native custom, English law is inapplicable to them. In other words, the Government recognizes that these customs are actually local laws, and that the parties must be tried in accordance with them, so long as they are fair and reasonable, and have not been specially barred.*

If, therefore, the tales are to have any scientific value at all, they must be related as nearly as possible in the very words of the original version, varied (according to the individual talents of the narrator) solely as regards the mode of recitation and gesture. The only real discretion allowed to the narrator should be the insertion of a few peculiar passages from other traditions—and in fact portions of variants are often introduced, as is mentioned in the notes—but even in that case no alteration of these original or elementary materials used in the composition of tales should be made, although it sometimes takes place. Generally (in theory) the smallest deviation from the original version will be taken notice of and corrected if any intelligent person happens to be present, but it is very difficult to persuade one Hausa to tell a story in the presence of another. However, this has not proved a very serious loss, for I have read the books written by other Hausa students, and have pointed out the variations where this seemed desirable.

At any rate, the reader may be assured that the tales have been gathered direct from the lips of illiterate story-tellers, and that they have been set down with accuracy and good faith. An authority says : " Every

---

* In this respect, Italy has set an example to the world, for the Italian troops were instructed in native beliefs before leaving their own country, so that they would not unnecessarily offend even the people against whom they were to fight.

turn of phrase, awkward or coarse though it may seem
to cultured ears, must be unrelentingly reported; and
every grotesquery, each strange word, or incompre-
hensible or silly incident, must be given without flinch-
ing. Any attempt to soften down inconsistencies,
vulgarities or stupidities, detracts from the value of the
text, and may hide or destroy something from which
the student may be able to make a discovery of importance to science."* Unfortunately some of the Hausa
vulgarities are unprintable, and where this is so, I have
purposely altered the offensive word, but in each case
it has been marked with an asterisk (*) so that no false
deduction may be drawn, *e.g.,* in Story 45.

I have examined carefully every story given here,
and have tried to get the most out of it, and, in addition, a great deal of other information (usually confirm-
ing or denying something in a tale) has been inserted.
One cannot depend absolutely upon the tales, for it is
sometimes difficult to distinguish between the original
event and pure fiction; slight changes take place, as
has been indicated; and lastly, stories (and here also
the people) travel, and pick up local characteristics *en
route.* Still, I hope that, in spite of its shortcomings, the
work will be of service—even of value—to the conscientious student of the people, whether he be an
administrator, or merely an amateur anthropologist,
and it is for this reason that so many figures have been
given in the text, for they can hardly fail to prove
useful in giving a good idea of the culture attained.
Probably, too, those general readers who have not
previously paid much attention to Hausa folk-lore, will
see that a fable may be more than a silly story if
analysed and understood.

---

* E. S. Hartland, *The Science of Fairy Tales*, page 21.

In *The Tailed Head-Hunters of Nigeria,* I en-
deavoured, by comparing the customs of some Nigerian
savages with those of civilized peoples, to show that,
after all, humanity, whatever the colour, has much in
common. In this book, I have striven to reach the
same end by a comparison of the folk-lore.*

THE NARRATORS.—Nearly all of the hundred tales
in this volume were obtained during 1908 and 1909
at Jemaan Daroro, in the Nassarawa Province of
Northern Nigeria. A few had been told me previously
(in 1906-1907) when in Amar, the headquarters of the
Muri Province, by Ashetu, a policeman's wife, but all
the subsequent ones were related by men. Women and
children are said to be the best story-tellers, and
naturally so, but I found them difficult to get hold
of, and nervous and easily tired, so I had to rely
mainly upon my own sex, the narrators being Privates
Ba Gu(d)du and Umoru Gombe, of the 1st Northern
Nigeria Regiment of the " W.A.F.F.," the Sar(r)ikin
Dukawa (Chief of the Leather-workers), and Momo
Kano and Mohamma, personal servants. So as to
distinguish them, each story is marked in the Table of
Contents with the initial of the person who told it to me.
The best Hausa was spoken by the last named, but
all were illiterate, and only two of them had even a
smattering of English. I urged Momo Kano to learn
the Hausa written characters, but he never got further
than learning their names, although merely on account
of this mild qualification, he wished to shave his hair
and wear a turban like a malam, or learned man. I

---

* At the same time, however much alike the early ideas may
have been, we must be careful to admit that the subsequent
development of white and black has been very different, and that
there is absolutely no reason to suppose that Europeans and
negroes can now be educated and trained upon similar lines.

hope that what he did proved useful to him on his way
to the next world—for he is now dead, I very much
regret to say.

DIFFICULTIES OF COLLECTING.—There are several
difficulties in the way of the collector. First, one has to
gain the confidence of the native, and that is an exceedingly difficult thing for an official to accomplish, because
even his most innocent inquiries are suspected.   Who
in England would give more information than he could
help to a person who was both judge and tax-collector ?

But that is not all by any means.   However hard
one may study the language, there will be many words
which one does not understand, and it is almost impossible for most students to keep pace with some of
the narrators.   To interrupt a native for an
explanation may often disturb him so much that
he loses the thread of the tale; to go on may
mean that one forgets to inquire afterwards,
or may not have the chance to do so again, as has
happened to me in several cases.   Then, many of the
speeches are sung in a falsetto voice, which alters
the sounds and even the accents of syllables, the latter,
in any case, being frequently carried along in Hausa
composite words, or in words followed by a pro-
noun.

But, as Mr. Hartland says, it is common for the
rustic story-teller to be unable to explain expressions,
and indeed whole episodes, in any other way than could
the immortal Uncle Remus, when called upon to say
who Miss Meadows was : " She wuz in de tale, Miss
Meadows en de gals wuz, en de tale I give you like
hi't wer' gun ter me."   I am not the only collector who
has discovered that when the tales had " sung parts,"
sometimes even they who sang them could scarcely

explain the meaning, especially when non-Hausa words had been introduced by some intermediate narrator. I sometimes found that, although several men would give certain sentences in exactly the same way, not one really understood what they meant, and I had to ask the assistance of the Alkali, or native judge—as being

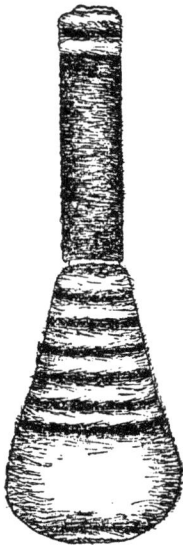

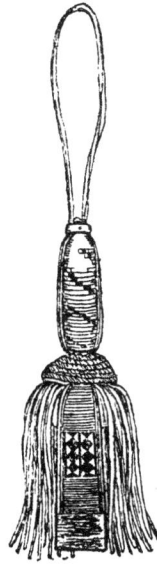

Fig. 2.   Fig. 3.

Fig. 2.—Antimony bottle of parchment, covered with alternate strips of hide (with hair left on) of white, black, and brown. H., 3¾ in.

Fig. 3.—Antimony bottle of parchment, covered with leather. The lower part is of red leather, with pattern in black, the upper part is of plaited green and black strips. The leather loop (to hang on wrist or girdle) keeps the bottle in position. L., of bottle 7¼ in.

the best educated man in Jemaa—to help me out of the difficulty. Thus, in Hausaland, as elsewhere, the popular memory may persist long after the proper explanation has disappeared. There are one or two words which I have been unable to translate, and, rather than make a guess, I have left them in the original Hausa,

so that others may see and perhaps be able to explain
them.   After all, how many English story-tellers can
give the meaning of " Fe Fi Fo Fum " ?

Again, the story-teller, if paid so much per tale, is
apt to skip certain parts which he thinks would puzzle
the listener, and, if paid by time, he may add on portions of other stories, so as to avoid the trouble of
thinking out a whole fresh one.   Or, perhaps the fault
may not be his at all; he may have heard only a
mutilated version, an example of which may be seen
in No. 39, and that is all, therefore, that he can hand
on.

In many Hausa tales a character is suddenly introduced, and as his name will probably not be mentioned
for some time, the listener is apt to become confused
when this sort of thing takes place : " He said, ' Take
this.'   He took it.   He said ' I thank you.'   He said
' Come again to-morrow.'   He said ' I give you this.'
He said ' Good-bye until to-morrow.'   He said ' I am
going home.'   He said ' Very well.'   He went home."
Sometimes, too, a good deal will be understood, *e.g.*,
" She said ' To-morrow you must go.'   As she was
travelling," &c.   The whole mention of her departure on
the following day has been omitted.   In these cases
I have supplied the missing information, but it appears
within square brackets so as to distinguish it from
remarks in parentheses actually in the story.

The Hausa squats cross-legged when telling a tale,
and although I tried to put the raconteur at his ease, so
as to watch his gestures, I never saw one move anything
but his eyes (and lips) during the narration.

AUTHORITIES.—Even a master of a subject cannot
afford to ignore the work of other writers, much less so
can one who is only a student, and I am indebted to

many authors for some of the matter in this book. First
of all (since the introductory chapters precede the tales),
I must mention Mr. Hartland's *The Science of Fairy-
Tales,* which is quoted so often that I have used an
abbreviation (S.F.T.), the number following the letters
in the text indicating the page.

The principal Hausa works consulted are *Litafi na
Tatsuniyoyi na Hausa,* by Major Edgar, and Dr.
Schön's *Maganna Hausa,* as revised by Canon Robinson, the abbreviations used in their case being (L.T.H.)*
and (M.H.) respectively, and the numbers being those
of the stories referred to. Unfortunately these will not
be of much use to any but the Hausa student, as they
have not been translated. All Europeans who wish to
speak the language are under a great obligation to the
two gentlemen named above, for by their early works
they have made it much easier for us who have followed.

A book such as this could have been expanded
indefinitely, for the short notes could have been increased in number and size, and more stories could
have been introduced. The illustrations, too, could
have been described at length. But a certain amount
of information regarding the Hausas has already been
published by me, and it would have served no good
purpose to have reproduced more than was necessary
to make the subject quite clear—besides, I am trying
to arrange that each book will supplement, not overlap,
the preceding works. Again, there is the question
of finance. My original intention was to publish some
200 tales both in Hausa and English, but that idea
had to be abandoned, and even in its present form this
work can hardly be expected to do more than pay its

---

* The first volume is meant unless otherwise indicated.

way, even if it does that.* However, although only 100 tales appear in full, by the aid of variants and notes, about 500 are mentioned, in fact most of the published work of others, and all of my own. An examination of those books and articles which have already appeared will certainly aid the student of folk-lore, and so I have referred to them wherever necessary. The abbreviation T.H.H. refers to *The Tailed Head-Hunters of Nigeria,* the numbers under ten indicating the numbers of the stories in Chapter xxiii, the larger ones referring to the pages. N.W.S. stands for *The Niger and the West Sudan,* the numbers being those of the pages. M. and F.-L. are abbreviations for *Man* (February and April, 1911) and *Folk-Lore* (1910-1911), respectively, the numbers being those of the stories, and as in these two journals the translation of the text is literal, the true form of the Hausa tale can be ascertained by anyone interested.

Many other books have been read, of course, in connection with this work, and they are quoted and mentioned *ad hoc,* but the above have been the most useful.

COMMENCEMENT AND ENDING OF STORIES.—Since the spider is the king of cunning and craftiness, all fables are told in his name. The narrator commences his story (*tatsunia* is feminine) thus :—

---

* In 1910 the Anthropological Section of the British Association appointed a Committee to advise and help me with the publication of my MS., but, unfortunately, without result. At the last meeting, at Dundee, a grant was made to a Committee, consisting of Mr. Hartland (Chairman), Professor J. L. Myres (Secretary), Mr. Crooke, and myself, in order to enable my MSS. to be typed (in Hausa) in a form suitable for preservation in certain University libraries, so students will eventually be able to compare the original texts with the tales given here. Published   by John Bale, 1914.

Ga ta nan, ga ta nan,	See her here, see her here,
or	
Ga tan, ga tanka,	See her (n is euphonic), see the account.

The listener then replies :—

Ta zo, ta taya mu hira,	Let her come and aid our conversation,
or	
Ta zo, mu ji,	Let her come, and let us hear,
or	
Ta zo, ta wuche.	Let her come and pass.*

And the narrator then proceeds with his tale.

When it is finished he says :—

Ku(r)rum bus kan kusu (or *bera*).	Finished (*Kurmus*-ashes) is the head of the mouse.†
En ba don gizzo ba,	Were it not on account of the spider,
da na yi ka(r)ria dayawa.	I should have greatly lied.
Da ma, ka(r)ria na yi.	As it is I have told an un- truth.
Ka(r)rian nan ta azu- zuka,	This lie is lucky, (for)

---

* There is a remarkable similarity in the tales from Sierra Leone, given in *Cunnie Rabbit, Mr. Spider*, and *The Other Beef* (F. Cronise and H. Ward, 1903), to many in my collection, even part of the Hausa introduction is seen, though in Sierra Leone the sentence is said at the end—" Story come, story go."

† Another translation of this (L.T.H., page 384) is, " The whole flesh of the rat has been consumed, only the head being left." *Kurungus, Kurunkus*, or *Kungurus*, meaning the cutting off of the head.

gobe da safe kaddan na tashi dagga kwana,	to-morrow morning when I arise from sleep,
en samu ta(i)kin kurdi chikke da kurdi ga bayan da(i)kina,	I will obtain a money-bag full of money behind my hut,
azurufa tinjim gizzo ya zubar.	a pile of silver (which) the spider has placed (there).
Idan ba asamu ta(i)kin kurdi ba,	If I do not get a money-bag,
asamu kurtu madoachi.	I shall at least get a bitter gourd.*

The story proper often ends with the words *suka zona* ("they remained"), an equivalent for our "they lived happy ever afterwards." The Hausa would not, however, bind himself to such a wide statement when he knows that the wife at any rate, being only one of four, will not be altogether content. Otherwise, why call her *Kishia?*

FIG. 4.—Koran cover of red leather, stamped designs, and black borders. L., 23 in.

---

* The du(m)ma, see note LVI, 3. It has an opaque inside skin which glistens like silver when dry.

FIG. 5.—Pillow of yellow leather, green ends (sewn with purple cotton) and yellow tassels. Pattern in red, with broad black, and narrow green border. L., 40½ in.

CHAPTER II.

SOME CHARACTERISTICS OF THE TALES.

Fondness for Tales and Proverbs—Similarities—Uncle Remus —Elaborate Traps and Easy Escapes—Chronology and Style.

THE Hausas are extremely fond of tales and pro-verbs, and almost every well-known animal and nearly every trade or profession is represented in the folk-lore of the people. Certain favourites of English children will be found to have their representatives in the Hausa stories; in fact, there seems to be very little which is absolutely strange to the student of anthropology, and here and there examples have been quoted to show that similar stories exist in one part of the globe or the other, the cast of characters being altered to suit local requirements. Nor is this surprising, for gods, ances-tors, witches, ghosts, and animals are believed by natives all over the world to possess powers exactly like those attributed by us to fairies and other super-natural beings, and to have natures and social organizations similar to those of mortals. Prob-ably all these superstitions have the same origin, namely, the belief in spirits, transformation, and witch-craft, and it will be easy to understand why similar legends should have been born in different countries if we remember that the highest nation has climbed the

very same ladder of culture on the lowest rung of
which the uncivilized people are still standing. In the
tales which follow, some of the steps in the ascent are
easily discernible.

SIMILARITIES.—The tale of Jack the Giant Killer
has its African representative in How Auta killed
Dodo (86), the sister following a creeper—the magical
growth of which recalls the Indian trick of causing a
mango tree to appear—and eventually obtaining riches
from the same mythical monster (56), reminding one
somewhat of Jack and the Beanstalk—and this story also
contains elements of Jephtha's daughter, and Moses
dividing the Red Sea. Dodo, no less than the giant,
can " smell the blood of an English (or Hausa) man "
(14 and 56).   The hyæna takes our wolf's place in
changing her voice, and pretending to be the mother
of the kids or puppies (F.-L. 22 and M.H. 21), but
the idea is the same. Cinderella was not the only one
who had shoes which would fit no one but her (86),
nor was it only Hop O' My Thumb who found a way
to save his brothers, at the expense of the children of
the house, by changing their clothes in the dead of
night (94).   Little Red Riding Hood is represented by
How Dodo frightened the Greedy Man, and in all probability, both are sun-myths. Dick Whittington's cat
brought him power and riches by catching mice, and
when Auta had lost his city (29), his pet recovered it
for him in a somewhat similar way. The variant
is even more like our legend. The white-ant
releases the lion in one story (T.H.H. 2), and was
rewarded much worse than was the mouse with us, but
the account of How the Spider obtained a Feast (78
and F.-L. 7) has an exact counterpart in an English
rhyme in which the crocodile asks the lion, wolf,

leopard, lynx, fox, duck and frog to his dinner party. Instead of a goose, the Hausa wife has a hen which lays golden eggs (though the white is silver), and she also kills it to see if there are more inside. The Hausa Half-man represents the " One-leg " of European tales, and the knife held by an invisible hand (75) is familiar, as also is that of the food serving itself (93).*

A reversed edition of Blue Beard—or rather the incident of curiosity in it—occurs in Story 82, and it resembles even more strongly an Annamite saga. The stories of *The Arabian Nights* are recalled when reading New Bags for Old (M.H. 83) and The Wonderful Ring (29, Aladdin), The Boy who Refused to Walk (70, The Old Man of the Sea), Dodo, The Thief, and the Magic Door (14, Ali Baba), and the story of the vanishing city (79); and a certain chief of Zanfara, Umoru, is said to have gone incognito amongst his people at night to find out their opinion of him, so that if it were unfavourable, he might kill them next day.

---

* In connection with these I must quote from a rather remarkable passage in *The Occult Review* (April, 1912, pages 193-4) to show that the Hausa stories are not so foolish compared with our own as they might at first seem to be. The writer states that such phenomena have been attested for a number of years by scientific men on the Continent, and he continues : " On one occasion, for example, a glass decanter was seen to be moved from the sideboard on which it stood on to the séance table, and thence rise and float about the room, no one touching it, and there being no possibility of any connection between it and any object in the room. Finally, the glass bottle held itself, or was held by invisible hands, to Eusapia's mouth, and she thereupon drank some of the water it contained." And, later on, " Sir William Crookes informs us that on several occasions a bunch of flowers was carried from one end of the table to the other, and then held to the noses of various investigators in turn for them to smell." The writer remarks : " Here, then, we have phenomena, attested by scientific men, happening within the past five or ten years, rivalling any of a like nature that are reported to have occurred in fairy stories ! "

The " Swan-Maiden " of Europe (who appears as a
seal-maiden of the Shetland Isles, a fish-maiden in
England, and a dove-maiden in other parts), becomes in
the Hausa lore a " Donkey-Maiden " (T.H.H. 4), and
she also is coerced into matrimony by the seizure of her
skin, but in this case she does not seem to be anxious to
escape again—or, at least, the tale does not indicate it.
It is evident, however, that the skin must be kept out
of her way, for in another tale (L.T.H., ii 59) the
husband throws away the dog-skin which his wife has
been inhabiting into a river, and it is only then that
she appears to the world as a woman.*

In European tales these maidens usually disappear
if reproached, no matter what they do ; in a Hausa story
(F.-L. 39) a dove gives a youth wives and a city to
rule over (though she herself does not marry him), on
the condition that he will not abuse or ill-treat her, and
immediately the tabu is broken the youth becomes as
poor as ever. There is a further resemblance, for
in a Hausa story (43) the maidens have to guess
the name of the youth at whom they have set their caps
—or perhaps one should say " head-cloths " considering the costume of the country ; in a Welsh tale it is
the man who must make the discovery.

The inevitable escape of the superhuman female from
her mortal husband is said to be due to the fact that
amongst savages the marriage ties are very loose, but
as civilization advances, prohibitions appear, and so the
wife must remain. If so, the Hausa story must be of
fairly recent origin compared to its European counter-

---

* She killed a dog and got inside its skin to escape from an
evil spirit, *Iska*, and arrived safely at a town. She lodged at a
house, and when the people were out she used to do the house-
work. But one day the son lay in wait, and saw her, captured
her, and married her.

III.—Praying for Rain.   IV.—Races at Ramadan.

The lower photograph is in remarkable contrast to those in the frontispiece. Islam is gradually obliterating the Pagan beliefs, and native spirits are shy of the European. *Vide* page 110.

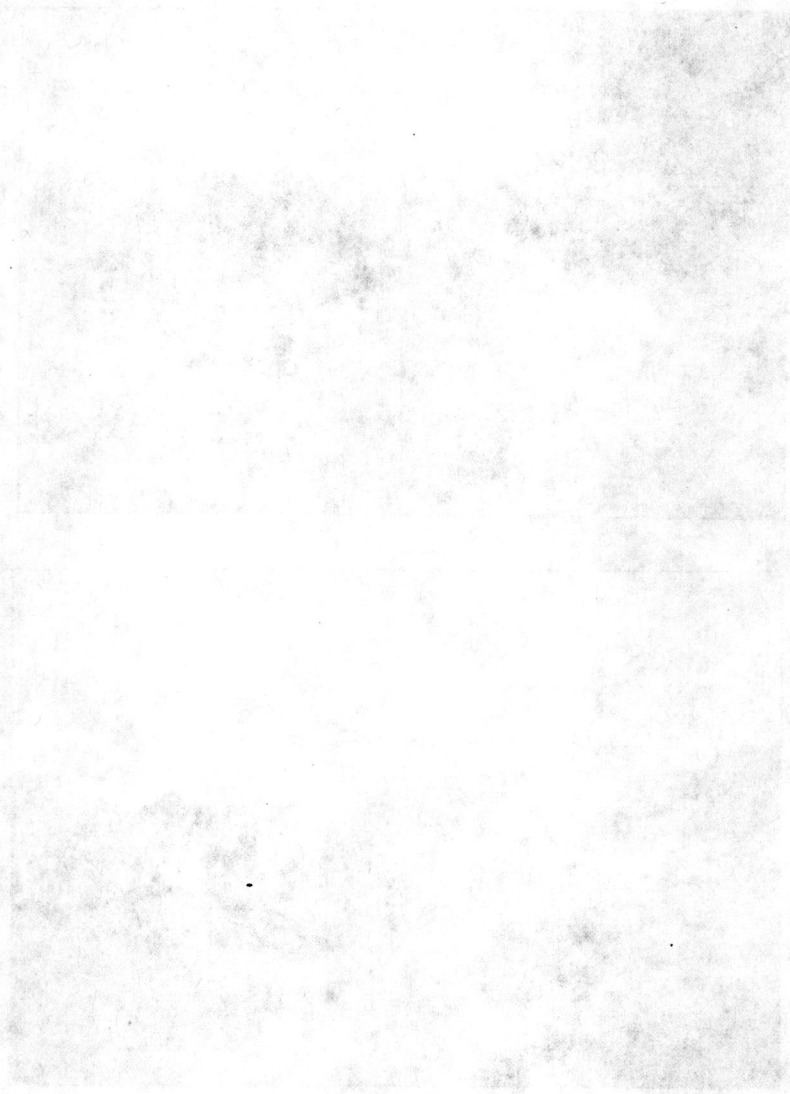

parts, and this is only what we should expect. Another explanation (page 120) is that the husband slights his wife's totem, and so she leaves him.

Jephthah's Daughter has already been mentioned; one is reminded of four other Bible stories in Why the Giant Lost his Strength (99, Samson), The King Who coveted his Son's Wife (55, David and Uriah), The Boy who became his Rival's Ruler (45, Adonijah and Absalom), and The Wicked Father and the Kind Stranger (the Good Samaritan, 68). Stories of Solomon are to be found (54 and variant), and some resembling those of other Israelitish patriarchs.

The two doves passing the eye to each other (F.-L. 36) put one in mind of the Graiai to a slight extent, except that there are only two of them instead of three; and the account of the manner in which the hyæna, after having been rescued from the well, rewards her pre-server (F.-L. 16) has its counterpart in many countries.

To many of Grimm's stories parallels can be found. In his tale of " The Twelve Brothers," the sister has to keep silence for seven years in order to have them changed back from ravens into men, and the king whom she has married is going to kill her owing to false accusations, which she is powerless to answer, brought by other women in the palace. But the seven years are completed just as she is to be burnt, the spell is broken, and the wicked women suffer instead. This has many points of resemblance to Story 30. In Hausa-land, again, jealous women substitute a dog for a baby in the queen's bed (page 94), and the queen is con-demned and imprisoned until the truth is known. The strong man who, in lieu of wages, receives permission to kick his master, reminds one of the price of the bull in Stories 76, F.-L. 4 and 5, and T.H.H. 7, while in Strong Hans, the hero, Fir-twister, and Rock-splitter, who are beaten by the dwarf when left behind on guard, we can recognize Awudu and his companions who wrestled with the Devil (88). The tale of Ferdinand Faithful and Ferdinand Faithless is much the same as that of Salifu (T.H.H. 6), especially at the end, where the captured princess kills the king by a trick and marries the man who had carried her off. Grimm's shepherd-boy is quite as good in repartee as is the precocious new baby (74), and the Youth who could not shudder may be compared, perhaps, with the people who could not sleep (83). The trick of setting up a corpse and making a person who hits it believe that she herself is the murderer is known to the simple Hausa (80). As in Europe, so in Africa (100), blood will tell—or rather speak.

As regards beings not quite human, we see that the promise to a supernatural of an unborn child, or of a living child in marriage, occurs in many tales (75 and 56). The robbers capture women for food in Europe, as do the many-headed cannibals in Africa (98), and the rôle of the dwarfs in saving a beautiful victim from her step-mother may be played by the *aljan* (L.T.H., ii, 88). It is always the youngest son who saves his brothers (94), and the youngest daughter who seeks for her long-lost sister (14 and 56), and the former may even change himself into an animal (*e.g.*, a horse, 49), and allow himself to be sold for the benefit of the family exchequer, only to change back again and escape when the money has been got safely away. The filling with water of a cask with holes in its bottom (or a sieve, 95) is common in the land of witches, and when chased by one of these creatures, European children might throw down a brush, a comb, or a looking-glass—which would change into a mountain—and by the time that she had gone home and got her axe to clear the way, they would be out of reach. Similar events are narrated in Stories 95 and 96. The magic bag, out of which different things appear which will be indispensable to the hero, is represented in West Africa by the magic handkerchief (T.H.H. 6).

In the animal kingdom, also, the similarities are numerous. The three crows in the tale of Faithful John talk together and are overheard in exactly the same manner as are the two doves in Story F.-L. 36, and all birds, whatever their " nationality," seem to know the healing properties of certain leaves (12). Many animals, birds, and fish reward the hero for sparing their lives (as in 3), and ants will sort out grain if kindly treated (as in 76). We thus see that the Hausa is with the European in emphasizing the fact that kindness to animals, especially in seeing that they are fed first (as in 79), will always bring its own reward. The fox and the wolf correspond to the jackal and the dog at the marriage-feast (F.-L. 29), for the jackal runs to the door from time to time and measures himself, so that he may not eat too much and swell, and be unable to escape; while in the contest of wits, the cat's place is taken by the dog, the jackal again playing the part of the cunning reynard (F.-L. 30).

Inanimate objects, too, are equally possessed of wondrous powers in Europe and in Africa, the story of The Straw, The Coal, and The Bean reminding one of The Dog, The Salt, and The Cake (F.-L. 2). The list of similarities could be continued almost indefinitely, but there is room to mention only one more here, though this may be given in fuller detail.

UNCLE REMUS.—Several persons expressed surprise

at seeing in *Fables and Fairy Tales* some stories resembling those of the immortal Uncle Remus, but surely one must expect to find such similarities in West Africa, for, although they were related and recorded in America, they had come originally from the former country in the days of the slave-traders.* The jerboa kills the lion here (25) instead of the hare (though the latter is the hero in M.H. 77), and the tar-baby of Uncle Remus becomes the rubber-girl in Hausaland, but the incidents are essentially the same. Even amongst the Hausas themselves, the spider and the jerboa are interchangeable, and sometimes even the jackal becomes the hero.

The " Tar-Baby Story," as it is popularly known, will serve to illustrate what I have said above about the existence of the same story in many parts of the world,† though the student who really wishes to study this particular phase should read the classics of Sir E. B. Tylor, Professor Frazer, the late Mr. Andrew Lang, Mr. Hartland, and others. It has been stated that at least three distinct African versions of the tar-baby episode in Brer Rabbit's career have come to light, but there are more than three. One writer‡ found two variants in

---

* An example of the contrary condition of things is seen in Dr. Schön's collection (M.H. 5) where our story of the mother and the stupid youth (who puts needles in the hay, butter in his sleeve, a puppy in a pot, and so on) has been translated into Hausa by a missionary boy, and is given as a tale of the country. The Dog in the Manger is also found there (M.H. 53), with a Hausa ending. " Because of that, whenever the dog sees the cow he chases her, and the cow tries to gore him. Whenever he barks she is frightened, and runs away."

† Mr. Hartland tells me that although it seems indigenous to Africa, it is a very widespread incident, being found in North America, quite independently of negro importation (Boas, *Indianische Sagen*, p. 44), and also among the Buddhist *Jataka* (*cf.* Jacob's *Indian Fairy Tales*, pp. 194 and 251).

‡ *Folk-Lore*, vol. x, page 282.

the Blantyre and West Shire districts, on the other side of the Continent, in one of which it was the cock which was overreached with tragic results by the swallow, in the other the rabbit's place was taken by the cat, and it was a small bird which was too sharp for her.

In a Shisumbwa tale the owner of the field cut a log of wood into the shape of a girl, adorned it with cloth and beads, and smeared it with gum. The rabbit came

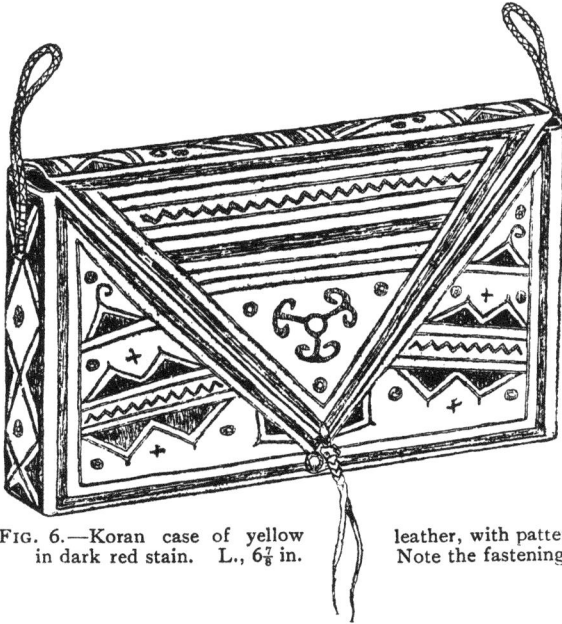

FIG. 6.—Koran case of yellow leather, with pattern in dark red stain. L., $6\frac{7}{8}$ in. Note the fastening.

up and addressed the girl, and, receiving no reply, behaved in much the same fashion as the spider in Story 15. But he escaped eventually through artifices similar to those employed by the spider in Story 18, and the youth in Story 90. In a Ronga tale the rabbit used to frighten the women away by blowing a war-horn, and, when caught by the gum-maiden, he saved his own life at the expense of the chief, in much the same way that the partridge saved hers in Story 24, and the boy his in Story 70. In an Angola tale a monkey also was caught, while in company with the rabbit, by a wooden image of a girl smeared with the gum of the wild fig-tree which had been set up by the leopard, the owner of the farm. They escaped and caught him, and then robbed and tortured him (thus causing his spots), and since then they have always had to sleep one in a tree, the other in a hole, so as to be secure from surprise.

In Sierra Leone the spider has a similar adventure with a virgin of wax. So as to be able to eat all the rice and yet escape the trouble of working, he said that he was ill, and having made his wife promise to bury him on his farm, he pretended to die. He was interred there, and soon afterwards the rice began to disappear in a mysterious manner, for every night (after the others had gone home) he would emerge from his grave and eat. His wife having sought advice from a " country-fashion-man " made a virgin of wax (from the *chockooh* tree), and the spider was caught as usual. All the people beat him, and that is why his body is flat nowadays; formerly he was " roun' lek pusson."*

In the Yoruba version† the hare is the victim of an image smeared with bird-lime. The animals were suffering from thirst, and at last they decided that each should cut off the tips of his ears, and that the fat from them should be sold so as to get money to buy hoes with which to dig a well. All cut their ears except the hare, and they dug their well, but by and by the hare came up, making such a noise with

---

* Cronise and Ward, *op. cit.*, page 109.
† Lt.-Col. A. F. Mockler-Ferryman, *British Nigeria*, page 288.

a calabash that all the other animals bolted away without waiting to see what it was. Then he slaked his thirst, but not content with this he bathed in the water, and made it muddy. After his departure the animals saw what had occurred, and they set up an image, and smeared it with bird-lime. The usual thing happened, of course, and the hare was well beaten, but at last he was allowed to go, and he has lived in the grass ever since. Thus he has longer ears than other animals.

Two distinct versions of the story as told in Northern Nigeria are given later on (15 and 15 v).

In all of the above, the tar-baby, rubber-girl, wax-virgin, or gum-maiden, whichever it may be, does not reply to the thief when he accosts her, but this is not always the case. In a Kongo story,* the gazelle protected his farm from the leopard by carving and setting up a wooden fetish called *Nkondi,* and when the leopard threatened to hit, kick and bite, the *Nkondi* dared him to do so. The leopard accepted the challenge, of course, and suffered in the approved fashion.

Now is this simply a " silly story " ? Has this tale become so widespread simply because of its power to amuse children ? Is it not much more likely that the fetish-posts which one sees in the fields—simply sticks to which rags or bunches of leaves are tied—are the representatives in real life of the tar-babies in the fables, especially since to them is ascribed the power of catching thieves? Is it not exceedingly probable that the tales have been built up to impress upon the listeners the magical power of these posts? Certainly, in most cases, the owner of the field has to depend for the preservation of his crops upon the respect in which the fetishes are held. The Hausa *Kunda* or *Kwanda*

---

* *Folk-Lore,* vol. xx, page 210.

(which sometimes has an inverted calabash on the stick as well as, or instead of, the leaves or rags) is supposed to cause the hands of the thief to fall off directly he sees it, and if it fails the executioner may perform the task when the thief is condemned (*vide* Note i, 2). It seems quite clear if we remember that not only does the ignorant pagan erect such charms to warn off human beings, but even the intelligent Mohammedan believes that similar objects will keep locusts away (see Note vi, 1), the only difference being that with the latter a sheet of paper is substituted for the leaves.

ELABORATE TRAPS AND EASY ESCAPES.—In some cases one is struck by the very easy manner in which captured men or animals escape (23, 26, and 90, and F.-L. 23)—possibly because they can make themselves invisible,* though this is not always stated. A favourite method is that of the youths in 89, or the hyænas

---

* Perhaps the original ideas of the wonderful escapes were similar to those regarding the " spirit cabinet " of to-day, in which a person bound and chained can move about, although discovered a minute later to be still in his shackles! Perhaps there is a more simple explanation. We know that even to-day persons mesmerised can see things or not see things, as directed, and it is quite possible that the idea of invisibility in the tales arose originally through this fact, the subject becoming in time the hero or the villain, as the case may be, the other being developing meanwhile into the antagonist, and the operator being even then credited with magic powers. The knowledge of hypnotism is old. Possibly the struggle between Moses and Aaron and the Egyptian sorcerers was simply a competition in the powers of suggestion, for a similar thing is said (*The Occult Review*, April, 1912, page 190) to have happened lately in Egypt —at any rate, there is a papyrus dated 3766 B.C. describing a séance in which a magician bound on a head which had been cut off, and made a lion follow him. As a fairly frequent modern example of appearance and disappearance, the case of sentries in war-time may be noted, for to a man tensely on the alert (even if he has no fear) bushes may move, and hostile scouts seem to come and go in a most realistic manner.

in 23, but often the Dodo, or whatever it may be, just lets the victim loose, and tells him to wait while he goes and gets fire with which to cook him, and is surprised to find, on his return, that the " meal-elect " has disappeared. In others, however, there seem to be unnecessarily elaborate means taken by the hero of the tale to secure the downfall of his adversary, or *vice versa;* thus in one story (T.H.H. 6), Slipperiness, personified, is summoned to cause the youths carrying food to the hero to fall down and so spoil it. Why could not the ants already there have eaten it? Again, a large force is sent out to kill a slave (19), whereas the King had the power of life and death over him, and could have ordered his immediate execution. Of course, a ram with magical attributes may be too much for a couple of hundred men, yet he is very easily overcome in the end, and by the very simple—but no doubt effective—means of an ordinary poisoned arrow.*

CHRONOLOGY AND STYLE.—The chronological order is not always strictly observed, for the ant speaks after it has been swallowed (T.H.H. 2), and a bird sings after it has been cut up and cooked (M.H. 45), even after it has been eaten!† That they can do this is not altogether surprising, for the dead ewe can hear the youth addressing her (79), and only comes back to life when she thinks that he is really going to commit suicide for her sake.

---

* It is interesting to note that the strength of the ram was in a wind (or spirit of the wind, *iska*) that attended him, and that the Egyptian god of the wind, *Kneph*, had a ram's head. But *Kneph* is identical with *Ra*, the sun, and the fact that the Hausa *Rago* (ram) goes away each day, and, in a variant, has birds to help him, suggests that the story is a sun-myth, borrowed from Egypt.

† A similar thing happens in a Sierra Leone story where the Devil turns Pigeon (Cronise and Ward, page 160).

Now and then the style is made much more graphic
by the narrator addressing the characters in the second
person as if actually present. An example will
be found on page 158, but a much better one
is given in L.T.H. 119, where in one of the
cases tried by the jackal, the narrator says " You, O
Dog, want to seize the Monkey. You, O Hyæna, want
to spring upon the Dog. You, O Dog, want to catch
the Wild-Cat." Another method is for the narrator to
interrupt his narrative to call attention to the position,
thus in F.-L. 49, " See, they alight together. There
is the fugitive, there is the one who wants to seize
him "; and there is another example in Story 15. The
changing of the person is extremely confusing at times,
for the narrator may commence a speech in the first person and finish it in the third, thus making the listener
uncertain as to whether the words are a quotation or a
description. Even a member of a Hausa audience
sometimes has to ask " *En ji wa* "—Let me know who
(it is who is speaking).

Parables are often introduced into the stories, thus
in the trial of a Ba-Maguje (pagan Hausa) who had
married his own daughter, his defence was that he
had inquired of a malam if it would be right. The
malam denied having been asked, but the other said " I
asked you that if a man had a mare with a foal, and
the mare died, could he ride the foal, and you said
' yes.' " In another, a chief desires the wife of one of
his slaves, and he sends the husband on a journey.
The wife is virtuous, wonderful to relate, shaming the
chief by saying that " the master does not drink from
the same vessel as his dog." The slave returns, finds
the chief's boots, and thinks his wife false, so he sends
her away. Her parents go to the alkali and demand

that their farm (the daughter) be given back to them, as it has borne no fruit. The husband says that he is afraid to go to the farm because he has seen the spoor of the lion there. But the chief assures him that the lion will not harm him, and so all ends happily. Other examples, also, remind one of Biblical parables.

Not only in substance is it that the Hausa story may call to mind an English tale, the monotonous repetition of The House that Jack Built, and The Old Woman and the Pig, find rivals in The Boy who was Lucky in Trading (27) and Story 78. Here at any rate is a " silly story " ! But is it ? Sir E. B. Tylor points out* that a poem printed at the end of the Jewish Passover services begins " A kid, a kid, my father bought for two pieces of money," and it goes on to describe how a cat came and ate the kid, a dog bit the cat, and so on, until " Then came the Holy One, blessed be He ! and slew the angel of death, who slew the butcher, who killed the ox, that drank the water, that quenched the fire, that burnt the stick that beat the dog, that bit the cat, that ate the kid, that my father bought for two pieces of money." The learned writer says that one interpretation of this is that Palestine (the kid) is devoured by Babylon (the cat), which is overthrown by Persia, and later on Persia is conquered by Greece, Greece by Rome, until at last the Turks are victorious. But in the end the nations of Europe will drive out the Turks (their territory is rapidly diminishing), the angel of death will destroy the enemies of Israel, and so that nation will once more be supreme. The Hausa story, also, may have a deep significance.

As has been said before, some parts of the stories are often told in a sing-song voice, and at any rate

---

* *Primitive Culture*, i, page 86.

many of the speeches are sung, especially if an animal
be speaking, sometimes in falsetto, always with a strong
nasal twang. In the examples which follow, the words
are intoned so as to resemble the actual sounds of the
animals concerned. The wild-cat wants the rooster to
come out to play with her at night, and calls out *Saidu,
Saidu,* which the rooster said was his name. The
rooster takes no notice, but at dawn next morning he
calls out " *Chikkakalike, Chikkakalike,* who has been
calling Saidu ? " The wild-cat comes again, and later
on has more success, the rooster falling into her clutches
and calling out in a choked voice, *Kurait,* as he is
being hurried off to the bush, the other roosters asking
what sort of *amana* (friendship) is this?   A variant
(L.T.H., 46) has a happier ending, the people of the
house driving off the cat, and thus saving the cock.

At one time the lion used to roar " *Allah Abin Tsoro*
(God is to be feared), *Za(i)ki Abin Tsoro* (the lion is to
be feared), but since his conquest by man (see page
31), he has substituted the word *Mutum* (man) for
Za(i)ki in the latter part.

In some recitals the words are intended to sound
like the barking of two dogs quarrelling, but one of
the greatest favourites is supposed to represent a
hyæna, some big dogs, and some puppies :

Ga tulun zuma.	(see the pot of honey) says the hyæna.
Enna, enna, enna?	(where, where, where ?) ask the puppies.
Ga ragon seyeruwa.	(see a ram for sale) says the hyæna.
Babu seye, babu seye.	(not buying, not buying) reply the big dogs.

Na ga ăbŭ bă(k)kĭ,   (I see something black, black,
    bă(k)kĭ, bă(k)kĭ.   black) say the puppies.

Duba dakeau.   (watch it well) reply the big
              dogs.

Ka(r)re zumuna.   (the dog is my cousin) says the
              hyæna.

Chan, chan, chan.   (go, go, go) exclaim the big
              dogs who are of a different
              opinion.

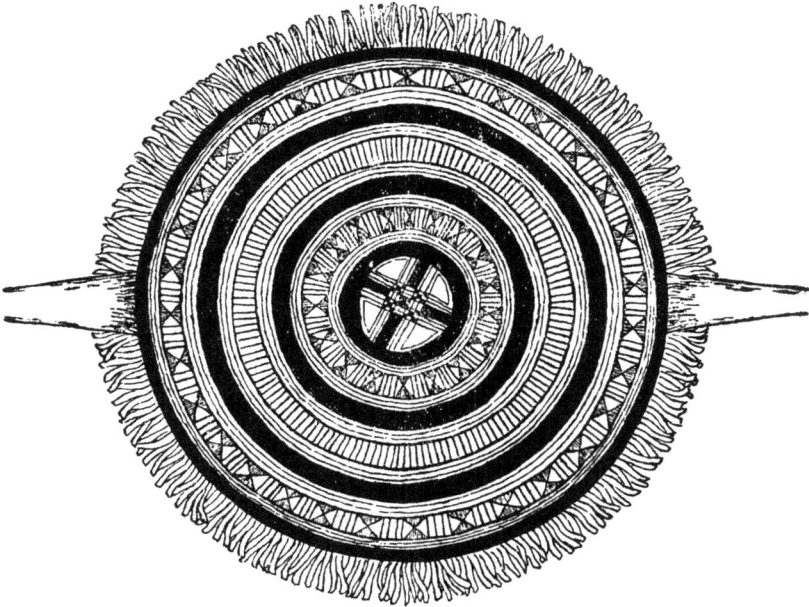

FIG. 7.—Leather cushion, with pattern picked out (and thus appearing white) and circles of black. D., 22½ in.

FIG. 8.—Book cover of red leather, part of pattern picked out, part stained black, edge sewn with yellow leather. L., 18⅜ in.

CHAPTER III.

ANIMALS IN THE TALES.

The Animal Community—The King of Beasts and Insects—Birds—Fish—Habits of Animals—Animals Resemble Human Beings.

ACCORDING to the Hausas, all the animals lived together at one time as members of a single community in a kind of Garden of Eden, but the sins of one of the number—usually the tricks of the spider or the thefts of the hyæna—destroyed the happy family. These animal communities were organized on exactly the same lines as are the human tribes to-day, of course, with chiefs, officials, and subjects, who had duties and dwellings such as are familiar to the narrator in his daily life.* One story shows how the lion was king before the arrival of man, and, so far as I am aware, there is no idea of a Hausa Adam naming the animals, for they seem to have been first in the world.

THE KING OF BEASTS AND INSECTS.—The hare

---

* Dr. Leo Frobenius (*The Childhood of Man*, page 410) says that although there are animals who build themselves houses, who clothe themselves, who rear live-stock, till the land, and have established orderly government, there are no animals which understand the use of fire, and he holds that " it is this possession that distinguishes the development even of the very lowest peoples from that of animals." From several of the stories given here, it will be seen that his remarks are not correct as regards Hausa Folk-lore.

(*zomo*) appears in a few of the Hausa tales, and is usually the victor (F.-L. 20), but the great hero is the spider (*gizzo*) who is the king of cunning, and, as has been seen, after each account the narrator excuses himself for his untruths by stating that the story has been told in the name of this insect. In one story (L.T.H. 20) the Hare agrees to go partners in a farm first with the Elephant, and then with the Giraffe, and makes them do all the work by pretending that he himself has done what each has accomplished in the others' absence. When all has been finished he frightens both of them away, and so has the farm to himself.

The King of Beasts is usually the lion, though he cannot conquer the leopard (*damissa*, 78), but sometimes the spider is said to possess the throne (F.-L. 2). Certainly, by reason of his having obtained a charm for popularity from a malam (T.H.H. 1), no animals will betray him, and his tricks usually go unpunished. However, *Za(i)ki* (lion) stands for power and dignity, and is a complimentary title for a chief, and there is no doubt that a leader would rather be known as such than as a *Gizzo*. At one time the lion was not afraid of man, it was only when his lioness had been killed by a poisoned arrow that he believed that man was greater than he.* Probably this tale arose after the discovery of poison for arrows.

The lion is no match for the spider in low cunning, he has to get the help of an old woman on the only occasion on which he comes off best (T.H.H. 2), the insect being shown at various times as outwitting not only him (F.-L. 11), but also the hyæna, the buffoon

---

* Kanta, the founder of Kebbi, is said to have issued a proclamation to the spirits and wild beasts to leave his people in peace, and they did so, whereas before this, men had been killed daily.

of the animal world (21 and F.-L. 2, 3, 11), the hippopotamus, and the elephant, and as being stronger than
these two beasts together (F.-L. 1); the snake (F.-L. 4),
the jackal (F.-L. 14), the lamb (F.-L. 13), all the animals
(F.-L. 3, 6 and 7), and even man (F.-L. 12), and young
women (72).   But he does not seem equal to an old
woman (83, F.-L. 14 and T.H.H. 2), and men often
pay him out in the end (17, F.-L. 9, 16 and 32), as
do certain of the animals, such as the tortoise (F.-L. 8),
the jackal (F.-L. 10), and the goat (F.-L. 13). There
is no sense of proportion, the spider carries a boy on
his back (70), and can lift any animal (F.-L. 6, 7, 8),
and eat it (36 and 78). But this is probably due to
the fact that he takes human shapes at times (15), and
may possibly be a giant. The female spider is called
Koki; probably it is a different variety, for such dis-
tinctions of sex are rare, though one may have been
made in the case of this particular insect to mark its
superior position. The spider is always represented as
being very greedy, even refusing to share a feast with
his wife whenever he can manage to do so, and considering the rapacious nature of the local chiefs, the
reason would seem to be that greed is one of the
attributes appropriate to royalty !*

---

* The character of this insect is so well summed up in
Cunnie Rabbit that I give it in full : " The Spider appears to be
the national hero, the impersonation of the genius of the race.
To him are ascribed the qualities most characteristic of the
people, or those most to be desired : cunning, sleeplessness,
almost immortality, an unlimited capacity for eating, and an
equal genius for procuring the necessary supplies. He possesses
a charmed life, and escapes from all intrigue. He is a tireless
weaver, and has spun the thread of his personality into all the
warp and woof of the national life. With him the adults
associate most of their traditions, while the children love him,
and push him tenderly aside if he chances to come in their way.
He is inclined to be lazy, and refuses to lift even the lightest
burden if it is in the nature of work; if it is something to eat,
he can carry the carcase of an elephant with the greatest ease."

V.—MALAMS, OR LEARNED MEN. MOHAMMEDAN PRIESTS, WHO (AS A BODY)
BELIEVE IN MAGIC. VI.—THE OLD AND THE NEW.

Note the rich embroidery on the dress of the shorter man, and the leggings (attached to the trousers) of the other.

The horsemen (Filani and Hausa) were all-powerful before the arrival of the Europeans, who trained the subdued races to conquer their conquerors

Dr. Rivers tells me that, in his opinion, the insect stands for some legendary hero, who, by reason of superior tactics and strength, overcame the indigenous inhabitants. This certainly seems to be the case in many stories (the Hyæna representing the conquered people, in all probability), but in others it would appear as if the spider were more nearly connected with the sun.

Sometimes the jerboa (*kurege*) takes the part of the spider, and often does much better, for, so far as I know, he is never outwitted. Thus he even kills the lion (25), and gets the better of the hyæna on many occasions (F.-L. 27); and he is too clever even for the jackal (F.-L. 26). Charms and aphrodisiacs are made from his body, his bite will cause madness, while if a man be touched in a certain part with a jerboa's tail, he will become impotent, it is said. In the stories here given, the variants which have come to my notice are mentioned, but there are no doubt many others; and the same thing applies in the case of other animals.

The jackal (*dila*) has a special *kirari*, or form of address, " O Learned One of the Forest " (6), and though he sometimes enters into contests with other rivals, such as the spider (F.-L. 10), or the dog (F.-L. 30), it is as a judge that we usually find him engaged (26, F.-L. 16), though his sentences are more clever than just.* His title of *Malamin Daji* is claimed also by a large species of wood-pigeon which is always making itself heard.

The leopard seldom finds a place in the Hausa folk-lore; if he does appear, it is merely so that he can kill

---

* In Northern India, too, the lion is the King of Beasts, with the jackal as his minister. *Vide* Crooke, *The Popular Religion and Folk-lore of Northern India*, 2nd ed., vol. ii, page 210.

the hyæna; he is never a friend of man. The monkey (*birri*) is sometimes mentioned, but not the baboon (*gogo*). I was told by men at Amar that if a leopard kills one of the latter animals his tribe will lie in wait, and if their enemy climbs a tree, and, crouches upon a branch, the baboons will drop down upon him and kill him.

The dog (*ka(r)re*) is considered anything but sagacious, perhaps because it is such a very poor specimen—resembling a mongrel greyhound. There seems to be only one breed, but some animals grow very much larger than others, and there may really be several varieties. Most are cowardly curs, and are therefore good watch-dogs; some of the bigger members of the family will attack hyænas—as did a little fox-terrier which I had for a time—but they are not used in war. Strangely enough, considering the low estimation in which they are held, they are supposed to kill witches and Dodo, but only if properly treated (M.H. 11). We find that throughout folk-lore dogs are associated with the spirits of the dead, and are regarded as being able to drive away evil spirits.* They are scavengers, and are not used at the present time for food, either ceremonial or otherwise, so far as I can ascertain, though they may have furnished a dish at one time (30), but the Magazawa eat them now, and certain tribes in the Jemaa district always include a dog in a marriage gift. Some say that the brown and white dogs were once used in hunting—certainly some kinds were (M.H. 52)—but that the black ones are regarded as evil spirits which cause blindness. The abhorrence of the black dog may be due to Semitic

---

* In England it used to be thought that a spayed bitch prevented a house being haunted. Crooke, *op. cit.*, ii, 222.

influence, for the animal was so much despised that the price of a dog was not accepted as an offering to God, and Mohammedans regard the animal as impure.* The dog is always in difficulties with the hyæna (F.-L. 20 and 30), and has to be very clever to get out of danger (F.-L. 21 and 22), and although on one occasion he manages to play a trick on her (F.-L. 33, which is a variant of 23), it is the goat which thinks out the plan. He is no match for the jackal (F.-L. 29 and 30).

The hyæna, as mentioned above, is the buffoon of the animal world, and is deceived by the goat (F.-L. 18, 23 and 33), the jerboa (F.-L. 26 and 27), the ostrich F.-L. 38), the jackal (F.-L. 30), the scorpion (F.-L. 15), the lizard (F.-L. 19), the dog (F.-L. 22, 33), even the donkey (F.-L. 25 and 28), and, of course, man (F.-L. 32); but he sometimes manages to avenge himself on the two latter (82 and T.H.H. 1). The hyæna is a noted thief, and has a bad name (34 and F.-L. 2), and she is very vain, being quite overcome by flattery (53 and F.-L. 11).† She is fond of dancing and of music, and she once (M.H. 38) returns a child to its mother because the latter has taught her a song. She has some magic power of appearing and disappearing (though this is not shown in the tales), and is sometimes called *amina*, the friend, though for what reason I could not discover. One man informed me that the name is given because

---

* But there is a Greek belief which is closer to the Hausa viz., that the sight of a black dog with its pups was unlucky. Compare also our saying of a sullen person that a black dog has walked over him—or is on his back.

† In India the tiger and even the *Rakshasa* (Dodo) are amenable to courtesy, and will release a victim if addressed as " Uncle." Crooke, *op. cit.*, i, 249. The Hausa calls a witch " Mother " (95).

she tries to come into a man's house at night, but it may be that the Hausa magician resembles his colleague in North-West Uganda in being able to make the hyæna take the place of a dog, and in that case *amina* would be better translated by "familiar," perhaps. Another man said that *Amina* was simply one of the names of the beast, she having taken several so that she may have an advantage in the division of food, as is shown in the following story. Some of the animals had found a carcase, and the hyæna, being the biggest present, said " I will divide it up." She took one quarter, and said " This is for Amina "; she took another fourth part, and said " This is for *Burungu* " (despoiler); she took a third quarter, and said " This is for *Maibi derri* " (Traveller by night); and then she took the remainder and said " Now the rest is yours."

The goat (*bunsuru* and *akwia*) and sheep (*rago* and *tinkia*) are not supposed to be at all foolish in Hausaland. The goat can outwit the lion (F.-L. 18), and the hyæna (F.-L. 18, 22 and 33); the sheep also is too good for the latter (F.-L. 15 and 16), and may kill even men (66). It is often said by newcomers that they cannot tell the difference between sheep and goats, because the former have hair like the latter, not wool, and even in the tales they are confused, but the animals are quite distinct in reality. There are several varieties of the sheep, a large kind from Bornu with a very Jewish nose being the most valuable. Nowadays, of course, rams are killed by the Mohammedans, but even in the old days sheep and goats had some sacrificial value, as will be seen later. The shivering of the goat is noticed in F.-L. 23, the animal pretending to the hyæna that he was God through being able to produce rain (by shaking himself) when all else was dry.*

The horse (*doki*) is said to have been introduced about 1000 A.D., but he does not appear to enter into the folk-lore to any great extent, though when he takes any active part at all it is always to help man against witches (95 and M. 2). The friendship is not always reciprocal, however, for in some stories (67 and 68) a man's affection for his adopted son is measured

FIG. 9.—Koran case, back of fig. 6.

by the number of valuable horses which he allows him to kill.

The donkey (*ja(i)ki*) is not altogether an ass (F.-L. 25 and 28, and L.T.H., ii, 2), though a very small specimen, and although he may not be able to deceive other animals in the way described in the stories quoted, he certainly can give a good deal

---

* In India the shivering is supposed to be due to an indwelling spirit, and the goat is made use of in disputes *re* boundaries. Crooke, *op. cit.*, ii, 224.

of trouble to his drivers by walking between trees and thus getting rid of his load. The Hausa traders own great numbers of these animals, and make them carry about 150 lbs.; they also ride on them occasionally. At one time the donkey lived in the forest (F.-L. 28), but in the end he took refuge in the town.

The two stories which I have obtained concerning the tortoise (*kunkuru*) show him to be well able to hold his own with either man (82) or spider (F.-L. 8). The elephant (F.-L. 1, 14 and 38), camel (*rakumi* 26), and hippopotamus (*dorina** F.-L. 1) are dull beasts, yet *Toron Giwa* (Bull Elephant) is a complimentary title of a chief. It is said that at first there was no elephant, but that God made every living thing give up a small piece of its body, and with these He made this beast. "That is why the elephant is the biggest." The monkey (*birri*) is foolish (F.-L. 16), and sometimes impertinent (26). The porcupine (*begua*) and the hedgehog (*bushia*), for they seem to be confused, are possessed of wonderful powers over men (2) and witches (M. 5), not only in this world, but also in the next (85), they can take people up to the sky (L.T.H. ii, 14)—as also can the wild-cat (64)—and are always on the side of right.

One does not expect to find the snake (*machiji* F.-L. 30), the scorpion (*kunama* F.-L. 15), the centipede (*buzuzu* F.-L. 44), or the locust (*fara* 87), acting as the friend of man, but it will be seen that such an opinion is not necessarily correct.† The names of certain snakes

---

* From *doki na rua*—water-horse.
† But the Hausas worshipped the snake, in all probability—though it does not follow that the 'sa in the name indicates this—and there were both good and evil serpents in Egypt. Most of the other animals, &c., named here are noted by Robertson Smith (*Kinship and Marriage*, pages 219 *et sqq.*) as being Arabic totems, so good offices would be expected from them.

are sometimes bestowed on warriors as a compliment! One kind of centipede is said to come out only at night, and to emit a light about four inches in length, and if it should walk over a person's hand, the hand will emit light afterwards. It is somewhat surprising that lizards (*kaddanga(r)ri*) but seldom find a place in the stories, for they are always present in the houses.* One kind is said to be killed and mixed with chaff to fatten cattle.

BIRDS.—Birds seem usually much more intelligent than animals (F.-L. 5, 6, 38 and 42), though not always (F.-L. 41), and they can give even Solomon a hint at times (54). They are almost always on the side of man, even at the expense of another human being; eagles (*mikia* 76), pigeons (*tantabbara* F.-L. 42), doves (*kurichia* 50 and F.-L. 36), and other birds (T.H.H. 7) backing him up whether he deserves it or not. Usually they protect a victim against his oppressor (12), or at any rate help those in need of aid (44). The domestic fowl (*kaza*) is usually a fool (21 and F.-L. 44), though the rooster (*zakarra*) may sometimes have his wits about him (20). The small first eggs of a hen are commonly attributed to the cock, and it is said that the white-breasted crow hatches her young from stolen hen's eggs.

---

* This agrees with Dr. Rivers' remarks (paper, Folk-lore Society, June, 1912). He believes it to be " a general rule that man has not mythologized about the domestic animals with which he is in daily contact, but rather about those he sees only occasionally, so that special features of their structure or behaviour have not a familiarity which has bred contempt and made them unfit subjects for the play of imagination." The author's definition of " myth " excludes stories which are purely fictitious, so the tales based upon the habits of familiar domestic animals (*e.g.*, the donkey and the dog) are not really exceptions to his rule.

There is, of course, a battle between the beasts of the forest and the birds of the air (22) as in our own fairy-tales, but I have not come across a story so interesting as one told in Southern Nigeria where the bat (*jemage*) could not decide to which side he ought to belong (to the animals as a mouse, or to the birds on account of his wings), and so has now to avoid both, by lying low in the daytime when birds are about, and by flying at night out of reach of the animals.

FISH.—Fish do not often find a place in the stories, though they can act the part of a fairy godmother to a Hausa Cinderella when they do (3). But they are not always grateful. One which was released by a malam for a similar reason given in (3), swam away to a safe distance and abused him, and its name, *Butulu*, has been a synonym for ingratitude ever since.

HABITS OF ANIMALS.—It is only natural that in some of the stories the peculiar habits of the members of the animal world should have been commented upon. So far from being too dull to think at all, the native has an inquiring mind, and he must invent a reason, where it is not apparent, for the events of everyday life. No doubt his thoughts run upon strange lines, but he certainly does think, let anyone who doubts this try to get the better of a Hausa or Yoruba trader!

The panting of the dog and his fondness for lying down are, of course, objects of notice (41 and F.-L. 20), and become tacked on to a good many stories (F.-L. 30). Thus when the hare and the dog are caught by the hyæna, and she asks which of them she had been chasing, the hare says " Why, surely he who is now panting," and the dog has to fly for his life. The fondness of hyænas for dogs and goats is not likely to go unnoticed by a people who value their pets and property (F.-L. 20 and 23), nor is the fact that hawks are partial to chickens (22), wild-cats to fowls (20, 21 and 45), and cats to mice (62 and 79). The wagging of the donkey's head deceives the hungry hyæna who thinks that he is biting at meat each time (F.-L. 25), and another story shows that he became domesticated because the hyæna discovered that what she had thought to be horns were in reality only ears (F.-L. 28). The hyæna was therefore no longer afraid of him, and the donkey had to flee into the town for protection, preferring to be a servant of man than to furnish a meal for his enemy. The thieving propensities of the hyæna are recorded (34 and T.H.H. 1), also those of the mouse (62 and F.-L. 34 and 38), and dog (79).

I have several times seen a snake trying to swallow a frog, and evidently the sight is not uncommon (F.-L. 45 and 50), although the frog is seldom seen in the day-time (39). The difference between the effect of the poisons of the snake and the scorpion is seen in Story 40. Although the spider remains still for a long time (hence his name *maiwayo*, for he is supposed to be thinking out some plan), he can get away quickly enough when one wants to kill him—the presence of such large numbers of the insect being explained in Story F.-L. 32. It is rather hard on him that the boy (70) and the partridge (24) both borrow his particular trick and beat him. Ants carry grains singly, so they may be used for sorting out different kinds (80), and their store-houses are useful to poor people (38 and F.-L. 45).

The fact that the note of the crow resembles the word *da* (son) is satisfactorily explained in a story about the origin of that bird (64). It will fly away at once if anyone prepares to throw a missile at it (F.-L. 40). The way in which doves (or wood-pigeons) will fly a little way along the road in front of a traveller and settle in the road, and then fly on again and settle again, until at last they fly back and leave him to go on alone, is shown in The Search for a Bride (F.-L. 36). Pigeons are easily tameable, and will come to eat grain if it be offered them (F.-L. 42).

Examples could be multiplied almost indefinitely, but this part of the subject is not particularly important, and the above will be sufficient, probably, to show that the Hausa is not altogether unobservant—even in matters not directly concerned with the food-supply !

ANIMALS RESEMBLE HUMAN BEINGS.—Many animals behave exactly like human beings, as regards, for instance, living in houses (24 and F.-L. 50) which have to be repaired (F.-L. 7). The familiar story of Little Golden Hair and the Three Bears conveys a similar idea, though this perhaps is not a good example of our folk-lore. The forest communities are organized on similar lines, as has been mentioned, and each species of animal may have its own quarter in a general city, or even a city to itself (F.-L. 20).

The Hausa animals also resemble the Hausa folk in visiting (24 and 34), courtship (F.-L. 27), marriage (F.-L. 12 and 27), feeding their young (3), spinning (F.-L. 33), grinding corn (163), marketing and fleeing from their creditors (167 and F.-L. 5, 7 and 50), working on the farm (15 and F.-L. 10) or in the smithy (41)—and it is not only the British workman who can invent excuses for the inevitable delays—dancing (F.-L. 11), wrestling (F.-L. 19), seeking revenge (F.-L. 18 and 50), fighting (22), and even going to the next world (85). Some of the highest human virtues are possessed by a few of the animals, particularly the horse, as, alas! are most of the vices!

As one would naturally expect, men and animals can converse, even without any transformation—though the former may not always understand (50 and F.-L. 36) —and, as has been mentioned above, sometimes even inanimate objects also can talk and act.* In fact, man is evidently very closely connected with every other living thing,† since one may marry the other (57, 58 and F.-L. 37, 38, 45 and 47), and have offspring (72 and F.-L. 48), even though the latter be not animate in the ordinary sense—perhaps such have the power of changing into human beings at will (71). As has been mentioned, a chief is often addressed as " Lion " or " Bull Elephant," these refer- ring merely to the man's power; but a closer connec- tion with the animal kingdom would seem to lie in the epithet " Son of a Wild Beast," which, strange to say, is considered complimentary! In addition to these forms of address, the name of some animal is often given as a name to a child, but this need not be treated further here, for it is considered under " Names " in Chapter VII.

In the case of monkeys, particularly the big baboons, it is just possible that the stories of marriage between animals and human beings were founded upon actual events. An Ijo cook whom I had

---

* This is found elsewhere, of course, though expressions like " Dead as a door-nail " and " Deaf as a post " point to a contrary opinion.

† For the reason I have used capitals in the stories for the initial letters of the names of animals, and even for those of things when taking an active part. The numerous capitals look somewhat strange in cold English type, perhaps, but they certainly reflect the idea in the mind of the Hausa. To him the characters are exceedingly real and personal.

in 1903 told me that the women of his country were afraid of monkeys assaulting them in the bush, and that some other tribes were the issue of such unions. Here, Son of a Wild Beast would be a true description. In Ilorin similar stories were told, but (as at Jemaan Daroro) it was always some other tribe which was the result. At the same time, I have never heard of an actual case—though it is not altogether inconceivable— and I suspect that either the husbands invented the tales so as to keep their wives from wandering in the bush, or else that the legend may be placed on a par with those of tail-bearing people, and that it is due simply to a wish to revile a less civilized tribe. I fear that not much stress can be laid upon the fact that the words for " aunt " and " baboon " are the same !

Although it may be usual to suppose that animals help man only because of some previous aid, this does not always hold good in Hausa Folk-Lore, for the animal or bird in question which proposes to do the good turn usually prefaces his remarks with the cheerful assertion : " You men of the world, you return night for day " (*i.e.*, evil for good), and the person benefited imme- diately proceeds to prove the statement true in many cases. It is gratifying to find that this is not a purely distinctive human failing, for the denizens of the forest treat each other in a similar way, and the animal-bene- factor may be maimed (F.-L. 16), or even killed (T.H.H. 2) by the one which he has placed under an obligation. Still, it is quite possible that parts of the stories have been lost, and that could the whole be traced, there would be found running through the vast majority the principle that " one good turn deserves another."

At any rate, kindness to animals is strongly insisted

upon. The wise ewe abundantly rewards the youth for always seeing that she was fed before he himself ate (79), the dog and cat (29) and other animals (80) well earn their keep, and the bull gives a good or bad report to the Mender of Men according to whether the bereaved mother has tended the herd well or ill (84). Other instances are quoted amongst the examples of gratitude in the following chapter.

Of course, accidents do occur even in the best regulated human-animal families, as where the snake in the end kills his benefactor after having previously saved his life (80), but this is plainly unintentional, and it does not appear in every variant of the story.

FIG. 10.—Purse of red leather with pattern in black ink. The lizard is outlined in stitches of white, blue, and yellow leather. The inside pocket is pulled down by the loop at the bottom. L., 5⅞ in.

FIG. 11. Money-belt of red leather, pattern picked out. L., 30½ in.

CHAPTER IV.

PERSONAL CHARACTERISTICS AND VIRTUES.

A Blind Man—A Woman's Tongue—Bravery—Honesty—
Debts — Indolence — Gratitude — Morality — Love — Dislike
—Drunkenness—Hospitality—Salutations—The Sign-Language—
Games, &c.—Riddles—Proverbs—Puns, &c.—Poetry.

A BLIND man is supposed to be very cunning, a
proverb running " If you gamble with jack-stones (cowries), do not do so with a blind man, for he is certain
to hide one under his feet." There are very many
blind people in Northern Nigeria, Kano being, I believe, the worst place for eyesight.

A WOMAN'S TONGUE.—Garrulous females are noted
in Nigeria, one saying is " A woman's strength
is a multitude of words," and there are others
to the same effect. When a woman is silent
it is evident that there is something radically
wrong (44 and 62). Very often the words can be ignored,
but not always, for a hairdresser is as famous there as
here, as is mentioned later under *kirari,* and her scandal
may cause trouble.

BRAVERY.—Courage is greatly admired, and naturally so in a people who have had to fight con-
tinuously for their very existence. There is a
proverb to the effect that even Death admires
valour, and that although she may kill the
body she cannot destroy that virtue. The Hausa

heroine often shows up well in the tales (65), but it is rather difficult to idealize the hero, for instead of going through his dangers and trials to win the maiden of his choice, his motive is more often (45) to commit adultery with someone else's wife! There are exceptions, however, for in one tale a chief's son wins the daughter of another chief by brave deeds, and she deserves all that he does for her, for she has already suffered indignities by having persisted in her wish to marry him at a time when he appeared to be poor. As the brave man is usually rewarded (10, 60 and 94), and the coward is punished (65), it is evident that the Hausas consider that courage covers a multitude of sins (86), and after all, some of the greatest generals of the European world have been anything but spotless in their private lives. A story like 86 variant is rather opposed to the stereotyped lessons one is taught in childhood about virtue and not evil-doing being rewarded. Lady Lugard* says that in an encounter between Songhay and Hausa troops in 1554, twenty-four of the former fought 400 of the latter, and at last they gave in, only nine being then alive, and all of them being badly wounded. The Hausas dressed their wounds, and when well enough, sent them back to the Askia with the courteous message that men so brave should not be allowed to die.†

HONESTY.—Fair dealing pays at times (12), but it is by no means always the best policy; indeed at times it is extremely unprofitable (11). To expect anything but

---

* *A Tropical Dependency*, page 213.
† It is rather sad to think how these people have deteriorated. Captain Hayward says (*Through Timbuctu and Across the Great Sahara*, pages 236 and 237) that the Sonrhais (another spelling), near Gao, are absolutely poverty-stricken, making no attempt to improve their position, and living on rotting fish and grass, so the Bambaras (once their slaves) hold them in great contempt, and say that they are more like sheep than men.

deceit from a woman is to invite disaster, and no
sensible man would think of courting one without giving
her false and exaggerated ideas of his wealth and position (L.T.H., 26).   An appropriate training is necessary in the gentle art of lying : A certain man said to
his son " Arise, let us go that I may teach you how to
lie, so that you may know how to obtain your living
some day."   They came to a large river, which they
entered, the father being in front, and he said to his
son " I have dropped a needle."   The son replied " It is
true, I heard the splash."   Next the father said " A
big fish has touched me," and the son replied " I have
just trodden upon it."   The father looking up and
seeing a small cloud, said " It is raining," and the
son replied " I am already wet through."   Then the
father said " That is good enough, you will do, you
can lie even better than I can."

Deceit and trickery seldom bring down any
punishment so long as the trick is sufficiently clever
(86 and F.-L. 12).   That certainly is the essential thing,
the Hausa admires a quick wit (20, 23, 25) and is quite
content to leave a fool to his fate (21).   Thus when a
man trying to steal growing gourds falls through the
grass roof, and pretends that he is an angel, and that
the people in the hut must hide their faces lest they
should see him, and he gets a present and goes off, the
people deceived are held up to ridicule.   Judgments
resembling those of Solomon are common.   Thus
(M.H. 80) a kind man had allowed a blind man to ride
on his bull, but when they reached the town the blind
man claimed the bull as his own, and complained to
the chief that the other (the real owner) was trying to
steal it from him.   The chief put them in separate
rooms, and said that he himself would keep the bull.

Food was brought to each, and the blind man ate, but the other said " How can I have any appetite when my bull has been stolen from me ? " The chief knew then that he was the real owner and gave him the bull. In another case (L.T.H. 17) where much the same kind of thing had happened, the one who had kept the property pretended to be deaf and dumb, and would not speak. " The King showed his hand to the Deaf-Mute in the manner that one questions a Deaf-Mute " [i.e., by the sign-language], and the Man replied (on his hands) that the property was his. Then one of the Councillors rose up and said " O King, see what the Deaf-Mute is doing, he is abusing you." The thief called out that this was not so, and by speaking betrayed his trick, and so he lost the case.

DEBTS.—In a country where trading is so general an occupation, debts are naturally contracted with great frequency, and it must be the constant study of the debtors how to avoid repayment. Of course, if a man is as cunning as the spider (77 and 78) he will probably manage comfortably, though even he may be brought to book at last (F.-L. 5). In two variants (L.T.H. 151 and 159) a man and a jackal respectively take the spider's place, but here, instead of having his creditors killed, the debtor allows each animal, except the lion, to escape from his particular enemy through a back passage, on his giving a discharge for the debt—and in the latter case even a promise of a payment also. There is a story (L.T.H., ii, 36) of a man who borrowed 500,000 cowries from an Asben, and made a farm on the road and caught two jerboas. The Asben came to demand his money, and the debtor loosed a jerboa which he had with him, saying " Go tell my wives to prepare food for the guest,"

4

and after a little they went to the house. They found
food ready (for the wives had seen the Asben), and on
the husband's asking where was the messenger, they
replied that it was tied up. The Asben was so taken
with the idea of having such a servant, that he bought
it (really the other jerboa) for the sum owing, and thus
released the debtor. But the mere ordinary man
must pay up and look cheerful (77), unless he has a
precocious child (74), or a member of the animal kingdom to aid him (76 and T.H.H. 7), or unless God comes
to his assistance (75), and at first sight it is rather difficult to see why the Almighty should help one who is
wholly undeserving, according to our ideas. But, then,
we are not Hausas!

INDOLENCE.—Laziness, though very wrong in a
wife (49), is not at all reprehensible in a husband (38), and, as a proverb says, "To volun-
teer for work is worse than slavery." This
entirely bears out what I have said elsewhere, that
though natives can work, and work well, they will never
do so unless there is some compulsion, either in the
form of a tyrant king, a hard-hearted husband or parent,
or the pangs of hunger. High pay in Nigeria has
produced the curious result that labour is harder rather
than easier to obtain, for directly a man has saved
enough money to have a holiday he leaves his work;
and the larger the wages he receives the sooner will he
be able to do so.

GRATITUDE.—It is very seldom that any moral
is expressed at the end of a fable, though this
does sometimes occur (91); usually the wrong
triumphs in a way that would scandalize the
children in our nurseries. Even a good deed
may be repaid by an evil one without any con-

demnation; thus the lion eats the white-ant which has
released him (T.H.H. 2). Sometimes, however, there
is a mild reproof for such conduct—as where the hyæna
bites the monkey's tail held out to help her out of the
well (F.-L. 16)—sometimes there is actual punishment
(F.-L. 39). There is seldom any forgiveness for an

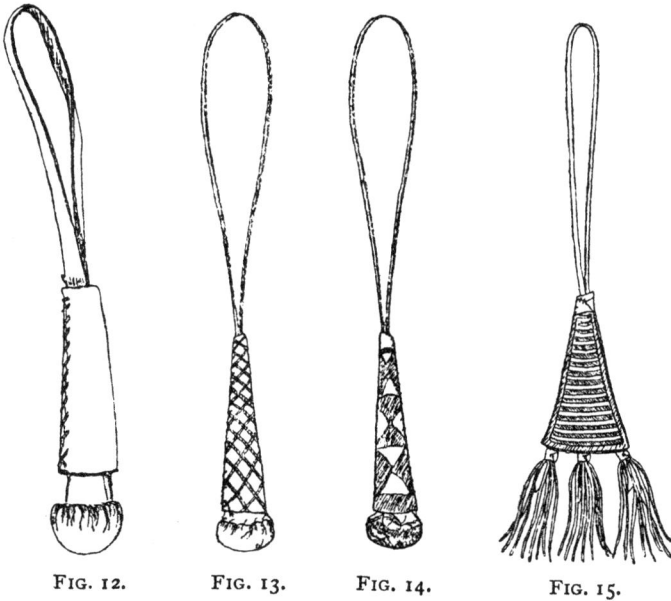

FIG. 12.   FIG. 13.   FIG. 14.   FIG. 15.

FIGS. 12-15.—Leather needle-cases. The sheath slips up and exposes the
cushion for the needles. Figs. 12 and 15 are of red leather; figs. 13 and 14
of yellow and green. L., 3¼ in.

evil deed, wives and parents usually losing their lives
when they do wrong.

A good deed does not by any means always
go unrewarded (3), however, and where there is what
is called an *alkawali*, there is evidently some necessity
to repay it. Thus the youth commits suicide because

his friend the lion has done so (8), the girl puts an end to herself because her mother has killed her preserver, the pigeon (F.-L. 42), and there are other examples.* In some cases, the debtor appears to deceive the corpse so that it will arise again (79); in others (65 and 99), the sentiment is more genuine. It would almost seem from Story 24 that if a person on a journey comes to grief, his fellow-traveller should share his fate; but this cannot be the case, for if it were, the Hausa nation would soon die out, considering the number of traders.

The story of The Ungrateful Men shows that when people have been partly cured of infirmities they ought to be thankful, and should not tempt Providence by expecting still more. Perhaps this idea was due to the pagan doctors who wished to save themselves from the consequences of their indifferent skill, but it seems more likely to be of Mohammedan origin.

MORALITY.—There seems to be no credit given to women for any moral ideas, the frail fair (or rather, dark) are stated to be tainted at birth, and the lover's chief difficulty is not to persuade the wife (for she is always ready for intrigue), but to avoid the husband.† The latter is regarded as being exceedingly foolish if he thinks otherwise, and attempts to prevent

---

* It is just possible that these ideas are connected with totemism, and that the human being must himself die if he has brought about—even indirectly—the death of his own particular protecting animal, *cf.* the mock sacrifice of a Hindu for having killed an ape. (*Vide* Frazer, *The Dying God*, page 217.)

† The Hausa's ideal woman is as follows. Her body should be of medium size, soft skinned, and well buttocked, though not too fat nor too thin; neither should it be too tall nor too short, though the fingers and toes should be long. Her voice should be soft (but she should not be too fond of using it—she should prefer to listen to the silver tones of her husband), her eyes bright, and her teeth should be well spaced.

N.B.—There is no idea of prettiness in the face!

the inevitable, for " the wiles of a woman [which are known to men] are ninety and nine, but not even Satan has discovered the hundredth." In some cases, the husband calmly accepts the fact, and trades on his wife's adultery. I have several stories on this subject, but they cannot be included here. Except as regards the wife of another, a man has practically no restrictions, and so there is no need for any standard of morality in his case.

Love.—There is nothing exactly corresponding to what we call " love," nor is there a word which definitely expresses such a sentiment, *so* meaning " like " or " desire," and to translate *Ina son ki* by " I love you " is absurd, for only the wish for possession and the animal lust are indicated by the words. Of course there are exceptions, especially in the tales; thus a father is described as being so fond of a daughter that " he seemed to wish to take her up and eat her." But usually, the wife who can give most is the most desired (44 and 59), and the same applies to the children (44). A mother might prefer another woman's son to her own daughter (59), and a Hausa chief may be content to replace his old family by a new one (7), and although this seems unnatural to us, we must remember that the same thing was done by Job who is held up to us as such a pattern. A maiden is wooed by riches (67), women generally are attracted by them (45), and a wife will desert her husband for any man who is richer (45), for, as a proverb delicately puts it, " With wealth one wins a woman." There is seldom any forgiveness for parents (64), and a wife will demand the death of her rivals (59), but children may be forgiven (44), and they may forgive others sometimes (63, variant).

DISLIKE.—Hatred, fear, and contempt are expressed in many ways. Spitting after or before a person is, of course, the most patent method, and although this may have been originally with the idea of getting rid of any influence exerted by the particular person to whom objection was taken, it seems to be done nowadays simply for the sake of showing hate or contempt. Sometimes a clicking noise is made with the tongue to indicate the latter. Gestures, too, may be insulting, as is stated later, and, needless to say, the Hausa is at no loss for an accompaniment of words which are appropriate, perhaps, but not polite.

The feeling of hatred is seldom mentioned in the tales, revenge being more often considered a matter of policy than of a balm to the wounded feelings. But many stories show how an envious rival wife or stepsister is punished.

DRUNKENNESS.—Drunkenness was not looked down upon before the Mohammedan Filani conquered the country, and in the unsubdued pagan districts it is still very prevalent (T.H.H., page 244). In one story it is related of a man that " he had no other occupation than drinking native beer."

HOSPITALITY.—Hospitality and courtesy to strangers are strongly emphasized (32 and 79), for, since the Hausa is such a great traveller, these virtues are very important to him, and they are, of course, imposed by Islam. So universally is the stranger regarded as a guest that the name for each (*bako*) is the same, though the Hausa visitor will not necessarily be entertained for nothing, any more than will the " guest " at an English lodging-house. A male stranger would not be expected to do any work in the house of his host, though a woman might help in the preparation of food (23), or in the gathering in of the harvest (86 variant). Greed is usually condemned (30 and 32), but the punishment seems to be rather an advantage in some cases (31). The giving of alms is much praised by the Mohammedan priests and others who live thereby, but the Hausa does not always give simply because of a thankful heart, or on account of his piety. There is a fever which breaks out when the guinea-corn is ripe, and the only way of avoiding it is to give presents of corn to the poor.

But the Hausa does not believe in too much economy, as is shown in a story of a Gwari and a Bassa (always butts for ridicule) who had a competition in making a little meat go a long way. The Bassa man ate a mouse-tail with his porridge, and yet managed to have a little piece left when the porridge was finished. But the Gwari capped this. He smeared butter on the remainder of the tail, stuck it on a spit by the fire, and with the gravy, which then ran down, he ate his porridge, thus saving the whole of his meat.

SALUTATIONS.—Numerous salutations are insisted upon, and a European who has a multitude of these will pass as a greater scholar than one who thinks more of the grammatical part of the language. No matter how often a couple of Hausas meet during the day they will always make the most minute inquiries after health, fatigue, and news, and I have tried to render graphically in the T.H.H. (page 210) the gradual decrescendo of question and answer.

THE SIGN-LANGUAGE.—Some motions have been mentioned under the heading of Dislike, but they do not by any means exhaust the vocabulary, of which the following are fairly representative :—

Come here.	(1) Hand (or both hands) held outwards, palm towards the person addressed, and the fingers closed and opened a few times, or
	(2) Hand waved with elliptical motion, back of hand towards person addressed, fingers close together.
	N.B.—If the person is not looking, a pebble may be thrown to attract his attention.
Go away.	Hand (or both hands) held out, palm towards person addressed, fingers close together and pointing upwards.
I am going away again.	Hands extended, and then swept upwards and outwards from the waist.
Will you return to-morrow?	Head laid on open right hand as if in sleep, and then face rubbed as if awaking.
I have been—days on the road.	Head as before, and fingers (of both hands, if necessary) then bunched, the number of fingers showing the number of days.
I am a chief.	Finger (usually of right hand) run round crown of head to indicate a turban, and then an imaginary beard pulled.
I (mounted man) greet my superior.	Clenched right fist raised to level of turban, fingers inwards, and waved.
I (footman) greet my superior.	Hand raised till elbow square, palm towards superior, and waved.
I (woman) greet my superior.	Hand on open mouth, and the *kururua* cry made (see T.H.H., page 252).
I am your inferior.	Hand placed on front of head, and head patted.
	N.B.—Kneeling is also a sign of respect (64).
I wish to marry you.	Woman first beckoned, then forefingers bent and then crossed.
	N.B.—The same sign, or a forefinger crossed over a thumb, indicates a less honourable avowal.
I do not understand.	One hand laid in the other, both palms upwards.
I refuse.	Arms lowered, hands upwards, palms towards person addressed, and waved horizontally.
Yes.	Head raised.
Certainly.	Head raised energetically, and eyebrows raised.

No.	Forefinger waved before the face, palm outwards.
Certainly not.	One shoulder raised, head lowered on same side and shaken.
That is so.	Forefinger and thumb touching the lower lip, other fingers closed, palm inwards.
I am angry or grieved.	Hands clapped, arms close to body.
I am pleased.	Arms extended, hands clapped.
I am horrified or surprised.	Hand curved like cup and placed over mouth several times, palm inwards.
I don't care.	Lips pouted and moved upwards, perhaps shoulders shrugged also.
I scorn you.	Lower lip protruded, or person spat at.
I despise and defy you.	Both hands held up level with face, fingers pointing towards the person addressed (probably to throw back the influence of the evil eye).
Your father is like——*	One forearm held up and grasped by the other hand.
Your mother is like——*	Outstretched forefinger and thumb of one hand placed against forefinger and thumb of other hand, forming a diamond-shaped opening.
(I have)—cowries.	Imaginary cowries collected on the ground in fives.
(I have)—pennies (half-pennies or tenths).	Imaginary circles of appropriate size drawn on palm of one hand with forefinger of the other, and (for the local coinage) hole punched in centre.
(I have) a three-penny piece.	Space of proper size marked off on nail of forefinger with a finger of the other hand.
(I have) a six-penny piece.	Second finger held up and nail of finger of the other hand run down, indicating a division into two.
(I have) a shilling.	Second finger held up.

There are many others, of course, some of which resemble our signs made to indicate similar ideas.

GAMES, &c.—Games of all kinds are exceedingly popular, boxing (99), wrestling (88), horsemanship (96), and *darra* (F.-L. 49), all being mentioned in the stories given here, while dances have been described elsewhere (T.H.H., pages 254-265). Even "Hunt the slipper" has its representative! The Hausa is an inveterate gambler, too, so there are many convenient ways of losing money, and alas! loaded cowries are not unknown, for it is not only a blind man who cheats. The Mohammedan Filani did all they could to put down this vice, but the native servant now asks why he should not play jack-stones if his master plays bridge! There are non-gambling games resembling " noughts and crosses," the " race-game," and " hi cockalorum," but there are much more sober amusements also, such as the propounding of riddles, quotation of proverbs, playing on words, counting-games, and, of course, the telling of tales.

RIDDLES.—Some of the best known riddles are :—

(1) I have two coats, the one which I always wear is new, the one which I do not wear is old. Answer: A road—which soon becomes impassable in West Africa if not used.

(2) I have two roads open, though I follow the wrong one, I am not lost. Answer : A pair of loose and shapeless Hausa trousers.

(3) The master is inside the hut, but his beard is outside. Answer: A fire, the smoke of which escapes through the thatch.

(4) The daughters of our house are always washing. Answer: The small saucers (gourds) used to bale out water from the large pots, and left floating in them.

(5) God has saddled him, but I shall not mount. Answer: A scorpion.

(6) The daughters of our house never go to the bush but they clap first. Answer : The wood-pigeons, which make a noise when flapping their wings.

(7) Red fell down, red picked it up. Answer : A ripe fan-palm fruit (see LXXX, 9), picked up by a Filani (called " red," as are Europeans).

(8) The house of the youths is full of meat. Answer : An egg.

(9) The great twins turned around, but they did not meet. Answer : The ears.

(10) I washed my calabash, I went east with it, I went west with it, but it did not dry. Answer : A dog's tongue.

(11) I have a thousand cows, but only one rope to tie them with. Answer : A broom—which is simply a number of twigs tied together.

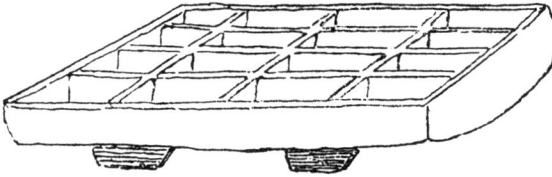

FIG. 16.

FIG. 17.

FIGS. 16 and 17.—Boards for the game of *darra*, which resembles back-gammon to some extent. The pieces may be specially made, or merely stones ; used sparklets are in great request. L., 15 in. and 25⅝ in. respectively.

(12) The cows are lying down, but the big bull is standing up. Answer : The stars and the moon.

(13) A very tiny thing can bind up the traders' loads. Answer : A packing-needle.

The list of riddles could be greatly extended, but these will be sufficient to give an idea of the Hausa train of thought; those who wish to see other examples are recommended to read the books already mentioned. Parallels to these could be given, but as I have no space to go more fully into this part of the subject, I will merely point out that numbers 3 and 11, and a variant of 9, have been noted in Sierra Leone (*Cunnie Rabbit*, page 193 *et seq.*).

PROVERBS.—But if riddles are numerous, what can be said of the proverbs? Some examples have been given already, but perhaps a few more will not be out of place, for they cover almost every subject imaginable, and many old friends will be recognized in spite of a dress suitable for the Tropics. Judging by the behaviour of most of the Hausas one meets, forethought is quite unnecessary; yet " The day on which one starts is not the time to commence one's preparations," which include the hollowing out of the gourd or traveller's water-bottle. " I • won't break the large pot (which corresponds to our tank) in the house until the new one has been brought," for " It is only when the quiver is quite full that it is necessary to pull some of the arrows partly out," so as to get at them quickly. The blind man cannot see our bitter grapes, although "Since he lacks eyes he says that eyes smell." But few normal people believe this, for " seeing is better than hearing," of course, although " The one-eyed man thanks God only when he has seen a man who is totally blind." Like a burnt child, " If the blind man has scorched his ground-nut once, he will eat it raw next time," instead of trying to cook it again. " Although the eye is not a measure, it knows what is small," and " Even without measuring (one knows that), a bridle is too large for a hen's mouth."

Since murder will out, " Dig the hole of evil shallow," else the wrongdoer may not be able to get out again. At any rate do not cry until you are out of the wood, for " If the bush is still burning, the locust will not congratulate her mother " on her escape, and be on your guard, for " The eye which sees the smoke will look for fire."

With us, a physician might have to be told to heal himself, and " If the hyæna had known how to cure

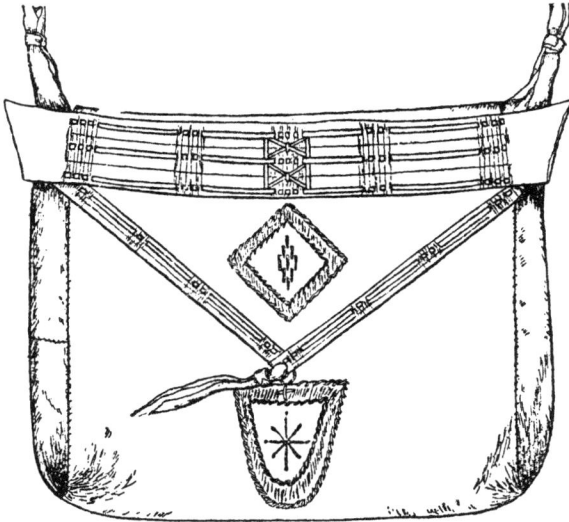

FIG. 18.—Haversack of red leather, turned inside out, black sides and border. The upper pattern is in green stitches on red, and in black stitches on green. Lower pattern in green stitches on red, and in black stitches on yellow; centre of lower pattern in black ink. 12⅝ in. × 9¼ in.

herself of small-pox, she would have done so." Still, all is more or less in vain, for " The man who must die, medicine will not save." At the same time, " He who is sick will not refuse medicine," and like the Devil, " It is when one is in trouble that one remembers God."

Although " The legs of another (man) are no good for travelling " in many cases, " He who is carried

does not realize that the town is far off "; at any rate,
" To have (a horse) is better than to be able (to ride)."
Certainly " An egg in the mouth is better than a hen
in the coop " where a wild-cat may get it. " Hurry is
not strength," and " The one who makes useless fuss
will meet with obstructions "; for it is only " By travelling ' softly, softly ' that you will sleep far away."

Even if his shoe does not pinch him, " The owner
of the house knows in what spot the water will drip
on him " from a leaky grass roof, and " He who runs
from the white-ant may stumble upon the stinging-ant,"
though he may not have a frying-pan on the fire.
Beware of great bargains, for " Whoever wants to make
an exchange does not want his own property," so there
may be something wrong with it.

Birds of a feather may fly together, but " Fire and
cotton will not be found in the same place," for the
latter would be burnt up if near the flame. Eggs and
stones also are not good neighbours, for there is
no connection between them, and " Who would compare a fish and a tick ? " Again, " A man will not enter
a slaughter-yard if he is afraid of the sight of blood,"
but " Evil knows where evil sleeps."

Although it may be quite true that " A chief
is like a dust-heap where everyone comes with his
rubbish (complaint) and deposits it," everyone likes
power, for " A wealthy man will always have followers."
In fact, according to the hen, " It is not the obtaining
of food which is hard, it is (the finding of) a place
where you can go and eat it which is so difficult." There
ought to be some consideration even here, for " Blood is
not demanded from a locust," any more than from a
stone. " The value of relationship lies in the feet,"
because if a relative does not care for you he will not

trouble to come to your house. The rich man, lest he be apt to belittle the sufferings of poor people, must remember that " The stone which is in the water does not know that the hill is (parched) in the sun."

" A man's disposition is like the marks in a stone, no one can efface it," or them rather, and " Everyone has his own peculiarities : a one-eyed man would look sideways down a bottle," for instance. Again, while " Some birds avoid water, the duck seeks it." This is quite natural, for as in the case of a house, " At the same time as the wall itself is built, the finger-marks on it are made," and a man cannot avoid his fate. Certainly " If there is a continual going to the stream (or well), one day there will be a smashing " of the pitcher, and " However hard a thing be thrown up, to earth it will fall " again, so it is a mistake that " The Dodowa (block of pounded black locust-tree seeds) calls the dark salt (from Bornu) black."

The Hausas, having no wagons, cannot very well hitch them to stars, but " If the vulture satisfies you, the guinea-fowl will fly off with her beautiful marks," for birds in such different sets could not possibly associate. Now, " Blood has more dregs than water," and since " We are mice of the same hole, if we do not meet when going in, we do so when going out," in fact, like father, like son, or rather, " The son and his father cannot be distinguished." Even if not as much alike as two peas, " On seeing them, one would say ' A calabash cut in half.' " One must be careful, for " If you despise (a man solely because of his) appearance, you may be sorry," " It is not the eye which understands, but the mind." Take the mote out of your own eye, for " Faults are like a hill, you stand on your own, and then talk about those of other people."

wanna takarda yafito waje alkali lokoja ‖ *yagaida*
This   letter   it comes from the (native) judge (of) Lokoja,   he salutes

   bature fulishi baya gaisuwana wanna ‖ *yaro*
the white man (i/c) police.   In addition to my greetings (I send you) this youth,

sunansa aliyu yafasa yarinyanakayi ‖ *jiya daderre niku'a*
his name Aliyu, (for) he broke the girl on the head yesterday at night.   As for me,

natanbayeshi   aikida shikiyi ‖ *ya gayamini shina'yi*
I asked him   the work that he does,   (and) he told me (that) he is doing

   aiki gumna   sabanda hakana banyimasa ‖
work (for the) Government. On account of thus (that)   I did not give to him

   hukunshiba   nakawoshi   gareka domin
judgment (I did not try the case).   I bring (send) him   to you   so that

   kayimashi ‖ *hukunshi baya gawanna engayamaka*
you may give him   judgment. In addition to this I report to you (that)

wani ‖ *mutumi da ankakama jiyadaderre wuri da*
a certain   man who was caught yesterday at night (in the) place where

ankayi gobara ‖ *anchi shiyasa wuta niku'a natanbayeshi*
there was a fire, it is said (of him that) he lit the fire. As for me, I asked him,

‖ *yachi bashiyasa wutaba niku'a nakaishi gida*
(but) he said it was not he (who) lit the fire. As for me, I put him in the house (of)

   dogari   domin ingari   yawayi   enkawo
the chief's police so that when the town was astir (day broke) I might bring

makashi ‖ *shiku'a yagudu gida dogari*
to you him. (But) as for him, he escaped (from the) house (of) the chief's police

   dudamarri
both he and the handcuffs.

---

wanna takarda yafito waje alkali   lokoja yagaida ‖
This   letter it comes from the (native) judge (of) Lokoja, he salutes

   bature kulfau   baya gaisuwa engayamaka ‖
the white man (i/c) the whips (police). In addition to the greeting, I report to you

wanga mache tazo gareni sunanta iyuwaje ‖ *sunan*
(that) this woman she came to me, her name (is) Iyuwaje, (and) the name of

   da uwantanan   amije   sungayamini ‖ *sarkin gubi*
her mother (with her is) Amije.   They told me (that) the Chief of Gbebe.

   yada'mesu   su ‖ *sunada shari'a da sarkin gubi* ‖
he is persecuting them, they, they have a case against the Chief of Gbebe;

yanzu nan   sunkazo   wurina ∴ *je* *   ‖ *dumin kazi(ji)*
only now   they have come to me,   so that you may hear

   abinda ke   chakaninsu ‖ *da sarkin gubi*
the matter which is (in dispute) between them and the Chief of Gbebe.

N.B.—The Alkali of Lokoja, or his clerk, does not write good Hausa, and there are several mistakes in his letters which are too obvious to need any remark here.

VII.—A HAUSA LETTER.

---

* The writer has omitted to mention the sending of the complainants to me.

وَنْسَ تَنْكُرْدَا يَا ايِطُو وَقِيَ الْقَاضِ لُوكُوجَا
يَاغِيْدَ بِنُّورَبِى فِلِيْش بَابَا غَيْشُوَرِسَ وَنْسَ
بَيْأَر سُوقَ نَمَسَ عَلِى يَابِسَ يَارِنْسَ ركَّى
جِتِى ءَ جَرَّكِى نِيكَا نَا تَمْنَبِيْش آنِيكَشِيكى
يَاغِيَمِى شِنْقِيرِ آنْكَ عَمْتَ سَمِبْتَدَكْنَا بِنْتِمَس
دَكَنْشِبَا تَاكَرُوَرْشِ غَبَرَمَكَ دُومِى كِيمَيْش
دَكَنْشِ بَايَا غَوَنْتَ إِنْغَيَمَكَ وَيْمِ
مُشْم ءَ دَنْكَكَام جِيءَ جَرْ وَوُرِ ءَ آنْكِمِ غَوَرْبَارِ
آڤِيْتِى شِيِيَسَلَاوُرْتَا نِيكَا نَا تَمْنَبِيْش
يَيْثِى بَاشِيِيَسَلَاوَرْتَابَا نِيكَا نَا كَيْمِيْش غِيدَا
دُوغَوِى دُومِى إِنْغَيَ يَاوَرَبِى إِنْكَاوَ دَكِيْش
شِيِيكَا بَاغُدُ غِيدَا دُوغَيِى دُودَمِرَ

_____

وَنْسَ تَنْكُرْدَا يَا ايِطُو وَقِيَ الْقَاضِ لُوكُوجَا يَاغِيْدَ
بِنُّورَبِى كُلْفُوا بَابَا غَيْشُوَرَا إِنْغَيَمَكَ
وَنْغَامِبَا تَادَقَ غَبَرِ سُوقَ نَتَ إِنْيُوَرَايِمَ
سُوقَ دَاعَوَنْتَنَ عَمِمَ سَنْ غَبَمَيْ
تَسَرْكِى غَوَرْبِ يَادَغَمُشَ شَفَ
شَتَ شَرِيكَا دَتَسَرْكِى غَوَرِ
بَيْعَنْتَ سَنْكَدَ وَوُرِ بِسَلَاجِمِ
دُومِى كَدَى آيِسَنَ بِى تَاكَايِنِشَ
دَتَسَرْكِى غَوَرِ

VIII.—A Hausa Letter.

Politeness will not do anyone harm, for " Bowing to a dwarf will not prevent your standing erect again." Nor will unselfishness, for " If you love yourself others will hate you, if you humble yourself others will love you." You must not expect rewards for nothing, " The prize for the race is given to the hare, and the frog must accept the fact." Remember that " God is the All-wise, not his slave " (man), for often " Lack of knowledge is darker than night," and " A fool is always a slave." Be content with what you have, " It is easier to plaster up (the old wall) than to build a new one," and remember that " There are three friends in this world— courage, sense, and insight "; and there are five of which a man should be suspicious, *viz.* : " A horse, a woman, night, a river, and the forest."

PUNS, &c.—Next we come to the plays on words, some being in the form of our " Peter Piper picked a peck of pickled pepper," some being merely puns. Of the first, the best known is probably the following about the seven crocodile-skins, and it must be rendered in Hausa, of course, to see the alliteration, the point being that in saying this over very quickly a word will probably be said in the wrong place, and so the sense will be altered.

Sa(r)riki ya aiko en kai ma-sa patar kaddan Kano bokkoi,
Ban kasshe patar kaddan Kano bokkoi ba,
Na kai ma-sa patar kaddan Kano bokkoi?
Bara da na kasshe kaddan Kano bokkoi
Ai na kai ma-sa patar kaddan Kano bokkoi.

A better one (L.T.H., page 292) runs :—
Da kwado da kato suka teffi neman koto,
Kwado ne zai ma kato koto,
Ko kuwa kato ne zai kwache ma kwado koto.

The translation is :—

A Frog and a Slave went to seek for food.
The Frog wanted to take the food from the Slave,
And again the Slave wanted to take the food from the
    Frog.

The following one is given in *Hausa Sayings* :—

*Kunun kuki, kunun kunkuki mutanen kuki, ga
    kununku.*
Ku uku, ku sha da sainyen safe.

Broth of the kuki-tree, broth of the kunkuki, O men of
    Kuki, behold your broth.
You three, drink it in the cool of the morning.

One (in *Hausa Proverbs*) runs :—

Babba ba ya babba baba ba.

Puns on words are met with. One is given in F.-L.
11, others occur in Story 74. One more is :—

Zumu Zumua ne   relatives are like honey.

But in the pronunciation of

Gata, iyaka ta kama gatan iyaka

The day after to-morrow your mother will catch the
    sentry on the boundary

great care must be taken, for a slight change will make
the last two words read " your mother's hinder parts."
There is a similar catch in *gatan birri*, a baboon.

A play upon words is not always appreciated, and
when a man who has promised to give a boy as wages
abinchin nama (food with meat in it) and he tries to
palm off *abin chin nama* (a thing to eat meat with,

e.g., a knife), he is taken to the Alkali (from the Arabic
Al kadi), and punished.

Even our celebrated word sequence to prove that " a
lie is nothing " (lie—story—tale, tail—brush—convey-
ance—jin, gin—spirit—ghost—shadow—nothing) has
its Hausa counterpart, though the latter is in the form
of question and answer. " How art thou ?—I am sick.
Art thou not reclining ?—I recline, am I a king ? Does
not one beat the drum for the king ?—Beat a drum for
me ! Am I a state-camel ?* Does not the camel carry
a load ?—Carry a load ! Am I a donkey ? Does one not
beat a donkey ?—I have a beating ! Am I a thief ?
Does not one tie up a thief ?—Tie me up ! Am I a
lizard ?† Does not one eat the lizard ?—Eat‡ me ! Am
I a market ? Does not the market rise ?—Rise ? Am I a
hawk ? Does not the hawk carry off the young chicken ?
—Carry off the young chicken ! Am I a wild-cat ? "‖
And so on,§ but there is no definite goal to be reached
as in the English proposition, the length of the game
varying in proportion to the ingenuity of the performers.

Some games seem to have a hidden meaning, and I
have two in one of my old note-books. One goes : " One
it is (1), two it is (2), they have been eaten (3) the white
(4) pumpkins (5), You (6), O Hen (7), what has brought
you (8) to the nest ? (9). An egg (10)." The meaning
is that the hen mistook the little pumpkins for eggs.
Unfortunately 1 was not able to go over the next one
during my last tour, and I cannot explain its full
meaning. It runs : " I ran away, with a *gurr* (1), I

* Some are furnished with drums as in our mounted bands.
† An edible variety.
‡ A play on the word *chi*, which means *inter alia* eat, and
hold (market).
‖ Both of these prey on the chickens, of course, as will be
seen in Stories 22 and 21, &c.
§ *Hausa Sayings*, page 60.

climbed a rock to the south (2), see me (3), I have finished (4). Truly (5), the drummers of the south (6) can sew (7) a drum (8) on top of (9) a bird (10)." This does not sound very illuminating, but that is my own fault. These two were said to be counting-games (hence the numbers in parentheses inserted in the places indicated by the narrator), and they may correspond in some degree to a Jewish poem, the last verse of which is " Who knoweth thirteen ? I saith Israel know thirteen : thirteen divine attributes, twelve tribes, eleven stars, ten commandments, nine months preceding childbirth, eight days preceding circumcision, seven days of the week, six books of the Mishnah, five books of the Law, four matrons, three patriarchs, two tables of the Covenant; but One is our God Who is over the heavens and the earth."* I do not say that there is any direct connection between the above, in fact, another man told me that the second saying was invented simply to confuse non-Hausas (*cf.* our selling sea-shells on the seashore), but there certainly is between the latter and the following : What is one in the world ?—There is no other one (God) but Allah. What are two in the world ?—There are no other two but day and night. What are three in the world ?—There are no other three but fire and food and water. What are four in the world ?—There are no four but the legal wives, whoever goes beyond four is punished. What are five in the world ?—There are no five but chieftainship, a horse, a cow, a son, and health. What are six in the world ?—There are no six but the shames (generally nine). What are seven in the world ?—There are no seven but the hand. What are eight in the world ?—There are no eight but the eyes. What are nine in the

* Tylor, *op. cit.*, page 87.

world?—There are no nine but that man is in the womb
nine months, he does not reach ten. When he has been
there nine months, if the mother has not miscarried,
he is born. What is ten in the world?—There is no
ten but a corpse (*i.e.,* finished).

"I met a man going to St. Ives" has some resemblance to the following: A man had a fowl, and the
fowl had forty chicks. The fowl and each chick had
forty eggs each and all were hatched. How many fowls
were there then?

Lastly, I might mention that there is a game in
which the players must give the names of an animal,
a bird, and a fish three times without any hesitation,
changing the name in each case thus: Lion, eagle,
frog-bellied fish; hyæna, vulture, cat-fish; dog, sparrow,
electric-eel—an easy thing to write, but difficult to
say quickly in the proper order.

POETRY.—It must not be thought, however, that the
Hausa has no better literature than word-games. Some
religious poems are given in Canon Robinson's
*Specimens of Hausa Literature,** the following extracts
from which will probably be sufficient to give an idea
of their beauty. It will be seen that the writers have
been influenced by their Islamic training:—

"Thou who art puffed up with pride because of thy
    relations, thy kingdom, or thy property, on the
    day when thou meetest with the angels, thou
    shalt be confounded. . . .
This world, thou knowest, is a market-place; everyone
    comes and goes, both stranger and citizen."

* Pages 2, 4, 24, 26, 28, 38, 46, and 80, respectively, a few
slight changes have been made. It is extremely difficult to procure any writings in Hausa, nearly all are in Arabic. The ink
is obtained from the fruit of the *farra-kaya*, a large white-thorn
tree, the pens are reeds or pointed sticks, the paper is imported.

" My brother, you know that we shall die; let us give
  credence, let us put aside quarrelling,
  For this world is not to be trusted; thou escapest to-
  day, have a fear for to-morrow. . . .
  A false friend will not become true, act thou not
  deceitfully, nor follow a fool. . . .
  My boy, I bid you be watchful, let the world flee
  away, refuse to cleave to it,
  Accomplish deeds fit for the next world, make much
  preparation; leave alone the things that belong
  to this world, which is to come to an end.
  Give up delaying, and saying that it will do when
  you are old; death may come before you are old."

" The fool would say ' This world is a virgin girl '; the
  wise man knows that the world is old.
  The wise man is a good friend, he would show to us
  the course of this world."

" My friend, repent truly, and abandon falsehood,
  abandon deceit, leave off drinking beer, and palm-
  wine, and honey-beer.
  Repent to God, cease from repenting like the wild-
  cat; it repents with the fowl in its mouth, it
  putteth it not down."

" Where is this greatness of thine and of thy lovers?
  To-day thou liest in the tomb.
  Where is the protection on the part of those who
  praised thee? To-day they carry thee to the place
  of burial.
  Truly it was falsehood they spake concerning thee,
  they loved thee not; though even had they loved
  thee thou wouldst have no power to-day. . . .
  A line (of men) is formed, a prayer is said for thee.
  Alas! thou knowest not what is done, thou
  fool. . . .

They wash their hands thus, and their feet; they all
  salute one another.
They scatter in silence, they leave thee in the grave;
  thou thyself criest, but there is no coming out.
Thy goods are divided, rejoicing is made, thy goods
  are given to thy children, each receives something.
Thou art forgotten, no share is allotted to thee; the
  suffering in the tomb is sufficient for thee."

Not only are there poems in prose, but there is even
one which rhymes. A rhyming *kirari* is often found,
and there are many couplets which quite satisfy the
Hausa ear, but in the following poem even the metre
is regular, and in some cases words have been clipped
or mis-accented so as to fit in, showing that in Hausaland as elsewhere, " poetic licence " is not unknown.
It is a war-song composed by Abdallah, the son of
Fodio, to commemorate the defeat of Yunfa, King of
Gobir, by Othman, the Filani conqueror, in an attack
upon the town of Ruga Fako, about 1804. Yunfa was
the most powerful king in the Hausa States before the
Filani conquest, but he was finally routed and killed
at Kwoto, Alkalawa, the capital of Gobir, then falling
into the hands of the victors.

The whole poem is given in Canon Robinson's
Hausa Grammar, the first and last verses are :—

Yanuwa mun gode Allah, Mun yi imanchi da salla,
Har jihadi don ka Jalla   Mun kasshe dengi na da(l)la.
    Sun sa(n)ni su sun yi tarki.

Wansu chan muzabzabina, Dukiassu ta fi dina,
Ga su, sun zam fasikina.   Mu, Amir-al-Muminina.
    Munka samu, mun yi Sarki.

The translation given in the *Grammar* (except for one trifling alteration) is :—

Brethren, we thank God, We performed acts of faith and prayer,

Even a holy war for Thee, We slew the breed of dogs. Exalted One,

They know (now) that their task was beyond them.

Some were waverers, Their wealth was more (to them) than religion,

Behold them, they have We, the Prince of the Be- become profligates. lievers,

We have found, we have made him King.

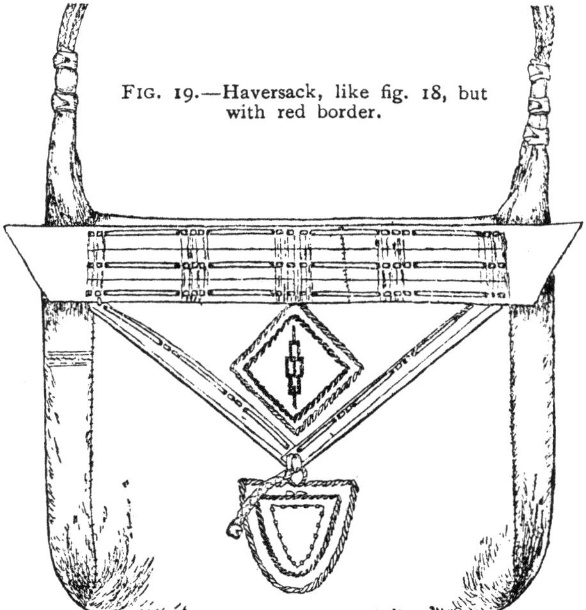

Fig. 19.—Haversack, like fig. 18, but with red border.

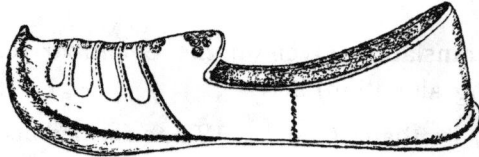

FIG. 20.

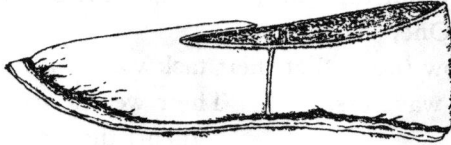

FIG. 21.

FIG. 20.—Slipper of red leather over black, which shows through.
FIG. 21.—Slipper of red leather, with black edging, and a green welt up side. Heel is usually turned down.

CHAPTER V.

THE LORE OF THE FOLK.

Meaning of the Tales—Courtship—Intimacy previous to Marriage—Marriage—Prohibited Degrees—Relation of Husband and Wife—Ceremonies—Avoidance—The Bachelor—Parentage—Miraculous Births—Childbirth—Infanticide—Relation of Parent and Child—Adoption—Organization—Descent—Tribal Marks—Development—Death and Burial—Inheritance.

IT is now time to try to find out from the stories something about the life of the people, and in doing so one has to be very careful not to see too much in them alone, but to confirm all deductions by information drawn from other sources. As the most important institution is the family, we may commence with that, showing how it first comes into existence, and the subsequent relations of its members.

COURTSHIP.—There seems to have been some test of fitness for marriage at one time, possibly the guessing of the name mentioned in 43 is one, the successful maiden gaining an influence over the youth by pronouncing it. Another story (F.-L. 12) relates how a father shut his daughter in a hut, and made a mound of filth in front, the suitor having to clear this away, without spitting or without drinking—hardships in a hot country—in order to win the bride, and after all the men had failed, the spider came, and succeeded by means of a trick.* In the cases where certain conditions are laid down, there appears to be no disgrace whatever in avoiding them, provided that the delinquent be not found out, so it is not always the case that only the brave deserve the fair; the cunning are often more successful. In another story (M.H. 7), the test is to ride a rogue camel, and all the suitors fall off but the right one whom the maiden has already chosen. Sometimes (especially in the case of witches) the bride is won by the man who can throw a stone so as to open a magic basket (95).

Women were not allowed to choose their own husbands, and a story is told of how a girl was punished who said that she would not marry anyone whose body was not free from blemish (F.-L. 44). No youth was found able to comply with the conditions (was the examination of the body another test of fitness?), and in the end she married a snake (or a Dodo in a variant) which had turned itself into a faultless youth for the purpose of deceiving her. She was saved by her younger sister, and after her escape, she swore that she would never again be so presumptuous as to wish to choose for herself; a very satisfactory conclusion to the parent who wished to make money out of his offspring !†

---

* Since writing this, I have read *Cunnie Rabbit*, and from a story there (page 40), in which the spider has to obtain the teeth of a lion, to extract palm-wine from the poisonous sasswood tree, and to capture a live boa constrictor, it is evident that the task was a test.

† In a Sierra Leone story (Cronise and Ward, page 178) the girl is deceived by a Half-Devil, who borrows half a body so as to look like a man. She is saved by her brother, and returns home ready to listen to the advice of others regarding the choice of her next husband.

Certainly the moral here is more orthodox than that of Story 61, where the parents had to give in to their determined daughter, and the sequel shows how little they relished doing so. Still, there is no denying that an adult girl has a good deal to say in the matter.

I am not certain who gave the bride away. Evidently the consent of the mother was necessary (56), although the bargaining was done with the father (64), and sometimes the latter would obtain a bride-price from several suitors at the same time (47), though he might not always be so lucky as the Kagoro parent in evading repayment to the disappointed lovers (T.H.H. 233), unless he had a malam to aid him (47 variant). Should there be no parents nor uncles nor aunts alive, elder brothers or sisters, or even protectors or hosts will arrange the marriage, and, since they thus act as parents, they will be called *suruku*. The girl in early times was promised before she had arrived at puberty, in which case she herself would let her fiancé know (if she liked him) when the proper time had arrived; the age is probably much later now, because her consent is usually sought. This is solely for the reason that if she objects to the husband provided for her, she will almost certainly be unfaithful; it is not due to any consideration for the happiness of the girl herself. Still, her wishes usually run parallel to those of her parents, *viz.*, on golden lines, the richer the suitor the more certain he is of success, for, as the poor youth bitterly complains, " Those who can give your parents presents can give you some also " (62). It is not only the father, however, who deceives the suitors. In one story (M.H. 41), a girl is sought by four youths, and she tells one to hide in a pot, and that she will run off with him. The next youth is told to take the pot to the bush for she will be inside it, and he does so, thinking that the person there is she. The two others are apparently told that the girl is to be carried off, and they follow, and seize the bearer. During the struggle which ensues, the pot is thrown on the ground, and broken, and the first youth appears instead of the maiden, and all give up the suit in disgust.

Kola-nuts are always sent to the female when the suitor proposes marriage or otherwise, and their acceptance or rejection signify her gratification or displeasure with the offer. As they are said to be aphrodisiacs there may be something symbolical in this gift. Cowries also may be sent when making the less honourable proposal (44), possibly they are a phallic symbol here.

INTIMACY PREVIOUS TO MARRIAGE.—Apparently, boys and girls were allowed to sleep together before marriage (94), though the complete act (*chi*) was prohibited, as is shown in another story which is unprintable. This was known as *Tsarenchi*, and it brought no disgrace upon either party. There was also a curious custom by which they were shut up together and left for some time. One writer* states that the custom was called *Fita furra*, and that several of each sex were shut up in the autumn in an enclosure, and left there for a month, food being taken to them by an attendant, the expense being borne by some rich man who thought that he was conferring a benefit on the community. At the end of this time any of the girls found to be *enceinte* were considered to be the wives of the youths with whom they had lived. A *jigo* or *gausami* (long pole) was erected inside the enclosure, and sacrifices of sheep, fowls, &c., were

---

* *Man* (R.A.I.), 1910, article 40.

made there to the deities *Kuri* and *Uwargona* so as to ensure fecundity in the clan.

The stories I have collected (64 and F.-L. 36) evidently refer to this, but in them not several, but only one youth and one maiden are shut up together, the time being a week, and it is related that during that period the former has to abstain from certain kinds of food. In each case the youth breaks the tabu, but being befriended in one case by a leper, in the other by a cat, he manages not only to escape the punishment—death, apparently—but even to make out that he had been in the right, and so win the bride.

MARRIAGE.—The first wife is the chief, the " house-mother," each of the others being called her *kishia*, from *kishi,* " jealousy," for an obvious reason.* I fancy that there was no limit to the number originally, except the length of the husband's purse. But this was only a temporary check, for a wife in Hausaland is an invest-ment, and, when once procured, she more than earns enough to maintain herself, and in addition furnishes sons who will work for their father, and daughters who will bring in marriage fees to the family coffer. The wives are usually quarrelling, and numerous tales of the triumph of the youngest are told, likewise of the infidelity of all of them to their husbands—but they cannot appear here. Should a wife run away with another man, the husband usually contents himself by enforcing the payment of a bride-price equal to the amount which he originally paid to the woman's parents. There is seldom much feeling aroused except anger, for a wife is regarded simply as property in

---

* For a similar idea on the other side of Africa, see Wester-marck, *The History of Human Marriage,* page 499, when he says that the Hova word for polygyny is derived from the root *rafy* —an adversary.

most cases, and so long as the injury done to the owner is paid for, there is no need to be annoyed. Still, there are exceptions, and, apart from any feeling of jealousy, a man of high rank would not so easily forgive such an insult by one in a lower grade.

Human beings may mate with animals and insects, according to the stories, and the unions are not always unhappy, not at any rate when the spider is the husband (F.-L. 12), in spite of the fact that there is necessarily deceit on one side or the other. In fact in one story (T.H.H. 5) the spider is described as being the best husband of all, though I fear that the reasons given would not convince us. In another (L.T.H., ii, 34) the ram proves himself to be a much better son-in-law than two others who are men. But except where the spider is concerned, such mixed marriages seldom seem to be a success, though the porcupine may make quite a good step-father (85).

PROHIBITED DEGREES.—Marriage with one's own daughter was never allowed, though if it had taken place there seems to have been no punishment formerly except the contempt of the other people. But the parents of a wedded pair could inter-marry (L.T.H., ii, 43). A man might not marry two sisters, though it is probable that, at one time, he could marry a wife of his deceased brother, even a widow of his father—except his own mother. Children of sisters or half-sisters may not marry nowadays; nor can those of brothers or half-brothers; but the child of a brother or half-brother may wed the child of a sister or half-sister. There is therefore no claim to the *bint ahn*; but other cousins may marry, and such unions are often encouraged so that the property may be kept in the family, and also because there is less likelihood of friction, the parents of both parties having an interest in preserving the marriage. In some clans men prefer to marry women who have the same totems as their mothers, but usually they are content so long as the women have not the same totems as they themselves have, *i.e.*, they are exogamous.

The women of a conquering tribe (*e.g.*, Filani) are **never** allowed to marry with men of the vanquished **race** (*e.g.*, Hausa), but the converse is exceedingly common, and a Filani conqueror always used to demand a Hausa princess of the defeated State in marriage.

Several stories show that neither a man (57, 58 and F.-L. 47) nor a woman (48 and F.-L. 45) should marry without knowing something of the history and the family of the other, nor should either marry out of his tribe (48). A man should not make anyone a member of his household unless he has full knowledge of his habits and character (41).

RELATION OF HUSBAND AND WIFE.—Obedience is naturally expected from the wives (50), and also hard work (49 and 57), but they ought to show some common sense when the circumstances are unusual (51). They should be cheerful at all times—for they ought to minister to a husband's pleasure, not make him dull—and they must answer when spoken to. The husband, on his part, must remember to share his pleasures (53), and to take care that he shall not, like Solomon, be ruled by women (54).

CEREMONIES.—The original Hausa ceremonies of courtship and marriage have been modified by Mohammedan influence, particularly so far as the marriage of a free virgin is concerned, the present proceedings being a mixture.

The youth would court the girl on the sly nowa-days, and give her presents, and try to win her favour generally. After a time, if she accepted him, he would tell his parents, and they would go first to her father's younger brother (he is the one appealed to in F.-L. 36), and to her mother and the younger sister of the latter, and tell them. On their consenting, the suitor's parents would go the round of the *fiancée's* whole

FIG. 22.

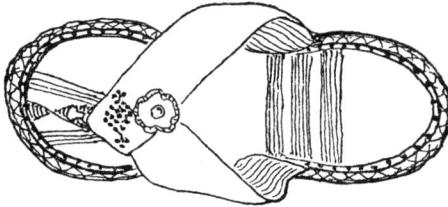

FIG. 23.

FIG. 22.—Wooden clog (left foot). FIG. 23.—Leather sandal (right foot), coloured red, yellow and black. Sometimes feathers are inserted under the "button" on the cross-straps.

family (61), though their consent was apparently un-necessary,* in fact, possibly the paternal uncle's word was sufficient. Then on a certain day, these would assemble, and the youth's parents would present a

---

* Perhaps they would give them presents, for "when the festival came he was told to go and pay respects to the relations of the girl's parents, both male and female, and greet them attentively. He was shown some twenty houses, and he paid them each man two shillings and each woman one shilling and sixpence." *Hausa Sayings*, page 73.

calabash of kola-nuts, and 10,000 cowries* to the girl's
father and mother, who would then say "We give
her," and the others would say "We accept her."

So much for the engagement; the subsequent ceremonies are best described by giving accounts of actual
marriages. When the wedding-day drew nigh, some
girl-friends were summoned secretly to the mother's
house, and on the bride's entering they surrounded her,
while the mother stained her with henna,† afterwards
bandaging the parts thus treated, the girl pretending
to resist. Then the bride and her maids all commenced
the women's cry, and went on for three days, the marriage taking place next morning, followed by a feast at
the bridegroom's house in the evening, and lasting all
night. At dawn next day she was taken to her new
home. During this time the best-man had been feeding
the bridesmaids with food supplied by the bridegroom's family. Then the bride's presents (household utensils, food, and garments) were brought and
examined, and both the bride and bridegroom were un-
veiled—for he also had been stained with henna.‡ His
friends came and brought him new clothes, and he
emerged and rode about with them until sunset.

What happens subsequently is as follows. In the
middle of the night the bridegroom and his best-man
enter the hut, and the latter tries to make the bride

---

* Equal in value to 10s. in the northerly districts, to 2s. 6d.
in Ilorin.

† In *Hausa Sayings* it is stated that the parents of the bridegroom supply the henna and leaves and staining rags, and that
they also give money to be divided up amongst the beggars; but
I think the above is correct. On further inquiry I am sure that
it is, though the bridegroom would obtain the henna for his
body from his own parents.

‡ It is somewhat unusual to find that the bridegroom is
anointed, but this occurs in India also, where a mixture of
turmeric is used. Crooke, *op. cit.*, ii, 29.

speak to him,* but as she will not do so he gives her kola-nuts " to buy mouth " (*i.e.*, speech), and he goes away. The husband makes advances, but gets a blow for his trouble, and then he and she wrestle until he finally conquers. If he finds that she is a virgin, he will give her money, and he will leave her, and hide in the best-man's house because he is ashamed of his own previous impurity, whereas she was undefiled. If, however, he finds that she is not innocent, he will break the big water-pot, and the sleeping-mat, and the drinking-bowl, and cut off some of the strings of the blind to shame her, and he will place a pot on a long pole, and set it up so as to give the news to the whole town.

Part of the foregoing is given in *Litafi na Tatsuni-yoyi na Hausa* (pages 246 and 426). There are some differences in the description in *Hausa Sayings,* but it is possible that the general account of the ceremonies is correct, and that there are slight variations in the different localities. This is only to be expected if we remember that the Hausas have been mixing continually with diverse tribes of indigenous negroes.

" In the evening the girl was bathed. The young man's parents brought some fifty large bowls of meal, and of cakes about twenty, and some twenty mortars full of *fura* were brought. When night fell the bridegroom's friend came with the horse on which he was to carry off the maiden.† To the bathing-place were brought fifty dates and fifty kolas, and about ten thousand cowries shell-money to be dispersed among

---

* In England it is often said that the best man has the right to kiss the bride if he can do so before the husband.

† There is no mention in this account of any actual abduction having occurred, I believe that it still occurs in the case of well-to-do people.

the youths. They brought new calabashes and soap. When the bathing was finished the girl was taken to her husband. After this they came and played at the husband's house—guitar, and violin, and devil-dancing,'' and drumming and merriment went on until six o'clock next morning.

During the festivity, the bridegroom sat out-side in a special chair, but the bride was inside (*vide* xcviii, 1). In the morning, after the departure of the elders, ''the young folk asked of the bridegroom's parents that food might be given them. So they were given two chickens, one in the daytime and one in the evening, and also salt,* and dodowa meal, and wood and corn.'' The bride's friends then put a stone in a calabash of porridge and took it to the bridegroom, and he gave it to his friends. But on the boys finding the stone '' they fall to abusing the girls, and they throw back at them their property, and the girls take it up and return to their own affairs. In the evening again they will behave like this, and again in the morning—even for three days. On the fourth morning the ' uncovering of the head ' will take place,† that is, the man and the

---

* Salt is widely recognized as a preservative against evil influences. The Hindus wave it round the head of a bride and bridegroom and bury it near the house door as a charm. (Crooke, *op. cit.*, page 198.) Roman Catholic priests still use it in baptism ; the Hausa mother says that her baby's flesh is salt, so that the witches will not take it, and the practice of putting salt in coffins was both religious and utilitarian. The other gifts probably symbolise plenty in the new household.

† The author remarks in a note that the covering and subsequent exposing of the head are widely employed in the preliminary ceremonies among non-Mohammedan tribes in Africa, Sir Harry Johnston (*Liberia*) mentions it as being practised among the Atonga of Nyassaland. There the bride's father must give a hen or a cock to the bridegroom's father immediately after the marriage to indicate his approval or disapproval of his son-in-law, and the gift of the two fowls mentioned above

woman take off their fine clothes and move about in public," and the bridegroom returns to his own house.

The following account of the modern customs was given to me at Zaria in 1905, and several differences will be noted. " If you want to marry a virgin, you go and ask her. If she agrees you go to her father, and if he gives his consent you get some money, perhaps 10,000 cowries, and take them to him. He takes some of it, perhaps 2,000 cowries, and gives it to his family, the remainder he divides into two parts, and gives one-half to the girl's mother, and the other to his relatives. That is how the engagement is arranged.

" Some time afterwards, say two or three months, if the girl is willing to marry, you go to her father, and talk over the price, and he will tell you what is the whole sum that you must pay. Perhaps you will then say ' Give me a month, my money is not sufficient as yet; wait until I have got it.' When you have got it you take it to her father, 20,000 cowries. He takes it and gives it to the girl's mother to buy cloths, and food for the feast, and food that she will eat during the marriage, enough for about two weeks. The white cloth also that she will wear during the marriage you will buy.

" From about five to seven days the bride remains in her father's house, she wears a white cloth, she covers up her face—her nails have been stained with henna. Other girls come and play with her, and she is taught things; these girls eat the food provided by the bride's father [at the husband's expense].

---

may have some connection with such a custom. Amongst the Rahazawa (pagan Filani) the girl is given a white cock by the bridegroom, and this she releases and it becomes sacred (*Man*, 1910, art. 40). Another reason given me for the gift of chickens is simply that the parents could not afford goats.

" After about seven days her relatives come to her house, and seize her, and take her to her husband's house. The husband does not come outside, his friends [groomsmen] come out and take the girl, and try to get her to enter the house, but she refuses. Then money is taken and given to the bridesmaids who have accompanied her to the house, and one takes her hand, another pushes her, until she has entered. All the women go in with her, all are singing and clapping. Then the bridegroom's friends enter the house and throw money amongst them. In the middle of the night, the adult women leave, but the bridesmaids stay in the hut.

" The bridegroom is not there; he has gone to his best-man's house, he will not return to his own house for five days or seven days. If he comes before the time is up the bridesmaids will drive him away, but about the sixth day he comes and gives the bridesmaids some money, perhaps 1,000 cowries, and says ' Return to your homes, the marriage ceremonies are ended.' Then the husband and wife eat food together*, and the

---

* The following account in the *Blackheath Local Guide* of May 11, 1912, will show that the Hausa customs are not so very strange to us after all : " The marriage of W——, son of W——, London, to R——, daughter of the late J ——, Monmouthshire, South Wales, took place on Saturday, the 20th ult., at St. Matthew's Church. . . . The choir received the bride [veiled, and in white] at the door of the church. . . . The organist played the accustomed bridal music. . . . An ' at home ' followed, and two old Celtic traditions (one distinctly Manx) were revived, the bridegroom carrying the bride over the threshold as indicating successful capture and possession, and the making of broth by the bride as the first act of formal betrothal and marriage, a custom in vogue in the Isle of Man within living memory and coming down from the days when the Celtic Empire dominated all Western Europe, over two thousand years ago, indicating the husband's duty to ' capture ' food for the pot on the slowrie and the wife's prerogative to cook it. Both drank from the same slig or shell, as custom had ordained." Amongst the Welsh, the bridegroom on the wedding morn would go with his friends on horseback, and carry off the bride. Westermarck, *The History of Human Marriage*, page 387.

shyness of each towards the other is ended, so they commence to talk."

According to another account, obtained at Jemaan Daroro in 1909, after the contracting parties have arranged matters as before, the relatives of both parties (but not the parties themselves) go to the malam, and the actual binding service is performed. The bride is smeared with henna four days before the feast, which takes place at the house of a relative of hers (? uncle), and the bride goes, but not the bridegroom. She is then taken to her husband's house wrapped in white cloths, and accompanied by bridesmaids, the husband having gone to another house for the time.

Next afternoon there is a feast at the bride's uncle's house, but she does not come to this one (nor does he), she is fed by her mother with the food which he has provided. In from two to seven days he returns to his house, and lives with his wife.

There are several changes therefore: the bride's father has ousted the uncle, the bride attends the feast (75), and the bridegroom does not live with her at once.* The fee seems to have been increased, but some of it goes to the provision of a gift in accordance with Mohammedan ideas (see T.H.H., page 231). There is one thing which ought to have been mentioned, and that is, that when the bride is taken to her husband's house she screams and pretends to resist, and this seems to be a survival of marriage by capture; especially as a horse was used formerly, and may be still in some districts. Her apparent reluctance is now ascribed to

---

* It may have been a compliment to stay away for seven days, for in one story (L.T.H., ii, 45) we find : " She was brought to the palace. The King rejoiced, and said that he would not go to her hut until seven days had passed." But it was not at all complimentary to stay away for longer than this.

shyness,* and it will be noted that such a feeling is insisted upon, the girl being expected to resist the application of henna, and the bridegroom being compelled to keep away from his wife. The henna is doubtless a Mohammedan introduction; formerly it would seem that oil or grease was used instead, for there is a proverb, "However cunning the bride, she will be smeared with oil."† These elaborate ceremonies are not necessary in the case of women previously married, nor is any shyness expected, the only exception being that the wives will still scream when going to their new home. If pots were still broken there would not be much water in the Jemaa houses; the late chief told me that there was not a virgin over the age of ten in the whole town !‡

AVOIDANCE.—It is difficult to understand to what extent the mother-in-law (*surukua*) has to be avoided by her daughter's husband. It is evident that there is some barrier set up, for he will not always eat food in her house (5)—though, perhaps, the objection is dying out

---

* A woman is said to have nine " shames," a man one—there being only ten in the world. She loses three on the morning after the wedding, three more after having given birth, and if she commits adultery she has not even one left.

† In Liberia, too, the bride is rubbed with animal fat. Johnston, *Liberia*, page 1038.

‡ The customs are kept up by people more to the north-west, however. The parents stand outside the house when the bridegroom enters, and two friends of his hold the bride's legs. If the bride is a virgin, a white cloth with the usual signs is exhibited to the parents, and presents are brought. If the bride is not innocent, the husband plants a pole in front of the hut, breaks her dishes, &c., and hangs them upon it. This is done on purpose to make the girl wish to leave, for if she goes away of her own free will, her parents must return the marriage fee, but they keep it if the husband drives her away. The men of Argungu, however, must serve on the farms of their parents-in-law-elect for some years, until the girls are ready for marriage, and must give annual presents also. (L.T.H., ii, page 416.) There the bride is smeared in henna for seven days, the bridegroom for four, and she is taken to his house by the best man.

(24)—and the word *surukuta* (the relationship thus established) has a second meaning of avoidance (7). Yet, on the other hand, the son-in-law is delighted when his wife's mother visits him (83); he pays her the greatest marks of respect which are due to an honoured guest, and when he goes to see her, the journey is considered to be of more importance than any ordinary trip (24). Great respect is due in any case to the wife's father (47, variant), though he may not always get it, for he and his wife are apt to make themselves nuisances to a generous son-in-law, since both of the woman's parents may eat in his house. A theft from either or from both of the parents-in-law is particularly vile (5 and 13).

I am informed that a woman also has to avoid her parents-in-law, but this does not seem to be correct— or it may have been an older custom—the general rule is for a husband to bring his wife to his own house or to that of his parents.

THE BACHELOR.—An unmarried man is looked down upon, so there is no need to extricate him in the stories from any danger into which he may have got himself (82), he may be killed without any regrets being wasted over him. Amongst the Hausas, if a man lives without a wife, although having money enough to procure one, he is regarded as being not quite normal. Besides this, he is expected to help in increasing the population, so there are not many unmarried adults. I do not suppose that there is a single woman who has not had relations of some kind.

A bachelor is the butt of many jokes, being known as "a man with a broom" because he has to sweep his own hut, and he is supposed to dream of nothing but house work, *i.e.*, women's work.

PARENTAGE.—The desire of motherhood is strongly
implanted in the Hausas, several stories relating how a
woman prayed to have offspring whatever it might be
(71 and 72), and even when it was abnormal the result
seems to have been quite satisfactory in most cases,
though there are exceptions (70).

MIRACULOUS BIRTHS.—Stories of miraculous births
are common, of course, and are mere fancy, but one
tale (M.H. 43), being somewhat out of the ordinary, is
worth noting; it is the story of a *Woli*.   The reason
why he was called " Consecrated " was that his mother
had died in child, and when she had been buried, she
gave birth in the grave.   Now the people near heard the
baby crying, and they took hoes, and opened the grave,
and brought out the child.   He was taken to the chief,
who said " He is the Servant of God," and gave orders
that he was to be brought up by a malam.   But no
sooner did the baby arrive at the learned man's house,
than he began reading the *Koran,* and the malam said
that he was to be taken back to the chief's house, for
he was already qualified.

Another version is given in *Hausa Sayings,* the
mother in this case being buried close to the dye-pits.
" During three subsequent months the dyers were
molested by an unknown person who repeatedly spilt
the dye, hid the dyeing poles, and generally made mischief.   By day nothing was seen of him, but a watch-
man placed at night in a *chedia* tree close by reported
next morning that he had seen a boy crawl out of a
hole in a neighbouring bank, play the same pranks with
the dyers' property as before, and finally return to his
hiding-place.   When the place was dug open the body
of the woman was found within with a live child beside
her.   Though dead, only one half of her body had

corrupted. The other half from head to foot had remained fresh and undecayed, so that her baby had been born and successfully weaned.* As they gazed at this remarkable sight the woman's body dissolved into dust. The boy under the name of Alfa dan Marinna survived to old age at Katsena, where until recently (1909) he was still living."†

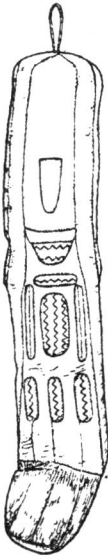

FIG. 24.   FIG. 25.

FIG. 24.—Long riding-boot. Height, 24 in. FIG. 25.—Boot of red leather, pattern picked out or stained black. Sole untanned. Height, 17 in.

The two stories seem to be the same, the first was written in 1856, and the events have naturally become more and more wonderful in the succeeding half-century.

---

* Generally two years or more, *see* the following section.
† Alfa is probably the same as Malam—it is so in Ilorin—and is akin to Woli, or better, Walli. Dan Marinna means Son of the Dye-pit.

The woman's cough becoming a child (85) is miraculous, undoubtedly, but, perhaps, no more so than the fact that the neighing of a horse carries away a man (96).

CHILDBIRTH.—When a woman has been *enceinte* about seven months, a stock of firewood is collected in her house—say, 20 loads or so—and from the day that she is delivered, or even before, she washes in warm water until about forty days afterwards. With the water is often mixed an infusion of the leaves of the *runhu* (a small tree with yellow blossoms), and the woman does not put her hands into the water to wash her body,* but takes a branch, and dips it in, and sprinkles herself. The actual childbirth is much the same as amongst the Kagoro—for which see *Journal of the R.A.I.,* January-June, 1912. Should the wood collected not be sufficient, the husband may have to get more (19). Should the mother die before being delivered, no attempt is made to save the child. After the child has been born, the mother remains for a week inside her hut, her female friends visiting and congratulating her, but on the eighth day the Malams and relatives are assembled, and kola-nuts are given to all. A special dish (*tuon suna*) consisting of corn, oil, &c., is prepared, and perhaps a ram or even a bull is killed and eaten, the midwives getting the head, legs, and skin, while the officiating Malam takes the saddle. After the child has had its head shaved, it is given two names, one of which is whispered into the child's ear, the other being announced to the company. The

---

* Professor Westermarck suggests to me that this is because she is unclean, and says that the washing for forty days is an Arab custom.

Malams then bless the child, ask God to preserve it from witchcraft, and bless the breasts of the mother.

The child is nursed for two years, during which time the mother lives apart from her husband, but on its being weaned she sleeps with him again. Boys will be circumcised when about seven years of age (*vide R.A.I. Journal*), though some of the pagan Hausas do it much earlier, but girls are not mutilated in any way.

INFANTICIDE.—I was told that albinos were once killed and eaten by an army before setting out to war,* and there is a fairly widespread practice amongst people in the southern part of the old Zaria province of throwing idiots and deformed children into the river.† It was not legal to kill them, apparently, though the result was exactly the same so far as I could see, and there does not seem to have been any idea of sacrifice in this act, though there was in another connection. Whether this custom was ever indulged in by the Hausas proper I cannot say, but I was told that the people of Argungu, on the other side of Nigeria, kept it up until quite lately. Certainly Story 73 would seem to point to the putting to death of abnormal infants. There is no suggestion in any of the stories which I have read that a child is a changeling. In the only instance given here of a father doubting his offspring (64), the question rests upon the son's legitimacy, not upon any fairy influence.

I do not think that there was any killing of twins,

---

* In Argungu the chief would kill perhaps five men, and cut up the flesh into small pieces and give them to his followers to be dried and kept until the outbreak of war. The bones were then pounded up and eaten in soup. (L.T.H., ii, page 420.)

† See T.H.H., pages 239, 240, for a description of this, and for an English parallel to the belief that the child changes into a pillar of fire.

there was none in recent times at any rate, and triplets would be considered lucky now, owing to the prevalence of sterility. Twins are supposed to have a special power of picking up scorpions without injury, but I have seen others do it who were not twins. Perhaps a malam had kindly provided them (on payment) with a concoction which when used both as a potion and a lotion renders the poison harmless! I have not come across any story which mentions twins, and at first I thought this strange, but, after all, our own folk-lore does not say much about them. Had they been put to death, I fancy the fact would have appeared somewhere, whether in the disgrace of the mother, or in the miraculous escape of the victims. In one story,* a woman gave birth to forty children at a time, and the rival wife killed them and substituted forty puppies. The children were buried, but came up as flowers which were eaten by a cow, and this animal re-bore the children, and they were at last restored to the King, much to the delight of the original mother who had been kept in the meantime in a fowl-pen. It is satisfactory to know that she was washed when she was taken out!

Another story (L.T.H., ii, 21), however, points to a different conclusion, for where a woman gave birth to a hundred children at a time both she and the husband ran away and left them, and they were brought up by her sister, their "Little Mother." Even a European father might have tried to disappear under similar circumstances!†   Perhaps these two stories show that any number above two were thought to be dangerous.

---

* *Hausa Stories*, Harris, page 1.

† The Countess Hagenan is said in old books on midwifery to have given birth to 365 at one time, but this case is now regarded as being one of "hydatidiform mole," or "vesicular degeneration of the chorion." *Vide* Whitbridge Williams, page 572.

RELATION OF PARENT AND CHILD.—Obedience from the children is expected, of course, but the parents have their duties also. They are usually kind to their children, but there are tales to the contrary, those of the step-mother variety being fairly plentiful. The daughter of a dead wife is usually badly treated by a surviving *kishia,* and is set to do some task which is thought to be impossible (93). She accomplishes it by reason of her sweet nature, and becomes rich; and the step-mother is so angry that she sets her own daughter a similar task, hoping for a like reward. In this case, however, the result is a failure, and so the ill-treated girl is avenged on her persecutors. Or the good girl may be aided by an animal (F.-L. 48), and marry the King's son. In Story 3 a fish acts the part of the Fairy Godmother.

Sometimes, however, the rival wife* treats the child better than his own mother does (60), but this is very rare, though the parent may be unnatural. In the end, he or she usually meets with death at the hands of the victim (64, 65, 68), though the narrator is not always sure that this is quite as it ought to be when the child must kill either the offending parent or a benefactor. In such cases he will ask " Now, did the child do right or not ? " If one says " Yes," he will exclaim : " What ! Is it right to kill your own parent? " If one replies " No," he will say : " What ! Is that how a benefactor should be rewarded ? " I found that the safest way

---

* Mr. Hartland has pointed out that co-wife would be a better word, especially in Story 52, but unfortunately he did not see the work until in print. However, if I err, I do so in good company (*e.g.,* with Robinson), and, after all, considering the amount of quarrelling, " rival " cannot be a very inappropriate description, especially as each wife has her own particular title, the first being " House-mother," the next " Lieutenant of the House-mother," and the last one " Bride."

was to refer the questioner to the spider, who, being the King of Cunning and of Folk-lore, no doubt delights in this sort of problem !

Needless to say, there is a certain rivalry between the different children, even when they are of the same mother (27), and, of course, this spirit is greatly increased when one goes outside the family, thus (in 45) a boy who is the rival of the King's son accomplishes various feats, and becomes King himself, and so rules over his rival. Sometimes, as in this case, the reason of the triumph seems most unsatisfactory to our ideas : perhaps some parts of the stories have been lost.

ADOPTION.—Sterility is common amongst the Hausas, and there seems to be no doubt that there was some form of adoption of sons to fill the place of natural-born ones. There is no mention of the adoption of daughters, and this and the fact that the adopted sons usually kill some animals (usually horses, 67 and 68), and also the intense desire for sons, even someone else's (59), seem to indicate that each father (and, possibly, each mother) had to have a son to perform some sacrifice or other rite for him. The son must be obtained in a proper lawful manner, with the consent of his natural parent if alive, but where none exists the boy can give himself (69). Even a woman can adopt, but whether she does this to herself or to her dead husband is not quite clear, though she evidently suffers by not having a son.

It is just possible, as in the case of the Hindus, that a son is necessary to carry on the worship of the Hausa ancestors, though the reason given nowadays is simply that if a man has no children his goods go to strangers. If any such custom be discovered, it will be more easy to understand why a perfectly true

IX.—GRASS FOR THE ROOF.
XI.—A VERANDAH.

X.—HUTS IN VARIOUS STAGES.
XII.—THE SKELETON OF THE ROOF.

The round hut of the indigenous native is giving place to a square house in many parts. *Vide* page 106.

(though undoubtedly impolite) remark on the manner of a person's birth is regarded as a much more deadly insult than anything said about his purely personal characteristics. Many Hausas (and indeed others) will say that they do not mind being abused themselves, but that they cannot bear anything derogatory to be said about their parents.

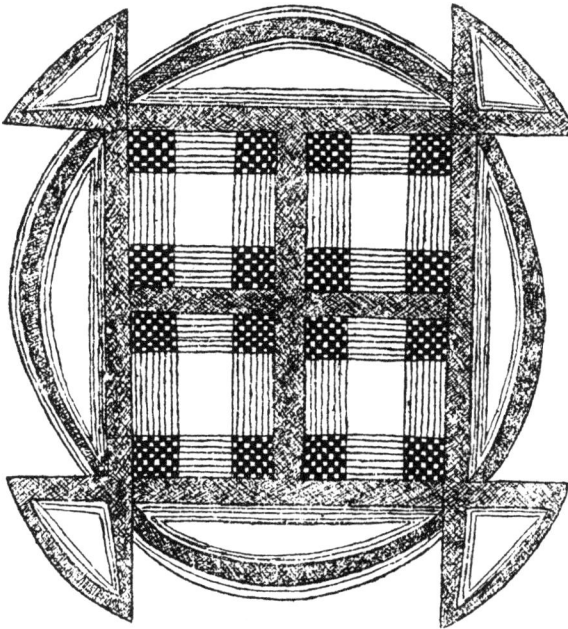

FIG. 26.—Pattern on boot similar to fig. 25.

ORGANIZATION.—The Hausas are very good agriculturists, and, as a people, are more inclined for peace than for war, though individually they are very good fighters when properly led. They have been, and still are, *the* traders of West Africa, always extending their sphere of operations, and forming new colonies in every direction. The language is thus widely spread, and, being fairly easily learnt, and rich, it often displaces the local tongues to a great extent.

The people were very good organizers, their system of revenue collection being adopted by the Filani, and this, shorn of its abuses, is what is practically in force now under us.

The Hausas seem to care but little what strange people rule the country so long as they can trade in peace, and keep their land safely, and yet they are great believers in leadership. A district is under an important chief or *Sa(r)riki*, under whom will be lesser chiefs over areas, and a chief of each separate town. But this is not by any means all, for the chief will have his deputies and other officials, and each of these will have his complete set of parasites. Not one of these exalted persons will do more work than he can help, he simply states that God will provide for him (or cause some kind person to do so), and sits down to wait for something to turn up Yet the Hausa can work when he likes, the intense agriculture in some parts shows this, and the traders have made a name everywhere in West Africa. The town itself will be divided into quarters, corresponding more or less closely with the nationality of the dwellers in them, the *Ungwal Yorubawa, Ungwal Nufawa,* &c., all of which have their respective head with its long neck. Every profession and trade, too, has its *Sa(r)riki,* the same word being used in every case, and even beggars and cripples have a recognized chief, while in Kano, at any rate, the blind have " Leaders of the Blind." This is really not quite so absurd as it seems, for the people like to have disputes and other matters settled by their own particular heads. Thus in L.T.H., 40—the snakes which were quarrelling refused to separate for a man, but did so when asked by Miss Snake. In court, a person always pleads through the head of his house or village.

In some of the tales it will be noticed that Kings of Lies, Truth, Good, and Evil are mentioned, but a man's wisdom and credit are measured usually by the length of his purse. A rich man may tell any lie and be believed, while even the most obvious truths of a pauper may be scoffed at. " If the King says ' it is black,' we exclaim ' very black,' if he says ' white,' we say ' pure.' " A story in L.T.H. (50) is identical in effect with a passage in the *Apocrypha* (*Ecclesiasticus* xiii, 23) which runs, " When a rich man speaketh, every man holdeth his tongue, and, look, what he saith, they extol it to the clouds : but if the poor man speak, they say, What fellow is this? and if he stumble, they will help to overthrow him." Even a person who claims to have some special remedy will find it difficult to see his patient if dressed in rags (80).

DESCENT.—The degrees of relationship are not well defined. A man will call a cousin or even a fellow-townsman my brother, or rather " son-of mother-of-me," while an uncle, a step-father, and even a protector is called father (45). To distinguish the real parent, a qualification is used after the word parent such as " he who begot me " (64), and a true child is called " my child, of my own flesh." Uncles and aunts have special words to denote them, for they are not always called fathers and mothers, the same words being used for the paternal as well as the maternal relatives, unless it is important to distinguish them, in which case they are called " younger brother of my father," &c. Except when used in the 1st or 3rd persons the words *uba* (father) and **uwa** (mother) are seldom heard, as " your

father " and " your mother " carry insinuations, and
are therefore terms of abuse in most cases.   The fact
that the word for a brother is " son-of mother-of-me,"
and not " son-of father-of-me," may indicate that descent was once traced through women ; for it would be
much more important in that case to remember the
relationship to the female than to the male parent.

Story 59 also (where the wives return to the homes
of their parents to be delivered) points to a system of
matrilinear descent, and the same may be said of
Story 64 (if the explanation be correct), where the son-
in-law lives in his wife's city, and inherits the chieftainship after her father's death.   Certainly it seems to
be so in some stories where the King gives the
hero his daughter in marriage, and one-half of the city to
rule over.   But the latter is not usual, for the bride in the
other tales is always brought to live in the husband's
town, and this indicates father-right.   The fact that in
many districts the inhabitants of villages which are
foreign colonies pay their taxes not to the local chiefs,
but to those of the district from which they have immi-
grated, shows that the system was based upon a tribal
and not a territorial bond, *i.e.,* that it was patriarchy.

TRIBAL MARKS.—During 1908 and 1909 I measured
over a hundred Hausas at Jemaan Daroro—at least they
said that they were Hausas—and the wearers of the
markings given later probably represent the average of
the people at present, except where the contrary is noted.
Many others presented themselves for examination, but
only those who could speak the language, and were able
to state that both parents were Hausas and were
" passed " by some of my men, were accepted, but even
so, I dare say that the patterns of some of these will
show their Hausa blood to be of very recent infusion.

At the same time, several tribes, although widely divergent in other respects, may have similar designs if these consist of a few lines only, and, in fact, even when the lines are numerous.* Nothing seems to have been done in the way of systematizing the markings—at any rate not in Nigeria—and these notes were written (for the *R.A.I. Journal* originally) in the faint hope of initiating the process.

A knowledge of marks might be very useful in certain circumstances, for they often indicate a man's special qualifications as well as the tribe to which he belongs; thus a river-dweller, especially a Nupe or a Kakanda (long sloping cut on each cheek), should be able to paddle and swim, an inhabitant of a district farther north (*e.g.*, Zaria) might know of donkey or even camel transport, a Cow-Filani (straight cut down forehead and nose) would understand the management of cattle, a man of Jemaa (various) possibly mat-making, and a native of Kano (several thin short sloping cuts on each cheek) perhaps leather or brass work. But sometimes a noted character will try to obliterate his marks; others add special ones as charms to bring good luck, as personal ornaments, or for the purpose of relieving or preventing pain, and it is just possible that cuts made at random at first may have developed into a stereotyped pattern when successful in such an object.

---

* As in the case with the Kagoro, Moroa, Kajji and other tribes, *vide* T.H.H., page 95. With regard to the accompanying figures and Appendix II at the end of this book (part of an article in the *R.A.I. Journal*, January-June, 1911), I ought perhaps to say that the outlines of the faces, &c., are not intended to represent faithfully the actual features; they are merely to show the position of the marks. These have been reproduced as much like the originals as possible, even the operator's errors being shown, though no attempt has been made to draw them exactly to scale.

Others again, may be enslaved, and, if young enough, be given the markings of the master's tribe, and lastly, small-pox may play havoc with the designs. Absolute dependence cannot be placed upon them, for that purpose, therefore, but they are usually a sure guide to identification.

Tribal marks generally are known by the Hausas as *zani;* they are usually mere simple cuts, but the *akanza* has blue pigment, or sometimes charcoal rubbed in. *Keskestu* are small dots in parallel lines; *kaffo* are ranks of short perpendicular cuts representing horns; *zubbe* are groups of fine slanting lines on the cheek; other names are noted as they occur. In addition to the cuts, the women paint lines on their faces, known as *katam-birri,* at times of feasts, special visits, &c., but it is doubtful if there are any strictly defined designs. Sometimes lightish coloured spots were seen on the chest and back, called *kasbi,* which are said to appear just before puberty, and to be a sign of a lustful nature.

I noticed occasionally that the top of the head was flat, and was told that this was due to the carrying of loads in childhood—tiny mites, hardly able to toddle, are often seen with pots of water. Sometimes the fore-head (and even all round the head) was very much wrinkled from the same cause. The carriers told me that anyone who carried too heavy a load for any length of time would sicken and die, and that was the reason given by independent witnesses in two or three inquests which I had to hold. I have seen men said to be ill from this cause, and they seemed to be wasting away gradually, although they had plenty of money for food, without showing visible signs of any disease. The Government is taking steps to prevent overloading, and no man may be compelled to carry more than 60 lb., and that this is very moderate is shown by the fact that Hausa traders will sometimes take a couple of hundred-weight of their own wares.

DEVELOPMENT.—A man settles down in the forest, near to some stream or other permanent water-supply, and there he clears the ground and makes a farm. Soon he has saved enough to obtain a wife, and she will take the produce to market and give him more time for his work. Then he obtains another wife, and he thus has someone to help him in the fields, and as he increases the number of huts, the place becomes known as *Giddan Mutum Daya* (The House of One Man). He soon gets other wives, concubines, and slaves, and his compound becomes a *kauye* or hamlet. Probably other men come to settle there, and as the original founder has at least four families growing up, the population increases by leaps and bounds. If the spot be near a trade route, and travellers can be induced to lodge there, other huts will be erected, and a market will be formed; if too far from the main road for this, parties of women will be sent to a spot on the road to sell *fura* and other light refreshments. In this way, the hamlet develops into a town, perhaps into a city, and even a poor man may have become a powerful chief in twenty years' time (or even much less under specially favourable conditions), with his train of officials, his attendants, and his slaves, exactly like those of his native-town (63). One of the legends of Daura makes a girl the foundress of the country of that name.

DEATH AND BURIAL.—In Gobir, Katsina, and Daura, when a chief began to fail in health or strength, he was throttled, and, after his entrails had been removed, his body was smoked over a fire for seven days. By

that time the new chief had been elected, and he was
then conducted to the centre of the town, and there
made to lie down on a bed.   A black ox was brought,
and slaughtered over him so that the blood ran all over
his body, and then the ox was flayed, and the dead
chief was put inside it, and dragged to the grave (a
circular pit), where he was buried in a sitting posture.
The new chief had to reside for seven days in his
mother's house, being washed daily, and on the eighth
he was conducted in state to the palace.   In Daura the
new chief had to cross over the body of his predecessor.*

I think that it is quite likely that the story of The
Youth and the Magic Ointment (*post,* page 132) has
some reference to king-killing, for the ruler agrees to
give up his life to his younger rival.   Another circum-
stance should be noted, and that is that in this tale (as in
Story 45) the new chief takes the wives of the one whom
he has supplanted; in fact, the hero having slept with
the wife (45) while the real husband was alive appears to
give him the right to the throne.†

Amongst certain people subject to Argungu (to the
north-west of Zungeru) the new chief was chosen as
follows : The bull was killed as soon as the old chief

---

* Frazer, *Totemism and Exogamy,* vol. ii, page 608.   A Yesko
(Hausa) chief has to wait much longer before he is installed, *vide*
T.H.H., page 125.   Black oxen seem to have some connection
with death and disaster, *cf.* our expression " The black ox has
trod on his foot," *i.e.,* misfortune has come to him.

† Such a mode of succession seems to have been known to
the ancient Israelites, for the offences of Reuben and Absalom
against their fathers denoted supersession; Abner tried to get
Rispah, the dead Saul's concubine; and in reply to Adonijah's
petition for Abishag, Solomon said, " Ask for him the kingdom
also," and put him to death.   (*Vide* Driver, *The Book of
Genesis,* page 382.)   Admiral Seymour claimed the English
throne because he married Katherine Parr.   Filani conquerors
demand a daughter of the conquered chief in marriage, and there
is, no doubt, a similar idea in this.

was dead, and the corpse was wrapped in it, and then placed on a bed, and carried out into the open. The dead chief's relatives were then made to stand in a circle around the body, and the elders of the town spoke thus : " O Corpse, show us who is to be chief, that we may live in peace, and that our crops may do well." The bearers then took the body round the ring, and it would cause them to bump against the man it wished to succeed. It was then buried seven days afterwards, and the new king was installed amidst rejoicings. It is probable that the man who had brought about the death of the old king was always chosen originally, as having proved himself the stronger.* At any rate, this happened in the case of one of the "*Hausa Banza*" (False Hausa States), for we are told that with the Korôrofawa, the king was allowed to reign only two years, and he was then killed by a member of the royal family. The internal organs of the corpse were then removed, and it was placed on a bed, and smeared with butter, a slow fire being lighted underneath. After two or three months, the chief men were assembled under the king-slayer, and they were officially informed of the king's death. The king-slayer was then given a whip and a cap (the emblems of chieftainship), and if he could turn his head smartly without making the cap fall he became chief. The dead king was then buried in a funnel-shaped grave.†

At the present time, on a death taking place, the

---

* An Indian custom seems to support this view. In the case of a suspicious death amongst the Gonds, the relations solemnly call upon the corpse to point out the delinquent, the theory being that if there had been foul play of any kind, the body, on being taken up, would force the bearers to convey it to the house of the person by whom the spell had been cast. Crooke, *op. cit.*, ii, 37.

† *Journal of the African Society*, July, 1912, page 40.

women of the family and friends assemble, and cry for one day, the mourners sometimes throwing ashes and dust on themselves, and drums beat the news. Narrow strips of *fa(r)ri* (white cloth) are sewn together to form a shroud, and the body is washed, and wrapped in it, and then in a mat (83), while outside this there may be a stiffening of sticks (82)—but there is no proper coffin. The grave may be made so that the corpse can be placed in a sitting posture, and may even be lined with sticks, but unless the deceased has been an important person, it will be simply a shallow trench* two to three feet in depth. It may be in the compound of the deceased's house, or even outside the town; there are no regular cemeteries.

The corpse is then carried on the heads of one or more bearers, and placed in the grave, together with a small branch, and perhaps some pots and treasures.†

---

* The rule that the shape of the grave (the abode of the deceased after death) follows that of the house which he inhabited during life is subject to some modification in Hausaland. The Mohammedans have introduced oblong graves, corresponding to the plan of the mosques and the houses of the chiefs and of the great men in the north. But in the south, although most of the people still live in circular huts, they may be buried in oblong trenches as has been mentioned above. Still, circular graves were used before the introduction of Islam, and this exception would seem to be merely a temporary one, and really helping to prove the rule.

† Possibly the Hausas were once buried in pots, for peoples on each side of them used this mode, *e.g.*, the Baribas of Borgu (N.W.S., page 69) and the Gwari (*Man*, 1911, art. 53.) With the latter tribe and some others, on the death of a chief, a concubine, a groom, and a favourite horse were slaughtered, and dressed in their best, and put in the grave (a circular hole with a porch above it) with the chief. Firewood, grass, and sleeping-mats were also put inside, and a bed on which the corpse of the chief was placed in a sitting posture, leaning against the wall. The corpse was then addressed, and the grave was closed, a large water-pot being placed on the top (L.T.H. ii, 95). For a somewhat similar custom amongst the Aragga, see T.H.H., page 187.

Loose earth may be thrown in then, and all will be over, but in the case of more important persons, grass might be placed next to the corpse, and perhaps sticks as well, and over this there would be built a cover of clay, the loose earth being heaped above. After the return of the mourners, the division of the inheritance is made.

It is related of one chief that he used to kill not only everyone who displeased him, but that he would even cut open living women with child so that he could see the stages of development. On his death a grave was dug, and he was put in it, but the earth threw him out again. A second time he was put in, but once more he was ejected, and a hut had to be built for the corpse. This is curiously similar to our own tales about tombstones which refused to remain standing.

INHERITANCE.—Two stories (80 and T.H.H. 6) relate that, on the death of the father, his property was arranged into lots equal to the number of sons, and that each elder son took his share, but that the youngest, who had promised to do this, took only a certain animal —which, of course, turned out later to be possessed of magical powers. But this was not known at the time, for on the youngest son's refusing his proper share, his mother abused him, and tried to persuade him to change his mind, so she evidently lost also. Now under the Mohammedan system she would have had her share independently of his acceptance, in fact it would have been increased by his refusal to partake, so the system was probably more like that of the Hindu, where a mother takes part of what her son inherits. But it could not have been this altogether, for in Story 81 we see that all children inherit their father's property equally,* and they are always anxious to know what he intends leaving them (85), though, as there is no mention of the wives receiving anything separately, each probably took part of her own child's share. The property of each mother is inherited solely by her own children, apparently (63). Although under the Moham-

FIG. 27.—Hat of straw partly covered with leather. Worn over cap, head-kerchief, &c., or allowed to hang down over the back. D. about 50 in.

medan law wills are allowed, it is evident from the above that they did not exist before the introduction of Islam.

---

* Mr. Evatt tells me that in Birnin Kebbi sons take more than daughters whatever their ages. Amongst sons, the elder ones take more than the younger, but daughters share equally with one another. If a girl were the sole heiress, she would take only about one-half, the other moiety going to the chief. Owing to the introduction of the Koranic laws, the details of the old systems are extremely difficult to obtain.

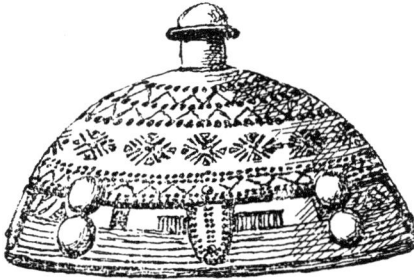

FIG. 28.—Lid of wooden calabash, decorated with brass.   D., 9¼ in.

CHAPTER VI.

CUSTOMS AND SUPERSTITIONS.*

Beliefs—Gods and Spirits—Nature Myths—The Next World—
Diseases—Totemism—Mythical Beings—The Half-Man—Dodo—
A Fabulous Bird—Wonderful Animals—Magic Ointment—Transformation—Sacrifice—Cannibalism—Ordeals, &c.—The Curse
and Blessing—Earth—Kola-nuts—Tabu—Bori—Hallucinations.

IT is evident from these stories, and from the account
of *bori,* given later, that various gods or spirits of some
kind were worshipped at one time, for a King of the
Thicket and a King of the Heavens are mentioned (64),
as well as *Dodo,* and spirits are said to live in the baobab
and tamarind trees. *Iblis* and the *Aljannu* have been
borrowed from the Arabs, and they sometimes take the
place of one of the local spirits; and since witches, too,
often play similar parts, it is very difficult to obtain a
clear idea of what the beliefs really were. In Story 90
the three beings which assume human shape are known
alternately as demons (or jinns, *aljannu*), or devils
(*iblisi*), and Death and a witch are also interchangeable,
as is mentioned later, while in another story (F.-L. 49)
Iblis is a female, the wife of a devil, and she sells charms

---

* Part of this and the following chapter, and some sections
of the preceding chapters, were read before the British Association at the Portsmouth meeting last year.

to enable the holders to transform themselves into animals, &c.   The demons are not always evil,* for they may do a good turn to a well-behaved girl (89), though they will punish one who is forward; they have cloven feet "like the hoof of a horse."   The *aljannu* live in families as do human beings, they work, and suffer hunger and thirst.   The prevalence of the Daura legend (see page 124) in districts unconnected with each other (it existed in Songhay), has made one writer† think that at some former time fetish worship extended much farther to the north than it does at present.   But the Hausas themselves had no fetishes; except for the posts set up in the fields, they worshipped the spirits themselves which lived in the wells or trees.

It is only natural that there should be a belief in evil spirits in a country where every tribe is the enemy of its neighbours, for stragglers near the boundaries often disappear, and—since they are probably sacrificed or eaten in secret—they are heard of no more.   But under conditions of increasing peace and enlightenment, these rites grow more rare, and the boundaries become more safe and defined, with the result that such disappearances can be sheeted home, usually, to some particular set of human beings, or even to individuals. These foreign spirits then retire (though those of ancestors may still remain, of course), and aid and redress are sought in the European court-house rather than in the mud-hut of the medicine-man.

At present, the vast majority of the people calling themselves Hausas are Mohammedans, but there are

---

* This is not surprising, for *daimon* once meant "god" or "divine being," but came to be employed specifically to signify secondary deities (or children of the gods), and finally the shades of the dead.   Toy, *Judaism and Christianity* (1892), page 155.

† Lady Lugard, *A Tropical Dependency*, page 260.

some communities which have remained pagan, and which keep up their pagan rites, though often much influenced by Islam, so that they now have what " is in fact, though not in name, a crude monotheism with some local spirit in the place of Allah."*

GODS AND SPIRITS.—The Magazawa (Sing., *Ba-Maguje*), as the Hausas are called who are still pagans, sacrifice to certain spirits, but they do not make images or fetishes of any kind. Some of these spirits are :—

Kuri, a male corresponding to Pan, another name being *Rago* (96); he barks like a dog, and wears a goat-skin. Possibly the baboon is responsible for this idea, as he barks; or *Kuri* may have come from *Kure,* a male hyæna. The proper sacrifice to him is a young red he-goat, but he eats human beings (96).

Uwardowa, a female, the goddess of hunting, the name signifying " Forest-Mother." The appropriate offering is a red she-goat, or a red cock.

Uwargona, "Farm-Mother," or *Uwardawa,* "Corn-Mother," also a female, goddess of agriculture. She prefers white-coloured victims. The spirit of corn is incarnate in a bull,† and at the first of the New Year a man will put on a horned mask, and dance, so as to promote a good crop.

Sa(r)rikin Rafi (or *Kogi*) is a water spirit, perhaps the same as Dodo, who is mentioned later. It would appear that a virgin was sacrificed to him at one time.

Ayu is a spirit living in the water, which drags people down. This name is also given to the manatee.

---

* Frazer, *Totemism and Exogamy,* vol. ii, page 601.

† As elsewhere, *vide* Frazer, *Spirits of the Corn and of the Wild,* i, 288. In Egypt, the time for ploughing was indicated by the sign of the bull, but oxen were not used in agricultural work by the Hausas.

Uwayara is a spirit which kills the mother and her new-born child.

The echo is attributed to a supernatural agency, in fact it is sometimes called *Iblis,* devil, or *Kurua,* meaning soul, spirit, shadow.

Fatalua and *Magiro* are evil beings of some kind, though I could not discover the exact meaning of the words. Canon Robinson (*Dictionary*) gives " ghost, hobgoblin, spectre " for the former, and " ghost, evil spirit " for the latter. *Kaura* is said to be an evil spirit which makes men fight.

Gajjimare is the god of rain and storms, which has the shape of a snake, and is double-gendered, the male part being red, the female blue. It lives in the storm-clouds (same name), but is supposed to come out at night, and it is also said to inhabit wells, and in fact all watering-places, so a pot is kept full in every house. *Gajjimare* (rainbow) may be represented by the water-serpent killed in the legend of Daura before referred to, but sometimes it is said to be the husband of *Uwardowa,* and the father of *Kuri.* Other names of the rainbow are *Masharua,* " water drinker," and *Bakkan gizzo,* " spider's bow."

NATURE MYTHS.—I thought at first that the story of the Fufunda (page 129) must have been imported—because the ending has a Mohammedan flavour—and Canon Robinson agreed with me, but it may not be altogether foreign, for the idea that the sun comes out of a great gate which the Heaven opens for it is known elsewhere in West Africa.* At any rate, the variant to Story 95 seems to be a sun-myth, of genuine Hausa origin. There the youth and the spider pass beyond

---

* On the Gold Coast, *vide* Tylor, *Primitive Culture,* vol. i, page 347.

XIII AND XIV.—HOUSES IN KANO WITH GRASS FENCES, AND IN SOKOTO
WITH MUD WALLS.

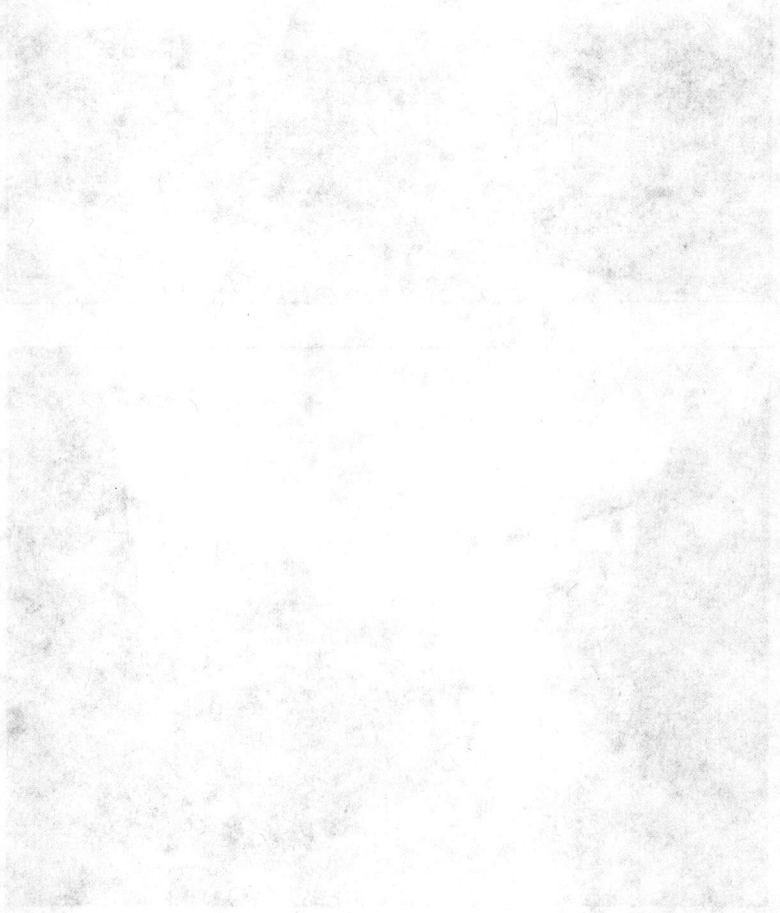

the world, and meet a witch, who tries to kill them, but her scheme is frustrated first by the crowing of a cock, then by the watchfulness of the spider. Witches or other man-eating monsters appear elsewhere as being connected with night,* so the idea is not strange in the case of the Hausas. The witch is able to kill the travellers only during the night, apparently, and although married to the youth in another version (95) she does not sleep with him, and he will not allow her even to enter his hut. The spider and the youth set out at daylight, the cock having announced the dawn, and cross a river of fire, which is probably the first flush of dawn; a river of cold water, possibly the mists; and a river of hot water, which might symbolize the warmth,† and they are safe only after having done this. The razors on the horse may have been introduced merely to "adorn the tale," or the tail may represent the bright fleeting clouds at dawn, pierced by the sun-rays.‡

But the night monster need not always be a female,

---

* Tylor, *op. cit.*, pages 335-342.

† This would mean a slight change in the order of the obstacles, but such an alteration should be permissible, for the myths are not supposed to be exact. In this very story, although the travellers had reached a place where "there was no land, nothing but wind, water, and darkness," the cock manages to escape capture by hiding "in the grass."

‡ Dr. Leo. Frobenius (*The Childhood of Man*, page 371) comes to a similar conclusion, and says : "When spiders break the witch's head at night-time, when her blood flows round about, we are decidedly reminded of Maui [N.Z.], who contends with the fire-god, or with other solar-deities, who rise out of a blood-bath in the morning. . . . In the form of rays the sun emits its sea of light; in the form of rays the spider, too, weaves its web. Thus the slender threads of the spider become solar rays, and the sun becomes the spider, which in artful ways ensnares the souls of mortals." The Bagos of West Africa represent the sun as "a thievish witch in the middle of a spider's web."

even in Hausa tales, for in another (L.T.H., ii, 77) a princess is married to a husband who is nothing but a ball of hair, and has eaten three previous wives. She takes a number of garments with her, and when left alone with him at night, she throws some in the fire each time that " he swells up and is going to eat her." He, not to be outdone, plucks some hair out, and burns that, and just before daylight, as she destroys her last garment, he pulls off his skin—all the hair having gone already—and " then the girl beheld a youth, red, red (white) was he; and he was shivering with the cold." She gave him clothes to put on (apparently quite ignoring the fact that they were all burnt), and then daylight appeared, and she was safe.

In other stories, too, there seems to be a sun-myth element, *e.g.*, where the girl is swallowed, and comes up again as shining metal (55 variant), and where the fiery Dodo catches the father and the boy, and they get out of the bag and escape (32), particularly as in the last case a witch is substituted for Dodo in a variant.*

The stars are supposed to visit each other and talk (M.H. 25). The morning-star in harvest time (which Canon Robinson thinks to be the *a* in Aquila) is known as the eagle-star. A constellation which appears at the commencement of the rains is known as *Kaza Maiyaya,* the Hen with Chickens.

---

* Dodo's Debt is evidently a sun-myth, although the bride herself is not swallowed, the story corresponding in many respects to the Basuto Myth of Litaolane. Dr. Frobenius observes (*op. cit.*, page 286). " It is very characteristic that the insular and coast peoples let the sun be devoured by a fish [*e.g.*, Jonah], since for them the sun sinks under the sea, while, on the contrary, the Basutos, living on the mainland, instead of the fish make the monster Kammapa responsible for the disaster." The Hausas, for a similar reason, make Dodo act the part of the destroyer.

Some myths of the sun and moon have been mentioned already, but there are many others. In the story of the hyæna and the bitch (F.-L. 22), for instance, the latter agrees to provide meals with all her six puppies, on the former promising to give her six cubs later, but mistrusting the hyæna, the bitch kills the cubs first and hides her puppies in a tree, giving them a rope-ladder to let down for her when necessary. The

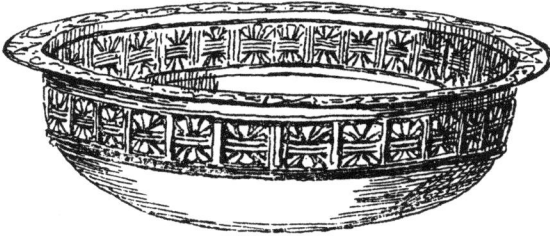

FIG. 29.

FIG. 30.

FIG. 29.—Brass basin, pattern stamped out from inside; corrugated bottom. D., 15¾ in. FIG. 30.—Pattern on upper face of lip of fig. 29.

hyæna, of course, tries to get at the puppies, but is not so successful as she is in the case of the girl in Story 84, and she chases the bitch until turned into wood. Another version is that the hyæna sank into the earth and was buried. This reminds one of a Malayan story noticed by Professor Tylor,* which is to the effect that both the sun and moon are women, both having stars as children. Each agreed to eat up her children, and the sun's stars perished, but the moon hid hers, and when the sun found this out she chased the moon to kill her. The chase is still going on, the sun sometimes biting the moon (an eclipse), while the sun still eats her own children (at dawn, when they fade), but the moon brings hers out only at night, when the sun is far away. I suggest that the Hausa story has a similar meaning, for—as Sir Edward Tylor shows—tribes far apart do have similar stories, and even Europeans preserve them.† The savage regards stars as being alive, or combines groups of them into mythical creatures, and even the modern astronomer finds the myths useful in mapping his celestial globe.

The following story (M.H. 33) would not seem to support the above suggestion, but it is impossible to say if the ideas were those originally possessed by the Hausas or not. " Some men say that the moon and the sun did not quarrel before the sun gave birth. Then the sun called the moon and asked him to hold her daughter while she went and washed herself. The moon took the sun's daughter, but was not able to hold it, for it burnt him, and he let it go, and it fell to earth

---

* *Primitive Culture*, vol. i, page 356.

† There is a story in Sierra Leone, however, of a similar agreement between the spider and the leopard regarding their offspring, and there seems to be no indication of any celestial myth contained in it. *Vide Cunnie Rabbit*, page 211. Here the spider escapes by frightening the leopard, and tying him up. Compare the spider and the lion in T.H.H., 2.

—that is why men feel hot on earth. When the sun returned, she asked the moon where her daughter was, and the moon replied "Your daughter was burning me so I let her go, and she fell to earth." Because of that the sun pursues the moon.

"But others say that the moon's path is full of thorns, while that of the sun is sandy, and on that account the moon cannot travel quickly, as does the sun. So when the moon can proceed no farther, he gets on to the sun's path, and the sun catches him. When the sun has caught him the people take their drums" and ask the sun to spare the moon.*

Judging by Indian analogies, Story 65 might refer either to the eclipse, or to the birth of the New Year, for both in the worship of *Rahu* and at the *Holi* festival, a tribal priest walks through the fire,† but sufficient proof is not forthcoming.

There is some virtue in being swallowed, for an ugly girl can be brought up again in a beautiful form, "half silver and half gold" (F.-L. 48). But if animals (M. 8) or insects (87) act the part of Jack the Giant Killer, they usually seem to kill their adversaries by cutting their way out of their hosts, as does the knife sent by God to the terrified bride (75). The swallowing of the victim, and his cutting his way out are well-known incidents in eclipse stories.

Once the sun and the wind had a quarrel about which was the more powerful, and they agreed to test their powers by trying to seize by force the tobe of a traveller. The wind first caught him, and blew off his

---

* The full translation is they "take their mortars, stretch skins over the openings, and beat the drums" thus formed, and so, says Frobenius (*op. cit.*, page 97), we see how the drum was invented.

† Crooke, *op. cit.*, i, 19 and ii, 317.

tobe, but he caught the arms and folded it up, and stooping down, avoided all further danger. Then the sun beat upon the man, and soon he was so hot that he would have thrown away his tobe, there was no escape from the heat, for he was far away from any shelter. Thus it was that the man said that the sun was the more powerful, and his opinion was accepted by the contestants.

THE NEXT WORLD.—*Dunia* (world) is often used, as with us, to denote the evil principle of this life. The next world is evidently a replica of this, since the families are together (85), and live in houses, and souls there have the same anxiety about what is to be left to them as do mortals here. It is above, probably (64), but there is a heavenly night and day (85). Animals go to it too, and the inhabitants die a second time. Souls may transmigrate from one human body to another, especially in the case of members of the same family, but they cannot enter animals. Some (*Garubawa*) believe that souls are good or bad, the latter being condemned to wander about, the former returning to the womb of a woman of the family, and reappearing, usually, in a grandchild of the deceased. Others (*Babban Dammo*) think that the souls will come to kill the living people if not placated or prevented, and so they place thorns on the corpse to prevent the soul escaping.*

DISEASES.—Several diseases seem to be personified, such as *Dan Zanzanna,* who gives small-pox to his enemies, *Dogua,* an evil spirit which injures the tamarind and baobab trees, and causes paralysis and death of people eating the fruit. The latter is also called *Maigidda biu* (the owner of two houses), because

---

* Frazer, *Totemism and Exogamy*, vol. ii, pages 604, 605.

when he becomes tired of one tree he goes to live in the other. Another meaning of *Dogua,* I was told, is Hunger, and to this also the description would apply, for if he had killed one person (*i.e.,* destroyed one house), he could always go to another.

TOTEMISM.—Although a doubt may be raised as to whether the pagan customs and beliefs of the Hausas should be classed under the head of totemism or not, it can be said, at any rate, that in many points they resemble true totemism very closely. The word for both totem (if really so) and tabu is *kan gidda* (that which is upon the house), and most of these totems are birds. Persons having the same totem or tabu constitute a clan, but these clans do not coincide with the political divisions of the country, for members of the latter are distinguished by scarifications on their faces, and these marks do not refer to the totemic clan. Some clans sacrifice the totem annually (*e.g.,* a hen), others will not do so, nor will they even touch it (*e.g.,* frog). A Hunter community of Katsina which has a short black snake as its totem will not eat anything killed by it, but it is friendly, and lives in the rafters, and comes down to the floor of the hut if a son be born. At least one community (*Babban Dammo*) claims to be descended from its totem, which is an iguana. The Magazawa were originally exogamous, but in some districts marriages within the totem may now take place.*

Some of the stories contain totemistic elements, probably Stories 3 and 3 variant refer to the mythical ancestors (a fish and a frog) of some clans, as likewise do F.-L. 42 and 47 (a pigeon and an elephant), and T.H.H. 7 (a bird). The Donkey-Maiden (T.H.H. 4)

---

* Frazer, *Totemism and Exogamy*, ii, pages 600-607.

and the Dog-Maiden (L.T.H., ii, 59), and possibly
also the Monkey-Woman (57 and 58), belong to the
class of which the tales of the Swan-Maiden and
Beauty and the Beast are types. The explanation of
these latter stories is that they referred originally to
the fact that husbands and wives would claim totems
of different kinds, and that they would resent, therefore, any taunts about their origin (58), for these would
be equivalent to injuries done to their animal kinsfolk.
Each husband and wife would revere his or her own
family totem, but would not be bound to respect that
of the spouse, and so quarrels would arise, and perhaps
end in permanent separation, one or the other becoming
the supernatural husband or wife who has mated for a
time with a human being.*

There is a story (L.T.H., ii, 280) strongly sugges-
tive of the primitive stage of " conceptional totemism "
which ought to be mentioned. A certain woman had
started out on a journey, when the leaf of a silk-cotton
tree fell upon her, and she returned home, sending to tell
those who were expecting her that she had been lucky.
The leaf she put under a water-jar, in a cool spot, and
it began to grow.   Then the woman said " Tell the
King that I have a son."   And when the King, her
brother, sent to ask his name, she said " It is Son-of-
a-Silk-Cotton-Tree."   Soon the tree grew as high as
the jar, and the jar was taken away, the tree being left
alone in the hut, and when it had grown up higher,
the roof was taken off. A slave was told off to look
after the tree, and four wives were brought, a hut being
built for each near the original one. The wives came
every morning to pay their respects to the tree, and
the youngest used to scrape the bark. One day the

* Frazer, *ib.*, page 571.

tree told the slave to get him clothes, and, when these
had been procured, the slave saw a man come out of
a hole in the tree, and put on the clothes. This being
visited his first wife that night and gave her bracelets,
returning to the tree in the morning, and then he
visited the others in turn, but he scratched the youngest

FIG. 31.—Brass jug, deep red colour, used for holding water for a chief,
especially at ceremonies; hinged lid. H., 11¾ in.

for having hurt him by scraping his tree. Then the slave
told the mother, and the son went through the proper
marriage ceremonies, "the King seized him and
smeared him with henna, while his mother seized the
King's daughter (the senior wife) and smeared her,"
and the husband and his wives lived naturally. Un-

fortunately there is no further mention of the tree, but it probably disappears, since the newly-formed family take possession of the house, and the slave says, " The-Son-of-a-Silk-Cotton-Tree has become a man."*

It is not improbable that other stories of miraculous births would be on similar lines to the above if fully told, for one can never be certain that the whole account has been preserved. Thus where a woman bears a mouse, a cake, or a household utensil,† she may have been touched by it or its type, in the original version, before conception. From other stories, it seems that the life of a tree in the compound may be connected with that of one of the sons of the house, and so the state of his health when absent can be told by the appearance of the tree.

MYTHICAL BEINGS, &c.—There are giants in the Hausa Folk-Lore (33,‡ 99 and 100), and many-headed

---

* Compare this story with those obtained by Dr. Rivers in the island of Mota, in the Banks' group. A woman in the bush finds a fruit (or animal) in her loincloth, and takes it home, and the people tell her that she will give birth. She replaces the fruit and builds a wall around it, and tends it every day. After a time it disappears, and is supposed to have entered the woman in some supernatural manner—but not by a physical impregnation. After a time a child is born, and it is regarded as being in some sense the (animal or) fruit which had been found, and tended by the mother. *R.A.I. Journal*, xxxix (1909), page 172.

Compare also the story of Batau who turned into two trees, and when being cut down at the suit of his faithless wife (who had married Pharaoh), made a chip fly into her mouth, and caused her to conceive. *The International Library of Famous Literature*, Ed. Dr. R. Garnett. Vol. i, page 81.

Tree marriages are not uncommon in India, a man taking a plant as his third wife (the third being unlucky) and a girl as his fourth. Girls, too, are wedded to trees amongst the Kurmis. Crooke, *op. cit.*, ii, 115.

† In India marriages to jars, nuts, &c., take place. *Vide* Crooke, *op. cit.*, ii, 117.

‡ According to the *Kano Chronicle*, Barbushe was a man of great stature and might, a hunter who slew elephants with his stick, and carried them home on his head. In this respect he resembles Bortorimi.

cannibals (98), but I have not heard of any dwarfs*
(unless the boys in 70 and 71 be exceptions), and
this is rather surprising, for Hausaland seems to
have been inhabited by " little black men " at one time.
It is just possible that this points to the probable origin
of the Hausas from the east across the desert—where
there was no such dense forest, and therefore no pygmy
race—for if they had gradually driven these little people
down the coast their folk-lore would surely have had
some mementoes of them ! The giants are represented
as being much more powerful than the average man,
and although it has been proved by scientific observers
that monstrosities are really weaker—for some part of
the body has developed at the expense of the rest—the
idea is natural.

THE HALF-MAN.—There is a somewhat unusual
creature in the " Half-Being " (*Barin Mutum* or *Bare-
Bare*) who appears in one of the stories as a half-man
(16), and in three others as a half-woman (16 variant,
84, and 100). I do not mean a being half-human, half-
animal, such as in Story 73, but half a human body,
" with one arm, and one leg, and one eye," as if
a person had been split up from the pelvis to the
skull.

Mr. Crooke tells me that the Hausa " Half-Being "
probably comes from the Arabic " Split-Man " (*Shikk*)
—who resembles the Persian " Half-Face " (*Nimchah-
rah*)—a kind of demon, like a man divided longitudin-
ally, which runs with amazing speed and is very cruel

---

* I refer to the pagan Hausas, but " in March, 1909, a man
named Awudu saw two black dwarfs, a man and a woman, each
about one foot high, emerge from a *rimi* tree and walk towards
him across a valley. They then disappeared as suddenly as they
had come." *Hausa Sayings*, page 96. This may be due to
Mohammedan influence.

and dangerous (*vide* Burton, *Arabian Nights,* Library Edition, iv, 279).*

Dodo.—*Dodo* is a mythical monster or bogey, in fact, the *giddan tsafi* (house of magic) is often called the *giddan dodo;* I do not think that he can be a crocodile, though I jumped to that conclusion at first, for one of his names is *Kadindi* (75), and I thought that this might be a corruption of *Kaddodi* (pl. of *Kadda*). Possibly he is a water-snake, for there are somewhat similar stories in regard to that reptile. Thus in the legend of Daura (a corruption of which is given in M.H. 15), a youth is represented as coming to the place, and killing the snake which lived in the well, and prevented the people

---

* Examples of the split or divided being occur elsewhere, for in a Sierra Leone tale (*Cunnie Rabbit,* page 22) a girl marries a half-devil who had borrowed half a body to supply his deficiency, but, on returning to his own home with his bride, the borrowed half fell away from him. In Uganda, too, the half-man is known, the Banyoro telling a tale of a man " who had only one eye, one ear, one leg, one arm, and one bull." (Kitching, *On the Backwaters of the Nile,* page 141.) He lived at the top of a hill, and after a youth of the Bahuma had trespassed, " Old One-eye" presented himself and his bull at his father's kraal to be buried, raising himself and returning each day, no matter what the mode of burial was. The Zulus go further, for they tell of a whole tribe of half-beings, who on finding a normal Zulu girl one day, say " The thing is pretty! But oh the two legs." (Tylor, *op. cit.,* i, p. 391.) Even in Australia, too, there is a being, *Turramulan,* whose name means " leg on one side only," or " one-legged " (Lang, *op. cit.,* vol. ii, page 30). The *Daitya* of India has only half a body, but he is not divided like the *Barin Mutum,* and I do not know of any tales of a half-being in our own folk-lore, for the one-eyed ogre had nevertheless a full complement of limbs. But a German story relates how a beaker was stolen from the underground folk, the thief (who was mounted) being followed first by " Three-legs," then by " Two-legs," and lastly by " One-leg," who nearly caught him. (Hartland, *op. cit.,* page 152.)

Professor Tylor says (*loc. cit.*) that these realistic fancies coincide with the simple metaphor which describes a savage as only " half a man."

drawing water, the youth then marrying the princess, and becoming the chief of the town (*cf.* Story 86). In fact Lady Lugard says that the youth did kill "the dodo or fetish lion." And she continues that "Dodo signifies the King of Beasts, and may apply equally to rhinoceros, elephant, or any other great wild animal."* Certainly, his keen sense of smell is an animal attribute, but not much reliance can be placed upon this tale, for, in another one, a bird is the fearsome object which "makes women afraid, and causes all men to run away." In fact, this type of story is found in many countries, even in Scotland.†

But although in some stories he is evidently a water-god (10, 56 and 75), and can give a charm or safe-conduct to a human being to enter water, and be safe from danger of drowning, in others he has a house in the forest (14 and 73), and he cannot cross running water (14 and T.H.H. 5), so there is evidently some confusion. Perhaps when he has once assumed the human shape he cannot readily transform himself again, and yet this would not account for his inability to cross a stream which women have managed without difficulty. Probably there are different species of Dodo, or else, when the human form has been assumed, water is tabu. Canon Robinson's *Dictionary* gives for Dodo an "evil spirit, spirit of a dead man which is supposed to walk about on the day of his death, but to rise and

---

* She remarks : " The myth may be taken to indicate that, in the time of the hero, the worship of the goddess was substituted for the worship of the fetish" (*A Tropical Dependancy*, page 260). But it may resemble the Babylonian myth of Marduk, and represent the killing of the wet season by the dry. *Vide* Frazer, *The Dying God*, p. 107.

† *Vide* Professor Frazer's Translation of *Pausanias's Description of Greece*, bk. ix, ch. 26, 7 (vol. v, pp. 143 *sqq.*), and *The Magic Art*, ii, pp. 155 *sqq.*

disappear the same evening; it appears at times in trees, and catches men." The fact that he is unable to cross running water also gives him a ghostly character.

However, whatever he is, he has the power of assuming human shape; one story (48) gives the converse also—he is even called "a man of men." Like a witch, he is afraid of dogs (51), and he takes her place in some of the stories (100). He is evidently a giant (T.H.H. 5), for he has to stoop to enter the houses (86), the parts of his body are very big (32), and he can swallow any number of people and animals (75). It is possible that he resembles a white man,* except that he has very long hair (55), and a tail (86).† He is too strong for the lion (48), and he roars.

He usually feeds on human beings (14 and 75), but sometimes he may treat them very well instead (56), and his human wife seems to be safe, at any rate so long as she does not try to escape (14 and 56). His offspring is evidently not desired (73), and it is possible that deformed children were attributed to him, and killed accordingly. If this is so, the girl could not have

---

* In Story 56, the girl is said to have been conducted into the river by the *mutanen rua*, who were described by the narrator as being white people with very long hair; these are Dodo's subjects apparently. Canon Robinson says that he is " hairy all over." He seems to correspond to the *Rakshasa* of Bengal. There is a female Dodo or *Dodoniya*, the common plural being *Dodonai*.

† This may have some reference to the pagan tribes to the south whose women wear tails. *Vide* T.H.H., page 107. It is said that when the Seyawa came from Dal to Bogorro, they found a man named Sangari who was covered with hair, had a tail, and knew not the use of fire. So they shaved off his hair, and cut off his tail, but even now his pure descendants will not eat roasted meat.

bathed so as to cause conception, though this is known in other countries where a water-god is married or worshipped.

The hero usually cuts off the head or tail of the slaughtered enemy as evidence, but in one story he also leaves his boots behind (86), and there is a competition

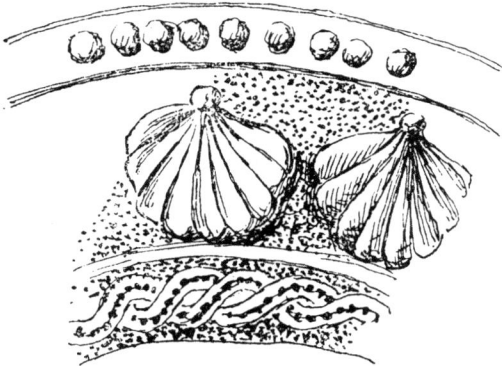

FIG. 32.

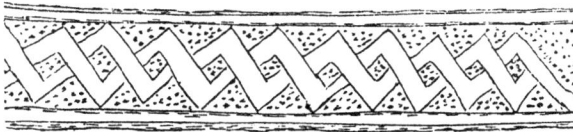

FIG. 33.

FIG. 32.—Pattern under body of fig. 29. The bold designs are stamped out from inside, the dots are stamped in from the outside. FIG. 33.—Pattern on handle of fig. 31.

amongst the warriors who pretend that they have done the deed, like that amongst the sisters in " Cinderella."

One Dodo story (M.H. 4) resembles some of the variants of the Swan-Maiden tales. Two girls claim to be the most beautiful in the city, and as they cannot agree, they set out into the world to ask the people of each city to vote for one or the other. They collect many presents while doing this, and at length return towards their own city, but at the river the elder makes the younger enter deep water and she is lost. After a time the maiden appears to her brother who tends flocks on the bank, attends to his hair (? a magic rite), and rubs him with oil. Then a youth volunteers to go and rescue her, on the condition that if successful he shall have her in marriage. The parents agree to this, so, having made himself appear like a leper, he enters the water and asks Dodo if he wishes to be shaved. Dodo does, fortunately, so the youth produces his razor (at which the water becomes white, and the watchers above are unhappy), and commences to shave him (at which the water becomes darkest black, and the watchers weep), and then cuts Dodo's throat (at which the water becomes red, and the watchers rejoice).

He marries the maiden, but she, being ungrateful, gives him dirty dishes to eat and drink from. At last he washes off his paint and a friend tells her that he was not really a leper, so she washes the utensils. But he will not now use them thus, and tells her that she must procure the tail of a young lion and wash them. So she sets off into the forest, and having made friends with a lioness, she hides in the den, cuts off a tail, and escapes with it, and all ends happily.

A FABULOUS BIRD.—In Story 44 (variant), a fabulous bird, the Jipillima, is mentioned, which feeds on human beings, and whose droppings have magical powers of healing. I asked the narrator whether the *jipillima* was the same as the *fufunda* (probably phœnix, mentioned in Canon Robinson's Grammar), and he said that it was; but another man whom I questioned on the subject informed me that both of them were *azenchin wofi* (lies).* I do not know if the fufunda story is genuine Hausa or borrowed from the Arabic, but it is at any rate interesting. A king wanted to send someone to see where the sun arose, and a poor man, named Ataru, volunteered to go. A horse was given to him, and after journeying for a month† he passed beyond everything, and came to the country of the storks, which, however, were men there. One knew Ataru, and took him to the King of the Stork-Men, and the other storks recognized him. He asked them where the sun came out, and they gave him directions how to proceed, so next day he took his departure and, after having passed a dark place, he reached a white place, a river of silver, a little of which he took and wrapped in his sleeve. Next he came to a red place, to a golden river, and after having done the same thing there, he continued his journey, passing a large gutta-percha tree, a large fig tree, and a large durumi tree. At last he arrived at a tamarind tree, and there he saw the *fufunda,* an enormous bird, and he rested that night. In the early dawn a cock‡ crew, and when the sun was about to come forth he crew again, and after a little he crew a third time. Then the Opener-of-the-Door came and opened the door, and said " The sun is coming forth," and he repeated " The sun is coming forth." Immediately Ataru galloped off, but before he had reached the City of the Storks the sun had scorched him, he could only just get along, and

---

* One description of the jipillima is a bird with a white head and wings, the rest of the body being mixed black and white.

† This makes a more Eastern origin probable. for many Hausas have been to Mecca, and they knew that to travel even as far as that takes several months.

‡ Not the phœnix, for the word *zakarra,* rooster, is used.

when he had dismounted they nursed him until he was well again.

The story ends with the information that the fufunda is the King of the Birds, it has only one egg; after the creation of the world it laid that egg and sat on it; it has not hatched it, it will not hatch it until the last day. He who is good will come under its shadow, he who is evil will remain in the sun's heat until his brains boil, he will see the shadow of the fufunda, but he will not enter it.

WONDERFUL ANIMALS.—A horse to which magic powers are likely to be ascribed in the near future is *Gunya*, the charger of Ismaila, one of the greatest fighting chiefs of Argungu. It is related (L.T.H., ii, page 346) that on going out to fight, the chief used to consult it, and if it neighed three times victory was certain, whereas if it did not do so, defeat was just as inevitable. It was given a state funeral when it died.

The *Zankallala* (87), although no bigger than two clenched fists, is a terrible enemy, for he carries a snake in his hand as a walking-stick, he wears a pair of scorpions as spurs, and a swarm of bees as a hat. He rides upon the jerboa, and flocks of birds attend him, to sing his praises, and to worry those with whom he fights.

Although there is no ghostly reaper in the Hausa tales, a man who possesses a *kwiyafa* is very lucky, as this animal will do all his farm work for him if controlled by the proper words of command (L.T.H., ii, 71). But the exact words must be used, else it will not commence or stop when required, and the person in whose possession it happens to fall may be injured, as in the case of the robber and the magic door (14). Sometimes the spirits of trees in the vicinity will help

(L.T.H., ii, 74), and with them, too, great care must be exercised. The dog-maiden and the donkey-maiden have been mentioned before; they can hardly be classed as wonderful animals, for they are really human beings temporarily in an animal form.

MAGIC OINTMENT.—The fairy unguent, so popular in European tales, appears but seldom in Hausa Folklore; in fact, I have come across only one instance (L.T.H., ii, 27). A man and his wife gave birth to four daughters in succession (about 2 years and 9

FIG. 34.—Brass bottle, with cap.   H., $5\frac{13}{16}$ in.

months between each), and as it happened that every one of them disappeared on the day that she was to have been weaned, the parents got the reputation of having eaten them. Last of all, a son arrived, and the mother decided to nurse him until he weaned himself. As he grew up, he found that the boys of his town would not play with him (see also 56), and one day, when he was out riding by himself, he came upon two black snakes fighting, so he took off his tobe, and threw it down, and they separated, and departed. Soon afterwards, he heard a voice calling him, and he saw an old woman, who gave him some lotion, telling him to rub his eyes with it. He did so, and immediately he saw a large house, and, on entering it, found his eldest sister. She made him welcome, and her husband, a bull, did likewise, and, when he left, the bull gave him a lock of his hair. He then found the other sisters, who were married to a ram, a dog, and a hawk, receiving hair or feathers from them, respectively, and after that he went home and told his parents of his adventure, and that his sisters were alive. Next day he went to a far city, and made love to the wife of the King (*vide* xlv, 8), and he persuaded her to make the King show his affection for her by " taking his own life, and joining it to hers." The King said " My life is behind the city, behind the city in a thicket. In this thicket there is a lake ; in the lake is a rock ; in the rock is a gazelle ; in the gazelle is a dove ; and in the dove is a small box." The Queen told the youth, and he made a fire behind the city, and threw in the hair and feathers. Immediately the bull appeared, and was told to drink up the lake ; the ram was set to break the rock, the dog to catch the gazelle, and the hawk to capture the dove. The youth thus obtained the box, and, on his return, found that the King was dead, having become unwell from the moment of the youth's leaving the city, and becoming worse and worse as his supplanter succeeded.* So the Queen married the hero, and he was made King, his sisters' husbands—who had become men—being given subordinate posts, and his parents were brought to live in the city.

TRANSFORMATION.—Instances of a human being

---

* Instances of the External Soul are exceedingly common, *vide The Golden Bough*, second edition, iii, pp. 351-389.

taking the form of an animal or a bird while preserving his original identity are numerous; for instance, he may become a horse, a scorpion, a snake, an eagle, a crow, or another kind of bird (F.-L. 49), or a frog, a mouse, a cat, or a hawk (19). He may also become an inanimate object such as an ant-hill, a stump, or a ring (F.-L. 46), even a part of the human body, such as the eyebrow or the pupil (19). It has been suggested that Story 71, where the prodigy is supposed to have been born in and to have lived in a clay pot, really means that the boy changed himself into a pot; but I do not think that this is so, for the cake in the following story seems to have no power to change into a human being, and to avoid being eaten by the mouse.

But the power of transformation does not belong to man alone, the contrary also holds, and members of the animal kingdom can become human beings for the time being, or at least that power is possessed by the buffalo (F.-L. 46), the gazelle (F.-L. 47), the monkey (57 and 58), the snake (F.-L. 45), the pigeon (F.-L. 42), and of course the spider (15 and F.-L. 12). When animals take human form the change is usually made to deceive some particular person, but sometimes it is for the purpose of benefiting him. Thus a witch, Dodoniya, a lion, or a buffalo becomes a beautiful girl, so that she can lure the hunter to the forest and destroy him (48 and F.-L. 46), a snake becomes a handsome youth so as to marry a girl who says that she will choose her husband herself (F.-L. 45), and that only a man whose body is without a fault of any kind will be eligible. On the other hand, in two stories (F.-L. 42 and T.H.H. 7) a bird saves a girl's life by taking her place, and I am not at all sure that this does not indicate some process of substitution in sacrifice; it is, at any rate, worth noting that when the change has been made it is complete in all respects, and that the newly made man or animal behaves as if he were really what he represents himself to be. But apart from this, inanimate objects sometimes have the power of speech (14, 72, 77, 91 and 100), and even of movement and action (2 and T.H.H. 6).

In some stories, a whole succession of transformations is effected by the hero and his adversary, the length of the sequence often depending solely upon the enthusiasm and imagination of the narrator.* Sometimes, again, the change is made for the purpose of profit; thus a boy becomes a horse, and after his brothers have sold him he becomes a boy again, and runs away (F.-L. 49). After all, why should not the Hausa believe in transformations, or even a series of them? The life-history of the butterfly is hardly less amazing than many of the tales. Indeed, the gentle change of the chrysalis into its wondrous final form, might well call to mind the Sleeping Beauty re-awakened to life by a kiss from the handsome prince.

Apparently the person or animal undergoing transformation must roll on the ground (57), and, if the former, must first remove any clothing or ornament appropriate only to human beings. Perhaps this has

---

* This is not peculiar to Hausa folk-lore, in a Finnish tale we find a similar idea. " ' If thou wilt not release me,' she said, ' I will change into a salmon and escape thee.' But Ilmarinen told her that he would pursue her in the shape of a pike. Then the maiden said first, that she would become an ermine, but Ilmarinen told her he would turn into a snake and catch her; and then she said that she would become a swallow, but Ilmarinen threatened to become an eagle." There are many other examples elsewhere.

some connection with the nudity charm, though nakedness is usually opposed rather than favourable to evil
influences.

It will be noticed that those persons who can transform themselves into animals, &c., have had some
charm or medicine given them (F.-L. 49), usually both,
and it has been suggested that the idea arose originally
because the medicine was some powerful soporific
which caused the patient to see visions, or else, perhaps, clouded his intellect, making him an easier subject to mesmerize. But this explanation ignores the
savage notion of the ancient animal kingdom, and
seems to be rather more elaborate than is necessary.
The witch who is mentioned in Story 91 was, possibly,
invisible, until she had spoken.*

SACRIFICE.—Story 56 indicates that there was
once a sacrifice to a water-god, and though he is
here called *Dodo,* that may not have been his original
name. The sacrifice was made, apparently, to prevent
an overflow of the river, though the first reason given
is similar to that in the Biblical tale of Jephtha
and his daughter, and there seems to have been
some disgrace attached to the victim, for the sister of
the girl who married Dodo's son is mocked by her
companions. In another story (L.T.H., ii, 51) the
sacrifice of a daughter of the chief is said to be made
annually to Dodo, so that the water-supply will be
plentiful. The Hausa St. George kills the snake, and
there are no more sacrifices. I am not sure that
this rite has any connection with the sacrifice of the

---

* In many cases, English witches were supposed not only to
have taken drugs internally, but to have rubbed unguents on
their bodies as well, sometimes parts of human bodies being
amongst the ingredients. *Vide* T.H.H., page 238.

Egyptian virgin to the Nile in order to secure a good inundation, but it is certainly not impossible.*

Infanticide and the slaughter of victims at war time have already been mentioned.

Story 99 suggests the burying alive of a wife with her husband, so that he may live with her again, and this is what one would expect. As the grave itself was turned into a palace, and there is no mention of the couple returning to earth, it is evident that it is the next world, and not this one, in which they settle down. But other relatives may be interred also (65),† and even persons outside the family may be sent to keep the departed spirit company (76), this referring, in all probability, to debtors and slaves purchased for the purpose. How long ago this custom (if it really existed) was discontinued, it is impossible to say; even the wild Kagoro have abandoned it, though it is

---

* The Egyptian custom was abolished by the Arab conquerors. Many instances of sacrifice or marriage to a water god have been noted by Professor Frazer (*The Golden Bough*, ii, pages 150-170). The Akikuyu of British East Africa worship the snake of a certain river, and at intervals of several years they marry the snake-god to women, but especially to young girls. In Timor a young girl was taken to the bank of the river, and set upon a sacred stone, and soon the crocodiles appeared, and dragged her down. In other parts, the offering was made to ensure a proper water supply, as in the Hausa variant. The hero who converts the pagans from this worship is saved by the Koran if a Mohammedan, by the Sign of the Cross if a Christian (as in the Rouen legend), and in later times it is he who is supposed to have killed the monster—*i.e.*, to have put down the sacrifice. A few writers have thought that some of the European scenic festivals represent the triumph of Christ over sin and death (Horner, *op. cit.*, gives a picture of Christ delivering souls from the *mouth* of the Hell-Monster), but Professor Frazer points out that the tale of the conquest of the dragon is older than Christianity, and cannot be explained by it.

† *Cf.* an Indian custom. " In Jesalmer, a curious variation of the *Sati* ceremony seems to have prevailed; mothers used to sacrifice themselves with their dead children." Crooke, *op. cit.*, i, 188.

reported to be still in existence among a neighbouring tribe.*

In Stories 67 and 68, animals were killed by a boy

FIG. 35.

FIG. 36.

FIG. 37.

FIG. 35.—Brass bowl or lid, fluted.   D., 8½ in. FIG. 36.—Brass pot, pattern stamped out. H., 5¾ in.   FIG. 37.—Brass pot (white tin colour inside), stamped pattern. H., 8½ in.

who is posing as the adopted son of the owner of the animals, and it seems extremely probable that this was

---

* See T.H.H., pages 178 and 187.   The Kagoro may place skulls on the grave even now.

a sacrifice to be performed only by a son. It is not merely a test of affection, for the owner is afraid that he will be disgraced if the truth be discovered, and prefers death rather than that. To make the offering the more efficacious, the father orders his adopted son to leave the saddle on the animal.*

Stories F.-L. 42 and T.H.H. 7 seem to indicate a form of substitution, for which see T.H.H., page 187.

CANNIBALISM.—Except in the case of albinos as mentioned before, cannibalism does not appear to be connected so much with sacrifice as with the taste of the flesh, and Number 97 reminds one very much of the well-known story in England concerning the flavour of a certain brand of stout. Evidently the victims were fattened up (98) before being eaten.†

It is just possible that the desire for the heads of enemies with which " to make cooking places " (59) may indicate some form of cannibalism amongst the Hausas themselves—or at any rate of head-hunting; certainly there is an idea of rendering service after death in Story 43 to the person possessing the skulls (compare T.H.H., page 153). It seems to have been the fashion to wear the skin of a slaughtered animal and to smear some of its fat on one's head, and then to dance before the assembled crowd who applauded the hero (F.-L. 11, and L.T.H. 31), and this certainly recalls the ovation to the successful Kagoro who had brought back a hot and dripping head.

---

* It is worth noting that in the Punjab when a horse was sacrificed it had to be saddled first. Crooke, *op. cit.*, i, 46.

† Dr. Frobenius (*op. cit.*, page 80) gives a story in which it appears that the Hausa escort of a European in the Congo captured and ate natives *en route*. But the account is too vague to be of much value.

ORDEALS, &c.—The only ordeal mentioned in the stories which I have read is that of stepping over the magic gourds (83), but the Hausas used poisonous decoctions as well, such as the *gwaska,* which seems to be much the same as the *sap* (described in T.H.H., page 201) of the Kagoro and others.

A modern test made by malams is as follows : The suspected persons are made to sit around a fire as close as possible. If a person shivers he is guilty, but should no member of the party do so within a certain time—about an hour—all are innocent, and another party is called up.

Another way is to cut a hole about the size of a sixpenny-piece in a small gourd and to fill it with ink. Each of the suspected persons then dips a forefinger into the ink, and those who are innocent will be able to withdraw again without trouble. But directly the finger of the guilty person enters, the gourd closes on it, and will not release it—not even if pulled or struck—until a malam has recited a portion of the Koran over it. This seems to be a mixture of Islam and Paganism.

Swearing on the Koran is often no more efficacious than is "kissing the Book" with us. Of old, oaths used to be taken on iron, and even now many of the less civilized Hausa people are tested with this metal, a bayonet being passed across their throats, and then between their legs. I found an even better method. A cartridge was put in a calabash of water, and the witness had to drink some. The rifle was rested upon his head for a moment, and then pointed at his heart, and he was told that it would thus know where to find its child (the cartridge being supposed to have communicated its properties to the water) if the swallower told an untruth. I have known this method to break up a case that had looked quite hopeless a few minutes previously.

It is related of a chief of Missau that, before making up his mind whether to quarrel or remain friendly with the Sultan of Sokoto, he set two rams to fight, saying that one was he, the other the Sultan, and, as the latter won, he determined not to break the peace.*

Judging by Story 7, the fulfilment of a promise is considered absolutely necessary, and is praiseworthy even if it results in the loss of wives and family. This may be some kind of pagan covenant too sacred to be broken, but it appears to be rather more like a Mohammedan oath, at any rate in form, and if so the story may not be a very old one—or this particular part may have been changed to suit the altered circumstances.

THE CURSE AND BLESSING.—A curse is feared, especially if the person pronouncing it be powerful. In 1906 the Mohammedan Sultan of Sokoto pronounced a curse on anyone rebuilding Satiru or tilling its fields, because a rising had been originated there.

A blessing, once given, could not be recalled, apparently, and one version of the legend of the origin of the Hausa states strongly resembles the story of Isaac, Jacob, and Esau.   Bawo (from Bornu), after having killed the snake which prevented the people drinking,

---

* Compare this with Dr. Barth's note on the Marghi, and " their curious ordeal on the holy granite rock of Kobshi. When two are litigating about a matter, each of them takes a cock which he thinks the best for fighting; and they go together to Kobshi. Having arrived at the holy rock, they set their birds fighting, and he whose cock prevails in the combat is also the winner in the point of litigation. But more than that, the master of the defeated cock is punished by the divinity, whose anger he has thus provoked; on returning to his village, he finds his hut in flames."   Benton, *Notes on Some Languages of the Western Sudan*, page 146.

had married Umma (or Daura) the queen of the city of Daura, and had had a son (called Kachi in one version, Bawo Bawo in another) by her, and other children by a concubine, namely, Kano, Daure and Yabuwu. When they had grown up, Bawo summoned them to bless them, and he told Kachi to come in the evening, intending to give him the "bottle of dyeing" (*i.e.*, the magic flask containing the charm or blessing which would make him supreme in that handicraft). But Kano, who was hiding, heard this, and came first, and said " Here I am, Father." So Bawo, who was blind, took the bottle of dyeing, and gave it to him, and that is the reason why Kano's dyes are so much better than those of any other city. Then Kachi arrived, and said to his father " Here I am," and Bawo said " What! was it not you to whom I gave the bottle? Kano has already been here," and he gave him (not being able to recall the bottle of dyeing) fire in order that he might set alight to the bush, his country to extend over all the space which the fire burnt, and all this became Katsina.

There is another version to the effect that Biram wedded a Berber maiden, Diggera, by whom he had six children, and when they grew up they were given special gifts: Kano and Rano were the dyers and weavers, Katsina and Daura the traders, and Zaria and Bauchi the slave-dealers.*

The Hausa utters a prayer after yawning, hiccoughing, or sneezing (compare our " Bless you "), but this may be due to Mohammedan influence—at any rate, the present invocations are Koranic in character.

---

* This is very much like a Llanberis legend (S.F.T. 327), according to which the eldest son became a great physician, the second a Welsh Tubal-Cain, while one of the daughters invented the small ten-stringed harp, and the other the spinning-wheel.

EARTH.—A white earth is sometimes eaten to secure easy childbirth, red is rubbed on the body—often smeared with grease—for the sake of adornment, and yellow or white lines may be drawn on the face either as a protection, or—especially when mixed with black strokes—so as to give an additional charm.

Mothers, if proceeding to another country, may rub the heads of their children with earth so that they will not forget their native land; sometimes the emigrants take a little of the soil of the country with them.

KOLA-NUTS.—Kola-nuts, brought perhaps from Ashanti, are in great demand owing to their stimulating properties, and a little of the first mouthful is spat on the ground. It is said to be "for Allah," but there would probably be no objection to the pieces turning into silver as in Story 44, and being secured by a human being instead. They are given to guests at marriages and births, and correspond to invitation-cards to the feasts. There is apparently some idea of a contract in the gift when made to a *fiancée* (see page 21), in fact *goro* sometimes almost equals *alkawali,* for the rooster's promise of chickens to the hawk in Story 22 is a *goro.* On being asked "What will you give me for my news?" the proper reply is "A kola-nut."*

TABU.—There seems to be a tabu in Story 82 corresponding to those common in the folk-lore of Europe and elsewhere—for the husband is not allowed to gratify his curiosity in regard to a certain thing. Story 4 may also have an element of such a prohibition in regard

---

* Kola-nuts have great significance all over West Africa; amongst the Mendi of Sierra Leone, members of the Porro society use two red nuts as a symbol of war, one white nut broken in two indicating peace (Haywood, *op. cit.*, page 30).

to the wife, who is of supernatural origin in both these cases, and a Kaffir tale (S.F.T. 328) will help perhaps to explain it.* The tabu on the mention of a name will be found under *Names.*

A man was not allowed to see his wife's younger sister at one time, apparently (14, 56, and F.-L. 44). But that prohibition no longer exists in Hausaland, although it does in other countries.†

In Story F.-L. 48, the elephant's daughter puts a ring in the food which she has prepared for the King's son, so that he may recognize her as the beautiful girl to whom he made love at another place. This idea of the fiancée serving in the kitchen is well known in Grimm's stories, and since, both in those and in the Hausa parallel, the girl had plenty of opportunities for addressing the prince directly, it would seem that there must have been some tabu against her doing so.

The mother will seldom allow the father to see her nursing her first-born on account of the " shame " which she is said to feel, though there is no such objection in the case of the others, though the tabu on the name may apply in their case also. In fact, the eldest child is known as the *kunya* (shame) of its mother. One girl, the eldest of her family, told me that her mother would not allow her to be anywhere near her when her father was expected. At the same time, the parents are very kind to their children, and are as fond of them as it is possible for a native to be.

---

* The woman was born because her human mother had eaten magic pellets given to her by a bird, and was married to a chief. It was noticed that she never went out in the day-time, but once, in her husband's absence, she was compelled (by her father-in-law) to do some work outside (fetching water), and she also was lost, disappearing into the river.

† *Vide* Frazer, *Taboo and the Perils of the Soul,* pages 338, *sqq.*

A wife must not allow her husband to see her eating. She first cooks his meal and serves it to him, out in the open courtyard unless wet, and later on she retires inside the house to eat with her daughters and young sons. The reason is said to be that she might open her mouth too wide, and so anger or disgust her husband. Probably, the original idea was that the soul might escape through the mouth at that time.

The men take it in turns to dip in the dishes, and they must not refuse to invite a friend or stranger to partake if one be present; it would be unlucky to ignore him. This is evidently due to the fact that the envious glances of a hungry man would injure the person eating. Many amusing tales are told of the means by which a person tries to avoid inviting the other to share his meal—even pretending to be dead— but all to no purpose.

There are some others. A few pagan Hausa communities may not eat food if iron has touched it, and may not eat what is saved of the corn after their village has been destroyed by fire. Some will not carry fire in a calabash, but only in an earthenware dish, others observe exactly the contrary rules, or carry it in two sticks. Restrictions regarding dress have also been noted, thus the Hausas of Maradi will not wear anything of a light blue colour* lest it cause poverty, and amongst the Katumbawa of Kano no unmarried boy may put on sandals.†

It is very dangerous for a human being, especially a woman, to mix with supernaturals unless invited to do so, as was the good sister in Story 56, or the woman in Number 51. Females are expected to hide themselves,

---

* See remarks *re* blue colour, page 164.
† *Vide Man*, 1910, Article 40.

XV.—A POTTER AT WORK.   XVI.—TYPES OF POTS.

Pots are made over a mould, by building with strips of clay, or by a combination of both methods.   *Vide* page 173.

and, if they do not do so, the demons may kill them (90), or at any rate they will be very much displeased (bad sister in 56). Probably the objection which witches have to being seen extends to all supernaturals. Even if a girl sees something extraordinary, such as the witch's back bursting open (93), she is expected to make no remark upon it unless asked.

BORI.—There is a peculiar institution amongst the Hausas known as *Bori,* and although it is not magic

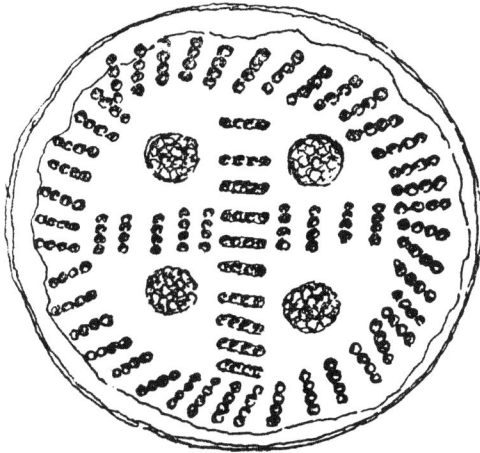

FIG. 38.—Pattern on knob of fig. 35.

exactly—being more like hypnotism, perhaps—it may be mentioned here conveniently, since it is regarded as uncanny by the more educated people. The ceremonies are usually described as a " dance," and although that term hardly describes the frenzied actions of the performers, I shall retain it for the sake of convenience. The Hausa word *rawa* means " to dance " as we understand the term, and also " to drill," so the range is fairly wide. The equivalent of *Bori* in Canon Robinson's Dictionary is given as "an evil spirit," "a demon," or "a delirious person," but it may mean rather the rites and ceremonies of a particular society, the members of which simulate the frenzied behaviour of insane persons. Probably "hallucination" is a satisfactory equivalent.

Bori dancing is said* to have originated in the Hausa States, previous to the introduction of Islam. At first merely a treatment for the insane, later on it was degraded into an objectionable form of dancing, though the origin was still apparent, since the actions of the dance simulated different forms of insanity. Each special division of *Bori* represents some kind of madness, and every *Mai-bori* ("actor," or "dancer," or "person possessed"), who may be either a male or a female in most cases, will profess one or more.

Bori was intended originally as a remedy for insanity, as has been mentioned above, or perhaps for inherited hysterical tendencies, the idea being that those who were really mad would be thereby less likely to commit acts of violence—it will be remembered that lunatics are never shut up amongst these pagan peoples, being regarded as people specially set apart by the gods, and, appropriately enough, the word for a person "touched" is *tabu*. Later on, the treatment was adopted by a class called *Karua* (consisting of disreputable males and females) in order to attract more attention. And later still, young children, generally girls, who were not thriving, or who were criminally or morbidly inclined, were subjected to the influence, for they were supposed to be possessed of some evil spirit which had to be exorcised. To be accused of *Bori*, therefore, is

* See T.H.H., pages 254 to 262, for a full description and the authorities quoted. See also extra note in Part III.

not necessarily a disgrace, though many men have objected to their wives practising it.

According to the account of Richardson, the explorer, *Bori* must have degenerated a long time ago, for one evening in 1850 " I found that one of our negresses, a wife of one of the servants, was performing *Boree*, the ' Devil,' and working herself up into the belief that his Satanic Majesty had possession of her. She threw herself upon the ground in all directions, and imitated the cries of various animals. Her actions were, however, somewhat regulated by a man tapping upon a kettle with a piece of wood, beating time to her wild manœuvres. After some delay, believing herself now possessed, and capable of performing her work, she went forward to half-a-dozen of our servants who were squatting on their hams ready to receive her. She then took each by the head and neck, and pressed their heads between her legs—they sitting, she standing— not in the most decent way, and made over them, with her whole body, certain inelegant motions not to be mentioned. She then put their hands and arms behind their backs, and after several other wild cries and jumps, and having for a moment thrown herself flat upon the ground, she declared to each and all their future—their fortune, good or bad."*

The person possessed often claims to foretell the future, but there is even more in the following account, which is mentioned in L.T.H. (page 242.) " There is a certain river at Argungu called Gandi, each year people come to fish in it. When they are about to go, all are assembled in the city, and then the chief woman drinks a potion and becomes possessed," and a man

* Benton, *Notes on Some Languages of the Western Sudan*, page 154.

named Makwashe goes into the water first, because the demons know him. "If the chief woman says 'Enter the water,' whoever enters will immediately fill his basket with fish, and then come out. If she does not tell the people to enter, whoever goes in, when he sinks, will not come out again, but will die. For it is said the river has many demons (jinns) in it." Perhaps the river has a varying current, and Makwashe tries it first and gives the woman the news!

After the conquest of the Hausa States by the Mohammedan Filani, at the beginning of last century, *Bori* was forbidden in the large cities, but it flourished in the smaller towns and villages. Later on, the *Masu-bori* (plural of *Mai-bori*) were allowed to practise their rites, even in the large cities, on payment of an annual tax, which was divided amongst the chiefs and headmen, and was really a bribe to ignore the practices. Under the British occupation the tax developed a more legal form, but serious steps have been taken lately to abolish the performances, and I am told that they are no longer held. It is said that there was a contest in the reign of Wake, chief of Gwari, between the malams, the magicians, and the *Masu-bori*. Wake secretly put a black bull into a hut, sealed up the door, and challenged the contestants to say what the hut contained. The magicians divined correctly, and the *Masu-bori* also gave the true answer, but the malams did not know, so they repaired to the mosque, and prayed that whatever the animal might be, God would turn it into a black horse. When Wake asked for their answer, and the malams replied "a horse," he was much cast down, for he was a Moslem, but lo! when the hut was opened, a black horse appeared, and since then "he who does not respect a malam does not respect God."

It is amongst the Hausa, Nupe, and Egbirra people that *Bori* proper is mostly held in favour, but there is another kind also, called *kwaga,* amongst the Kanuri of Bornu, which seems to be purely a state of hysteria in some cases, of fever or other sickness due to exposure in others, especially in the case of one who has sat under a tree, or near to water, " where a bad spirit lives."

Anyone of any age may learn it on payment of the usual fees, so the right to initiation is not hereditary, *i.e.,* there is no strictly observed caste of *Masu-bori.* The initiation or treatment may be carried out at the house of the District Head of the sect, the *Ajenge,* or at that of the patient, except among the Nupe tribe. In addition to the varying tuition fee, and the necessary accommodation, the following are necessary : A large new pot, four fowls (a white cock and hen, a red cock and a black hen), money for the *Uwar Tuo* (literally " mother of porridge ") who supplies the food, one large ram, one small black he-goat, one white cloth, one black cloth, and three grass mats—one each for the candidate, the *Maigoge* (the violinist, the chief musician) and the *Uwar Tuo.*

Some days are auspicious, others not, apparently, and so a consultation takes place between the *Ajenge* and the *Maigoge* in order to fix the date (always a Friday) on which to commence the treatment, and when this has been decided upon, the *Ajenge* goes into the bush, and collects the necessary herbs and bark, and prepares his medicines. Two days later, the candidate enters the house, clothed in white, and accompanied by a couple of selected tutors, and certain ceremonies take place which are at present unknown to us.

When the period of initiation has been completed,

the candidate, followed by a crowd of fully qualified *Masubori,* is led to a selected tamarind tree, around the trunk of which has been wrapped the black and white cloths before referred to. The small black goat is killed near the tree, the meat is cooked and eaten, and playing and dancing go on all the time round the tree. Then the initiate is carried home, and more dancing, the final rite, takes place near some big tree, a baobab if possible, probably for the object of propitiating the evil spirits which dwell there, all *Masu-bori* being afraid of them. After it is over, the initiate's friends are informed as to the particular kind and the number of the degrees conferred, and the newly-made member may then perform in public, and give way to his particular hallucinations. The initiate is then said to be "baked," whereas he was only unbaked before, like the unfinished clay pot.*

Each spirit has a special colour or object which is called its *tsere* (protection, refuge, &c.), into which it will pass instead of into the possessor, and these objects and colours are prized by those who wish to escape from the influence, or at any rate induce it only when required.†

---

* There is something derogatory in being not properly cooked. Abdurahmani, Sultan of Sokoto, was known as an Unbaked Pot, because of his evil deeds. It is just possible that this has some reference to cannibalism.

† It may be of interest to note that in Morocco the jinns are supposed to have special colours by which they are attracted. A regular *ginn-cult* is practised by the *Gnawa,* a regularly constituted secret society, the members of which live on amicable terms with the *gnun* (jinns). By ascertaining the day when a *ginn* has entered a man, his colour can be determined, for the ginns of each day of the week have a special colour, and the *Gnawa* dress themselves and the patient in the colour required. If the day of seizure is not known, perhaps the whole seven colours will be used. The *Gnawa* not only expel *gnun,* but can attract them at will, for by inhaling the smoke of a certain incense, and by dancing, they can induce the *gnun* to enter their bodies, and when thus possessed, they can foretell future events. *Vide* Westermarck, *Journal of the R.A.I.,* July-Dec., 1899. The Gnawa and the masubori resemble each other to some extent.

Thus the *Sa(r)rikin Rafi* has as its *tsere* a kola-nut and a small chicken, the *Wanzami* (barber), a razor, and so on, the connection being obvious in most cases.* There is also a special vocabulary employed by the *Masu-bori*, but as the performers are frowned upon by the authorities, both Christian and Mohammedan, the latter regarding *Bori* as being converse with the powers of evil, it is difficult to obtain information of the spirits themselves, or of the spirit language. Some words are given in the book quoted above, however, *malam* (a learned man, priest, magician) becoming *maiwalwala* (the troublesome one) for a reason which appears to be obvious considering that he is a Moslem; *ga(r)ri* (town) becoming *jan garu* (red walls); *berichi* (sleep) becoming *kankanana mutua* (little death), and so on.

When a *Bori* headman dies, a red goat and kid, a black kid, and a red and a speckled cock are killed. Speeches are made at the foot of one of the haunted trees, or a rock, and then the body is buried. After this, the goats and fowls are eaten, together with porridge, milk, and honey.

HALLUCINATIONS. — In some stories (93), the Israelitish ideas of lands " flowing with milk† and honey " is expressed, and not only this, but food cooks itself and asks to be eaten, and houses appear (50), and perhaps run away (59). In some cases fowls ask to be destroyed, as does a bird in M.H. 45, and it will be remembered that in European tales animals beg human beings to kill them, *e.g.,* Beauty and The Beast. But in the latter, the animal is really a man or woman com-

---

* *Vide Hausa Sayings*, page 103.

† The picture of the river of milk may be due to pagan Filani influence, for in India " the sacred portion of the Phalgu is said occasionally to flow with milk." Crooke, *op. cit.*, p. 21.

pelled by a witch to take a lower form until delivered
from the spell; there seems to be no such notion in
the Hausa stories.   I suppose that the idea arose
through mirages and the hallucinations of hungry
and thirsty travellers in the hotter and dryer countries to
the north-west.   Certainly the desert to the north near
Aiwalatin was waterless, and caravans frequently
perished of thirst in former times.   The mirage was
common there, and the desert had the reputation of
being haunted by demons says the authoress of *A
Tropical Dependency* (page 89).   And yet, perhaps, I
ought not to say this, considering that even with us
(see footnote, page 15) glasses of water hold themselves
up to one's mouth !   Possibly the idea may apply more
to the next world, especially if the witch (93) is the same
as Death (79), but it is no more surprising than that of
the appearance of a city in a place where before there
had been only a few huts.

FIG. 39.—Brass bowl, patterns in dots.   D., $9\frac{1}{16}$ in.

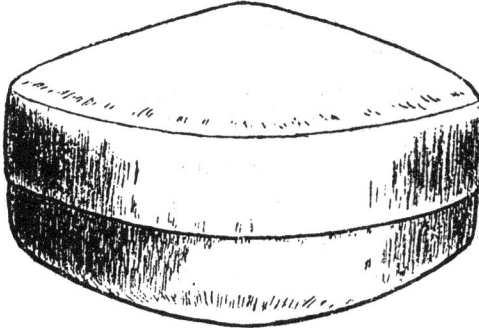

FIG. 40.—Parchment box.   D., $2\frac{5}{16}$ in.

CHAPTER VII.

CUSTOMS AND SUPERSTITIONS (CONTINUED).

Evil Influences—Witchcraft—Visits to the World of the Im-
mortals—Lapse of Time—Magic and the Evil Eye—Lucky Days
— Rites — Conjuring — Charms and Potions — Magical Gifts —
Forms of Address—The *Kirari*—Names.

THE belief in evil influences generally is well
developed, both sexes being represented. Old women
are considered to be very cunning, though I have never
heard of any, whether old or young, being accused of
possessing the power of witchcraft, except perhaps
temporarily. But in the tales any woman may become
a witch (91), and she is liable to do so by drinking a
brew of the leaves of the locust tree. All females
are supposed to be very clever in deceiving men ; there
is a proverb " A woman is more crafty than a king."

But charges of witchcraft were not confined to
women, for Malam Jibrella was expelled from a Mohammedan state in Northern Nigeria on this account in
1888. He afterwards declared himself the Mahdi in
Gombe, and was defeated and captured by a British
force fourteen years later. A mother will often say that
the flesh of her baby is bitter or salt, in case there may

be any witches about. A white man's flesh is supposed to be very salt.*

WITCHCRAFT.—In 1906, when in Amar (Muri Province), the native police-sergeant one day brought three constables before me who accused their wives of being witches. I laughed at the time, and told them to go back to barracks, but soon afterwards the sergeant reported that the men were preparing to desert, for they really believed that what they had stated was a fact. I therefore summoned the women, and asked them if the charge were true, and on being informed that it was, I placed them under a guard, not knowing quite what to do with them. Next day I put a galvanic battery on to each in turn, telling them that they would feel the evil influence pass right out of them, and, as they thought that they did so, the matter ended happily. A simple trick may be much more successful sometimes than the most learned judgment!

Witches can, of course, change into anything they like, and they often feed on human flesh, their chief mode of obtaining victims being to turn themselves into beautiful girls. A variant makes a buffalo do a similar thing in order to avenge her tribe on a family of hunters; a *Dodoniya* may do the same.

All witches have many mouths which they can cause to appear all over their bodies at will, and the owner can turn them back into one by slapping herself. The mouths both eat (M. 95) and drink (93 and 95), and they are the sign of the possession of unholy powers, for the owners do not like being seen in this state.

This is not at all surprising; a similar objection is

---

* Salt seems to be very generally regarded as being particularly inimical to evil spirits, the idea being based probably on its power of preventing decay. The *gnun* of North Africa are afraid of salt and steel, says Professor Westermarck, *loc. cit.*

found in European tales, the Peeping Tom usually losing his eyesight.* In the Hausa tales the death of the Peeping Tom is often desired (95), although he is never blinded, but in one case (94) the hero's brother loses his eyes, and it is probable that he himself (though not a Peeping Tom) escapes simply because he will not put himself into the witch's power of his own free will. Even the Half-Woman (15, variant) will not allow herself to be seen nor talked about.

A witch is usually powerless in the towns, and must entice the victims to a distance to work them ill (95, 96 and F.-L. 46), though this is not always so (91 and 94). But she can never seize her victim whenever she wants to do so, he must first voluntarily place himself in her power. Sometimes she is malignant only when roused by an offending party who has jeered at her (M. 95), and this touchiness is not confined to Hausa witches, for we find (S.F.T. page 46) a similar incident in a Harvey Isles tale.† The Hausa witch can give charms

---

* Thus in Southern Germany and Switzerland, on Twelfth Night, a mysterious being goes abroad named Dame Berchta, who is the relic of a heathen goddess, a leader of the souls of the dead. Once a servant boy hid himself and watched her come to the house of his master who had laid a repast for her (as was the custom), and her followers blew through the hole and blinded him, and from this and other similarities Mr. Hartland (S.F.T. 90) concludes that the legend and procession of Lady Godiva are survivals of a pagan belief and worship located at Coventry; that the legend was concerned with a being awful and mysterious as Dame Berchta, or even Hertha, who killed a mortal every year, and was worse than Diana.

† The hero, Tekonæ, having pretended to eat the food (live centipedes) yet manifested no burning thirst, and at last Miru (the horrible hag who ruled the shades) said " Return to the upper world. Only remember this—do not speak against me to mortals. Reveal not my ugly form and my mode of treating my visitors." This, however, is not universal, for in *Finnish Legends*, M. Evind tells us (page 129) that " evil things cannot bear to have their wicked origin told, and if, therefore, one sings the source of any evil, one makes it harmless at once," exactly the opposite of the Hausa idea.

for ailments (30 and 94), and in fact, if properly treated, she may be even exceedingly benign (93), the best means of securing her favour being to rub her back while she is washing. This simply means that women like to get someone else to perform the office for them, and witches—being lonely creatures, but still women—greatly appreciate little services from ordinary mortals, when such services have been duly invited. Witches seem to be somewhat simple at times, in spite of their magical powers, for they may be deceived rather easily (90). Apparently there is no objection to their addressing their husbands by name (95).

Witches do not appear to be afraid of iron, for they sharpen their knives, and although one is cut down by a sword (94) the danger to her was not in the substance of the weapon, but in its shape, and even so, it does not finish her off completely. The same applies to the iron club in the variant to Story 95. Witches also touch the legs of horses, but as the animals are not shod in Hausaland we learn nothing from this, and in fact, I was told by another man that any touching of iron was fatal.* They are, at any rate, afraid of dogs (95), as is Dodo (51), and the belief in the peculiar power of dogs in this respect is not confined to the Hausas—see Story 96, variant.   Do not we ourselves say that dogs can smell death?

The animals guarding the palace in Story 45 would seem to have been bewitched, for the dogs eat grass and the horses meat, and it is only when the boy gives them their proper food (and thereby breaks the spell?) that they let him pass in peace.

---

* The Hausa seems not to fear iron now, although he did so once in all probability. For the respect shown by pagan tribes to Hausa blacksmiths, see T.H.H., p. 136.

VISITS TO THE WORLD OF THE IMMORTALS.—There are several stories concerning the visits of a youth to a witch (*Maiya*), but one makes him go to the house of Death (*Mutua*) instead, and as the main parts of the tales are almost identical, perhaps there is some connection between the two in the Hausa mind, especially as the hero does not die before setting out upon his journey. Other stories show that a witch and Dodo are often interchangeable. Usually, of course, to eat of the food in the land of spirits is to acknowledge one's union with them, thereby renouncing all hope of returning to mortal abodes, for joining in a common meal often symbolizes some union, even if it does not actually constitute one. Strangely enough, however, the Hausa mortal may eat the food provided there (though he does not always do so, 95 and M. 2), and he may return none the worse for it (93 variant and 96), though it is evident that this is very dangerous, and people may refuse to touch any food the price of which is the death of the purchaser (76). The youth's intelligent horse sometimes saves his master (95 and 96), but at others the spider acts the part of the preserver (M.H. 20). When a witch is killed, every bit of her must be destroyed, for even a single drop of her blood can kill the victim (95 and 100, variant).*

LAPSE OF TIME.—It ought to be noted, perhaps, that there is no supernatural lapse of time during these visits to Death, or to a witch, *e.g.*, that the visitor is detained a year when he thinks that it has been only a day, a feature so strongly marked in European tales. I have never heard of any local Rip Van Winkle. The Hausa hero does not suffer through having carried off

---

* In Grimm's tales, too, drops of blood can talk.

the food, and, on his return, he finds everything as he left it. On the contrary, time seems to pass much more quickly in the other world than in this, as is shown by M.H. 67, the following being a free translation of the principal incidents. There were once three students, the eldest of whom was not quite sincere. On the day of the feast of *Idi,* the other two came to his house, and said " Let us go to our teacher." He said " Very well, but stay and eat first," and then he told his wife to place water behind the house so that he might wash. When she had done so she entered her hut to get some cakes, and he went to where the water was. He took off his clothes and squatted down to wash,* but when he had put his hand into the water, it became a sea, like the Mediterranean. " See him squatting on the shore ! " Then angels said to him " O thou at the waterside, if thou art a woman, thou wilt become a man ; if a man, thou wilt become a woman." And by the power of God, he immediately became a beautiful girl !

She saw a city ahead of her, and entered it, and went to the Chief Priest (*Limam*), and said that she was to be a daughter to him, and three months afterwards she married a student whom he chose from about forty who wished to marry her. She conceived, and bore a son, and, after she had carried him for two years, she weaned him, then she bore a daughter. She had four children in all, two sons and two daughters, and she lived twelve years in the city.

The day on which she weaned the younger

---

* The Hausa squats down to wash (unless he be right in a stream) and throws the water over himself with his hands. He washes outside his house, for he uses only a calabash, there is no kind of bath to catch the water. In this story the magic water is first a sea, then a river.

daughter* was a Friday, and she came to the river-
side and washed her cloths, and she was happy, for
that night she was to return to her husband.† But lo!
she became a virgin again, and as she was squatting
by the side of the river, she heard the angels say to
her " O thou at the waterside, if thou art a woman,

FIG. 41.—Wooden mortar and pestle for pounding corn, &c.
H. about 18 in.

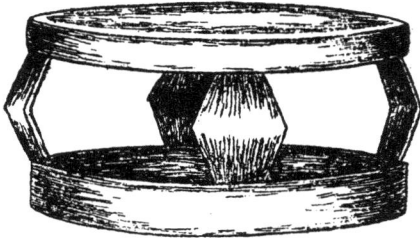

FIG. 42.—Wooden stool.

thou wilt become a man; if a man, thou wilt become a
woman." Immediately she became a man, and there
he was squatting behind his house, " see the water, see
his tobe and other clothes." He dressed himself, and
entered his house, and saw the students who asked

* This would really be just over eleven years, but the year in
which she came and the one in which she went would be counted,
so the time would be correct according to Hausa ideas. In any
case, one does not look for exactitude in a story.
† She would not live with him while nursing her child. See
T.H.H. 239, and *R.A.I. Journal*, Jan.-June, 1912.

" Have you washed ? " And he found that his wife
had not yet come out of her hut, and when she saw
him she was annoyed at his not staying longer so as
to give the cakes time to cool. After that they went
to the mosque, and the eldest student, Sheku, then
really believed.*

A magical appearance is attributed to Shefu
Othman, son of Fodio, the Filani conqueror of Hausaland. It is said that a man named Dodo, coming from
Gwanja, was crossing the Niger when he was nearly
upset, and he called out " O Shefu, son of Fodio, help
us." Immediately a man appeared, and righted the
canoe, and then disappeared again, and when Dodo
had reached the other bank he vowed a gift of five
calabashes of kola-nuts. On his arrival in Sokoto
twenty days afterwards, Dodo took three calabashes,
but Shefu said that five was the number vowed, and
the man admitted it. But there was stronger proof
than that, for at the very hour when Dodo had called,
Shefu was in the council chamber, and he left it for
a moment, and on his return the councillors saw that
his clothes were wet through. When they asked the
reason he said that they would know it in twenty days'
time.

In one story, the *Mutanen Lahira* (People of the
Next World) are described as living at the bottom of a
well, and a mortal, who falls in, has to give them
presents of clothes before they will take him up again.

---

* Professor Frazer has kindly pointed out a parallel in a
Turkish tale quoted by Addison in the *Spectator*, No. 94 (June,
1711), and he there refers to a similar story in the *Koran*. The
other stories which my informant noticed are an Indian one in
the *Katha Sarit Sagara*, translated by Tawney, ii, pp. 326 *sq.;*
and a Sumatran tale given by Van Hasselt in his *Volks Beschrij-
ving van Midden Sumatra*, pp. 78 *sq.*

MAGIC AND THE EVIL EYE.—The women paint rings
in red, white or yellow round their eyes to avert the
evil eye. The praising of a woman's beauty by any
man except her husband is a serious injury, and the
proper reply to complimentary remarks, however sin-
cerely made, is "*Ba ruana, Ka ji?*"—"I don't
care, do you hear?" At the same time, an air of
prosperity in a man is not by any means despised, for
"a good appearance means good fortune."

An amusing instance both of the fear of the evil eye
and sympathetic magic came to my notice in 1907, when
at Amar. I made a life-sized target to represent a man
firing, and set it up in the barrack-square, so as to be
able to give the men instruction in aiming, before
transferring it to the rifle-range a little distance off.
The next day I was implored to have it removed,
for some of the police constables' wives had seen it, and
feared a miscarriage in consequence, and I was solemnly
assured that if it were left there no births would occur
that year amongst the women in barracks. I was also
asked to keep the face free from any lines or spots, for
I was told that if there were any tribal marks on it, those
men having scarifications, marks, or tatuing resembling
them would die if the target were pierced. Of course I
complied with their wishes, for the fear was evidently
genuine, the target being set up in the butts at once,
and the face was painted white to resemble that of a
European, so that the natives could shoot at it in peace
and comfort of mind, and have the knowledge of a
good deed done on the few occasions on which they
managed to hit it.

It seems that not only lines and dots resembling
tribal marks are to be feared, but any spots at all (37
and F.-L. 8), and of course animals are as much afraid

of them as men. Perhaps spots have a religious significance. In an old print in which Our Lord is depicted
as rescuing souls from Hell,* his body is covered with
spots, though they do not appear on those of the demons
or souls. But in other cases the spots are probably
used more as a decoration (though there may still be a
religious element) as in the case of the women in Sierra
Leone, and the men of the Gan tribe in Uganda.†
Possibly spots represent the evil eye. They are often
used to avert the power, but in the stories mentioned
here the animal using the spots does not wish to avoid
the harmful influence issuing from another, but to
terrify him.‡   In fact, one man said that the spots
were eyes, showing that the object could see in all
directions, and, judging by the analogy of the *Kunda,*
detection is followed by immediate punishment if
necessary.

I could not hear of anyone having injured his enemy
by operating on an effigy, but I am quite prepared to
believe that this is done, considering the above
anecdote, and also since a charm can be written so as
to injure another. The girl scooping up the water
in a calabash, and thus emptying the streams, in
Stories 61 and F.-L. 17, seems to be a case of
sympathetic magic, as also does the healing of the
boy's eye by that of a goat in Story 94, and perhaps
also the annihilation of the pagans by dashing the

---

* *Ancient Mysteries Described.* By William Hone (1823).
William Reeves, London. Page 140.

† *On the Backwaters of the Nile*, page 231.

‡ Dr. Seligmann tells me that the peasants in the Kandian
district of Ceylon hang black pots, decorated with white spots
and circles, in their farms to protect their crops, and these must
be intended to harm would-be thieves. Mr. Crooke tells me
that the peasants in Northern India hang up old pots, black
with soot, and smeared with patches of whitewash. Here, also,
the idea seems to be rather to work injury than to escape from it.

sweat from the brow (64) and the destruction by the girl who escaped from Dodo of the gifts which he had given her (73). An example in L.T.H. (106) is perhaps even stronger, for there a woman who wishes to make her husband love her has been told by the malam to get dust from the chief's house. The chief, who is very unpopular, finds the woman doing this, and thinks that she is trying to injure him. There may be special properties in the earth on which the intended victim has trodden, as is pointed out in Story 4 and Note IV, 4.

I could never get the chief of Jemaan Daroro to tell me who would succeed him, nor would the recognized heir (the present chief) nor anyone else enlighten me, so there was evidently a reason against doing so, in fact I was told that such things are not spoken of. As there was no doubt that we should appoint the heir, there was no need for me to press the point after I discovered that there was an objection to giving a reply. This is evidently due to some fear that the person so named may never come to his own (after all, we ourselves can understand that), but whether the belief is Filani or Hausa I am not certain, for the family was mixed. It does not seem quite in keeping with the ideas of the latter, for they are confirmed fatalists (28), some of the proverbs already quoted showing this point well. It may be for quite another reason, however, viz., that the mention of the chief's death is tantamount to ill-wishing, the mere expression of the idea being considered to show that the event is desired.

LUCKY DAYS.—There are lucky days and unlucky days which are now indicated by the malams (F.-L. 36), but a European official cannot always defer to a "conscientious objector," and when a chief refuses to travel on important Government work simply because the stars are not propitious, or there is some similar obstacle, one has to explain that although the signs and portents may be against a native doing his own work, a different system of astronomy applies to ours, and that he must therefore rely on our reading for that particular occasion. To wash or shave on certain days, or at certain hours, is dangerous, for the person himself, or his wife (or her husband), would soon die, and these tabus remind one of the jinns of each week-day in Morocco.

RITES.—There are certain ceremonies for the bringing back to life of men (4, 62, 65 and 99), and even of animals (79). Both have a place in the next world—which is very much like this (85)—but when they die there they can never rise again.

The goat usually seems to play a part in these magical rites (70), especially a black one (*e.g.*, in *Bori*), in fact the colour black seems to have particular properties. Thus when Awudu, Chief of Zaria, was engaged in a war which ended in the conquest of the Katab country in the south-west of his kingdom, he gave the people a black bull to sacrifice on the Dutsin Kerrima to appease the demons there (see T.H.H., page 99).* With some tribes in the Sudan the word "black" is avoided because it is held in horror as being of evil omen,† the words "blue," "green," &c., being used instead, but with the Hausas almost the contrary is the case, for all cloths darker than royal blue are called *ba(k)ki*. I think, however, that this is due simply to laziness, not that there is any objection to

---

* He thus resembled the Greeks who sacrificed black oxen to Pluto and other infernal deities.
† Yacoub Pasha Artin, *England in the Sudan*, page 160.

naming the colour blue, at the same time some Hausas
will not wear cloths of that shade. Certainly some
persons (possibly Mohammedans) do not like the word
" black," although they have no objection to " white,"
and that is strange considering that the latter colour,
and not the former, is connected with death in Hausaland.*

A magical creation of white crows is related in
L.T.H. 57, where the Chief of Gobir took a small bag
of medicines, and threw a little of the powdered condi-

FIG. 43.—Earthenware jug, incised pattern, used to hold water for ceremonial
ablutions. H., 6¼ in.

ment on to a pot of live cinders, and when the smoke
had risen some hundred white crows appeared.

The liver has special virtues. It may be used as a
remedy for illness (80), it has magical powers of

---

* The following Arabic legend is interesting in this connection. The King of China once came upon a white and a black
snake fighting. He killed the latter, and the former turned into
a lovely lady whose sister married him as a reward for his help,
and gave birth to the Queen of Sheba. Hartland, *op. cit.*, page
316. Compare this with the story of the magic ointment in the
preceding chapter.

becoming alive (66—is it the seat of life?), and it is a
name for the man who divided the inheritance in Story
81. It is often specially mentioned even when there are
no magic rites (17 and 34). Canon Robinson says* that
he was told that in the event of a man being bitten by a
mad dog, the animal was at once killed, and the victim
ate the liver, an elaboration of " the hair of the dog
that bit you." In one story (L.T.H. 41) the blood of
the liver restores the sight of a blind man.

I do not know whether haruspication was practised,
but probably it was (and still is?) for one story (L.T.H.
129) relates how a jackal took a goat to the house of a
hyæna (against which he had a grudge), and persuaded
her to accompany him to the forest because he was
going to kill the goat, and perform magic rites. He had
previously warned his pups to steal the liver, and when
it could not be found he drew a knife across the throat
of each in turn, but as it did not hurt them he pronounced them innocent. The hyæna, seeing that a slur
was cast upon her, offered to undergo the same ordeal,
and, of course, the jackal killed her.

Divination was also practised, patterns being drawn
in the sand—previously smoothed down—or by looking
in a heap of sand for special signs. The following
tale will show how useless it is to try to avoid one's
fate. A man consulted a malam as to his end, and
the malam read in the earth that a buffalo would cause
it. The man then went away, and of course kept out
of the way of this animal. One day, long afterwards,
there was a big hunt, and the man was going to join
in it, but, remembering the result of the malam's
divination, he hid in a corn-bin instead. After the

---

* *Hausaland,* see page 144.

hunt was over, the booty was distributed, and as it happened, the owner of the bin was given a head. Wishing to hide it, he threw it into the bin, and the horns pierced the man hiding in there, and killed him. Next morning the dead man was found, and the people, remembering the prophecy, said " That which a man will obtain, and that which will happen to him, from his birth are they fore-ordained."

There is also a kind of fortune-telling, and dreams are interpreted. The *bori* women pretend to tell fortunes, as mentioned before.

Another story of Othman's magical powers is told of an Asben who had lost his camels. On appealing to the *Shefu* (sheik), he was told to look, and he saw them to all appearance quite close. He went after them, but he took 30 days to reach the place in which they were.

It is just possible that the song of the birds in Story 87 is a necromantic spell which enables the zankallala to kill Dodo; an example occurs in Sierra Leone in the story of Goro the Wrestler, where the song of incantation chanted by the mother enables the child to overcome all the animals, so such spells are known in West Africa.* There may be some connection between the idea in this and the singing of the snake-charmers mentioned later.

CONJURING.—Of course there are conjuring tricks such as the gourd from which water drips or not at the command of the operator, the needle and the cotton which pass through the youth, and the magic hoe-shovel which cannot be held down on the ground—there being a slight hypnotic element in this—but they are described

---

* Cronise and Ward, *op. cit.*, page 14.

in full elsewhere (T.H.H., pages 207-209), and the accounts need not be repeated here. There was a female
snake-charmer in Lokoja, but I never saw her do more
than make the reptile coil around her body and uncoil
again. The skilled performers, who wear a lot of hair
on their heads, are said to be able to charm the reptiles
by singing to them.

Snake-charmers were not always popular. It is
related of one chief that he was so much annoyed by
their music that he decided to rid himself of their atten-
tions for ever, so, pretending to be glad to see them, he
invited the leader into an inner room. Here he cut off
his head, and had it placed in a food-calabash, the body
being removed. Then the remaining charmers were
asked to come to the feast, and were left alone in the
room. Soon, one wished to see what had been prepared, and, uncovering the calabash, he saw his
leader's head! Hurriedly replacing the mat, he made
his escape, followed by the others, and the chief was
not troubled again.

I have seen it stated that a guinea-corn plant can
be made to grow from a seed, and that a child can
be apparently killed, chopped up, and brought to life
again as in India, but I have never heard of these
things myself, so I cannot say whether such is the case
or not.

CHARMS AND POTIONS.—Charms are used of course,
but I doubt if many of purely pagan origin now exist
in the Mohammedan districts, for the malams naturally
wish to substitute verses of the Koran written and sold
by themselves, and wrapped in small leather cases.
These are worn all over the body, and may be tied to
the manes or tails of horses and other animals. There
are special kinds for special objects, and once, when I

was about to go out with a small patrol, I found a malam offering great bargains in charms which would invariably protect the wearers against wounds from arrows or other weapons. I offered to let him wear all the charms he could put on to his person, and to give him half a sovereign if I failed to wound him first shot, but he was much too modest and retiring to accept the offer! I hoped that this would have the effect of making my men save their money, but I dare say the malam explained to their satisfaction that a white man was rather outside the influence of black man's magic. At any rate, all the men were covered with them when we did set out. I was told that the fruit of the small *dundu* tree if ground up and drunk with water will make it impossible for the drinker to be wounded by a sword; other decoctions are of more use against arrows or clubs.

There was a special kind (*sha bara*) which had a great vogue when the European first began to conquer the country, its virtue being that by its means the white man's bullets would not only cause no harm to the wearer, but would even rebound and wound the one who had fired the rifle. Considering the number of casualties, it is strange to think that the trade still flourishes. My cook had fought against our troops at Kano, and had been defeated, but his faith in native charms was as strong as ever.

On another occasion, I saw a girl sitting on the wharf, with a calabash of very dirty-looking water beside her, and I was informed that a malam had written a verse or two on a prayer-board (resembling the boards at College on which the grace is written), and had then washed off the ink with water, and it was this mixture which was to cure her of the fever from which she was suffering! I gave her some quinine, and next morning I heard that she had recovered, but the malam claimed the credit, though he had advised her to swallow the quinine lest I should be offended! Or it may be that he really believed in the efficacy of his treatment, for in certain respects Mohammedanism does not seem to be much of an advance on paganism, and the native —even the household servant and the soldier—will often prefer a charm of local manufacture to the best European medicine.

The above treatment must not be derided, however, for it has been proved over and over again to the entire satisfaction of numbers of the Hausa folk, that if a man have the hiccoughs, and the names of seven liars be written on the board, and the ink washed off and drunk by him, he will be cured at once!

There are charms for childbirth (21) amongst other things, the head of a young demon being particularly potent (L.T.H. 71), but I fancy that herbs play quite as important a part in these (59) as the malam's ink, for the Hausas are adepts at prevention, and possibly in the opposite direction also. But in a good many cases, it seems to be that the rite to be enacted is the important thing (45), *e.g.,* in Story 70, where a boy is made to walk. Many of the tatu marks are charms, as is mentioned later, and the *Tsuguna ka chi dawa* (squat down and eat yams) which makes all seeing it rush off immediately and offer the wearer food, is deservedly popular.

It is not only for causing or saving life that charms exist. For if in a mixture of ink and water, as described above, there be soaked—with the appropriate words, of course—a piece of wood taken from a tree which has been struck by lightning, a very powerful potion is produced.* If a person washes his own body with this, his enemy (not he himself) will die, and this is very convenient, for the enemy would not give him the chance of washing *his* body.†

Charms are also made to give the wearer the power of making himself invisible, and these are particularly useful to thieves—for the priests have no hesitation in taking fees from whatever quarter they are offered. A policeman of mine was covered with them, as I discovered when I at last found him out and put him in prison, and his nickname in Jemaan Daroro was " King of the Door-blind," because (I was told) he could pass his body into a house without disturbing even that flimsy protection. There is a potion which will give the gambler success if he washes his hands (which throw the shells) and mouth (which says the word *sabi* at the same time) with it.

There are love-philtres which will create desire when drunk by the person selected, or certain rites may be performed to accomplish the same desirable end, and last, but not least, certain tatu patterns make the wearer quite irresistible. The fruit of the *begeyi* tree will reconcile husband and wife, if eaten.

A high level of reasoning is shown in L.T.H. 34, where a woman seeks a charm to give her the power of ruling her husband. The malam tells her that she must bring him some buffalo-cow's milk, and she gets this after having gradually made the beast accustomed to her presence. When at last she brings the milk, the

---

* Robinson, *Hausaland*, page 141.
† The Hausa is not the only one who kills with a written charm. Only last year I heard of an English society lady who had hidden a paper in a drawer for some time with a wish written upon it, in order to cause an injury to someone who had offended her, and she quite believed that it would act!

malam asks " How did you get it ? " " By strength of
will, by luck, and by coaxing," she replies. " Good,"
says the malam, " by the same means that you obtained
the buffalo's milk will you be able to rule your husband."

For some affections, the cure is more a rite than a
charm. Thus, for a swelling on the throat, one should
tie a mortar behind (like an infant) and walk about the
house; while for a certain kind of boils there is nothing
so efficacious as kneeling to a dog ! As these boils are
mainly on the knee, there is more sense in this than is
apparent at first sight, for the kneeling might burst
them.

MAGICAL GIFTS.—Presents (as apart from charms
which are purchased) from supernaturals are not common in Hausa folk-lore—though, as certain gifts have
magical properties (29), they may have come originally
from other than mortal donors—but members of the
animal kingdom sometimes reward a hero and take the
place of the fairies in the tales of other countries (12
and 62). There is no philosopher's stone, but there is
a tree which will turn what it touches into money,*
and there is also a magic carpet, though this last has
almost certainly an Arabian origin.

---

* It is called *Jato itachen kurdi* or *Jato na arzikki*, and " the
approach to it is guarded by phantoms—fearful men and animals,
leopards, hyænas, and enormous snakes. . . . The writer
was entirely incredulous of every property attributed to the lucky
tree until May, 1909, when one night, looking in a direction
where there was nothing but uninhabited bush, he saw at a distance of between 500 and 1,000 yards a ruddy light which
hovered unsteadily in the air, appearing and disappearing at
intervals of about a quarter of a minute like a large will-o'-the-
wisp. The natives unanimously recognized it as the light of the
Fortunate Tree, but declined to explore in its direction. It is
probably an electrical manifestation at the tips of the branches
similar to the St. Elmo's fire seen at the extremities of ship's
masts in certain conditions of atmosphere." *Hausa Sayings*,
page 93.

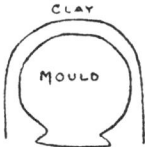

Fig. 44.　　Fig. 45.　　Fig. 46.　　Fig. 47.　　Fig. 48.

The five figures, Nos. 44 to 48, show the stages in one method of pot making.
Illustrations XVII. and XVIII. correspond with the third and fourth diagrams.

FORMS OF ADDRESS.—It is worthy of note that the personification of animals is emphasized in the tales of some tribes by an honorific prefix corresponding to "Brer Rabbit," "Miss Cow," &c., of the Uncle Remus stories. This does not apply to the Hausa versions, but there is a form of address or *kirari* used for certain members of the animal kingdom. For instance, that of the lion is "O Strong One, Elder Brother of the Forest" (6), the hyæna is addressed as "O Hyæna, O Strong Hyæna, O Great Dancer," and on hearing this the animal at once begins to dance, and will go away (53). The dog has a long *kirari*, part of which is unprintable, it is "O Dog, your breakfast is a club, your *fura* a stick (*i.e.*, a beating), O Dog, you spoil a prayer (because if a dog's shadow touches a man while praying it ruins the supplication),* you are the hyæna's perquisite, your ribs are like the plaits in a grass mat, your tail is like a roll of tobacco, your nose is always moist." That of the jackal has already been mentioned (6).

The horse is known as "O Prancing One, that which the Great Man rides; O Horse go carefully; O Offspring of another, I have you."

A small species of crocodile is addressed thus, "O *Tsari,* you causer of anger, if you are chased you fall into the water."

The spider is *Gizzo Gizzami,* which seems to mean "O Spider of Spiders," but he is usually known by

---

* Mr. Crooke thinks that this has been borrowed from Islam, as dogs are regarded as unclean animals. According to a tradition by Abu Hurairah, Mohammed said that when a dog drinks in a vessel, it must be washed seven times, and that the first cleansing should be with earth (*Mishkat*, Book iii, chap. ii, pt. i), quoted by Hughes, *Dictionary of Islam*, page 91.

his nickname *Maiwayo*, the Crafty One, or less often *Munafikin Allah*. The butterfly's *kirari* is most appropriate, "O Glistening One, O Book of God, O Learned One open your book," *i.e.*, your wings. The common locust is not at all a favourite, but there may be a particular species which is harmless, "O Locust of the *tumfafia* tree, you are not eaten, and you do not eat anything."

Birds, too, have their *kirari*, the hen's is "O Fowl, you foul your own nest." A turkey is prized, "O Turkey, you are too valuable to be killed for a stranger's feast." There is one small house-bird which nests in the inside of the grass roofs of entrance-halls or unused huts (where there is no smoke) which, if caught and held by the back of the neck, like a kitten, will swing to and fro. The holder will sing "O *Chada*, swing, I will give you your mother, O Yellow Beak," and this means that the bird is not to be afraid. I have forgotten the rest, unfortunately; the bird is a kind of swallow, I think. A small bird like a sparrow, renowned for its twittering, is addressed "O *Suda*, you are full of news, you tell it though not asked." I called a Court messenger Momo Suda for a reason which I considered most appropriate, but he was not at all pleased. The eagle is supposed to be a wise bird, "O Eagle, you do not settle on the ground without a reason," *i.e.*, that there is something there to eat. The belief that the White-Breasted Crow rears chickens has been mentioned elsewhere, "O White-Breasted Crow, make the offspring of another become yours," is its *kirari*.

I do not know if many fish have been immortalized in this way; the mud-fish (or lung-fish) is addressed "O Mud-fish, eat your own body," from the fact that it lives in the mud during the dry weather, and does not get any food.

Persons and bogies also have their proper titles. Dodo is often known as *Mijjin Mazza,* "Man of Men," not what one might expect considering his general reputation. A bachelor is said to dream of the grinding and pounding corn that he will have to do next day. But an old woman has the least complimentary titles : "O Old Thing, you are thin everywhere except at the knee, of flesh you have but a handful, though your bones would fill a basket." Another is "Bend down your head, Sword, I'll kill your lice, and you will end my married life." The first is obvious, the meaning of the latter is that when one woman does another's hair (a tedious operation, for it has been up for weeks probably, and will not be done again for some time) they usually talk scandal, and so the young wife will hear tales of her husband, and probably quarrel with him.* The word sword refers to the old woman's sharp tongue, and has a familiar sound.

The general *kirari* of a wife and husband is "O Woman whose deception keeps one upon tenterhooks (thorns), your mouth though small can still destroy dignity. If there were none of you there could be no household, if there are too many of you the household is ruined." Another version is "O Woman, your deception is a cloak of pain, without you there is no household," &c. But this *kirari* is a double one, for

---

* The hair is worn in a single hard ridge on the top of the head, and as it is plastered thick with grease it soon becomes full of vermin. It is so firm that the women sometimes hide English silver coins in it. (*Vide* note xciii, 5.) Beriberi women also wear a ridge, but the hair is arranged in a number of tiny plaits. The Filani (whose hair is much longer, and not curly) wear long curls on each side of the face.

it continues : " O Chief when I came to you what did you give me ? I brought my goods to your house, and when you had seen them you squandered them, now you wish to get rid of me."   The first part will be clear from what has been said in Chapter V, but the last part requires a little explanation, being built upon the following story. A rich woman took pity upon a poor man and married him. He was fond of her, and at first he would not touch her property. But one day he asked for money to buy a new tobe, and she gave it to him. One success spurred him to further efforts, and soon he had spent all her money in new clothes for himself. When he saw that she had nothing more to give him (and he had the clothes, which are a form of currency) he began to illtreat her, and so she sang this pathetic song.

In addition to the general *kirari,* every celebrated man has a special individual nickname resembling our Richard, the Lion Heart.   But sometimes the titles (real or false) are strung out to almost endless lengths, for as each professional flatterer must live by his tongue, he will take care to make as much use of it as possible.

It is not etiquette to refer to the members of a man's family individually—unless, perhaps, one be ill—though a general salutation such as " Are all your household well ? " is quite correct. The forms of address and the descriptions vary for an important person and for a poor man, thus one says " The beggar is dead," but " The Chief is missing "; an enemy may be " ill," but a friend is " not well." And while a common woman about to become a mother might " make belly," her sister in more polished circles would have " two selves."

There is also a distinction between human beings

and animals, in spite of the fact that they can transform themselves, for while it is correct to say " the man is lame," the horse is described as being " without a leg "; my brother may be " blind," but my dog, if in the same unfortunate state, " has no eye."

NAMES.—There is evidently some magic in names, and the first-born child is usually, if not always, known by a nick-name, for all Hausa children have a secret and a public name, the first being known only to themselves. Thus the wife of one of the Court Messengers (native runners) was always known as Yar Jekada (Daughter of the Tax-Collector), her real name —almost forgotten even by the owner herself—being Ashetu. This prohibition applies even to adopted children, for Story 69 relates how a boy offered to let a childless old woman treat him as her son on condition that she would not even tell anyone else his name, and, as she could not keep the secret, she died childless.

Children are often named according to the day on which they were born, thus *Lahidi* because born on the first day, Sunday; *Laraba,* on the fourth day, Wednesday; *Bi Salla,* because they appeared on the day after the Feast, and so on.*

The names may commemorate some special incident, such as the arrival of a European, but in that case, if girls, they are usually called *Matan Bature,* or " *Wife* of the White Man," though the reason is not evident unless there is some idea of betrothal in infancy. Twins would probably be named in pairs thus Al Hassan and Hassana, Husein and Huseina, and so on.

---

* This corresponds to some extent with our custom of christening children born on Christmas Day, Noël (and even Melbourne, Tasma, &c., after the name of the place where the interesting event occurred).

Again, they may simply show the order in which the owners were born, for instance, a son after two daughters is known as *Tanko*, a daughter after two sons as *Kandi*, and the next child after twins might be called *Gumbo*.* The sole survivor of a family, the members of which had died in infancy, would probably be known as *Berau* (left).

The names of animals are sometimes used, *Kura*, the hyæna, being fairly common (another occurs in Story 81), and it has been suggested that when such a name is given in infancy it indicates a survival of totemism.†

When several children of one mother have died in infancy, means must be taken to avert a similar fate in the case of those born subsequently, and it is lucky for them that these measures are not so elaborate as those on the Gold Coast, which are quite sufficient to kill the child right off (see T.H.H. page 173). First a special name is given, *Ajuji* being a favourite in the case of both males and females; next a special charm (consisting of a leather belt ornamented with brass rings) is worn on neck and waist until the child is grown up; and sometimes the hair will be shaved or dressed in a special way. The mother, too, may partake in the last; if three children have died she will shave one side of her head; if four, the whole. Very often in the case of other peoples, an opprobrious name is chosen for a child born after the death of others, so as to depre-

---

* We may compare with these, perhaps, our own names of Tertius, Decima, and others. Even the celebrated " Elizabeth, Betty, Bessie, and Bess " has a Hausa representative in Ayeshetu, Ashetu, Ayesha, and Shetu or Shatu.

† This is probably correct, though not invariably so nowadays. An Englishman would not necessarily be in the totemistic stage simply because he lived in, say, " The Pines," and called all his daughters by the names of flowers—an actual case in Ballarat.

ciate it, and make the evil influence less likely to be
exerted against it. In India *Kuriya* (" Dunghill ") is
a common name for a male,* and it is exceedingly likely
that *Ajuji* has come from *juji* which has a similar
English equivalent. Possibly, too, instead of indicating
the order of birth, originally, *Tanko* may have come
from *tankoshe* (repelled), *Kandi* from *kandilu* (cow-
dung), and *Gumbo* (also spelt *Gambo*) from *gambu* or
gyambu (lame, sore legged).

Wives must not address their husbands by name,
not at any rate their first husbands, nor must they tell
it to others (56); there is a song " O God, I repent, I
have spoken the name of my husband." They usually
call him " Master of the House,"† or perhaps use some
nickname, or his title if any. But the prohibition does
not seem to apply to witches, or at any rate they can
pronounce it with impunity (95), and this is only to be
expected if the origin of the tabu was due to the fear of
sorcery. Although the name is in this case considered
to be part of its owner, it is a vulnerable point of attack
only by an evil-disposed wife, but care is taken to ensure
that nail-parings, hair, &c., shall be buried, for not only
the wives, but anyone else can work the owner
harm through their agency. I am not sure if
the prohibition against a wife mentioning her
husband's name applies before marriage or not,
but I think so, for, although in Story 43 only
the maiden who could guess the name of the
unknown youth could become his wife, and then the

---

* Crooke, *op. cit.*, p. 187.
† Or " Master of our House." No one but the master himself
would use the term " my " when referring to the house, family,
or possessions. So the Hausa servant speaks of his European
master as " Our Whiteman," and to tell him that his baggage
is arriving, he would say " There are our loads."

name was a fictitious one; in Story 42, the bashful girl
was beaten for pronouncing it to the owner. But the
unmarried girl may perhaps tell the name of her
beloved to her parents (61), without evil consequences.*

Men are often known as So and So, Son of So and
So (e.g., Othman dan Fodio, the Filani Conqueror),
but in Story 86, variant, the hero is addressed by his
sister as " Auta, Brother of Barra."

Nicknames are very common, especially those suggested by some physical characteristic, such as *Babban
Kai* (Big Head), and *Maika(r)rifi* (the Strong One). Or
they may commemorate some act, the " Burier-alive "
in T.H.H. 7, and Rice and others in Story 43, or some
speech such as " There-is-no-King-but-God " (1). The
words Lion or Bull Elephant when applied to a chief
are not really nicknames, they are forms of address;
but sometimes the names of other animals, such as Giwa
(elephant), may be when given later in life, for they
probably point to some physical characteristic.

Slave-names correspond to some extent to our
" Praise God Barebones," though the sentence is often
much longer, part being spoken by the person calling,
and the rest by the owner of the name when answering.
Thus " *Ku(l)um Safia* "—and the person addressed

---

* Perhaps the Hausa has a similar reason to that of the Hindu
for the tabu " by which a Hindu woman is prevented from using
the name of her husband. To this, however, there is one notable
exception—' At marriages, coming of age, first pregnancy, and
festive days .   .   . . it is usual for the women to recite or sing
a couplet or verse in which the husband's name occurs. At
marriages . . . . an old man or an old lady gets close to the
door, and refuses to allow the young women to go unless they
have told their husband's name. [This is either] part of a
ceremony whose object is to drive to a distance any spirits whose
influence might blight the tender life of the unborn child,' [or it
may be] a survival of the custom of distinctly admitting
maternity and paternity." Crooke, *op. cit.*, ii, 6.

replies " *Ina Godia,*" meaning " Every morning—I give
thanks." Again, " *Bia Maradi—Allah,*" " The Giver
of Joy—is God." Others still are in the form of a question, as " *Mine ya fi dadi?—Dan uwa,*" meaning
" Who is best off ?—He who has a mother " (to look
after him). *Allah Keauta* is exactly our Theodore.
Some of course are shortened, and are difficult to understand, such as " *Kun so* "—and the reply " *Na samu,*"
which in its proper form is " *Kun so en rassa* "—" You
wanted me to go without "; " *Allah ya sa na samu* "
—" but God caused me to obtain." A common name
is *Allah bai*—which is really " *Allah shi ba baba mu
samu* "—*i.e.,* " God give our chief plenty, so that we
may have some of it "—there is no unnecessary reti-
cence in the Hausa invocations ! !

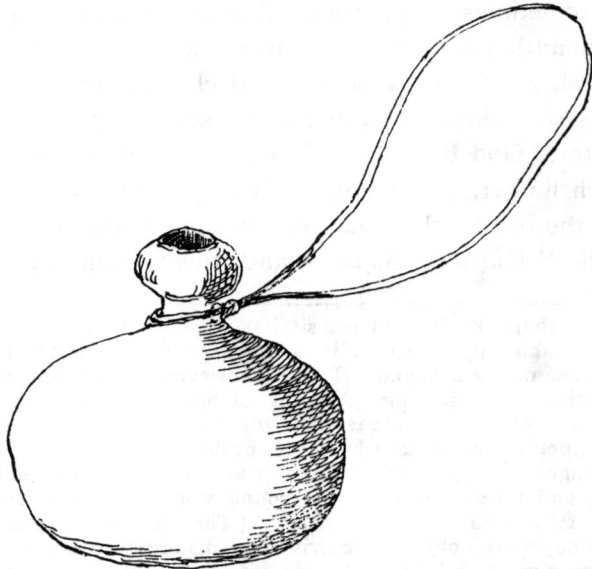

FIG. 49.—Gourd used by travellers.   Can be grown in various shapes.

FIG. 50.—Decorated gourd, pattern left in relief and stained purple.
D. 3⅝ in.

PART II.
Hausa Tales, Variants, and Parallels.

I

THERE IS NO KING BUT GOD.

When one [who is an ordinary Person] comes to the council, he says " May the King live for ever," but a certain Man came and said " There is no King but God." Now he was always saying this, and at last the King became very angry with him. So he took two rings of silver and gave them to him to keep for him, with the intention of avenging himself upon him. So [the Man whom everyone now called] " There-is-no-King-but-God " took the two rings, put them into an empty Ram's horn, and gave it to his Wife to keep for him.

About five days afterwards, the King said " O, There-is-no-King-but-God, I am going to send you to

a certain village," and the other replied " It is good."
And when the King sent him, he said " Tell my
People to come in and help to build the city wall."
No sooner had he gone, than the King said [to his
Attendants] " Go to the Wife of There-is-no-King-but-
God," and, he continued, " Offer her a million cowries,
offer her a hundred body-cloths, and a hundred head-
cloths, if she will give the King that which There-is-no-
King-but-God gave her to take care of." When the
Wife heard this, she said " I agree," and she brought
the horn and gave it to them, and when the King
had received it he opened it, and looked inside, and
saw his rings there. So he replaced them in the horn,
and pressed them down, and said " Take this, and
throw it into a certain lake that can never dry up."
But as it happened, just as the Attendants had arrived
at the lake, and had thrown in the horn, a great Fish
swam by, and swallowed it.

Now on that very day There-is-no-King-but-God
returned from his journey, and when he had arrived,
he met some men of his city who said that they were
going off to fish with nets at the lake.   And he went with
them, and lo ! he caught the very same great Fish, and
as his Son was cleaning it, the knife struck the horn
with a *keras*. Then he said " Opp, there is something
inside this Fish." " What is it ? " asked There-is-no-
King-but-God, and the Son said " Well I never, there
is a horn in its inside." Then his Father said " Pull
it out that we may see it," and the Son pulled it out,
and gave it to him. So he opened it, and looked, and
what did he see but the King's rings which he had
given him to keep for him ! Then he said " Truly
there is no King but God."

Just as they had finished cleaning the Fish, the

King's Messenger came and said " There-is-no-King-but-God, when you have refreshed yourself (1), the King wants you." So he replied " I come." And when the Messenger had gone, he said to his Wife " Where is that thing which I gave you to take care of ? " She replied " Oh, I don't know, a Mouse must have taken it." Then he said " There is no King but God."

When he had refreshed himself he took the path to the court, and when he had come he sat down. And the Councillors began saying " May the King live for ever," but he said " There is no King but God." Then the King told all the Councillors to be silent for he was going to talk with There-is-no-King-but-God, and he asked " Is there no King but God ? " And the other replied " Yes, there is no King but God." Then the King said " I want immediately that thing which I gave you to keep for me." And as he spoke, the Guards arose and stood about him, so that if he could not give back the thing, they would take him to be impaled (2).

But There-is-no-King-but-God put his hand into his pocket, and pulled out the horn, and held it out to the King, and when the King had opened it he saw his rings. Then he said " Truly there is no King but God," and the Councillors saluted There-is-no-King-but-God. Then the King divided his city into two, and gave him half to rule over.

In a variant (L.T.H. 92) the King gets the King of the Thieves [a recognized individual] to steal the rings on the advice of a Leper. The ring was thrown into the water, and the Fish which swallowed it was bought by There-is-no-King-but-God. Other trials are imposed like those in Story 80. In another (L.T.H. 113) the Man catches the Fish at a ford on his way home.

This is one of the many versions of a tale first recorded by Herodotus, iii, 40, *sqq.*, where the adventure is attributed to Polycrates, despot of Samos in the sixth century B.C. Variants are very numerous. The story occurs in the *Arabian Nights* and throughout the East as far even as Japan (*Nihongi*, Aston's Translation, 1, 92, *sqq.*). In Africa it has been recorded in Senegambia by Berenger-Féraud (*Contes Pop. de la Sénégambie,* 145), and in Morocco by Doutté (*Magie et Religion dans l'Afrique du Nord,* 157), where it is a Mohammedan tradition. It has also been reported by Miss Kingsley (*West African Studies,* 565) from Old Calabar, where it seems to be a native tale. It is localized in many parts of Europe. The arms of the city of Glasgow commemorate the tale as a miracle of St. Kentigern, the Apostle of Strathclyde. (H.).

In India, it appears in Kashmir (*vide* Knowles, *Folk-tales of Kashmir,* p. 27, and in *North Indian Notes and Queries,* iii, 11 ff.). (C.).

2

THE PUNISHMENT OF THE SABBATH-(1)-BREAKERS.

A number of Men went out to fish with nets, and on the way they met an Old Man, and the Old Man asked " Where are you going ? " They replied " We are going fishing." Then he said " Ah, to-day is not the day for fishing," for it was the seventh day, but they answered that they were going all the same, so he said " Very well, go." And they went, and began to cast their nets.

Soon the Hedgehog made a noise like thunder, and said " Are you equal to me ? " But they said in their hearts that there was no one who would stop them now. Then the Boys [who were standing on the bank ready to catch the Fish when thrown to them by the Men in the water] were turned into Pelicans, and the Men became big Monkeys, and they could not return home.

You know that the seventh day is the one on which the Fishes pray.

———

This appears to be a corruption of the story in the Koran, a Hausa version of which is given in M.H. (9), the reason of the Men refusing to listen to the Messenger of God being that the Women derided them for even thinking about it.

————————

3

THE TENDER-HEARTED MAIDEN AND THE FISH.

A certain Man went to the river to catch Fish, and he brought one home, and gave it to his Wife, so the Wife said to her Step-Daughter (1) "Get up, go to the river, and wash the Fish, but if you let it go, when you have come back I will thrash you."

So the Step-Daughter went to the river, and had begun to wash the Fish, when it said "O Maiden, will you not set me free that I may go and give my Young Ones suck?" (2). And she replied "Very well, go," and she waited. When the Fish returned, it said (3) "Now, pick me up, and let us go," but she replied "No, no, you may go free." Then the Fish said "I heard what was said to you, that you would be beaten [if I escaped]," but she replied "Fish, swim away." And the Fish said "Good-bye until to-morrow, you must return in the morning." So the Maiden went home, and she was seized, and beaten, until at last her Father said "Leave her alone, God will give us another to-morrow."

Next morning she got up, and went to where she

had left the Fish. Now the Fish had summoned all its Relatives to come and see the Maiden who had set it free, and all the Relatives came, there were many of them. Then the Fish called the Maiden, and said " Come here," and when she had gone up close, the Fish continued " Now, see the One who has saved my life. I was caught, and it was decided that I should be cooked, so I was given to her that she might come and wash me, but she set me free. That is why I said " You come, all of you, and see her, and thank her." Then it said to her " Go home, whenever you are hungry come here, until the first night of the feast " (4).

When the first night of the feast came, all of the Family [except the Step-Daughter] were going off to the dances, to those which the Young People perform, and the Fish said " When they have gone, you come to me." All of the Others went off to the dances—an old cloth had been chosen and given to the Step-Daughter, although the Wife's own Daughter had been given a new cloth to wear—and so she went to the Fish, wearing the old cloth. But the Fish brought her a heap of finery, and the Maiden went to the dance looking splendid.

Now when the King saw her, he sent to tell her that she was the Maiden whom he wished to marry. But she replied " Very well, but go to my Father's house, I was not born in the playground " (5). So the King ordered his Messengers to go to the Father's house (6), but the Father said " What! It cannot be. I have no Daughter such as the King would wish to marry." Now his Wife [heard them talking, and she] said to her Daughter " Go, run home, do you not hear that the King wants to marry you?" But the Girl replied " No, no, it is not I, it is another, the King noticed her at the dance." So the Messengers came, and arranged for the marriage, and the King gave the Rival Wife (7) riches, and the Parents said " Let her oe carried away and taken to the King." In the evening she escaped, and ran to the Fish and told it, and said " I have been married to the King." And the Fish replied " Thanks be to God, go to the King's palace, and to-morrow we will come." So she said " Very well," and went, and in the morning all the Fishes assembled, and the Fish told its Relatives what had happened. So they collected grain, and in the evening when the night had come, they sent word saying " Let nobody from the King's palace go outside at night " (8). Then they took the grain and brought it to the Maiden, and they collected cloths, and brought them to her.

Now, that night, the Women of the King's palace seized the Maiden's hands, and cut them off, because of their jealousy, and they said derisively " Look at the King's Wife, she has no hands ! " But she roused her Chamber-Maid, and said " Go to the Fish, and tell it what has happened to me, the Women have cut off both my hands." When the Fishes had heard, they said " Since she did not bring grief upon us, she also shall not have any." So at midnight the Fishes took the road, and came to the palace, and restored her hands to her (9).

Next morning the Women said " Let them be given guinea-corn to pound up," and they continued " Let the Bride be called to come and pound." So the Bride came out, they thought that she had no hands, but she took hold of the pestle, and they saw that she had hands. Then other People, who had heard them say that she had no hands, laughed at the jealous Women, and they were made fun of until they were shamed. But the Bride merely ignored them, and returned to the King (10).

———

A variant (L.T.H. ii, 69) is even more like Cinderella, for the Maiden leaves her boot of gold behind, and next morning she is the only one whom it will fit, in fact, the boot runs to her, and puts itself on her foot. In this case, the Frog acts the part of the Fish in return for food which the Maiden has given him, and the other Wives of the King's Son are good to her. The Step-Sister, however, tries to take her place in the palace, and is killed on being discovered, while the rightful Wife comes back to her own.

———

4

The Spider, the Old Woman, and the Wonderful Bull.

Once there was a certain Old Woman who used to boil herbs and take them to the market to be sold, and at last she had saved up enough money to buy a Bull-Calf, and when she had bought him she took him to her compound, and looked after him. She tended him until he had grown into a great Bull.

One day the Spider saw the Bull, and he went and told the King. He said "O King, how many ears have you?" And the King replied "I have one ear." The Spider said "Cut off the one and give it to me to eat, and you will hear some news" (1). And the King said "I have done so, what have you seen?" The Spider replied "I have seen a Bull in the Old Woman's house, a very big Bull." Then the King sent Men to go and loose the Bull, and they tried to do so, but he refused to allow them. Then they said "Beat the Spider [it is he who brought us here]." But the Spider said "If you beat me you must beat

the Old Woman also." Then the Old Woman said to
the Bull " Go up to the heel-peg (2), the Councillors are
possessed with evil, even for the smallest thing they
will haul one to the Court." So the Bull went off, and
was brought to the King's palace. Then they tried to
make him lie down, and as he refused, they cried out
" Beat the Spider." But he said " If you beat me
you must beat the Old Woman also." So she said

FIG. 51.—Lid of fig. 50.

" O Bull, lie down, and let them slaughter you." So
he lay down, and they slaughtered him.

When they had slaughtered the Bull, they gave
the Old Woman the entrails, and then she went home.
Now the Old Woman had left some cotton boles at
home, and when she returned she saw that the cotton
had been spun. So she hid in her hut [to see who had
done it], and soon she saw some Young Girls appear
and commence spinning again. But when they saw

her they began to change into entrails so as to [disguise themselves and] hide from her, but she said " Remain as you are," and they replied " Very well."

Now one day the Spider came along again, and he met the Beautiful Girls, so he went and told the King that he had seen Beautiful Young Girls at the Old Woman's house. So the King said to his Messengers " Go and bring the Old Woman and the Girls." So they came, and the Old Woman was told to return home with all but one whom the King had chosen as his Wife.

After a time the King began preparing for a campaign, and he told his Bride to give up going outside the house, for if she did any work she would melt ; and when he had said this, he went off to the war. Now when he had gone, the Women of the household who had been there before she had come, told her to come outside and work (3), so the Girl did so and began to work, but she melted near a fire. Then a Pigeon was summoned, and they said to her " Go and tell the King that the Bride has melted." Thus the King heard the news, and returned home, and said " Whatever made the Girl go outside and work ? " And they replied " The Women of the house made her do so."

Then the Old Woman was summoned, and, when she had beaten the ground in the place where the Girl had melted (4), the Girl rose up. Then the King said " What made you go outside and work ? " And she replied " They made me do so." Then the King put to death all those Women of the house, and he summoned the Old Woman and gave her presents, and he lived with the Bride.

———

In a variant (L.T.H. 160) the Young Girls are known as " Of-the-Stomach," " Of-the-Liver," " Of-

the-Heart," " Of-the-Kidneys," " Of-the-Fat," according to the part which gave each birth, and it was the
last-named whom the King married. The Old Woman
resurrects her by putting the spots of grease in a pot,
pouring in water, and leaving the pot closed until the
morning.

5

THE FALSE FRIEND.

A certain Youth said to his Friend " Come, accompany me to my Wife's People's house," so the Friend
went with him, and they took the road, and started
travelling. When they had come to the Mother-in-Law's
house, the People said " Oh, welcome, welcome." The
Husband had taken his Mare with him.

Well, food was brought to them, but the Youth said
that his Friend could eat, but that he himself could not
do so, as they were in his Mother-in-Law's house (1),
and they said " Very well." The mid-day meal was
brought also, and the Friend said " Come and eat," but
he replied " No, no, you eat, I shall not eat anything,
this is my Mother-in-Law's house." So the other ate
it, and when the evening meal was brought, the Youth
refused that also.

Now in the middle of the night, he was seized with
hunger, and he roused his Friend, and said " I am very
hungry, there is plenty of millet at the farm, and here
is a rope. I shall tie it to a post in this hut and
take the other end with me (2), and go and get some of
the bundles." So he did so, and went, and got some
bundles. But while he was away, the Friend untied the
rope, and made it fast to a post in the Mother-in-Law's
hut; so when the Youth had got his millet, he felt his
way along the rope until he had come [and entered]
his Mother-in-Law's hut. When he had got inside, he

said " I have been, I have got my bundle," and he
continued " This year these People have a great quantity
of millet, and I have taken some." Now the Father-in-
Law was lying there, and had been watching all this
time ! But the Youth thought that it was his Friend,
so he pulled off the ears of corn, and when he had
finished the lot he cooked them and ate them. When
he had had enough, he said " O Friend, where is the
water ? " and the Father-in-Law pointed with his hand,
but did not open his mouth lest he should betray
himself. When the Youth had drunk, he said " Make
room for me to lie down," but the Father-in-Law
said " O Youth, this is not your hut." When the
other had looked, he saw that it was his Father-in-
Law, and he left the hut, and went and put on his
saddle, and mounted his Mare, although it was night,
and started off. Before day had broken he had come
near his own town, but just then his Mare (3) bucked
him off, and returned to the Mother-in-Law's house,
and when she had arrived they caught her, and tied
her up.

Then the Wife's Father came out, and went to the
Mare, and opened the saddle-bags and put in his hand,
and—would you believe it?—the Friend had half-filled
them with dirt.* When the Father-in-Law had put in
his hand, he brought out the leg of a fowl, but when he
put it in again he stuck it in the dirt.

The Youth [was so much ashamed that he] would
not go back to his Wife's town, nor would he go and
get his Mare, both of them he abandoned to his Father-
in-Law. As for the Friend, he went his own way next
morning.

That kind of friendship is not pleasant.

———

In a variant (L.T.H. 101) a Malam takes a Boy with him to hold his Mare, and (although there is no mention of his refusing any of the food offered) in the night he steals three Fowls, and rides off. At daybreak, the Malam dismounts to say his prayers, and the Mare gets away from him, and returns to the house of the Parents-in-Law. The Malam follows, and pretends that he was put out of the house, and accuses the Boy of stealing the Fowls, but no one believes him. If this change is due to Mohammedan influence, it is rather strange that the Malam should be much worse than the Youth.

6

A LIE CAN GIVE MORE PAIN THAN A SPEAR.

A Jackal once lived with a Hyæna, and whenever he stretched himself he would say " A lie can give more pain than a spear." But the Hyæna would reply " A spear does more harm than a lie."

One day the Jackal went to the market, and bought honey-cakes and then took them to the Lion's lair, and on his arrival he said " O Great One, Elder Brother of the Forest, see here is something nice that I have brought for you "; and he gave him the cakes (1). The Lion took them, and tasted them, and found them delicious, so he said " O Wise One of the Forest, where did you get these very nice things? " " I got them at the Hyæna's house," the Jackal replied, " they are her tears*; she will not give any to you, however, but only to us young ones." Then the Lion asked " Where is the Hyæna? " and the Jackal said " She is at home."

So the Lion started off for the Hyæna's house, and on his arrival he said to her " Shed some of your sweet tears for me." So she shed some, and he tasted them, and found that they were not sweet, and he said " No, no, not that kind." So she tried again, and he found them bitter also, and then he got angry, and seized her, and squeezed her, and he kept on squeezing her, and she kept on shedding bitter tears, until he had almost killed her. Then he left her, and went home.

Soon afterwards, the Jackal arrived, and she exclaimed " Truly a lie can give more pain than a spear." Then he said " Oh, you have found that out, have you ? " And she replied " I have."

In a variant of this story (F.-L. 23) the Goat deceives the Lion by a false description of the Hyæna's products.

7

The King who fulfilled his Promise to the Leper.

A Blind Man and a Female Leper married, and after that, they gave birth to a hundred Children, and amongst the whole lot there was not one who could walk; some dragged themselves along the ground, some crawled about, some could not raise themselves at all.

Soon after the hundredth Child had been born, an Enemy's Force came and attacked the city in which they lived, and the Man said [to his Wife] " You take fifty and I'll take fifty of the Children, and let us go and hide them " (1). So the Woman took one and put it on her back, and she took another and put it on her breast; the Man took one and put it on one shoulder, he took another and put it on the other shoulder, and he took a third and put it on his chest; and they went off with the five Children, and began running. Soon the Hostile Horsemen spied

them, and followed them at a gallop, and they ran on
until they had come to the brink of a river. Then
the Man plunged in and became a Bull-Hippopotamus,
and his three Children became young Hippopotamus-
Calves; the Woman also plunged in and turned herself
and her young into Crocodiles.

Just then the Enemy arrived and halted at the
brink of the river, and the Hippopotamus came close
up and, with his chest, caused the water to overflow, and the wave carried off twenty Horses, the
Riders only just escaping. Then the remainder
returned to the " War-Mother " (2) and said " See,
there is something in the water which is too
powerful for us." " Can one Man be too strong?"
asked the King. " Let us go and see him," he continued, so he started off and came to the bank of the
river. When he had arrived, and had stopped, the Hippopotamus took up the water and hurled it at them, and
about fifty Horses and Men were killed. Then the
War-Mother said " Truly that is not a Man, it is a
Devil." So they started off, and left the place, and
returned to besiege the city.

Then the Hippopotamus and the Crocodile came
out of the water, and changed themselves back
into Human Beings again, and they went on and
hid their Children afar off on the other side of the
river. And after that, they returned, and followed behind
the Enemy, and re-entered the city. Then they went to
their King, and said " See, we have ninety-five
Children here, in the name of God and his Messenger
we claim your protection for them, for we are going to
escape." And the King replied " I will answer for their
safety." So they arose and fled.

Soon afterwards, the Besiegers attacked and took

the city, and, when the King saw that the city was
lost, he said " A pledge in God's name is difficult of
fulfilment." For was he to rescue the Offspring of his
own body and leave those of the Blind-man and the
Leper, or should he fulfil the promise that he had
made [for he could not save both his own and theirs].
But he abandoned his own, and put their ninety-five on
Horse-back, and he escaped with them. And the
Enemy looted his palace and captured everyone of his
own Children.

Now after the Enemy had departed again, the Blind
Man and the Leper returned with their five Children, and
the King came back with the ninety-five, and said
" Here are your Children." And now the King
possessed nothing but his own life, he had no property
of any kind. But when the Children grew up, one of
the Maidens amongst them became very beautiful, and
the King said that he wanted them to give her to him
in marriage, and they said that she was his.

Now when he had married her, the Girl would bring
forth* from her body 10,000 cowries in the morning,
and 20,000 in the evening, so the King bought Slaves
and filled his palace with them, until his household was
even larger than it ever was before (3). And there
was avoidance (4) between him and the Leper (5).

8

THE FRIENDLY LION, AND THE YOUTH AND HIS WIFE.

There was once a certain Hunter, and whenever he
went to the forest he would kill some Beast and bring it
back for himself and his Wife to eat. But one day he
returned without having shot anything, and they went

hungry. Next day he went out again and wandered about, but got nothing. But at last he caught a Locust, and wrapped it up in leaves, and brought it home and put it down (1). Now when the Wife saw the parcel of leaves, she thought that it was meat, so she lit her fire, and put on the pot to boil, and then she undid the leaves, and while she was doing so, the Locust jumped up with a " boop " and went off. Then she said to her Husband " The Thing which you brought has disappeared." And he abused her, and said " You

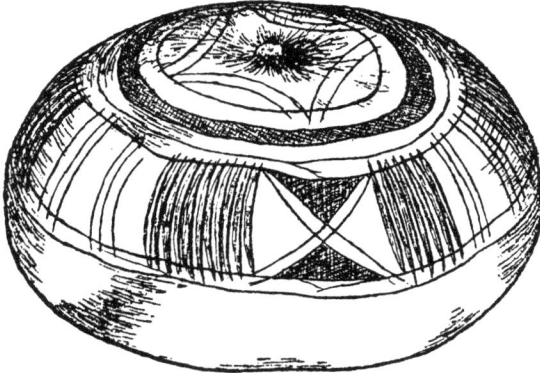

FIG. 52.—Decorated gourd, pattern cut on red ground, small lid at top.

go too, and wherever it goes you must follow and bring it back." Now the Wife was with Child, but she took the road, and followed the Locust. Just as she was about to catch it, it jumped up, and went on as before, and so she had to follow on again, and every time she tried to catch it, it escaped and went on further.

Thus it continued, she could never catch it, and at last she became tired, and night was at hand. So she looked for a hollow tree, and no sooner had she found it and entered, than she felt the pains of labour, and she gave birth in the hollow tree to her Child, a Son. Then she put him on her back and went out to seek food (2).

They lived on there for some time, and the Son began to understand a little, and he used to walk about, and go even to the den of a Lioness which had a Whelp. Whenever the Lioness brought meat, the Boy would get his share, and take it to his Mother in the hollow tree, and soon the Whelp got to know them both, and they used to play together.

But one day, the Lioness, while out hunting, saw the Boy's Mother, and she sprang upon her, and killed her, and took up the corpse, and brought it to her den. The Whelp recognized the body, and refused to eat of it, and he told the Boy; so they dug a grave, and buried the Mother. And, when the Whelp had grown up into a Young Lion, he killed his Mother the Lioness, and told the Boy [who was now a Youth]. But the Youth refused to eat the flesh, and so they dug another grave, and buried the body.

After a time, the Youth said to the Young Lion " I am going to the town to live and marry," and the Young Lion replied " Very well." Then the Youth said " But I want a tobe, trousers, and a turban also, and money, and other things," and the Young Lion replied " You are right." So he went to the edge of the forest, and lay in wait on the road, and when the Traders were passing he sprang upon them, and killed them, and they fled and left their loads (3). Then the Lion took them, and carried them to the Youth, and the Youth went off to the town with them.

When he had settled down, he married, and he lived in the town, and the Lion used to come at night and enter the Youth's house. But one day the Wife saw him, and she was afraid, and ran away crying

out " There is a Lion in our house." Then the Lion's
heart was broken, and he returned to the forest, and
went and lay down at the foot of a tree. And he said
to the Youth (4) " If you hear me roar only once you
will know that I am dead, if you hear me twice you will
know that I am still alive." And the Youth said " Very
well." And the Lion went off (5).

Soon the Youth heard the Lion roar, and as it was
only once he knew that the Lion was dead. So he
arose and followed the Lion's spoor, and came to the
place, and found the Lion dead. Then he said " Since
the Lion is no longer alive, my life is of no use to me,"
and he took his knife and stabbed himself, and fell.
dead on top of the Lion. So they were quits (6).

In a variant, the ending is not so sad, for when the
Youth went to look for the Lion, a Guinea-Fowl told
him to take her dirt from the foot of a tamarind tree,
and to mix it with water, and when he had done so,
" he came and he gave it to the Lion, and the Lion
drank this, and came to life again." But he said " O
Youth you go to your house and live there, but I will
go to the forest."

In another variant, a Female Friend of the Wife
who is staying with her during the Husband's absence
sees the Lion drinking milk out of a calabash which
has been placed ready for him, and the Lion, thinking
himself ambushed, rushes away, staking himself so
badly on a fishing-spear blocking the gateway that he
dies of the wound and of a broken heart. On the
Husband's return, he goes to the den and rips open his
inside.

The Hausa story has not much resemblance to the
Roman legend of Romulus and Remus, but some can
certainly be seen in a Southern Nigerian version (given
in *British Nigeria*, page 283). In the days when Iddah
(7) was but a village, a Woman from Ohimoje found

her way there, and brought forth a son in the forest, and left it there. A Leopardess found him and reared him with her Cubs, and when he grew up, th Leopardess, having observed the customs of Human Beings, was troubled about his nakedness, so she way-laid a Man, and took his clothes, and brought them to her Foster-Child. Later on, she decided that he must associate with his own kind, so she took him to the out-skirts of Iddah, and left him there. The Youth entered the town, and, on finding some of the People fighting, he took upon himself the position of Arbiter, and so much impressed were they, that he was proclaimed King on the spot. He was thus the first King or Attah, and by marrying with Women of the town, he had children as bold as Leopards. After a time, the Leopardess, knowing that she was about to die, came to bid him farewell, and the Attah begged her to remain with him, but she ran away to the forest, and died there. The Attah followed, and flung himself upon the body, and the People who followed found them both dead, so they buried them together.

9

HOWEVER POOR YOU ARE, THERE IS SOMEONE EVEN WORSE OFF.

There was once a certain Man, and he was very poor, he had no food, no tobe, nothing but a loin-cloth. So he arose and went to the King, and said " O Lion (1), I am weary of life so kill me (2); I have no food, I have no tobe, I have nothing but a loin-cloth, my poverty is too much for me." So the King said " Very well," and he ordered his Attendants to take him and put him to death.

But just as they were about to kill him, another Poor Man, who was quite naked, saw him, and said " I have a favour to ask; when you have killed this Man, give me his loin-cloth." Now the other heard this, and he said " Stop, do not kill me, take me back to the King, I want to say something to him." So he was taken back to the King, and they said " Oh, this Man has something to say." Then the King said " Well, let him come and say it, so that I may hear." And the Poor Man said " Well, I want you to let me go alive, to-day I have seen one who is even poorer than I, for he wants my loin-cloth. Now that is what caused me to ask that I might be brought before you again. I do not wish to die." Then the King said " Very well, go your own way, and give thanks, you have seen One who is even poorer than you."

This is finished.

10

THE BOY, THE GIRL, AND DODO.

A CERTAIN Boy used to go to a village to escort a Girl to his town. Now there was a river between them, and one day when they arrived at the bank of the river, he saw that it had risen, and he said " Stay here, and let me go and see if it is very deep or not " (1). So he went and entered the water, and was just about to come out [on the other side] when he heard a Father-Dodo asking " Have you caught him? " and just then the Young Dodos came and grasped his foot, but he kicked them off, and got out. Then [he heard the Father-Dodo speaking again], he said " Never mind, he will return."

Just as the Boy had crossed, he heard the cries of Hyænas, about twenty of them were rushing on to the Girl. The Hyænas were on the other bank, the Dodos were in the water; was he to take the road to the town and escape, leaving the Girl to her fate, or was he to return to help her? And he wondered whatever he should do. But at last he said, "If a Man must lose his life, let him die for Someone-else's sake," and he threw himself into the river, and swam across and got the Girl.

But when they were crossing again, Dodo seized him, both he and the Girl were caught, and they were dragged down under water. He struggled with them for about twenty days, and during that time his Parents were searching for him, but could not find him, and the Girl's Parents were looking for her, but could not find her. But on the twenty-first day he conquered the Dodos, and he and the Girl both emerged from the water, and he took her home.

The Parents were glad.

For a variant (which is at the same time a contrast) see the variant to Story 53.

II

FALSEHOOD IS MORE PROFITABLE THAN TRUTH.

This is about certain Men, the King of Falsehood and the King of Truth (1), who started off on a journey together, and the King of Lies said to the King of Truth that he [the latter] should get food for them on the first day. They went on, and slept in a town, but they did not get anything to eat, and next morning when they had started again on the road, the King of Truth said to the King of Lies "In the town where we shall sleep to-night you must get our food," and the King of Lies said "Agreed."

They went on, and came to a large city, and lo, the Mother of the King of this city had just died, and the whole city was mourning, and saying "The Mother of the King of this city has died." Then the King of

Lies said " What is making you cry ? " And they
replied " The King's Mother is dead." Then he said
" You go and tell the King that his Mother shall arise."
[So they went and told the King, and] he said " Where
are these Strangers ? " And the People replied " See
them here." So they were taken to a large house, and
it was given to them to stay in.

In the evening, the King of Lies went and caught a
Wasp, the kind of Insect which makes a noise like
" *Kurururu*," and he came back, and put it in a small
tin, and said " Let them go and show him the grave."
When he had arrived, he examined the grave, and then
he said " Let everyone go away." No sooner had they
gone, than he opened the mouth of the grave slightly;
he brought the wasp and put it in, and then closed the
mouth as before. Then he sent for the King, and said
that he was to come and put his ear to the grave—
meanwhile this Insect was buzzing—and when the King
of the city had come, the King of Lies said " Do you
hear your Mother talking ? " Then the King arose ;
he chose a Horse and gave it to the King of Lies ; he
brought Women and gave them to him ; and the whole
city began to rejoice because the King's Mother was
going to rise again.

Then the King of Lies asked the King of the city
if it was true that his Father was dead also, and the
King replied " Yes, he is dead." So the King of
Lies said " Well, your Father is holding your Mother
down in the grave, they are quarrelling," and he continued " Your Father, if he comes out, will take away
the chieftainship from you," and he said that his Father
would also kill him. When the King had told the
Townspeople this, they piled up stones on the grave (2),
and the King said " Here, King of Lies, go away ;

I give you these horses," and he continued that so far as his Mother was concerned, he did not want her to appear either.

Certainly falsehood is more profitable than truth in this world.

———

In a variant, a Man dies, leaving Falsehood, a Son, and Truth, a Daughter. They have plenty of corn, but they hide it, and go begging. Truth tells what they have really done, and so she gets only abuse, but Falsehood says that they are Orphans, and starving, and so he is given plenty. "Falsehood will procure food more quickly than truth."

————

12

VIRTUE PAYS BETTER THAN GREED.

Once the King of Good and the King of Evil (1) started off on a journey, and the King of Evil said "O King of Good, you bring your food, and we will continue eating it until we have finished it, and then we will eat mine." So they travelled on and on, until the food of the King of Good was finished, and then he said "You now, King of Evil, bring your food." But the King of Evil refused to do this, so the King of Good wasted away.

They travelled on and on, until one night they slept at the foot of a large tree. Now there was a Bird's nest at the top of the tree, and the Bird up there said "The leaves of this tree"—the King of Evil was sleeping but the King of Good could not do so, for hunger was troubling him—the Bird said (2) "This is such a tree, that if a Person gathers its leaves, and rubs the eye of a Blind-man [with the juice] it will be healed." Then the King of Good arose quietly, and went and picked the leaves of the tree, and threw them into his bag, and he continued gathering the leaves and throwing them into his bag until dawn came.

When it was light they arose and went on, and came to a certain city, and lo, the Son of the King of this city was a Blind-man. Now the King of Good went to the King of the city, and asked the King to find him a Blind-man and he would heal him. Then the King said " Are you able to heal the eyes ? " and he continued " How much shall I have to give you if you heal my Son's eyes for me ? " " A million cowries," replied the King of Good. And the King said " Agreed ; but wait till to-morrow."

When day had dawned, the King of Good said " Let them be taken to another hut, the two of them only; besides himself only the King's Son could be present." So they were taken to another hut. Then the King of Good asked them to give him a little water in a gourd, and he took some medicine and mixed it, and rubbed the Blind-man's eyes, and lo ! at last they were healed. Then the King of the city said " Since you have healed my Son's eyes for me, you shall be my Deputy." So the King of Good was made the Deputy-Ruler of the city; half the city came under the Deputy. And as soon as he could, he took the King of Evil and killed him (3).

The Borlawa (a people of Bornu) have a tale which resembles this, but in it the Bad Man plucks out the eyes of the Good Man. The events occur as in the above, but the Good Man is kind to the Bad Man when he next sees him. The latter, however, tries to get some of the magic leaves for himself, and is killed by the Birds.

The conference overheard by the hero takes place frequently between demons or other supernatural powers. Skeat and Blagden (*Pagan Races of the Malay Peninsula,* ii, 359 note) quote from Goudinho de Eredia, a Portuguese writer of the early part of the seventeenth century, a statement that "at the equinox, especially the autumnal, on the day called *divaly* [probably the South Indian or Tamil feast called *Thivali*] trees, herbs, plants talk and disclose the remedy for every malady. To hear them people hide in the forest." (H.).

N.B.—In Northern India it is *Divali* (Crooke, *Popular Religion and Folk-Lore of Northern India,* 2nd ed., ii, page 295).

13

The Victim does not Always see the Joke.

A certain Thief lived with his Wife, and whatever he stole in the town he brought to her. So they went on for a long time, until one night the full moon was shining almost like the sun, and the Wife said ".Well now, see, that full moon makes it easy to walk about, are you going to stay in the house?" and the Husband replied " Oh, all right, I'll go." So he started off, and went to his Father-in-Law's house, for the Father-in-Law had a certain big Ram, there was none like it in the whole town. The Thief went and took it away, and brought it to his Wife, and said " See what God has given us to-day " (1). Then she said " Good, but kill it now, lest when day has broken the Owner should see it, and know it to be his " (2). So he said " Very well, and he killed it, and skinned it, and cut up the flesh into small pieces.

When day broke, the Woman saw that the skin of the Ram was exactly like that of her Father's Ram, and she said to her Husband " Hullo, Owner-of-the-

XIX.—A HAUSA CHEAP-JACK. XX.—MATS.

The Hausa is widely known as a trader, his cloths, metal-work, and grass mats, as well as other manufactures, being greatly in demand.

House, where did you get this Ram, is it my Father's?" But he replied "Poof, is your Father's Ram the only one in the town? Truly, I merely caught this Ram loose." So she said "Oh, all right." But while they were sitting there, the Thief's Mother-in-Law arrived, and said to the Wife "Have you not heard the News? Last night a Thief got into our house, and stole your Father's Ram." And the Daughter said "Indeed." But when her Mother had gone, she said to her Husband "As for you, you knew quite well that it was your Father-in-Law's Ram, and yet you went and stole it, and said that it was not his," and she began to cry and to weep. Then he said "Well, did not you yourself tell me to go and steal? So far as you are concerned, had I stolen from another Person's house you would not have cried about it, it is only since you knew that it is your Father's Ram that you have done so." And he continued "A Tatuer does not like to be tatued himself." Then she said "Well, my heart is broken," and she went out of the house, and returned to live with her Parents.

In L.T.H. 116 the Wife tells the Husband that the Moon almost seems to be saying "Go and bring something," and after the Thief has acted upon the suggestion, the Mother comes to summon the Wife to condole with the Family on the loss; otherwise the story is the same.

14

DODO, THE ROBBER, AND THE MAGIC DOOR.

This is about Dodo, he lived in the forest, and was always wandering about looking for People to eat. One day he caught a certain Woman, and brought her to his home and married her, and he made her live there with him.

Now after a long time, her Sister said that she was going to find her, so she took a creeping-gourd (1) and planted it, and said that wherever her Sister was the gourd would guide her to her. So the gourd-plant crept on, and on, until it reached the door of her hut and [the Girl followed, and when she had arrived] the Sister said "What has brought you here?" Then the other replied "I waited for some years but did not see you, and that is why I planted this gourd to guide me to you." Then the Sister said "Yes, but what about Dodo, he eats People?" The other replied "Well, can I not be a Younger Sister to you?" So the Sister took her, and put her in a binn of cotton-boles. But when Dodo returned, he said "Ambashira, whence have you got a Human Being to-day? [I can smell one]." Then she replied "It is I, have you become tired of me, do you wish to kill me and live alone?" (2). So Dodo was silenced, and at daybreak next morning the Sister packed her Younger Sister's bundle, and told her to go home, but to return in a week.

When the seven days had passed, the Younger Sister returned, and as Dodo had gone to the forest, they slept together, and next morning at dawn they tied up their bundles and went off, and they got across the river. But as they were leaving the house, Ambashira spat* (3) on the floor.

When Dodo returned from the forest, he called "Ambashira," and the Spit answered, but when Dodo entered the hut he could see no one, there was only the Spit. So he went off along the road, and followed their footprints. But when he came near, they had

already crossed the river, so Dodo stopped on his side
of the river, and he returned home.

Soon the Women met a certain Robber who said
that he was going to commit a theft in Dodo's house.
So they said " When you go, say to the door ' *Zirka,
bude* ' (4), and when you have stolen what you want, and
have gone out again, say ' *Zirka Gumgum.*' " So he
went to Dodo's house and said " *Zirka bude,*" and the

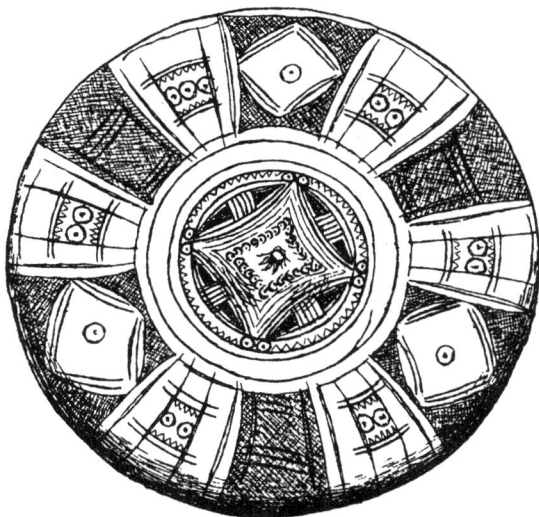

FIG. 53.—Decorated gourd, pattern in relief in brown.

door opened. And he went in and stole Dodo's riches,
but when he was ready to go away again he forgot the
words, he could then remember only *Zirka Gumgum,*
and immediately he had said this the door jambed more
tightly than ever into the wall. Then he tried, and tried
to get out, but he could not do so.

Now the Women from where they were standing
[knew this, and they] began singing " O Mad Robber,
we gave you the chance to steal, but we did not give

you forgetfulness," and they went off home. So Dodo when he returned caught the Robber in his house, and he killed him, and stuck his body on a spit. Soon the flesh was cooked, and then Dodo ate it.

In a variant (L.T.H. ii, 16) a Man and his Wife and Children have to go to the forest and eat herbs because they are so poor. The Wife finds a way of catching Guinea-Fowls, but the Husband ruins it. She then tricks Elephants into supplying her with Fish, but the Husband again interferes with disastrous results. Then she finds Dodo's house, and sees him come up, and say " Baram," and the door opens. When he has entered, he says " *Zarga gungun,*" and the door closes again. She does the same for a week, and steals Dodo's food, but when the Husband goes, he is caught. Dodo makes him show him where his Family is, and he takes all of them to his house, intending to eat them, but the Wife hides herself and her Family in a Mouse-hole, and saves their lives, the end of the tale resembling that of F.-L. 24.

15

THE DECEITFUL SPIDER, THE HALF-MAN, AND THE RUBBER-GIRL.

The Spider one day told his Wife to measure him out some ground-nuts (1), and said " Peel and cook them." So they were peeled, and cooked, and salt and oil were mixed with them, and then he said that he was going to sow (2).

So he took his hoe, and started off, but he found a cool, shady spot near the water, and he sat down, and ate his fill; and, after he had had a drink, he went off to sleep. When he awoke, he got some mud and plastered it on his body, and then he returned to his wife, and told her to bring him some water with which to wash, for he had come back dirty from his work.

This went on every day, until at last the Wife said that she had seen ground-nuts ripe in everyone's farms, and that those which her Husband had sown must be ripe too, so she would go to the farm and grub them. But the Spider replied " No, no, it was not you who sowed the ground-nuts, 1 myself will go and dig them " (3). Really, he intended to commit a theft on the Half-Man's farm, and he went there, and stole some ground-nuts, and brought them back to his Wife.

Now when the Half-Man came, and saw that he had been robbed, he said that he would make a trap with a Rubber-Girl (4), and catch the Thief. [So he did so] and when the Spider came again, he saw a Beautiful Girl with a long neck, and fine breasts (5). Then he came up close and touched her breasts, and said " O Maiden," and the rubber held his hand. Then he exclaimed " Ah ! Girl, let me go, you must want me badly." He put his other hand on her and it stuck also, and he said " You Girls, are you amorous enough to hold a Man ? I will kick you." Then he kicked with one foot, and the rubber caught it, and he became furious, and said " O Base-born of Your Parents." Then he kicked with the other foot, and the rubber held him all over, so that he was bent up. Then he said " Very well, I am going to butt you," and he butted, and his head stuck (6).

Just then the Half-Man, from where he was hiding, saw the Spider, and he said " Thanks be to God." Then he got a switch of the tamarind tree, and put it in the fire, and he brought some grease, and rubbed it in (7), and he came up, and rained blows upon the Spider until his back was raw, his whole body was raw. Then he released the Spider from the Rubber-Girl, and said " Look here Spider, if you come here again, I, the Half-Man, will kill you."

———

In a variant (L.T.H. ii, 72) the Spider is caught by a female " Half-Being," but she lets him go on condition that he does not say anything about her.   He breaks his promise, and she tries to kill him, but he escapes.

———

For parallels, see Chapter VI.

———

16

THE RICH MALAM, THE THIEVING SPIDER, AND THE HYÆNA.

This is about a Malam who had riches of all kinds; Cattle, Horses, Goats, all of these he had.   One day the Spider came to him, and said " Peace be upon you," and the Malam replied "And on you too, be peace " (1). Then the Spider said " I want to tend your flocks for you, I will also sweep the place where the Sheep are kept."   And the Malam said very well, that he agreed.

So the Spider lived there, and every morning he would clean up the rubbish and throw it away, and sweep the place. Now when the Spider had first come, he had taken a big basket, and had said that he was going to put the sweepings into it, but really, every morning he would kill a Goat, and put the body in the basket, and cover it up with sweepings, and then he would take it to the forest, and eat it.

But one day the Malam saw that the animals were being diminished, and he said to himself " I wonder if the Spider is playing me some trick," and he said

"Well, I must watch him closely." Next morning
the Spider killed a big Ram, and put it in the basket,
and then found that he could not carry it. Just then
the Malam saw him, and he came up and said "Let me
lift it on to your head," but when he felt the weight,
he said "You must lighten it." Then the Spider said
"No, no, I can manage it, do not touch it." But the
Malam replied "You cannot do so, it must be light-
ened," and he put in his hand and threw out some
of the sweepings, and then he touched the body of the
Ram, and pulled it out. When he had done so, he
said "Oh indeed, that is how you are acting towards
me, is it?" And he seized him, and tied him up to the
entrance of the pen, and beat him all over, and left
him there.

During the night the Hyæna came along, and when
she had come close, and had seen the Spider, she said
"What has happened that you have been tied up?"
And the Spider replied "Opp, I was tending this
Malam's flocks, and every day I killed a Goat that he
gave me, and ate it, but I said that I was tired of it,
and was going to run away." Then the Hyæna, the
Greedy One, exclaimed "Good gracious, does one obtain
so much in the Malam's house that he becomes tired of
food?" and she continued "Now as for me, I should
like to have such abundance." "Opp, that is easy,"
replied the Spider, "all you have to do is to loose me,
and I will tie you up in my place." So the Hyæna
said "Good," and she loosed him, and he tied her up,
and then said "Well, I am going to the forest," and
off he went.

In the morning the Malam came, and when he saw
the Hyæna he beat and beat her until she was nearly
dead. But at last she managed to slip her bonds, and

she ran off, and went to the forest to look for the Spider.

That is all, the Spider and the Hyæna both escaped.

In a variant (M.H. 3) the Jerboa is the Villain of the piece, and it is the Malam's Daughter who finds him out by helping him with the load—and this would certainly be the case if there were a daughter, for no Malam would do any work when there were others to do it for him. In the variant, the Hyæna is not told that the Jerboa is going to run away.

In another (L.T.H. 150) the Hyæna takes the place of the Spider, and the flocks are owned by an Old Woman who is helped by a Lion.

This story is widespread, being found also among the Masai (Hollis, *The Masai,* 214), the Bechuana (Arbousset and Daumas, *Exploratory Tour,* Eng. Ed., 59), and in the Cameroons (*Journ. Afr. Soc.,* iv, 63). Outside the Continent, it is found among the Bisayans in the Philippine Islands (*Journ. Amer. Folk-Lore,* xxix, 108), being possibly an importation from Europe, where it is common. In North America it is combined by the Yuchi Indians of Oklahoma with the Tar-Baby (Speck, *Ethnology of the Yuchi Indians,* 152). It is also told by the Uraons in India (Rep. Brit. Assn., 1896, 661). (H.).

17

LITTLE FOOL, OR THE BITER BIT.

Certain Parents had a Son, and his name was " Little Fool." One day they went to their farm, and when they returned they said " Have you not cooked even a single bean for us ? " But he replied " Oh no, you did not say to cook you any." So they said " Very well, to-morrow cook a bean for us " (1).

When morning came [they went off again, and] he
took a single bean and put it into the largest jar (2) and
cooked it. And when they returned and saw the big
jar, they said " Little Fool, what are we going to do
with all these beans ? " But when they had opened the
jar, and had seen that there was only one bean inside,
they said " O Little Fool, is it only a single bean that
you have cooked for us ? " Then he replied " Well,
you did not say to cook ' beans,' you said ' a bean.' "
So they said " Very well, to-morrow cook beans."

Next morning [they went off again, and] he got
inside the barn, and called others to help him, and
they cooked every one of the beans. So when the
Parents returned they saw pots of beans right from the
door of the entrance-hall up to the centre of the compound. Then they said " O Little Fool, whatever shall
we do with all these beans ? " And he replied " Ah !
are you the only ones to eat ? I can easily find others
to help." Then they said " Do so," and he went to
the forest and brought back ten Gazelles, and said
" See, here are your Fellow-Feasters."

Well, next morning when the Parents went to the
farm they left him at home with the Gazelles, and it
happened that the Spider arrived on a trading trip, and
gave the salutation " Peace be upon you," and Little
Fool said to him " Welcome." Then the Spider said
" Let us slaughter your Gazelles, and I will take the
meat and sell it for you." And Little Fool said
" Agreed." So they slaughtered all the Gazelles, and
they put the meat into the saddle-bags, and these were
put on to the Spider's Donkeys.

[As the Spider was going off with them] Little Fool
said " Ah, this bag is not full," and he continued " You
must stay here now and wait for my Parents who have

gone to the farm, and I will go on with your Donkeys and get some more meat to fill these bags." But the Spider said "Oh Little Fool, come now, you know that a real Friend would not behave badly." Then Little Fool replied "Truly I shall not act except as a Friend would," and the other said "All right."

When Little Fool had gone off with the Donkeys, he took off the bags, and [removed the meat, and] he took dirt* and filled them, and he put pieces of liver on the top. Then he brought the Donkeys back, and said "See, now the bags are full, I have made a profit." So the Spider said "Good, now let me go." Now as he travelled along, the [hoofs of the] Donkeys were saying "Dir-ty-muck, dir-ty-muck, dir-ty-muck," and the Spider said "O You of Evil Origin, say 'Meat-it-is, meat-it-is, meat-it-is.'" So he went on home, and said to his Wife "Quick, quick, unload the Donkeys," and she did so. Just then the Cat said "Um yau," and the Spider said "Excuse me, will the liver suffice to fill you?" Then he put his hand into the bags (3) and pulled out the pieces of liver and gave them to the Cat, and she ate them.

But when he put in his hand again he found nothing but dirt. Then the Spider said "Opp, Little Fool has tricked me; because of his cunning he has found me out," and he continued "I'll leave it at that."

In a variant (L.T.H. 83), the Spider returns to ask for an explanation, and finds Little Fool covered with ashes. "Oh dear!" he says, "those Gazelles which we seized belonged to the King. He has sent for my Father, and has told him to bring them at once, and I do not know what to do." Then the Spider said "May God preserve you, I am off." In another (L.T.H. 157) where Little Fool was sent by God in answer to an Old Woman's prayer, both she and he deceive the Spider.

18

How the Spider ate the Hyæna-Cubs' Food.

One day the Spider went to the Hyæna's house when he knew that she was out for a walk, and began talking to the Cubs. He asked one what his name was, and the Cub answered " Mohammadu." Then he said to another " And what is your name? " and he replied " Isa." Then the Spider asked a third Cub his name and he said " It is Na-taala." When he had asked them all, he said " Now, look here, your Mother-Hyæna asked me to come here and live with you, so you must know my name, it is For-you-all." Now whenever the Hyæna brought food she used to say " It is for you all," and [so after that] the Spider would at once exclaim " You see, it is all for me only, you heard what our Mother (1) has said." So the Spider would eat up all the food.

This went on for about a month, and as the Spider had always taken the whole food, the Cubs by this time had wasted away. Then one day the Hyæna said "Come out of the den, My Children, and let me see you." Now when they appeared, she saw that they had become very thin, and she said " Whatever has happened to you, O My Children, to make you so thin? " " Ah," replied they, " you have brought us no food." " What! " she exclaimed, " What about all that which I have been bringing for you all? " " Oh," they replied, " For-you-all has eaten it, he is in there." Where is For-you-all? " she said. " Let him come out and show himself." Then the Spider pushed forward his ears until they were sticking out of the hole (2), and said " Catch hold of my boots first, then I will come out and you can see me." Immediately the Hyæna seized hold of the ears, and angrily threw them behind her, and the Spider [for his whole body had been pulled out] got up, and ran away. Then she said " Where is For-you-all ? " And her Cubs said " It was he whom you threw over there behind you."

Now the Spider ran on to the house of the Dog where he was weaving, and he sat down. But soon the Hyæna approached, looking for the Spider, and she came upon the Dog and the Spider sitting there by the loom. Then she said " Of you two, whom was I chasing ? " And the cunning Spider at once replied " Look at the Dog's mouth, he is panting tremendously, that is proof that it was he who has been running away " (3). Immediately the Hyæna sprang towards the Dog, but the Dog got away in time, and the Spider also ran away, so both escaped from the Hyæna.

———

In a variant (M.H. 2) the Jerboa plays the part of the Spider, in another (L.T.H. 5) the Hare takes his place, and manages to make the Dog pay the penalty.

———

19

THE SLAVE WHO WAS WISER THAN THE KING.

There was once a certain King who had three male Slaves, and each was married and had a Son. One Son was called " He-who-will-not-see," another was called " The-Gift-of-God," and the third " You-are-wiser-than-the-King," and they were brought to the King for him to see.

They lived with their Parents until they grew big, and when they were adult, they went to the King to work for him. So a bundle of guinea-corn was brought and given to "He-who-will-not-see," and a bundle to "The-Gift-of-God," but only a bundle of husks was given to "You-are-wiser-than-the-King." And the King said "Now, next year, let each bring three-hundred bundles." So they said "We will obey," and they went away [to make their own farms].

When the year had passed, and the harvest had been gathered in, He-who-will-not-see brought his 300

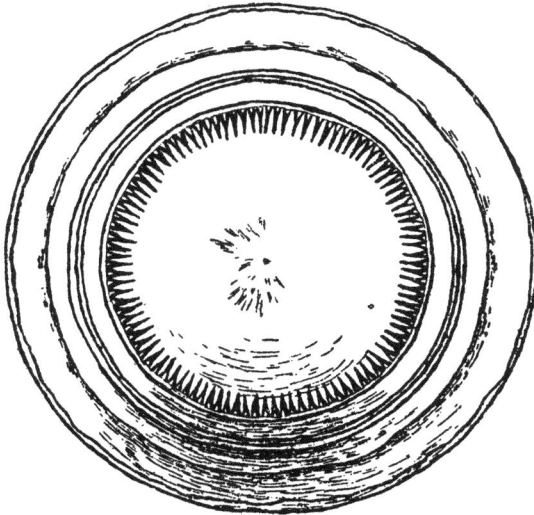

FIG. 54.—Inside of fig. 53.

bundles, and The-Gift-of-God brought his 300, but You-are-wiser-than-the-King brought a basket of husks. And when they had come into the King's presence He-who-will-not-see said "Here are my 300 bundles," and The-Gift-of-God said "Here are my 300 bundles," but You-are-wiser-than-the-King said "There are mine also." Then the King said "Why have you not brought me 300 bundles?" And he

replied " Well, the bundles of husks that you gave
me I planted, this is what came up." So the King
said " Oh, I see." So he brought a Cow and gave it
to He-who-will-not-see, and another to The-Gift-of-God,
but he gave a Bull to You-are-wiser-than-the-King.

Next year He-who-will-not-see brought two Calves,
and The-Gift-of-God brought two Calves. But
You-are-wiser-than-the-King took his axe, and hung it
on his shoulder (1). There was a dead tree behind the
King's palace, and he climbed it, and began cutting
the wood. Then the King said " Well, each of the
others has brought his two Calves, where is You-are-
wiser-than-the-King ? " Then the Attendants said
" Ah ! there is Someone like him chopping wood,"
and then they exclaimed " It is he." Then the King
said to him " O, You-are-wiser-than-the-King, what
are you doing here ? " and he replied " I am cutting
wood for my Father who has given birth." Then the
King said " What, can a Man bring forth a Child ? "
and You-are-wiser-than-the-King replied " Oh, so you
knew that a male could not bring forth young, yet you
gave me one, and told me to bring you two Calves ? "

Then the King said " Ahem, what shall I do with
this Boy ? " Then the Courtiers said "Opp, kill him" (2),
and they continued " Give him a blue-striped tobe (3),
and blue-striped trousers, and a turban with a border
of embroidery. Then choose a good Horse and put
caparisons on him." They said that the King's own
Son should put on an old tobe, old trousers, and an old
turban. " Then send them out on the road, but order
the Gun-men (4) to go on in front, and to wait in
ambush, and tell them to kill the one whom they see
in grand clothes, for he is You-are-wiser-than-the-
King " (5).

Now You-are-wiser-than-the-King when he had seen through this, sent a Man on ahead with ten gourds of pito, and ten of pure water, and when he and the King's Son overtook the Man, You-are-wiser-than-the-King said to the King's Son " Let us have a drink of water." Then he took the gourd of beer, and gave it to the King's Son, but he himself drank water. Then the King's Son began rolling about (6), and when they had gone on a little further, You-are-wiser-than-the-King said " Let us have another drink of water," and so they drank again, and the King's Son collapsed. Then You-are-wiser-than-the-King said " O King's Son, I will not leave you thus," and he continued " Take this blue-striped tobe and put it on, these blue-striped trousers, and put them on, this turban, and put it on, and I will leave my Horse, and you can ride it." So the King's Son said " Very well," and You-are-wiser-than-the-King gave the King's Son his Horse and all his trappings, and he himself put on an old tobe, and mounted a broken-down Horse.

So they went on, and came to where the Slaves, the Gun-men, were hidden, and when they came up the Slaves shot the King's Son, and he died. Immediately You-are-wiser-than-the-King galloped back and saluted the King, and said " Who is the equal of You-are-wiser-than-the-King ? ' Then the King answered " I am," and he jumped up to seize him, but You-are-wiser-than-the-King changed himself into a Frog. Then the King changed himself into a Snake to swallow the Frog, but You-are-wiser-than-the-King became a Mouse. Then the King changed himself into a Cat, but the other became a Red-Bird, and the King became a Hawk. The Red-Bird flew against an Old Woman who was sweeping the courtyard, and fell into her eye,

and became the pupil, then the King became the eyebrow. And even now they are like that, the pupil of
the eye is afraid to come out lest the eyebrow should
catch him (7).

That is the end.

20

THE COCK BY HIS WIT SAVES HIS SKIN.

One day the Cock started off to condole with the
Mourners at a burial, and as he was going along, he met
a Wild-Cat, and the latter said " Where are you
going ? " The Cock replied " I am going to condole
with the Mourners." " Where ? " asked the Wild-Cat.
" At the house of my Relatives " was the reply. Then
the Wild-Cat said " Oh really, are there to be two
deaths then ? " But the Cock replied " Oh no, neither
two nor three, I live with the Dog " (1).

They went on a little way, and then the Wild-Cat
said " Really, Cock, you are a very laughable Person,
but I must go off on my own business." So he departed, and the Cock went on.

In a variant (L.T.H. 132) the Cock replies " There
will be two or three [Mourners] " (2).

21

THE HEN SEEKS A CHARM FROM THE WILD-CAT.

A certain Hen went to a Wild-Cat, and said that she
wanted a charm for childbirth, so the Wild-Cat said
" Go and pluck the feathers from your head, and put

on salt and pepper (1), and then come back and I will give you the charm for childbirth." And [when she had gone] he lit his fire and put on logs, and the fire caught them. The Hen went and plucked the feathers from her head, and she rubbed on salt and pepper, and then returned, and said " I have done it, and I have come for you to give me the charm for childbirth." So he said " Very well, let us go close to this fire, you go in front, and I will go behind and follow you. While we are going round and round the fire, you must keep on saying :—

" ' A charm for childbirth I am seeking,
A charm for childbirth I am seeking.' "

So they went up to the fire, and began going round it, the Wild-Cat behind, when suddenly he seized her, and threw her on to the fire, and ate her.

———

In a variant, the Wild Cat can change into a Malam, and it is in this shape that he prescribes for the Hen, who is told to pluck her whole body clean.

————

22

THE BATTLE BETWEEN THE BEASTS AND THE BIRDS.

A Rooster and an Elephant kept house together. But one day the Elephant went and caught hold of the door-post of the Rooster's hut, and broke it. And the Rooster went and took a lot of rubbish and threw it inside the Elephant's hut (1). Then the Elephant said " O Rooster, I am going to fight you," and the Rooster replied " Very well, let each assemble his Relatives." So the Elephant went and called out all the Beasts of the Forest, and the Rooster went and mobilized all the Birds, and when the latter had come near to the battle-field, the Hawk said to the Rooster " I am the Commander of your Army " (2).

Now the Hyæna was detailed as a Scout by the Beasts to see if the Birds' Force was drawn up, and the Birds said " O Ostrich, you go on in front of us." And it happened that as the Hyæna was approaching the Birds, the Ostrich was working towards the Beasts, and they met, and watched each other. Then the Hyæna said " O Ostrich, is your Army ready ? "   " What about you ? " asked the Ostrich, " is yours ready ? " And when the Hyæna had replied " Yes," the Ostrich said " Go back and tell them, and I will report to mine."   But when the Ostrich had turned round, the Hyæna saw her flesh through her feathers,* and she was immediately overcome with greed, and said " Ostrich, wait, let us have our little fight first, just you and I." " Very well," replied the Bird, " You beat me three times, and I will return the blows three times."   So the Hyæna came close up, and beat the Ostrich three times, and then the Ostrich stood up, and said " Now let me have my turn," and she beat the Hyæna with her wings, she kicked her with her feet, and she pecked her with her beak.   " That is the three times," cried the Hyæna, but the Ostrich said " Oh no, that is only once."   So she again pecked her with her beak, and pulled out her eyes, and then she said "Now let each go back."   When the Beasts of the forest saw that the Hyæna had been blinded, they said " What is the matter ? "   " Do you see that my eyes have been plucked out ? " she asked.   " We are not able to fight them."   She was overcome with fear.   But the others said " Come, let us advance."

Now the two armies arrived on the battle-field at the

same moment, and the Rooster said "Let us attack."
Then the Commander of the Birds came and saluted
the Rooster, and, when the forces had approached each
other to fight, the Hawk took a string blind (3) and a
Hen's egg, and flying on to the Elephant, he broke the
egg on her head. Then the Hawk called out "The
Elephant's head is broken, the Elephant's head is
broken," and when the Elephant had touched her head
with her trunk, she said "Oh! dear, my head *is*
broken!" Then the Hawk threw the string blind over
her, and called out "Her inside is falling out, her
inside is falling out," and when the Beasts of the
Forest had come close and looked [they thought that it
was true, so] they all ran away.

Then the Rooster went off home, and said "To you,
O Hawk, will I give a present for fighting so well,
whenever my Wife has Young you come and take one.
That is my obligation (4) to you."

In a variant (F.-L. 38) the Elephant and Cock both
woo a Woman, and it is on account of their rivalry in
love that they fall out. In another (L.T.H. ii, 4) the
Birds help a Bull against an Elephant, and they fly in
the eyes of the enemy while the Bull gores him. In
this story, the Hyæna, the drummer, escapes in time,
and returns later to find the Elephant dead, and then
she eats him. She never stays to fight.

23

THE GOAT FRIGHTENS THE HYÆNA.

This is about a Goat which was living with her
Kid, a Male. One day they started off and went for a
walk, and they had lost their road, when just before
sunset they saw a house ahead of them. So they came

to it, and found the Hyæna there talking to her Cubs, and the Hyæna said " Welcome."

Now when they had come in, and were conversing, the Hyæna arose and took some grain, and began grinding it. Soon the Goat said to her " O Hyæna, let me relieve you," but the Hyæna replied " Oh no, does a Guest grind ? " Then the Goat said " Oh, let me do it, a Female is not treated as a Guest " (1). So she took the stone, and began grinding and grinding, and the Hyæna watched her. Then the Young Goat became afraid, he thought the Hyæna was going to seize him, and he came and stood close to his Mother, the Goat. Then she said " Now, when I sing you must take up the chorus " (2), and the Kid said " Very well." So the Goat began her song, saying

" I have killed ten Elephants," and the Kid said " It is true."

" I have killed ten Lions," and the Kid said " It is true."

" I have killed ten Leopards," and the Kid said " It is true."

" I have killed ten Hyænas,"——

And the Kid said " Hush, O Parent, do not speak thus, if the Hyæna hears that she will run away and leave us without any food " (3). But the Hyæna did hear (4), and said " What did you say O Goat ? " And the Goat replied, singing

" I have killed ten Elephants," and the Kid said " It is true."

" I have killed ten Lions," and the Kid said " It is true."

" I have killed ten Leopards," and the Kid said " It is true."

" I have killed ten Hyænas,"——

Then the Hyæna said " Oh, let me send my Cubs to get water for us to drink," but when she had entered her hut she said " O Cubs, run off, escape, and do not return, this is too much for us." So they fled, and disappeared into the forest.

When they had gone, the Hyæna returned to the Guests and sat down, but after she had waited a little while, and the Goat was still singing, the Hyæna said " Well, O Guest, I sent the Cubs to get water, but see, they have not returned, excuse me while I go and look for them." Then the Hyæna went off at a run, and did not return, and so the Goat took the Hyæna's goods and chattels, and she and her Kid carried them off.

In a variant (F.-L. 33) the Goat and the Dog frighten the Hyænas off in a similar way. They then hide in the house, and when the hyænas return the intruders make strange noises, so the owners leave the house for good, and the Goat and Dog live there instead (5).

24
THE SPIDER, THE GUINEA-FOWL, AND THE FRANCOLIN.

The Francolin said to the Guinea-Fowl " Will you go with me on a journey?" But just then the Spider arrived, and said " Come with me, I am going to visit my Mother-in-Law." Then the Guinea-Fowl said " Your journey is the more important, let us go together, you and I." So they started to go to the town where the Spider's Parents lived.

While on the road, the Spider said to the Guinea-Fowl " See this grass, if when we have arrived at the town, they bring me some ground-nuts, you come back here and get some of this grass so that we can roast them." " Very well," said the Guinea-Fowl.

They went on, and as they were travelling, the Spider said " There is a spoon (1), if when we have arrived at the town they bring me porridge, you come back here and get the spoon so that we can eat it " (2).

Soon they arrived at the house, and porridge was made and brought to them, so the Spider said to the Guinea-Fowl " Go, get the spoon and bring it." As soon as she had gone to bring the spoon, the Spider ate up all the porridge except for a little bit, and when she returned, he said " O you Sluggard, you have been a long time going, the People have since come and taken away their porridge."

Then he said " But see, they have brought ground-nuts, get that grass and bring it here so that we may roast them." So she went off to get the grass, and when she returned she found that the Spider had eaten up all the ground-nuts. He said " You have been so long that the People took away their ground-nuts."

Next morning they said " Now, we must go home." So the Spider's load was tied up, and that of the Guinea-Fowl also, and they started off on the road. Soon they came to the bank of a big river, and the Spider lighted a fire, and said " Stop here, I am going over there, if you hear me fall into the water, you throw yourself into the fire " (3). So he went on, and took a stone and threw it into the water so that it made a sound like *pinjim*. When the Guinea-Fowl heard this, she said " The Spider is dead," so she threw herself into the fire so that she also might die. Then the Spider came and pulled the dead Guinea-Fowl out of the fire, and plucked her feathers out of her body, and ate it. Then he took the Guinea-Fowl's load, tied it on to his own, and went off home.

Some time afterwards he went to see the Francolin,

and said " O Francolin, will you not also accompany
me on a journey ?" And when she had agreed, off they
went. As they were travelling they came to the grass,
and the Spider said " See this grass, if when we have
arrived at the town they bring us ground-nuts, you
come back here and get this grass so that we can roast
them." But the Francolin picked some grass on the sly
and hid it.

Then the Spider said " There is a spoon, if when we
have arrived at the town they give us porridge, you
come back here and get the spoon." " Very well,"
said the Francolin, but she took it then, and hid it.

Soon they arrived at the town, and porridge was
brought, so the Spider said " Go and get that spoon."
The Francolin said " Oh, you said to bring it, here it
is." Then the Spider was very angry, and said " Very
well, take the porridge yourself and eat it." So the
Francolin took it, and ate all but a little bit which she
gave to the Spider to eat.

Then ground-nuts were brought to them, and the
Spider said " Go and get some grass that we may roast
them." But she replied " Oh, here it is, I got it long
ago." Then the Spider was furious, and he said
" Take the ground-nuts and eat them." But when
she had roasted them, and had eaten all but a few, the
Spider snatched them away and ate them.

Next morning they said " Well, we must go home,"
so the Spider's load was bound up for him, and the
Francolin's for her, and they took them and started off.
Soon they arrived at the bank of the river, and the
Spider lighted a fire, and said " Stay here, I am going
over there, if you hear me fall into the water, you throw
yourself into the fire." " Very well," said she. So he
went and took a stone and threw it into the water, and

it made a sound like *pinjim*. Then the Francolin went
and got one of the Spider's long boots and put it on
the fire, while she herself crawled inside the Spider's
load, and hid. Soon the Spider came and searched in
the fire, and took out the boot and ate it. " Well," said
he, " The Guinea-Fowl was certainly more juicy than
this Francolin " (4). So he took the Francolin's load
and tied it on to his own, and started off home.

Then the Francolin, who was inside, said " The
Spider is a fool, he has eaten his boot," and when the
Spider heard this he was so frightened that he ran away,
he thought that he heard the Francolins' war-drums
beating (5).

When he had returned home, he untied the load,
and he had begun putting the contents into a calabash,
when the Francolin flew out and settled on the Spider's
Wife's head. Then the Spider said to his Wife " Stand
still, do not move," and he picked up the wooden pestle
to strike the Francolin, while on the Female Spider's
head, but the Francolin flew off, and the Spider missed
him, but killed his Wife. Then the Francolin settled
on his Son's head, and the Spider struck at him but
killed his own Son. Then the Francolin settled on the
head of the Spider's Baby, and the Spider took the
pestle and missed, and killed his Baby in the same way.
Then the Francolin settled on the head of the Spider
himself. The Spider ran outside and climbed up and
up a tree until he had come to the top, and then he
bobbed his head so that he might throw the Francolin
down and kill her, but she saved herself with her wings
and the Spider fell down and was killed.

Then the Francolin went and seized all the Spider's
possessions, and went away (6).

In a variant (F.-L. 13), the Spider kills the Lamb, but the Kid plays the part of the Francolin.

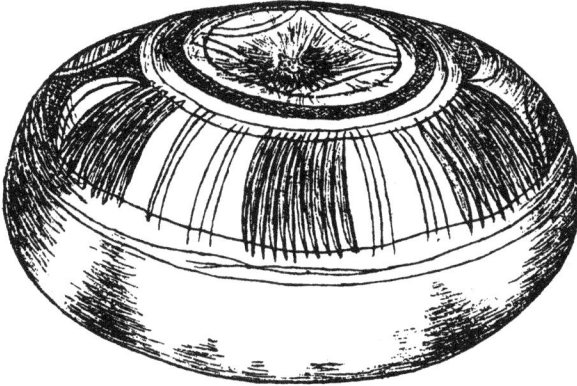

FIG. 55.—Decorated gourd, like fig. 52.

25

HOW THE CUNNING JERBOA KILLED THE STRONG LION.

This is about the Beasts of the Forest. The Lion was killing and eating them so fast that one day they said " Look here, the Lion will soon annihilate us, let us take counsel to see what we can do to save ourselves." So they all assembled, and went to the Lion, and said " O Great One, Elder Brother of the Forest, we have something to ask you," and they continued " We will bring you one of our number every morning to eat if you will leave the rest of us alive." Then the Lion said " Very well," and they went off.

Next morning they drew lots (1), and the lot fell upon the Gazelle, so the others seized the Gazelle and took her to the Lion. Then the Lion killed her and ate her, and did not hurt any of the others. The following morning the Beasts did the same thing, and they took the Roan Antelope to the Lion, who killed and ate him.

This went on every day, until at last the lot fell upon the Jerboa, and the others seized him, and were about to take him to the Lion, when he said " No no, leave me alone, I will go to the Lion of my own free will." Then they said " Very well," and they released him. Now would you believe it, the cunning Jerboa was going to kill the Lion !

The Jerboa went to his hole and fell asleep, and did not go out before noon. But the Lion in his den began to feel hungry, for nothing had been brought to him, so he arose, in anger, and went to look for the Beasts of the Forest, and he was roaring. The Jerboa came out of his hole and climbed a tree near a well, and watched the Lion from afar off, and, when he had passed, the Jerboa said " What is making you roar ? " The Lion replied " Ever since daybreak I have been awaiting you, yet you have brought me nothing." Then the Jerboa from the top of the tree said " Well, look here, we cast lots, and the lot fell upon me, and I was coming to you, and bringing some honey for you that you might enjoy it also, when another Lion in this well stopped me, and stole the honey from me." Then the Lion exclaimed " Where is this Lion ? " and the Jerboa replied " He is in the well, but he says that he is stronger than you are." Then the Lion was furious, and he ran to the well, and stopped on the brink, and looked in, and saw another Lion in the well looking at him. In reality it was only his reflection, not a real Lion. Then the Lion abused him—but there was only silence. Again he abused him—silence. And then he became mad, and sprang upon him in the well, and he sank in the water and was drowned.

So the Jerboa returned to where the Beasts were, and said " Well, I have killed the Lion, so you can feed in the forest in peace, but I am going to live in a hole." So the Beasts said " Well done," and they continued " Cunning is better than strength, the Jerboa has killed the Lion."

———

In a Malayan story (Skeat, *Fables and Folk-Tales,* page 28) the incidents are almost identical, but it is a Tiger which is killed, the Chevrotain being the hero in that country, as he is also in Sierra Leone (Cronise and Ward, page 17).

———

26

THE CAMEL AND THE RUDE MONKEY.

One day a Jackal climbed a *kainya* tree (1), and began eating the fruit, and soon a Camel came up, and said " O Jackal," and the Jackal said " Yes." " What are you eating ? " asked the Camel. " I am eating *kainya* fruit," was the reply. The Camel said " Pick some for me too," and the Jackal did so, and then descended from the tree and went home.

The day passed, and next morning a Monkey arrived and climbed the tree, and began eating the fruit, and the Camel seeing him there said " Will you not pick some for me to eat ? " and the Monkey gave him some. The Camel asked again and again, and the Monkey picked more for him, but at last he became tired of doing this, and said that he would give him no more, and called him a humpback. Then the Camel abused him and called him a Beast with deep-set eyes. Now this made the Monkey very angry, for he was ashamed of his deep-set eyes, and he said that the Camel had no hind-quarters. Then the Camel seized him (2), and bound him, and carried him off.

As he was going along he met the Spider who said " O Camel, what has caused you to seize the Monkey ? " And the Camel replied " Ask him himself." So the Monkey said " I was up the *kainya* tree when he asked me to pick some fruit for him, and then more, and then more, and I got tired of it, and said ' O Humpbacked One.' He replied that I had deep-set eyes, and then I said ' O One with the tiny behind.' " Then the Spider said " The Monkey was wrong, do not loose him," and they passed on.

Next they met the Lion, and the Lion said " O Camel, what has caused you to seize the Monkey ? " And the Camel said " Ask him himself." So the Monkey said " I was up the *kainya* tree when he asked me to pick some fruit for him, and then more, and then more, and I got tired of it, and asked if he had no shame. He replied that I had deep-set eyes, and I said ' O Humpbacked One, with a rump like as if you had drunk *kimba* (3).' " Then the Lion said " The Monkey was wrong, do not loose him," and they passed on.

Then they came upon the Jackal sitting outside his hole, at the foot of a tree, and he said " Come here and I will arbitrate between you." Now the Jackal was the Monkey's Friend [and he knew what a nuisance the Camel was], but the Camel did not know this, for the Jackal is very cunning (4), so they came close, and sat down, and the Jackal said " Loose the rope from him first (5)," and the Camel did so.

Now the Monkey was sitting on the Jackal's right side, the Camel on the left, and suddenly the Jackal said " My judgment is that you, O Monkey, shall climb that tree, while I enter my hole." Immediately the Monkey sprang up into the tree, the Jackal dived into his hole, and the Camel was left sitting by himself.

That was all, the trial was finished, so the Camel went off.

———

In a somewhat similar tale (F.-L. 16), the Hyæna seizes the Monkey, although the latter has done her a good turn.

———

27

THE BOY WHO WAS LUCKY IN TRADING.

There were once a certain Boy and his Father, and the Boy said that he was going on a trading expedition, so the Father said " Here is a little Scorpion, you can have it for food." The Boy took it and started off, and soon he met some Farmers, and they said " Bring that little Scorpion here," and when he had done so, they killed it. Then he said " O You, Farmers, give me my little Scorpion." " Which little Scorpion ? " they asked. " The little Scorpion which my Father gave me as food for the journey," he replied. And [in order to keep him quiet] they took a sickle, and gave it to him.

So he went on, and soon he met some People reaping guinea-corn, and they said " Bring us your sickle that we may reap with it." So they took the sickle, and when they had done so, and had reaped the corn, he said " O you Reapers, give me my sickle." Then they said " Which sickle ? " And he replied " The sickle which the Farmers gave me." " Which Farmers ? " they asked. " The Farmers who killed my little Scorpion," he replied. Then they said " Which little Scorpion?" And he answered "The little Scorpion which my Father gave me as food for the journey." So they took some millet-flour and gave it to him, and he went on.

As he was travelling he met a Filani Maiden who was selling sour milk, and she said "Hey, Boy, bring me your millet-flour that I may mix it with my sour milk" (1), and he gave it her. So she mixed it with her milk, and drank the lot. Then he said "Oh, I say, Filani Maid, give me my millet-flour." Then she said "Which millet-flour?" "The millet-flour that the Reapers gave me," he answered. "Which Reapers?" she asked. "The Reapers who took my sickle." "Which sickle?" she asked. And he replied "The sickle which the Farmers gave me." "Which Farmers?" she asked. "The Farmers who killed my little Scorpion," he replied. Then she said "Which little Scorpion?" And he answered "The little Scorpion which my Father gave me as food for the journey." So she gave him some butter.

As he was travelling on and on, he met with a Man carrying tobacco, and the Man-with-the-tobacco said "Hullo, you have some butter, bring it here that I may mix it with my tobacco and pound it up." So the Boy gave him the butter, and he fried it, and mixed the tobacco with it. Then the Boy said "Alas! alas! O Man-with-the-tobacco, give me my butter." But the other said "Which butter?" "The butter that the Filani Maiden gave me." "Which Filani Maiden?" asked the other. "The Filani Maiden who drank up my millet-flour," he replied. "Which millet-flour?" asked the Man. "The millet-flour that the Reapers gave me," he answered. "Which Reapers?" he asked. "The Reapers who took my sickle." "Which

sickle ? " he asked. And he replied " The sickle which
the Farmers gave me." " Which Farmers ? " he
asked. " The Farmers who killed my little Scorpion,"
he replied. Then he said " Which little Scorpion ? "
And he answered " The little Scorpion which my
Father gave me as food for the journey." So the Man
gave him some potash (2).

As he was travelling along with the potash, he

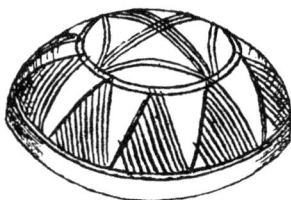

FIG. 56.

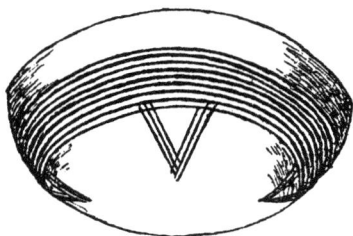

FIG. 57.

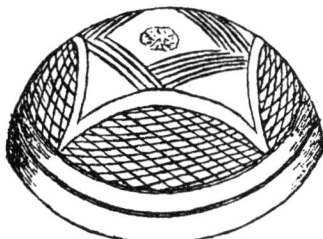

FIG. 58.

FIGS. 56-58.—Decorated vessels of wood or gourd, pattern cut on purple
ground, D. of largest, 3⅝ in.

met a Filani Youth (3) who was tending Cattle, and
the Filani Youth said to him " Here Boy, bring your
potash here that I may put it in the water, and give it
to the Cattle to drink." So the Boy handed it to him,
and he gave it to the Cattle, and they drank. When
they had done so, the Boy said " Alas ! alas ! O Filani
Youth, give me my potash." Then he said " Which

potash?" And the Boy replied "The potash that the Man-with-the-tobacco gave me." "Which Man-with-the-tobacco?" asked the other. "The Man-with-the-tobacco who used up my butter," he replied. "Which butter?" asked the other. "The butter that the Filani Maiden gave me." "Which Filani Maiden?" asked the other. "The Filani Maiden who drank up my millet-flour," he replied. "Which millet-flour?" asked the Youth. "The millet-flour that the Reapers gave me," he answered. "Which Reapers?" he asked. "The Reapers who took my sickle." "Which sickle?" he asked. And he replied "The sickle which the Farmers gave me." "Which Farmers?" he asked. "The Farmers who killed my little Scorpion," he replied. Then he said "Which little Scorpion?" And he answered "The little Scorpion which my Father gave me as food for the journey." So he chose a Bull and gave it to him (4).

The Boy went on and on with the Bull, until he came to a certain city, and he lodged at the house of the Chief Butcher (5), and the Chief Butcher said "Hullo Boy, bring us your Bull that we may slaughter it." And when the Bull had been slaughtered, and the meat had been sold, the Boy said "Alas! Chief Butcher, give me my Bull." And the other said "Which Bull?" The Boy said "The Bull that the Filani Youth gave me." "Which Filani Youth?" asked the other. "The Filani Youth who took my potash," he replied. "Which potash?" asked the other. And the Boy replied "The potash that the Man-with-the-tobacco gave me. "Which Man-with-the-tobacco?" asked the other. The Man-with-the-tobacco who used up my butter," he replied. "Which butter?" asked the other. "The butter that the Filani Maiden gave me."

XXI.—Butchers. XXII.—A Blacksmith.

Any meat not sold immediately after the kill is stuck on spits, and exposed to the sun. The skins are pegged down to be cured.

A Hausa blacksmith is often found in a village of another tribe which even the Hausa trader could not enter.

"Which Filani Maiden?" asked the other. "The Filani Maiden who drank up my millet-flour," he replied. "Which millet-flour?" asked the Chief Butcher. "The millet-flour that the Reapers gave me," he answered. "Which Reapers?" he asked. "The Reapers who took my sickle." "Which sickle?" he asked. And he replied "The sickle which the Farmers gave me." "Which Farmers?" he asked. "The Farmers who killed my little Scorpion," he replied. Then he said "Which little Scorpion?" And he answered "The little Scorpion which my Father gave me as food for the journey." So the Chief Butcher took two Slaves and gave them to him, a Male and a Female.

When he had got them, the Boy returned to his Father's house, and said to his Father "The trading has been successful, I have returned." He had obtained two Slaves for his little Scorpion!

That is the end of this.

———

With this story and numbers 77 and 80, may be compared one from Sierra Leone (Cronise and Ward, page 313) to account for the origin of the axe.

> "Dah breeze take me wing, eh!
> De wing wey de 'awk done gie me;
> 'Awk done yeat me fis', eh!
> Deh fis' wey wattah gie me;
> Wattah take me pot, eh!
> Dah pot wey de bug-a-bug gie me;
> Bug-a bug yeat me corn, eh!
> De corn wey dah girl bin gie me;
> Girl yeat me bird, eh!
> Wey mese'f bin ketch um."

The breeze then gives him fruit, but the Baboon steals it, and has to give him an axe instead. The King takes the axe, but has to give him great riches for it.

———

This is a very favourite tale throughout Africa,

it exists among the Damara (Bleek, *Reynard the Fox*, 90), the Zulus (Callaway, *Nursery Tales*, 37), the Kabyles (Rivière, *Contes Pop. de la Kabylie du Djurdjura*, 79, 95), the Anyanja (*Folk-Lore* iii, 92 ; xv, 344). It is found in Europe from Malta (*Archivio perlo Studio delle Trad. Pop.*, xiv, 459) to Brittany on the west (Sébillot, *Contes Pop. de la Haute Bretagne*, i, 346) and among the Cheremiss of the Russian government of Kasan on the east (Porkka, *Tcheremissische Texte*, 63). (H.).

28

ONE CANNOT HELP AN UNLUCKY MAN.

There was a certain Man, a Pauper, he had nothing but husks for himself and his Wife to eat. There was another Man who had many Wives and Slaves and Children, and the two Men had farms close together.

One day a Very-Rich-Man who was richer than either came, and was going to pass by on the road. He had put on a ragged coat and torn trousers, and a holey cap, and the People did not know that he was rich, they thought that he was a Beggar. Now when he had come up close, he said to the Rich-Man " Hail to you in your work," but when he had said " Hail," the Rich-Man said " What do you mean by speaking to me, you may be a Leper for all we know !" So he went on, and came to the Poor-Man's farm, and said " Hail to you in your work." And the Poor-Man replied " Um hum " (1), and said to his Wife " Quick, mix some husks and water, and give him to drink." So she took it to him, and knelt (2), and said " See, here is some of that which we have to drink." So he said " Good, thanks be to God," and he put out his lips as if he were going to drink, but he did not really do so, he gave it back to her, and said " I thank you."

So he went home and said " Now, that Man who was kind to me I must reward." So he had a calabash washed well with white earth (3), and filled up to the top with dollars, and a new mat (4) was brought to close it. Then the Very-Rich-Man sent his Daughter, who carried the calabash, in front, and when they had arrived at the edge of the bush (5) he said " Do you see that crowd of People over there working ? " And she replied " Yes, I see them." He said " Good, now do you see one Man over there working with his Wife ? " And she replied " Yes." " Good," he said, " to him must you take this calabash." Then she said " Very well," and she passed on, and came to where the Poor-Man was, and said " Hail," and continued " I have been sent to you, see this calabash, I was told to bring it to you."

Now the Poor-Man did not open it to see what was inside, his poverty prevented him (6), but he said " Take it to Malam Abba, and tell him to take as much flour as he wants from it, and to give us the rest." But when it had been taken to Malam Abba, he saw the dollars inside, and he put them into his pockets, and brought guinea-corn flour and pressed it down in the calabash, and said " Carry it to him, I have taken some." And the Poor-Man [when he saw that there was some flour left] said " Good, thanks be to God, pour it into our calabash (7), and depart, I thank you."

Now the Very-Rich-Man had been watching from a distance, and [when he saw what had happened] he was overcome with rage, and said " Truly if you put an unlucky Man into a jar of oil he would emerge quite dry (8). I wanted him to have some luck, but God has made him thus."

In a story given in L.T.H. (14) a Son of the King
of Katsina gave orders that the Poorest-Man was to be
brought before him, and when he had come, the Prince
heaped riches upon him, "ten Goats, ten Asses, ten
Mules, ten Camels, of all the things in the world he
gave him ten each." The Poor Man was then given a
house to live in, and told to go to it, but just as he had
arrived he fell down and died. Then the People said
" Whatever good a Man proposes to do to you, if God
does not wish it, it will be all in vain."

29

THE WONDERFUL RING.

This is about a certain Woman who had two
Children, both Sons. One day they left home, and went
into the world to try their fortune (1); the Elder took
three cloths, and the Younger took three cloths, and
with these the Elder bought a Goat, the Younger a
Scraggy Dog. When they returned, their Mother said
" Welcome to you," and the Elder said " See what I
have gained, a Goat; and the Younger said " See what
I have gained, a Scraggy Dog." Then she said [to the
latter] "O, you, may God curse you, whatever made
you buy a Scraggy Dog? " And the Elder Son said
" Opp, will he be able to do as well as I ? "

Soon afterwards, they prepared to go away again,
the Elder took four cloths (2), the Younger three, and
off they started. The Elder obtained a Bull, but the
Younger got only a Skinny Cat. When they returned
their Mother said " Welcome to you," and the Elder
said " See what I have gained, a Bull; and the Younger
said " See what I have gained, a Skinny Cat." Then
the Mother said to him " May God curse you, whatever
made you buy a Skinny Cat? " And the Elder Son
said " Opp, will he be able to do as well as I ? '

" Ah," exclaimed the Younger Son, " I am storing up favour with God."

Once more they made ready to go off, and the Elder Son took ten cloths, while the Younger again had three, and on their travels the Elder gained two Slaves, two young Girls ripe for marriage (3), while the Younger got only an Old Woman, wizened up, and with breasts like long boots (4). So they returned, and their Mother said " Welcome to you," and the Elder said " So far as I am concerned, this is what I have gained, two young Slave-Girls." And the Younger one said " I have gained an Old Woman, wizened up." Then the Mother said " May God curse you, whatever made you buy an Old Woman wizened up (5) ? " The Elder Son said " Opp, will he be able to do as well as I ? " But the Younger Son said " Ah, I am storing up favour with God."

Now, as it happened, the Old Woman was really the Daughter of the King of the city to which they used to go to trade, and the King had no Son, and no other Daughter but her, the Old Woman. She had been taken prisoner during a war, and had been lost to the King, and now the Younger Son had bought her. One day a Man of her city came to the Boys' city—she had been given flour and water and was selling it—and while she was calling out its good qualities and saying " Here is *fura,* here is *fura* (6)," the Man from her city said " Bring it." When she had done so, and he had seen her, he grasped his body, and said " What ! Gimbia ! You have been sought for from town to town, and not found." Then she said " I have been here, a certain Boy bought me, I am kept in slavery." Then he said " Indeed !" and he continued " Let us go, take me to your Master that I

may see him." So they went, and she called the Boy
aside so that his Mother should not hear, and said to
her fellow Townsman "Here is my Master." Then
the Man from her city said "If you agree, follow her,
and go to her city, go to her Father, the King of the
city, and he will ransom her." So the Boy said "I
will," and he went and told his Mother. But she said
"Oh! go, Luckless One, go, and they will take from
you even the Wizened Old Woman." But he said
"Ahem, perhaps, but I will go."

So he put his Slave in front of him (7), and they
went to her city, even unto the door of the King's
palace, and the whole town was excited, saying "Gimbia has returned." Then the King rejoiced, and he
took the Younger Son to a house, and said that he was
going to slaughter a Bull in his honour, but the other
said that a Ram would do.

Now the Slave said to her Master "See here, if my
Father offers you a million cowries, say that you do
not agree; if he offers you a thousand head of Cattle,
say that you do not agree; if he offers you a thousand
Horses, say that you do not agree; if he offers you a
hundred Slaves (8), say that you do not agree." And
she continued "What he must give you to ransom me
is nothing else than the small ring on his little finger."
The Younger Son said "I see." She said "It alone
he must give you to ransom me, if you get that ring, it
is the spirit (9) of the city, you will rule the whole
city." And he said "I understand." So when the
King said "Here is the ransom, a million cowries,"
he said "I will not accept them." The King said "I
will give you a thousand head of Cattle," but he replied "I will not accept them." The King said "I
will give you a thousand Horses," but again he said

" I will not accept them." " I will give you one hundred Slaves " said the King, but once more the Younger Son said " I will not accept them." At last he said " What you must give me to ransom her is that small ring on your little finger." Then the King said " If I were to give you this ring at once, the whole city would arise and follow you on the road, and kill you," and he continued " I will give you the ring, but I will first give you a certain Charger which can outstrip all the other Horses of the city in a race." Then he said " See, here is the ring, put it into your mouth, and as soon as you are outside the door start galloping."

Now to go from this city to the Boy's city took thirty days, but he was going to gallop and get there in one day. Just as he emerged from the gate of the city, the whole of the People rushed up and raised the alarm, and put on their saddles, and as soon as they came they followed the Boy at a gallop. They galloped, and galloped, and galloped, until they almost caught him (10), but he managed to enter the gates of his own city and leave them outside. Then they said " Well, if you follow a man and he escapes, and gets into his own house, you must leave him alone " (11).

No sooner had the Boy arrived at home and had dismounted, than the Horse fell down and died, and then his Mother said " You see, I told you that you are unlucky, see now the Wizened Old Woman has been taken from you, and though you were given a Horse in exchange, it is dead." Then the Elder Son said " Will he be able to do as well as I ? " But the Younger Son replied " I am storing up fortune with God," and he left the city, and went and lived in a booth in the forest.

Now the ring was on his finger, and when he lay down to sleep he heard sounds of *dit, dit, dit,* the earth was moving, a city was coming! And when day broke, lo! there was a big city with walls, and flat-roofed houses, and women without number. Then he went and called his Mother, and made her a house for herself, the Scraggy Dog and the Skinny Cat had their houses built for them, and the Elder Brother had his (12).

Some time afterwards a certain Bad Woman heard the news, and said that she would have no one but him, and he said that he wanted her. So he lived with the Bad Woman, and he gave her everything that she wanted, whatever it might be that she wished for he gave it to her.

One day when dawn came she started crying, and she cried, and cried, and at sunset she was still crying. She said "Is it true that you do not love me?" "Why do you say I do not love you?" he asked. "What has come between us is this," she replied, "if you love me, give me that ring to keep on my hand for a day." But when he had given it to her, she took it to her Paramour, and so when night came, the city arose and settled down around the Paramour's house, and the Younger Son was left with only the Scraggy Dog, the Skinny Cat, his Mother, and his Elder Brother.

When morning broke he saw this, and began crying, but the Dog asked "What is it you are crying for?" And he replied "You see what the Bad Woman has done to me." Then the Cat also said "What is it you are crying for?" And he replied "You see what the Bad Woman has done to me." Then they said "Opp, that is easily remedied, did you not bring

us here so that we might one day do you a good
turn ? '' (13).

Now the Dog and the Cat departed for the city to
which the Bad Woman had taken the ring, so that they
might steal it. But [just outside the city] they came
to a large river which barred their progress. Then the
Dog said " Opp, I can swim, you, O Cat, get on my
back." So he took the Cat on his back, and they
crossed the river, and it was now sunset. Then the Cat
said " Now, O Dog, go into the city, steal food and
eat your fill (14), and then return and meet me here."
So the Dog entered the city, and stole and stole food
until he had had enough, and then he returned and
met the Cat at the brink of the river. " Now," she
said, " You stay here, while I go into the city." And
when she had entered into the house to which she first
came, she killed a thousand Mice. She left that
house and entered another, and killed another
thousand, then she went to a third house and killed a
thousand Mice there also. Then the King of the city
heard the news—the one who had the ring on his
finger—and he said " Bring me that Cat, so that she
may come and kill the Mice in my palace." And when
she had been brought, she killed a thousand of them.

Then the Princes of the Mice came to her, and said
" What crime have we committed that you are killing
us thus ? " And she replied " My Master's ring is
here, in the possession of the King of the city, if you
do not steal it and bring it to me, I will kill every one
of you." Then they began to make plans, and plans,
but they did not get the ring, and she said " As you
have not got it for me your trouble is upon your own
heads," and she killed five hundred of them straight off.

Then one of the Mouse-Kings said " Now, our kind

cannot get it, but the Roof-Mouse can," so they went to the house of the King of the Roof-Mice (15), and called him, and the King of the Mice said " O King of the Roof-Mice, you know what evil has happened to us, order your People to steal for us this ring so that we may be free from being slaughtered thus." Then the King of the Roof-Mice said " Opp, that is a simple matter."

Now the King of the city used to sleep with the ring in his mouth all night, and the Roof-Mice came, and began searching and searching in the hut, but they did not get it, and at last they climbed the bed. The King was sleeping with his mouth open, and, as it happened, the ring rolled out of his mouth, and fell close by him. Immediately one of the Roof-Mice picked up the ring, and another bit the King on the tongue so that he awoke (16). And when he awoke he began feeling about until the Bad Woman said " What is the matter ? " Then he said " A Mouse has bitten me in the mouth." And she said " Let me know the worst, has it taken the ring ? " And he felt about, and said " No, no, we shall see it in the morning."

So the King of the Roof-Mice took it to the Cat, and she put it in her mouth, and she went back to the Dog, and the Dog carried her on his back, and they re-crossed the river, and returned home. Then the Cat said " O Master, leave off crying, it was an easy task, see the ring !"

When he arose next morning, he saw that the city had returned, and when day broke the Bad Woman saw that she had no city, and that but for her and her Paramour there was no one. Then she said to him " May God curse you. If you put an Unlucky Man into a pot of oil he would come out quite white, but a

Lucky Man will find someone to buy water, even on the banks of the Niger " (17).

In a variant (L.T.H. ii, 80) the Old Woman is obtained in a somewhat different way, and she turns out to be the Mother of the King of a distant city, who ransoms her for one of two little balls, which he keeps in his mouth. In this case the Hero is not pursued, nor is there any mention of the temporary loss of the city which he founds.

In another story (L.T.H. ii, 42), a Man is going on a trading trip, and each Wife gives him something to take. The fourth Wife—who has never done any work at all—giving him only a tin with an Insect in it. The Husband sets out, and at the first town, a Cat steals his tin, and eats the Insect, and on his complaining, the Cat is handed over to him in conformity with a code resembling the *lex talionis*. He goes on until he reaches a city where Cats are unknown, and during the first night she kills numbers of Mice. The King is told of this, and he and his People buy the Cat for 200 Slaves. The Husband returns, and gives them to his fourth Wife, and turns out the other three (18).

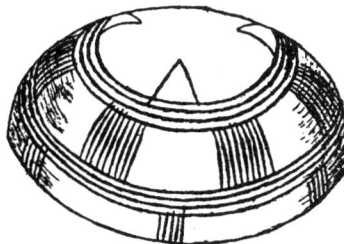

Fig. 59.   Fig. 60.

Figs. 59, 60.—Decorated vessels, like fig. 58.

30

THE GREEDY GIRL AND HER CURE.

This story is about a Girl who was so greedy that whatever she saw she would take and eat it. Even bones a hundred years old she would take and eat. At last her Parents said "Get ready and go away, we love you no longer, you are so very greedy."

So she went to a Girl-Friend, and said "See, my Parents have told me to go out into the world, they love me no longer because I am so very greedy [come with me out into the world]," so they both started off, the Girl and her Friend. Now as they were going along, they came upon nine Dogs in the road, and immediately the Girl seized them, and ate them. When she had eaten the Dogs, she said to her Friend, who was standing in the road, that she was going a little way into the forest,* and when she had returned, and her Friend asked her where she had been, she could say only " *Um, um*," she could no longer speak human words, only those of the Dog.

Now they went on to a certain far city, and came to the King's palace (1), and when the King saw the Girl he said that he would make her his Wife, but she spoke not a word, she could only bark like a Dog. So she was married to the King [and everyone remarked how] very beautiful she was. As for the Friend, the King's Brother married her. So they lived thus, the Girl could not talk, but only bark, and though the King tried and tried to make her speak, she could not do so. And this went on until it was ordered that all the Women of the town should assemble and pound grain together at the King's palace, so that the Girl's speech should return (2).

Now in the middle of the night the Girl-Friend came and roused the Girl, and they returned to the place where she had eaten the Dogs, and thence they went to the house of a Witch. Then the Friend said to the Witch " O Parent (3), will you not make me a charm for a Girl who has eaten Dogs? " And the Witch beat and beat the Girl's back, and lo! all the nine Dogs emerged. Then both of the Girls returned home, to the King's palace.

Next morning, at daybreak, all the Women of the town assembled at the King's palace to pound corn, and they began pounding and pounding, and as they were doing it the pestles sang :—

> " O Dogs, come out quick-ly,
> O Dogs, come out quick-ly " (4).

When they had finished, the Girl came out of the palace with a pestle of silver in her hand. Then the Sun said " Oh, oh, oh, she *is* beautiful." And the Earth asked " Shall I give way and give you room to pass? " But she said " If you give way where shall I tread? " So she went to where the Women were pounding, and began to beat. Then she said to the King " Draw me your sword, if one is not happy in his position, he will try to change it "(5).

The King hearkened unto her words, and he lived with her as his sole Wife, and they ruled the world. He killed all his other Wives (6).

––––––––––

In a variant (L.T.H. ii, 78) the Girls are Step-Sisters who were so much alike that they could not be told apart. A dead Dog was found and " Little-Eve " ate it with a similar result as in the above, but she was cured by a Dodoniya (or She-Dodo), who brought seven Dogs out of her throat. The other Wives, Concubines,

&c., had complained to the King that she could only
bark, but when asked to speak she did so, and their
heads were requisitioned as stones for the cooking-place.

31

THE GLUTTONS.

Once Bankammi and his Wife Barrankamma
built a house in a certain town and lived there.
When he went to the forest he used to kill an
Elephant and eat it, and if when he had carried one
home, he called his Wife and said " Here Barrankamma," and gave it to her, before he could go inside,
turn round, and come out again, he would find her
with only the bones left. Every morning at daybreak
she would grind a whole barn full of corn, and give it
to him, and when he had [mixed it with water and] (1)
drunk it, he would go off to the forest.

Now the King of the City heard about them, the
People said " They are of a truth great eaters, both
the Husband and his Wife."   So the King said
" Summon them here," and he said to the Citizens
" Let everyone pound corn, and make porridge, make
pudding, and bring it to the King's palace."

Then the King said " See, we have two Guests
in the town."   Then the porridge and the pudding were
taken to Bankammi and Barrankamma and they ate
every bit, and they told the King that they were still
hungry.   Then the King said " Bring them a tank (2)
of water," and it was brought, and they drank it, but
they said that they were not satisfied.   Then the King
said " Indeed! You must try to get along with that,"
and he continued " Now, you can sleep here to-night,

but to-morrow I shall send you away, we cannot put up with you."

So next morning he brought four Slaves and gave them to the Gluttons saying that the Slaves could farm for them (3).

———————

32

How Dodo frightened the Greedy Man.

There was a certain Man who had a Son, an Orphan, without a Mother. Now the Father had a Bull (1), and he said " I am not going to kill it where there are Flies to settle on it to eat some." So they went far into the depth of the forest, and he told his Son to hold up some bad smelling meat to see if there were any Flies about. So he did so, and not a Fly came, so they killed the Bull there, and prepared to eat the whole of it.

Now, as it happened, they had forgotten to bring fire (2), so the Father climbed a tree, and afar off he saw a red glow like fire—which was really Dodo's mouth*—and he said to his Son " See there is fire over there, go and get some." But when the Son tapped Dodo's mouth *ket, ket, ket,* as if to get some embers, Dodo said " Who is that ? " and the Son replied " My Father says that you are to come."

Then Dodo took up his leather bag, that in which he used to store his meat—the bag was like a hill in height—and he came to where the Father was, and said " Who has summoned me ? " Then the Father said " It was I," and [pretending that he had invited him to the feast] he took a forequarter of the Bull, and gave it to him. Dodo put it in his bag, and said " Does a Man invite his Friend to a feast on account of a tiny

morsel like that?" So the Father took the other forequarter, and gave it to him, and Dodo put it in his
bag, and said "Does a Man invite his Friend to a
feast on account of a tiny morsel like that?" Then the
Father cut the Bull in two and gave him half, and
Dodo put it in his bag, and said "Does a Man invite
his Friend to a feast on account of a tiny morsel like
that?" Then the Father gave him the rest of the meat,
and Dodo put it in his bag, and said "Does a Man
invite his Friend to a feast on account of a tiny morsel
like that?"

Now there was nothing left but the hide, the
hoofs, and the head (3), and these the Father collected and gave to Dodo, but he put them in his bag,
and said "Does a Man invite his Friend to a feast on
account of a tiny morsel like that?" Then the Father
said "Alas, there is no more." But Dodo replied "Oh
yes there is, you also are meat." So the Father seized
his Son and gave him to Dodo, and Dodo put him in
his bag, and said "Does a Man invite his Friend to a
feast on account of a tiny morsel like that?" Then the
Father said "But really there is nothing left." But
Dodo said "What about yourself?" and he put the
Father inside the bag.

Then he pulled out the Son, and told him to
watch the bag because he was going away to get some
wood to roast them. But when he had gone, the Son
took a knife and ripped open the bag, and the Father
emerged. Then they ran away, leaving the meat there.
So when Dodo returned, he found that they had run
away, but that they had left the meat, so he roasted it,
and ate it.

Now when the Father and Son had returned home,
they said that they repented, they would never be so

XXIII.—A MALE TRADER.

XXIV.—FEMALE TRADERS.

The shape of a man's load and that of a woman often differ considerably. Skins, rubber, cloths, &c., are to be found in the former, while pots and pans, and food, held together by a net, always form part of the latter.

greedy again, and that if they saw a Man passing along the road, even if he were not close to them, they would invite him to share their meal. They said that greed was not right, that they would not indulge it again (4).

———

In a variant, it is the Witch who glows like fire, but the rest of the story is like numbers 48 and 51.

————

33

BORTORIMI AND THE SPIDER.

There was once a certain Man whose name was Bortorimi, a Giant was he, there was no one like him in all the world, for, when he used to go to the forest, he would kill some twenty Elephants, and bring them home for his meal. One day the Spider sent his Wife —the female Spider—to Bortorimi's house to get fire (1). So she went, and while she was there, they gave her a great piece of meat, so she took it home with her. Then the Spider said "Who has given you that meat?" And she replied "I got it at Bortorimi's house." Immediately the Spider said "Put out your fire." And when she had done so, she returned to Bortorimi's house, and said that the fire had gone out (2). So more meat was given to her.

Then the Spider himself went to Bortorimi's house, but when Bortorimi gave him some meat he ate it all up at once, and did not bring any home. When he had eaten it, he said to Bortorimi "Where do you get this meat?" And the other replied "Over there in the forest, a great way off." "I see," said the Spider, "may I accompany you next time?" And Bortorimi

said " Very well," but that he would not be going until
the next morning, [so the Spider went home].

But the Spider could not wait until the dawn had
come, so he pulled the roof off his hut (3), and set it on
fire, and this made the whole place as light as if day
had broken, although it was really not even dawn, but
midnight.   Then the Spider ran to Bortorimi's house,
and stood outside, and called out " Hey, Bortorimi,
Bortorimi, awake, awake, it is dawn." But Bortorimi
replied " Oh ! come, Spider, now I was watching you
when you took the roof off your house and burned it."
So the Spider went home again.

Soon afterwards he mounted a rock and made the
first " Call to Prayer " (4), and said that dawn had
come.   Then he went and roused Bortorimi, saying
" Everyone is astir, they are calling to prayer, wake
up."   But Bortorimi said " Oh ! dear Spider, can you
not have patience ? " and he refused to go.

Now Bortorimi's nose was as big as a house, there
was a market inside it.   At daybreak they started off,
and when they had come to a certain great river,
Bortorimi said to the Spider " Drink your fill."   And
when the Spider had drunk all he wanted, Bortorimi
pouted his lips and drank up all the water, leaving only
the mud.   Then they went on, and at last they reached
the depths of the forest where the Elephants used to
feed.

When they had arrived at the spot, Bortorimi said to
the Spider " Go and spy on the Animals there, and
abuse them, and when you have done so, and they
chase you, run and get inside my nose."   " Very well,"
said the Spider, and off he went and abused the Elephants, calling out " Hey, you Animals, you are not
properly born " (5).   Immediately they charged down

upon the Spider, but he went off at a run, and jumped into Bortorimi's nose, and Bortorimi captured the whole herd of Elephants, and killed them.

Now as soon as the Spider got inside the nose (where there was a market) he began his tricks, saying that he was a King's Son, and so he ought to have a

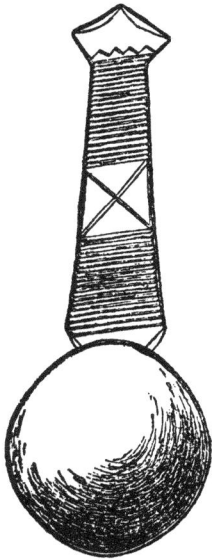  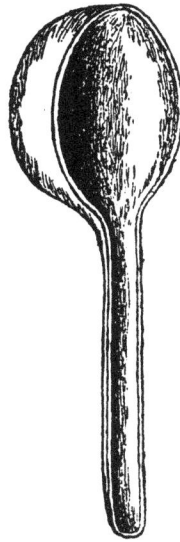

FIG. 61.   FIG. 62.   FIG. 63.

FIG. 61.—Spoon of white cottonwood, incised pattern, L., 12⅛ in.
FIG. 62.—Brass spoon, stamped pattern, L., 9$\frac{5}{16}$. FIG. 63.—Ladle made by splitting a gourd.

present of ground-nuts to eat, and the Old Woman selling them there gave him some (6).

Just then Bortorimi finished killing the Elephants, and he began calling out " Spider, Spider, come out." So the Spider emerged, and Bortorimi said to him " Now choose the Elephant that you are going

to take." But the Spider said that he could not carry
one (7), so Bortorimi heaped them all together and
carried the lot. When they had got home, Bortorimi
said " Now Spider, here is yours," and the Spider
skinned the Elephant, and roasted it, and ate every bit,
he would not give any to his Wife.

As soon as the Spider had eaten it, he returned to
Bortorimi's house, and said " O, Bortorimi, are you not
going back to the hunting-ground ? " But Bortorimi
said " Umm, I shall not return, this is enough for me."

In one variant (L.T.H. 144), *Butorami* is described
as a certain kind of large Beast. In another one (L.T.H.
90) Futaranga, takes the Hyæna to draw the Elephants, and she hides in his nose. Then the Hyæna
takes the Dog hunting and builds a large nose of mud
for him to enter when chased. But he breaks it, and
has to flee, and when the Elephants catch the Hyæna
she says that it was not she who had abused them, and
so they leave her. Both of the hunters escape, but they
have to be content with a dead Gazelle for their bag.

In a Sierra Leone story (Cronise and Ward, page
233) the Frog plays the part of Bortorimi, but instead
of hunting Elephants, the Frog used to jump down the
throat of a Cow which considerately opened her mouth
for the purpose, and let the Frog get some fat from
her inside. The Frog tells the Spider about it, and
invites him to join in the feast, saying that he " mus'
come to-morrow mawnin', early in de mawnin'." The
Spider cannot sleep, and wakes the Frog at midnight,
but the Frog will not go. Soon afterwards the Spider
crows like a Cock, but still the Frog is not deceived.
Next he sings like the Morning-Bird, but is again
unsuccessful, and the Frog and he do not set out until
day has really broken.

34

THE HYÆNA AND THE SPIDER VISIT A CHIEF.

This is about a Hyæna and a Spider. The Spider said " O Hyæna, buy honey, and let us go and do homage to the King," and the Hyæna replied " Agreed." So they bought honey, and they were travelling on and on, when the Hyæna said to the Spider " I am going into the bush for a minute." Then the Spider said " Very well, but put down your pot of honey and leave it here until you come back."* But the Hyæna replied " Oh no, surely it is my own ! " So she went into the bush and drank the honey, and when she had done so she placed some dirt in the pot instead, and then she returned to the Spider.

When they had arrived at the city, they went and saluted the King, and they were made welcome, and were given a lodging in the palace. Then they took their pots, the Spider took his pot, and the Hyæna hers, and they said " Here is the offering which we make to the King." So the Hyæna's pot was taken and placed in the house, and the Spider's was placed in the entrance-hall, and when the Hyæna's pot was opened, dirt was found in it, but when the Spider's pot was examined the People found honey. So they went and told the King, and said " Lo ! in the Hyæna's pot is only dirt," and the King answered " Oh, very well, they have come to get something good from me, I know what kind of a good thing the Hyæna will get."

In the evening, sleeping-mats were brought, and the People said " These are for the Hyæna to sleep upon." Then skins also were brought, and they said " These are for the Spider " (1). Now the Hyæna would not agree to this, but the Spider said " Look here

Hyæna, they said that I was to sleep on the skins, and you on the mats. You say you will not agree, you want to eat the skins, that's why." But the Hyæna replied " No, no, a real Friend would not act thus," and so the Spider said " Very well, but look here, if you eat the skins you will make me ashamed of you." So he gave her the skins, and she gave him the mats, and he went and lay down.

During the first sleep she arose, and started eating the skins, and the Spider called out " Oh, so you have begun eating them ? " But she replied " No, no, it is a Mouse." Before dawn had come she had eaten the skins all up, there was nothing left of them. And then the Spider said " All right, O Hyæna, how are you going to excuse yourself, how are you going to get out of the scrape ? " But the Hyæna replied " Opp, cannot we say that a Thief has been here and has stolen the skins ? " " Well, Hyæna, even if you do say it, the King will not believe you, he will know it is you," said the Spider. " I found a way in, I will find a way out somehow," was the reply. So the People told the King, they said that a Thief had stolen the skins. But he replied " Oh no, I know quite well that the Hyæna has eaten them."

Then the King said " I will say Good-bye to them, to-day." And he brought a Bull, and said to the Spider " On account of the present which you brought to me, I give you this Bull." But an old He-Goat was brought and given to the Hyæna. Then the Spider said that he thanked the King, and the Hyæna said that she also thanked him. So off they started, and they were travelling on and on, the Hyæna was dragging the old He-Goat along, when she said " Let me eat a leg, you can become lame, you are lame now." So she pulled off a leg and ate it, and kept saying to the He-Goat "Travel with three-three, travel with three-three." Then she pulled off another leg and ate it, and kept saying to the He-Goat " Travel with two-two, travel with two-two." Then she pulled off a third leg and ate it, and kept saying " Travel with one-one, travel with one-one." Then she pulled off the remaining leg and ate it, and kept saying " Travel with none-none, travel with none-none." Then she took the rest of the body and ate it, but she left a small piece of the liver which she gave to the Spider, and he ate it.

Now they were travelling on, and on, when she said " Give me my piece of liver." Then the Spider pointed out to her the sun, which had nearly set and was very red, and said to her " See, there is fire over there, go and get some and return, and we will eat the Bull." So the Hyæna went off at a run, and ran on and on, but the sun was always afar off. And when she had gone, the Spider killed the Bull and took off the hide, and climbed up a tree with the lot, not even the skin or a bone did he leave, and he covered up the blood on the ground.

When she had become tired, the Hyæna returned, and kept calling " Where is the Spider, where is the Spider ? " At last she sat down on her haunches by a tree, and lo ! it was the very tree in which was the Spider. After a little he threw a bone on to her head, and she said " Well, I never, will God give me food at the foot of a tree ? " But when she had eaten the bone, she looked up and saw the Spider, and said " Oh, so it is you ? I thought that it was God," and she continued " Spider, for God's sake give me one of the legs." But the Spider said that he would not do so, and she replied " Very well, you are very brave because you are up in the tree, aren't you? I will get one who is taller than you to come and seize you in the tree.''

Then she went and found the Ostrich, but when the Ostrich came, the Spider made a noose of tie-tie, and he caught her, and as he dragged her she let fall an egg. Then the Hyæna pounced upon the egg and ate it, and called out '' O Spider, drag her, so that the eggs will fall out.'' But the Ostrich said '' Opp, Hyæna, is that how you would treat me? Release me O Spider.'' And the Spider did so. Then the Hyæna said '' Now let us have a race,'' and she went off at a run, and the Ostrich followed, but she just escaped.

As for the Spider, he descended from the tree, and went home.

———

A Malayan tale (Skeat, *op. cit.*, page 7) has similar incidents. A Shark catches the Chevrotain in the water, but allows him to go on his promise to teach him magic. The Chevrotain ties up the Shark (much as the Spider does the Lion in T.H.H. 2) and kills him. Just then the Tiger arrives, and wants the meat. The Chevrotain first sends the Tiger to wash the meat, and then to get fire, and then to get drinking-water. In the meantime the Chevrotain has taken the whole of the meat to the top of a she-oak tree, and on the Tiger's return he finds that both Friend and feast have disappeared.

———

35

THE HYÆNA CONFESSES HER GUILT.

All the Beasts of the Forest had assembled, and they took council, for they said '' Our guinea corn has disappeared; on Friday let us come in the morning and punish the Thief.''

So when the Friday came, in the morning, about eight o'clock, they all assembled in one place, all except the Hyæna, who refused to come. They waited and waited for her until late, but she did not arrive, and then they got tired of waiting, and separated again.

That night they saw her coming " softly softly," and they said " O Hyæna, we came and looked for you, but did not see you, [how is it that] you have come only now ? " Then she said " As I did not come, whom did you punish ? " And they replied " We did not punish anyone." Then she said " It is true, I am the Thief."

And since then even until now the Hyæna has admitted her evil deeds, whatever theft has been committed you may be sure that it is she who has done it (1).

In another story (F.-L. 2) the Spider steals the corn belonging to the Animal Community, and places some dirt of the Hyæna in the empty bin. On finding this, the Hyæna is blamed, of course, and she is driven out.

36

THE GREEDY SPIDER AND THE BIRDS.

This story is about certain Birds, Magpies. They used to go to the middle of a lake where they could get food in the mud, the fruit of a small *kadainya* (1) like mangoes. They did this every day, and once they let fall one of the fruits just by the door of the Spider's house, so next morning at daybreak the Spider found it (2) and ate it. Then he said " Ahem," and he went to the house of the Birds and asked them about it, he said " Where do you get this ? " And they replied " Over there far away." Then he said " When you are going next time will you not ask me to go too ? " So they said very well," [and he went home].

By this time the People were walking about, and the Spider went again to the Bird's house, and they took the wing of one of their number and put it on the Spider, and they took the wing of another and put it on the Spider's other side, and then they started and flew away. When they had arrived at the tree, every fruit that the Spider saw was ripe he claimed as part of his share, and they let him have it, and so not one of them got any, for the Spider ate them all.

Now when the Spider had finished, they let him go to sleep in the tree, and when they were ready to start, they pulled the wings from him, and went off home. And as they went the Spider awoke from his sleep [and was going to fly off, but he found that he had no wings] and he said " Oh dear." Then he picked off a small twig and threw it into the water, saying " If the water is deep here, the stick will sink." But when he had thrown it down, it rose to the surface, so the Spider said " Opp, the water is shallow," and jumped in. But the water was deep, and he sank, and was drowned.

37

THE HARE OUTWITS THE HYÆNA.

Once the Hare and the Hyæna went out hunting, and whenever the Hare killed a Beast, the Hyæna would take it and put it into her own bag. At last the Hare went and killed a Spotted Deer, and the Hyæna came up, and said that it was she who had killed it, [and she took it] (1). So the Hare left her and went off at a run, and returned to the road towards home.

Then he got some red earth and plastered his body with it, and he got some white earth, and smeared it on, so that the whole of his body was spotted, and when he had done this, he climbed up on to a high ant-hill and sat there. Soon the Hyæna turned to go home, and when she had come back [a part of the way], she saw a Something on an ant-hill, and she said " O Something-on-the-ant-hill, I have been out hunting with the Hare," and she continued " shall I give you all the meat which we have obtained ? " So she pulled out one of the Beasts and gave it to him (2), and then she said " May I pass ? " But the Hare said only " *Umm, umm.*" Then the Hyæna pulled out another and threw it to him and said " May I pass ? " But the Hare said only " Umm, umm." Then the Hyæna pulled out another and threw it to him, and now all were finished except the Spotted Deer. Then the Hyæna said " May I pass ? " But the Hare replied " You still have some meat." So the Hyæna pulled out the Spotted Deer and threw it to him, and he let her go free and she went past.

Then the Hare went and washed the whole of his body and took the meat.

In a variant (F.-L. 8) it is the Tortoise which deceives the Spider.

38

EVERYTHING COMES TO HIM WHO WAITS.

There were once a certain Man and his Wife who had nothing to eat, and they used to dig out the holes of the Ants so that they might get the grains of corn there, and eat them (1). One day they had returned, and were lying down in their hut, when the Husband noticed a Lizard which fed itself by simply opening its mouth and letting the Flies fall into it. Then he said " I am not going to wander about outside, digging out those ant-holes, and looking for food, see that Lizard, he only lies down, and yet he gets his fill (2). So his Wife said " Oh, very well."

But she went out and walked to an Ant-hill, and dug, and lo ! what did she see but a cooking-pot, closed up, and when she had opened it she saw that there were dollars inside it. Then she replaced the covering, and closed the hole, and went and told her Husband, and said " Let us go together." But he replied " Not I, I am not coming, go and call your Family to help you." So she went to her Brothers and Sisters, and told them. But they replied " It is a lie, were it any good you would have told your Husband." But she said " Very well, let us go, however, and you will see."

Now when they had come, and had opened the pot, they saw only a Snake inside, and they said "There you are, see, it is exactly as we said. If it had been any good you would have told your Husband. But we shall be avenged," and they went home.

In the night they took the pot carefully, and went and placed it by the hut, they pushed the door ajar, and then they went home again. And just as dawn was about to break, the Husband awoke and saw something shining by the door, and he said " The food has come." So he went and opened the pot, and he saw that it was quite full of dollars. There were so many that they had enough for themselves, and the Wife even took some and gave them to her Family (3).

A similar transformation of a snake into gold, when placed in a house for an evil reason, takes place in L.T.H. 133, where a scoffer tries to kill a malam.

39

THE LAZY FROG AND HIS PUNISHMENT.

Once a Frog and a Fowl lived together. Every night the Fowl would say " O Frog, to-morrow you must go and get wood for the fire." But when the morrow had come the Frog would go off and sit idly in the sun, and would say " I shall not get wood now, see the sun is up." [So the Fowl had to do all the work] (1).

One day a Hawk flew down and seized the Frog, and the Fowl said " Take him, the Stiff-Backed One," so the Hawk flew off with the Frog, and the Fowl had the house to herself.

In a variant (L.T.H. ii, 21) the Frog first refuses to help to build a hut, although a tornado has come on, and he enters a hole, leaving the Fowl outside. The water fills the Frog's hole and he hops over to the hut which the Fowl has built, asking for shelter, but she refuses until he threatens to summon the Wild-Cat. The Frog then lights a fire and gets up on her bed, and annoys her generally, until she at last asks him to get on the roof and pick some pumpkins to eat. Immediately the Frog climbs up, a Hawk seizes him, and the Fowl cries out as above.

That even a story like this may not be quite as absurd as it appears to be is shown by Dr. Haddon (*op. cit.*, page 343), for the Kenyahs tell this to illustrate the dilatoriness of the Sĕbops. The Monkey and the Frog were sitting in the rain. The Monkey said that they would beat bark-cloth next day, and the Frog

agreed.   But the next day was fine, so the Frog
refused.   As it was cold again at night, he again
agreed, but refused when warm once more, and at last
the Monkey became disgusted, and left him.   The Frog
still hoots and howls when the rain comes down, but
sits silent in the sunshine.

40

THE SNAKE AND THE SCORPION.

One day a Scorpion went to a Snake, and said that
she wanted such a poison that if she stung a Man he
would die at once.   But the Snake said " Oh ! Scorpion,
I will not give it to you, you are very hot-tempered,
and you would kill off Everybody."   Then the Scorpion
replied no, no, she would use it only now and then.
So the Snake said " Very well, go now, come again
to-morrow and I will give it to you " (1).

Now next day, the Snake went out for a walk, and
the Scorpion came while he was still out, so she went
inside his hut, and lay down on one side of the door.
Soon the Snake came in, and while he was getting
through the door he squashed the Scorpion, and when
she felt hurt she stung him.

Immediately he felt the pain, he wriggled in and
wriggled out, he wriggled in and wriggled out of the
hut, the pain was driving him mad.   Then the Scorpion
said to him " O Snake, what has happened to you ? "
And he replied " Welcome, when did you come ? "
She said " Oh, I came sometime ago, before you
returned."   Then he exclaimed " For God's sake
don't bother me, something in the hut has hurt me."
So she said " It was a sting, O Snake, it was I," she
continued, " when you came in, while you were enter-

ing you squashed me, and as I felt a movement I stung you; is it my sting which has given you pain?"

Then the Snake said "Get out, get out, leave my hut, I will not give you any of my poison, you would kill Everybody."

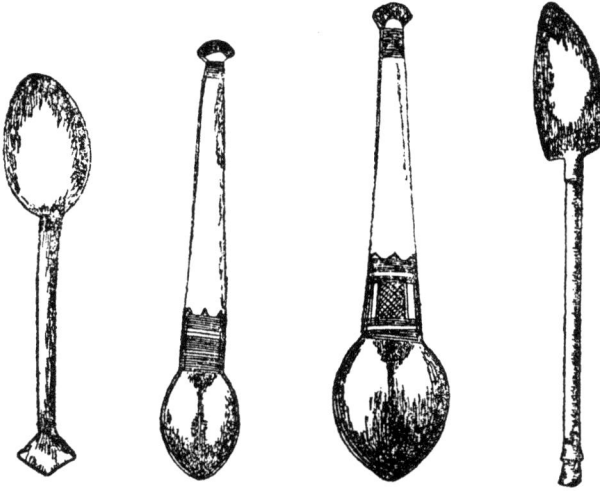

FIG. 64.   FIG. 65.   FIG. 66.   FIG 67.

FIGS. 64 and 67.—Wooden spoons for stirring food while being cooked. FIG. 65.—Wooden spoon, pattern burnt, L., $9\frac{3}{4}$ in.   FIG. 66.—Ditto, L., $10\frac{9}{16}$ in.

41

THE SPIDER WHICH BOUGHT A DOG AS A SLAVE.

One day the Spider went to the market and saw some Dogs for sale, so he went home and thrashed his guinea-corn, and said that he was going to buy a Slave with it. So he did so, and brought the Dog home.

Then he went and bought a hoe, and gave it to the Dog, and told him to go and work on the farm (1), but the Dog only lay still and took no notice. So the Spider seized the hoe and they went off to the forest, but when he told the Dog to get up and work, the Dog only lay still, and said nothing. Then the Spider pointed out the limits of the day's work, and said that when they had done so much they would return, but the Dog only lay still and said nothing. So the Spider himself began digging, and said that as the Dog was panting so hard he must be tired, so he could lie down.

Now as the Dog was lying there, a Hare passed by, and immediately the Dog arose, ran off, and caught the Hare. And then the Spider said " Well I never, so my Slave is a Hunter, he who can kill with his teeth," he continued, " will do better with an arrow." So he took the Dog's hoe, and brought it to the Monkey, the Smith, and told him to make arrow-heads out of it (2), so that he could give them to the Dog. And he and the Dog returned home.

Now the Spider was always going to the Monkey's forge, and asking would the arrow-heads be finished that day (3), and one day the Monkey said to the Spider " Have you obtained a Slave ? " And he replied " Yes, it is for him that I want the arrow-heads, so that he may enjoy the chase." Then the Spider said that he would bring the Dog, but the Monkey asked him not to do so. The Spider was always going to the Monkey and complaining that the arrow-heads were not being done quickly, until at last he became angry, and brought the Dog, and the Dog when he saw the Monkey, began stalking him, and when they had come close the Monkey ran away, and the Dog ran after him and caught him. As he was bringing the Monkey back, the Spider said " Let him go, it is the Smith, do not seize him," and then [being afraid that he too would be seized] he fled, and he ran on past his house, not stopping to go inside, and called out to his Wife " Get up, and run away, see the Dog is seizing people, and eating them."

Now as they had run away, they had left the house with no one to claim it except the Dog, so he took it for his own, and the Spider and his Wife disappeared into the forest (4).

42

THE WOOING OF THE BASHFUL MAIDEN.

There was once a certain Boy, the King's Son, who used to play with the other Boys of the town, and his name was Musa (1). And there was a certain Beautiful Maiden who wanted to marry him, but he did not want her, and so she was shy and avoided him (2).

Now one day all the Maidens went to the river to bathe, and they had taken off their cloths, and had begun to bathe, when the Boy came and seized all the cloths on the river-bank, and climbed a silk-cotton tree. So as each one came back from bathing and looked, she could not see her cloth, but when she searched she saw him, and said " Musa, give me my cloth." Then he let it fall down to her, and she went home. And when she had gone, another came out of the water, looked, and did not see her cloth, and then said " Musa, give me my cloth," and he dropped it down to her, and she went home.

At last there was only one Maiden left, she who loved him, [and when she had looked and had seen Musa with her cloth, she re-entered the water], and

she said " So and So, So and So, give me my cloth,
please." But he refused, and lo! the water rose to
her knees. Then she said " So and So, will you not
give me my cloth?" And he replied " I will not give
it to you until you have spoken my name—Musa."
Now the water had reached her neck and was still
rising, but she did not want to come out naked, for
she was ashamed, so again she said " So and So, give
me my cloth." But again he refused, and the water
rose over her head, and she was about to be drowned
when she called out " Musa, give me my cloth," [and
then she came out of the water]. So he let down her
cloth to her, but he [himself descended from the tree,
and] pulled out a whip, and began to beat her.

After that, he seized her and took her to his house,
and then he found that he desired her, so they were
married.

43

The Maids of the City and the Unknown Youth.

This is about a certain Youth, there was no one so
handsome as he in the whole city, and his name was
Denkin Deridi (1). Now all the Maidens were in love
with him, so he said that only she who knew his name
should be his Wife; for in the whole city there was
no one who knew it except a certain Old Woman.
And all the Maidens started to cook special dishes, the
first boiled rice, the second grilled meat, the next
made a porridge of guinea-corn flour, the next Maiden
one of millet, the next boiled bitter roots (2) like pota-
toes, another bread-fruit, and the last made a dish of
evil-smelling *dadawam basso* (3).

Now the Youth built a hut, and closed it up in every direction, there was no way in (4). And when the Maidens were on their way to where he was, the Old Woman stood in the middle of the road, and to each Maiden, as she was about to pass by, the Old Woman said " Come here and rub my back." But each Maiden replied " What! leave me alone, I am going to the Youth whose name I do not know." And the Old Woman said " Very well." All the Maidens had gone by except the one with the evil-smelling *dadawam basso,* and when she had come close, the Old Woman said " O You, Maiden, come here and rub my back," and she replied " I will." So she put down her load, and rubbed her, and when the Old Woman had finished washing (5), she said " Good, the name of the Youth is Denkin Deridi," and the other replied " Thank you."

Well, all the Maidens arrived at the hut, and the one who had boiled the rice—she was in front—came up, and said " O Youth, come and open the door for me that I may enter." " Who is there that I should open the door for her to enter? " asked he. And she replied " It is I, Rice (6), the sweetest food." Then the Youth said " Well, I have heard your name, now you tell me mine." But she replied " I do not know your name, O Boy " (7). And he said " Very well, go back again," and she retired crying.

Then came the Maiden who had grilled the meat, and said " O Youth, come and open the door for me that I may enter." " Who is there that I should open the door for her to enter? " asked he. And she replied " It is I, Grilled-Meat-with-Salt, the most delicious food." Then the Youth said " Well, I have heard your name, now you tell me mine." But she replied "I do not know your name, O Boy." And he said "Very well, go back again," and she retired crying.

Next came the Maiden who had made a porridge of guinea-corn flour, and said "O Youth, come and open the door for me that I may enter." "Who is there that I should open the door for her to enter?" asked he. And she replied "It is I, Porridge-of-Guinea-Corn-Flour, the sweetest to swallow." Then the Youth said "Well, I have heard your name, now you tell me mine." But she replied "I do not know your name, O Boy." And he said "Very well, go back again," and she retired crying.

Next came the Maiden who had made a porridge of millet-flour, and said "O Youth, come and open the door for me that I may enter." "Who is there that I should open the door for her to enter?" asked he. And she replied "It is I, Millet, who makes the best-tasting flour." Then the Youth said "Well, I have heard your name, now you tell me mine." But she replied "I do not know your name, O Boy." And he said "Very well, go back again," and she retired crying.

Next came the Maiden who had boiled the bitter roots, and said "O Youth, come and open the door for me that I may enter." "Who is there that I should open the door for her to enter?" asked he. And she replied "It is I, Bitter-Roots, the cure for hunger." Then the Youth said "Well, I have heard your name, now you tell me mine." But she replied "I do not know your name, O Boy." And he said "Very well, go back again," and she retired crying.

Next came the Maiden who had cooked bread-fruit (8), and she said "O Youth, come and open the

door for me that I may enter." "Who is there that
I should open the door for her to enter?" asked he.
And she replied " It is I, Bread-Fruit, well steamed" (9).
Then the Youth said " Well, I have heard your name,
now you tell me mine." But she replied " I do not
know your name, O Boy." And he said " Very well,
go back again," and she retired crying.

Now all had tried except the Maiden who had made
the dish of evil-smelling *dadawam basso*. But when
she came up, the other Maidens said to her " What !
You, O Evil-born One ! the good foods have not succeeded, much less can you, O Stinking One." But
some said " Oh, let her go, let us see what she will
do." So she came up and said " O Youth, come and
open the door for me that I may enter." "Who is there
that I should open the door for her to enter?" asked
he. And she replied " It is I, Dadawam Basso, the
sweet-scented food " (10). Then the Youth said
" Well, I have heard your name, now you tell me
mine." And she answered " Your name, O Boy, is
Denkin Deridi." And immediately he said " Come
into the hut, O Maiden." So he opened the door, and
said that she was the one who was to be his Wife.

Then the one who had brought rice said let her
head be cut off, and let it be one of the stones for a
cooking-place. And the one who had brought grilled
meat said let her head be cut off, and let it be one
of the stones for a cooking-place. And the one who
had brought a porridge of guinea-corn flour said let
her head be cut off, and let it be one of the stones for
a cooking-place (11). The rest of them said " I will
draw water for you," or " I will get wood for you,"
or " As for us, we will grind flour for you " (12).

The incident of the maidens going to seek fortune or perform a task, and one of whom is kind to a beggar or a supernatural being and in consequence attains the object desired, while the others are punished, is very common. The story of the Three Heads of the Well (Halliwell, *Popular Rhymes and Nursery Tales,* 39) is one of a large number of European examples (H.).

44

THE SON OF THE KING OF AGADDEZ.

There was once a certain Man who had two Wives, and each one had a Daughter, but he did not love the Mother of one, so a hut was built for her and her Daughter on the edge of the dunghill, where the sweepings were thrown, and they had to go and live there, and all that they had to eat was boiled husks.

Now one day the Husband was going to bargain in the market, and the Daughter of the Disliked Wife said "O Father, see here are some cowries, buy me the Son of the King of Agaddez" (1). Then he cursed her, but she said again "When you go, buy me the Son of the King of Agaddez." So he took the money —five cowries (2).

Now when he had come to the market, he said "Where is the Son of the King of Agaddez?" Then the People fell upon him with blows, and said "O Evil-born, why do you ask where is the Son of the King of Agaddez?" And they covered him with blows until he was unable to stand. Then they said "Good, leave him thus, and let everyone go home." But as he was about to rise, the Son of the King of Agaddez said "When you go, tell the Maiden that I will come on Friday." So the Father said "Good," and went home. And when he had arrived, he called his Daughter, and seized her, and tied her up. Then he took a whip, and began to beat her, and he kept on beating her until he was tired (3). Then he said " Prepare, he is coming on Friday." And she said " Very well," and went off crying.

So on the Thursday she swept her hut clean, she could not do it well enough, and she spread mats on the floor. On the Friday he came and alighted on the roof of the hut, while the whole city was asleep, only the Maiden being awake, so he came through and alighted on the bed. She had bought kola-nuts and scent, and had put them by, so now she took them, and gave him them, and he began to eat. And as soon as she had given him them, wherever he spat there would be silver, and the Girl picked it up. She was picking it up, and putting it in a cooking pot, and covering it up [all night], and when he saw that it was enough, he arose and went home.

Now he was always coming and doing this, but one day, when they had let the Girl go out for a walk, they saw that she had filled all the cooking-pots with silver. Then the Women of the house came, and put needles in the bed, they put about a hundred needles there. So that night when he had come—the Girl herself was not there—and had alighted on the bed, all the needles pricked him, and he died. Soon afterwards the Girl came in and found him dead, and she commenced crying, and saying what would she do, the Son of the King of Agaddez had died in her hut.

Now the Boy's Father heard the news, and the Girl said to him " O hear me, hear me, I did not know." Then they sent and seized the Parents, but left the Girl, and they tortured the Parents until they died.

And when they were dead the Girl was summoned, and the King said to her " Iss, you must not do that again, it is not right," and he continued " you see, you have made me lose my Son. Now, shall I kill you or let you go?" Then she said " Ah! whatever you do, it is all the same to me, if you kill me I will have brought it upon my own head." So the King let her go, and he gave her a hut in his own compound, and he gave her presents, so she lived there. He pitied her.

————

A variant in which *Ba-Komi* (" Nothing ") takes the place of the Son of the King of Agaddez (the girl having asked her father to buy her " nothing "), is to the same effect as the first, second, and fourth paragraphs above—though there is no beating—but the ending is different. In this case the daughter of the rival wife put thorns on the roof. In the evening, Lahidi heard the wind *bip, bip, bip,* and so she spread her mats, and lit her lamp. But when Ba-Komi came, he alighted on the thorns, and they stuck into his flesh. Then Lahidi [who did not know] said " Welcome "—but there was no reply. " Welcome "—silence. Then he said " *Chip,* I am going home," and he gave her one tobe [instead of 10 black tobes, 10 white tobes, 10 pairs of trousers (4), 10 turbans, and 100 bowls of grain, as usual]. He had two of each there, but he would not give her all, for his heart was broken [and he went off].

Well, at daybreak, Lahidi saw the remainder of the thorns, and she guessed that her Step-Sister had put them there to prick him, and she knew that he must be ill. So she shaved her head, she split up her body cloth and made a tobe and trousers, and set out to seek for medicine to take to the King's Son.

As she was travelling in the depths of the forest, she came to the foot of an enormous *Kainya* tree, and she squatted down there. Just then a *Jipillima,* the biggest one, flew up and settled in the tree, and said " Ah me! To-day I have not been fortunate, I have eaten only 99 Men, I left the other one because he was a Leper."

Then a second arrived, and said "Ah me! To-day I have not been fortunate, I have eaten only 79 Men, I left one because he was a Leper." [Then other Jipillimas arrived and the narrator gives 59, 49, 39, 29, and 19, as the numbers eaten]. Then another arrived, the smallest of them, and said "Ah me! To-day I have not been fortunate, I have eaten only 9 Men, I left one because he was a Leper." Then he saw the Girl squatting, and he said "But I, Auta [know one thing], there is a certain King's Son who is so ill that he is

FIG. 68.—Basket of grass, stained red, white, and black.   H., 6½ in.

almost dead, but if our droppings be taken and given to him to drink, he will recover" (5). Now Lahidi heard this, and she went and gathered their droppings, and wrapped them in her tobe, and ran away. She ran, and ran, and ran until she arrived at the city where the King's Son was.

So she came [to the door of the palace] and called out "The Disciple asks for alms" (6). But the Attendants exclaimed "What kind of senseless Disciple is this to come when the King's Son is so ill that he is almost dead? Bring a sword and kill him." But others said " No, no, let him beg." Then Lahidi said " Ba-Komi, Lahidi salutes you," and when he heard this he raised his head, and said " Let that Disciple come here." When she had come close, Lahidi undid the Jipillima droppings, and said " Here is medicine, give it to him to drink." Now, when he had drunk it, the King's Son began to vomit, and as he vomited, the thorns came out, and lo! at last all the thorns had come out! Then the People said " Well, what shall we give this Disciple?" The King's Son said " Let me give you 100 Horses," but she said that she did not want them. He said " Let me give you 100 Slaves," but she said that she did not want them. He said " Let me give you 100 Head of Cattle," but she said that she did not want them. He said " Let the city be divided into halves," but she said that she did not want it. Then she said " The little ring on the King's finger [is all I want]," so it was pulled off and given to her. Then she returned to her home, and would you believe it, no one knew that she was a woman.

As soon as the King's Son had recovered, he took a large sword, with the intention of killing Lahidi. So he went at night and entered the door, and she said " Welcome," but he drew his sword. Then she said " For the sake of the Disciple who gave you the medicine which cured you, and to whom you gave a ring, spare me." Then he trembled, and put back the sword in its sheath, and said " How did you manage to find out that a Disciple had cured me?" And she replied " It was no Disciple, it was I," and she showed him the cloth that she had split up to make trousers, and the cloth with which she had made a tobe, and the ring that he had given her.

Then he said that he wanted to marry her, and the parents said " Very well, but if she marries who is going to bring us water?" So he brought 100 Head of Cattle and 100 Slaves, and said " Here are your Water-Carriers." Then she was given to him in marriage, and thus the Father became rich all through the Daughter whom he did not love."

In a Sicilian tale (Pitrè, *Bibliotica*, iv, 342) a queen procures repeated interviews with an emperor's son by means of a spell consisting of 3 golden balls put into a golden basin with 3 quarts of pure milk. One day a servant breaks a drinking glass and puts the fragments into the milk. The prince appears covered with blood and vanishes, nor does she recover him until she learns the remedy by overhearing the conversation of some demons (see Story 12, variant), which enables her to heal him, and he marries her. In a Danish tale (Grundtvig, *Danische Volksmärchen*, i, 252) belonging, like the foregoing, to the Cupid and Psyche cycle, the heroine is persuaded to stick a knife in the bedstead. Her husband scratches himself with it and she loses him for the moment. (H.).

The commission to the father appears also in Sicilian tales (Pitrè, iv, 350; xviii, 70). Cf. *Folk-Lore*, vi, 306, a tale apparently from the south of England, and an Indian tale from Mirzapur, *N. Ind. N.* and 2, ii, 171, No. 633. (H.).

45

THE BOY WHO BECAME HIS RIVAL'S RULER.

A certain Man once had a large household, so far as Wives and Slaves were concerned, but he had no Son. So he was always going to different Malams, and saying "Give me a charm that I may beget a Son, for I have none." But all to no purpose, until at last he went to a certain Malam who said to him "You must go and live in the forest, and you must plait hobbles for Horses, and sell them until you can buy a Slave-Wife, then when you have built a house you will have a Son."

So he went into the forest, and lived there, and when he had made enough money, he bought a Slave-Wife, and she conceived and bore a Child, a Son.

Then the Father arose and went to the town, and made more and more money, and stored it there, but he still lived in the forest.

The Boy soon began to understand, and grew up, and then he used to wander about in the town, leaving his Father outside. Now one day he met one of the Sons of the King on the road who said " Hullo Boy." And he replied " Well." " Will you not come with me ? " asked the King's Son, and the Boy said " Very well." The King's Son was courting,* and he made the Boy hold his Horse for him while he went inside the house to woo the Girl.* After a time the King's Son came out again, and they started off, and when they had come to the road again, the King's Son said " Well, you go your way, and I will go mine." So the Boy went home, and his Father said " Where have you been since dawn ? " And he replied " I have been wandering about in the town."

The next day the Boy again went to the town, and the King's Son again met him, and said " Hullo Boy, come, let us go again to where we were yesterday," so the Boy went off with him. Now as the King's Son was dismounting, some of the Women of the house came out, and said " Hullo, look at this most handsome Youth, is he fit only to hold a Horse ? " This made the King's Son so angry that he came out again from the doorway, and mounted his Horse, and went off. When the Boy had come home, he said to his Father " Why do you make me go about as if I were a Slave ? I have no tobe, no trousers, no turban, not even a cap." So the Father arose, and went into the town at night, and opened his treasury, and took out some clothes, and gave them to the Boy.

Next morning the Boy took the road, and came

to the place where he had before met the King's Son. When the latter came, he said " Hullo ! where did you get a loan of those clothes, or are they your own ? " and the Boy replied " Um." So they went off to the house, and when the King's Son had dismounted he told the Boy to hold the Horse, but he refused to do so. So they both entered the house, and saw the Women. When they had come out again the King's Son said " Look here, Boy, to-morrow let each show what he has to eat at home," and so they parted.

Now when he had arrived home, the King's Son said " Make me some guinea-corn porridge, and some of millet, and of dark rice, and of *acha,* and of white rice, and of black millet also." And these were made, and the King's Son ate them. As for the Boy, he said " Bring me sour milk in a calabash," he also told them to bring him a heap of silver, and they brought it. So, as he drank the milk, he threw the silver into his mouth, and swallowed it.

Next morning the Boy took the road, and came to the meeting-place. The King's Son also came, and said " O Boy, have you come ? " He replied " Yes." Then the King's Son said " Good, let us go." So they went to the Girl's house. When they arrived there, he said " Now, let each show what he ate yesterday," and he began to vomit, and the black rice, and *acha,* and white rice, and everything that he had eaten fell out, so that the Girl might see that there was plenty in his home. Then the Boy said " Good, have you finished? Give me room now." Then he did the same, and the Women of the house began scrambling for the silver which was thrown on the ground, and praising the Boy. As for the King's Son he ran away, he felt so ridiculous.

Then the Boy went home, and said to his Father
" Let us leave this village and return to the town (1),"
so they arose and went.

One day the Boy asked " Has the King's Son a
Mother ? " And they said " He has, she is still living." So the Boy ordered two handfuls of silver to
be brought to him, and he took them to the Smith, and
told him to make him ten spindles, and he got his
Father to bring purple cord and to plait it into a
blind (2). Then he went down the street, holding the
spindles and ten kola-nuts in his hand. He went as
far as the road leading to the river, and there he sat
down, and asked someone to point out to him the
Slave of the Mother of his Rival. When he had spoken
to her, he gave her the ten silver spindles and the ten
very large kola-nuts, and told her to take them to her
Mistress.

Now when the Girl had returned, she called out to
her Mistress " Help me to put down this water." And
the Mistress said " You are always bringing water,
have I never helped you before that you should cry out
so ? " When she had come out of the hut (3), and had
caught hold of the calabash, and had felt that it was
not heavy, she was going to make a fuss, but the Slave
whispered " Silence." Then they entered the hut, and
when she had uncovered the calabash she saw the
spindles inside, and the ten kola-nuts as large as Robbers' heads (4). Then she said " Who sent you to me
with these ? " and the Slave replied " A certain Youth
said that I was to tell you that he would visit you later."
Then she said " But how will he manage it ? "

Then the Slave went back to the Boy, and said
" How will you manage it ? " The Boy said " What
is there to hinder me ? " She replied " Our house has

three entrance-halls. In the first are ten Watch-Dogs, in the second are ten Slaves, in the third ten Horses. The Horses are given Ox-bones to eat, the Dogs are given grass, and the Slaves smoke nothing but potash "(5). He replied " Very well," [and gave her the blind to take to her Mistress].

When night had come, the Boy persuaded his Father to kill ten Bulls, and the heads were cut off. Then he sent ten Youths to cut grass, and he got ten tobes and ten rolls of tobacco, and he went off towards the King's palace. He entered the first hall, and spread out the bundles of grass for the Horses, and the Horses said " Ah ! see, that which we most desire has been given to us to-day." He passed on and entered the second hall, and the Dogs said " *Wu, wu, wu,*" but when the Bulls' heads had been thrown to them, they said " We are not eaters of grass, and see to-day God has given us meat." Then the Boy passed on and came to where the Slaves were (6), and all rose up with cutlasses in their hands. But he gave each of them a present, everyone got a tobe and a roll of tobacco. Then he passed on, and searched for the door where his blind was hanging, and when he saw it he went in, and found his Rival's Mother there. He had a bottle of scent in his hand, and he sprinkled the contents in all directions, and then he sat down.

In the morning, the King went out, and he saw all his Slaves with tobes. He passed on, and found the Dogs eating Bulls' heads. He passed on, and found that the horses had grass (7). Then he said to the People outside " Go in and tell the Boy who is inside that he is King, I abdicate to-day (8), he who does not wish to serve the Boy as King may follow me, she who does not care for me any longer may keep away from me."

So, you see that the new King of the town was the Boy, and the Son of the ex-King came and did homage, and said " O Great One, I hope you have slept well." And the Boy said " See, my Son has come." And the People said " See, they were Rivals for the affections of Women, now the Boy has taken the place of the other's Father."

———

In a variant (L.T.H. ii, 48) a Youth sets out to get the King's Chief Wife, and several Persons join him in his quest. He sends the Old Woman in whose house he lodges with scent to the Wife, and she sends him kola-nuts, and directions how to reach her. He gives kolas to the Male Slaves guarding the entrance, cloths to the Females who next accost him, and bones to the Dog, and grass to the Horse as here. He then sees the tree, hut and blind indicated to him, and reaches her. The ending is different, however, for the King suspects something, and has a search made. However, by the help of his Companions, they escape, the Robber getting them out of the city, the Soldier keeping back the King's troops until Another has cut out a canoe, and so on.

———

The incident in folk-tales of appeasing animal and other guardians with food or some other requirement is often found, especially in tales belonging to the Cupid and Psyche cycle. Sometimes these guardians are already furnished with food which is inappropriate; and they are then appeased by changing it, as above. So in an Arab tale from Egypt, the hero, going to seek the singing rose of Arab Zandyg, finds tied up at the palace gate a kid and a dog. Before the kid is a piece of flesh, and before the dog some clover. He changes them, putting the clover before the kid and the flesh before the dog, and thus is enabled to accomplish the object of his quest (Spitta Bey, *Contes Arabes Modernes,* 143). (H.).

XXV.—FIREWOOD. XXVI.—COTTON.

In the larger markets almost anything may be bought, from rough sticks to wooden matches, from raw cotton to the finished (and often inferior) cloth from Manchester.

46

THE WILD-CAT AND THE HEN.

This is about a certain Hen which was going to marry a Wild-Cat. The Wild-Cat had told her to summon all her Relatives to take part in the marriage-breakfast, so she invited them accordingly, and the Guests came in large numbers. Now the Wild-Cat hid in the house, and as each Fowl arrived, she looked up at the house, and saw his eyes [but she went in all the same].

At last, when all the Guests had assembled, the Wild-Cat prepared to kill them, and he sprang upon the Fowls and killed them. And that night he told his Wife [the Hen] to go to bed, and when she had lain down, he twisted her neck, and ate her (1).

———

Usually the Victims are deceived by the Villain of the story pretending to be dead. Thus the Spider frightens the Mourners so much that the Elephants and other big Beasts trample upon the smaller ones in their anxiety to escape (F.-L. 6), or the Cat may deceive Mice in a similar manner (L.T.H. 78).

———

In a Southern Nigerian tale (*British Nigeria,* page 287) the Bush-Cat sought to avenge herself upon the Monkey for having tied her tail to a tree while she was asleep. The Monkey, however, was wily, and he escaped when she sprang at him, but since that time he has always lived in the trees. Except for the fact that it is the Rabbit which escapes instead of the Francolin, a Sierra Leone story (*Cunnie Rabbit,* page 221) is almost exactly the same as the Hausa one (F.-L. 6).

———

47

The Dishonest Father.

A Girl and her Friend went out to make love, and when they had gone, the Girl herself found a Lover, and she took him, but she prevented her Friend from doing the same, so the Friend became angry and returned home.

Now the Girl's Father was very dishonest, and he said " Let us go away from here," he said that he had cheated too much. So he told the Girl to grind corn [to make flour for the journey]. As she pounded, she sang :—

> " Grounding rations now I do,
> Father has cheated Men of money,
> In the morn or in the even
> We will flee and leave the town."

The Father wondered what would he do, his evil deeds were many.

So they went to another town, and there he gave his Daughter in marriage, one Daughter to four Suitors. Then the drummers were summoned, and they beat sentences saying that he must leave off evil-doing. Then he asked if he left off evil-doing how would he live? And they said " Well, one Husband will pay all the money." And one of them did this, and lived alone with his Wife.

———

A variant of this (L.T.H. 76) gives a much better story, and shows what a mutilated account one's own narrator may give (1). In other cases, my versions show to advantage. The variant relates how the Father had promised his Daughter to three Suitors, and wonders what he would do, and continues : " So he arose and went to an old Malam, and said ' Malam, I have a favour to ask,' and the Malam replied ' Well.' The Father said ' I have only one Daughter, but I have taken money from three Suitors, I have told each that I would give her to him, and the Girl is now ready for marriage.' The Malam replied ' I see. When you depart, go and pray, and draw your sword and place it close to your head. When you have bent down, lift up your head, and if you see a Bitch come and cross in front of you, make haste and take your sword, and

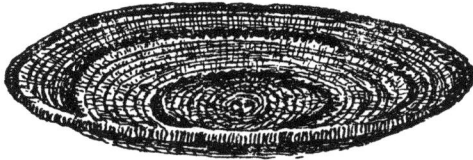

FIG. 69.

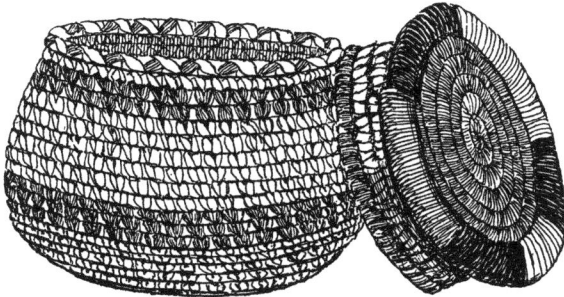

FIG. 70.

FIG. 69—Mat of red, white, and black grass, used as cover for calabashes having no lid. D., 11⅝ in. FIG. 70.—Basket of coloured grass, like fig. 68.

cut her down and divide her into two. Then you will obtain what you are seeking.'

" When the time for prayer came, the Father arose and prayed, and he had bent down and raised his head, when, see, the Bitch came, and crossed quickly in front of him, so he made haste to take his sword and cut her in two, and immediately two Young Girls appeared, as beautiful as his own. So he took them home, and smeared henna upon them together with his own

Daughter, and he gave each Suitor one, and so ended the trouble.

" After a time he wanted to know which was his own Child amongst them, so he set out on a round of visits. The first Daughter whom he found was quarrelling and called the Father names, the second had become immoral, but when he came to the house of the third and saluted, they responded, and he was given a fine lodging, and he rested. He was made much of, for him was prepared porridge with meat, sour milk mixed with *fura* was presented to him, everything was brought which was proper to his position, and then he knew that he had found the one who was the Daughter of his own blood."

48

The Contest for Dodo's Wife.

There was once a certain Woman who was the Wife of Dodo—for Dodo had emerged from the forest and had become a Husband—[and she wanted a human victim]. So she came to the town bringing a small basket with a lid to it, and she placed it on the brink of a dye-pit (1) where the People were dyeing. And when she had placed it there, she said " He who can knock over that basket may have me for his Wife " (2).

So the Men all began to throw—they did not know that she was already married to Dodo—for they saw that she was very beautiful. The Great Men threw first, but they were unable to knock it over and open it (3), and all threw, until at last only a certain Small Boy was left to throw. Then they said " Pick up a stone and throw." But he said " My Betters have tried and tried, and have failed to open it, much less shall I be able to do so." But he took a small piece of gravel and threw it, and the basket opened! So the People said " He is her Husband," and they were married.

Three weeks went by, and then the Woman said that she ought to go to her own town and see how her People were, so the Boy said " Very well." Now the Boy's Father was a Hunter who knew the whole country, he could transform himself into an Elephant, or into a Lion, or into anything at all. And he knew that the Woman was Dodo's Wife, as also did the Boy.

Next day the Boy and his Wife started off and into the forest, and when they had come into the middle of the forest she said " Look away for a moment."* No sooner had he done so than she became a Dodo, and rushed up to eat the Boy. But he changed himself into a Lion. She made as if to spring upon him, but he became a Snake, and then she let him alone, and the Boy became a Bird, and flew off.

At last he reached home, and he spoke of what had happened, and his Parents said " Ah, we told you not to marry her." And they added " When you marry a Woman do not tell her the secrets of your family." And he said " I see."

There is evidently a good deal missing from this story; it is a variant of M. 8 and F.-L. 46. He ought to have told her that he could change himself into a Lion, and into a *Ma——*, and his Father ought then to have interrupted him, and to have prevented him from saying *Machiji* (Snake), so that she would not know next day that the Snake was he.

In a Sierra Leone tale (Cronise and Ward, page 261) an Elephant becomes a Girl and marries the Hunter who tells her that he can turn himself into a tree, or an ant-hill, and is then stopped by his Mother who has

overheard the conversation. Next day the Hunter and
his Wife go to the forest, she becomes an Elephant
and charges at him and he turns into a tree. She
charges again and he becomes an ant-hill. She charges
again and he gets up and " he go fa' down inside
wattah, he turn dat t'ing wey (which) turn fas', fas',
'pon top de wattah. He loss f'om Elephan', but he
bin broke all de bone w'en de Elephan' 'mas' um. . .
So ef ooman come to yo', no tell um all de word wey
yo' get inside yo' heart."

49

THE MAN AND HIS LAZY WIVES.

A certain Farmer and his three Wives used to work
on their farm, but one day the Women said that they
would not do any more hoeing, that they were tired of
it; so the Husband said " Very well." But he
concocted a trick. He made three loin-cloths (1), and
hid them, and next morning he called his Chief Wife
aside, and said to her " See this loin-cloth, I give it to
you to tie on, but do not tell the others, for there is a
certain charm for child-birth in it, and if you tie it
on, you will have a Son " (2). So she replied " Very
well, good," and she put it on.

When she had gone, he called the Second Wife
aside also, and said " See this loin-cloth, I give it to you
to tie on, but do not tell the others, for there is a certain
charm for child-birth in it, and if you tie it on, you will
have a Son." So she replied " Very well, good," and
she put it on.

Then he called the Youngest Wife also, and when
she had come, he said " See this loin-cloth, I give it to
you to tie on, but do not tell the others, for there is a
certain charm for child-birth in it, and if you tie it on,

you will have a Son." So she replied "Very well, good," and she put it on.

So they all went off to the farm, the Husband and the three Wives, and when they had arrived, and had started hoeing, the Husband began to sing, saying :—

"Quickly, quickly, Loin-cloth Wearers,
Quickly, quickly, Loin-cloth Wearers."

Then they went faster and faster, they tried hard, and worked in all truth. They beat the earth like one Man, and they all rose up again together (3).

After a time the Chief Wife's loin-cloth became uncomfortable (4), and she pulled it off, and said "I cannot work with that on." But when she had taken it off she became thoroughly tired, and she said "Oh indeed, so I was given the loin-cloth to make me work hard, well, I'll wear it no more." When the others heard this they said "Opp, is it thus that we have been tricked?" So they also undid their loin-cloths, and pulled them off. Then the Husband said "Well, had I not done that to you, you would not have worked so hard," (5) and he continued "Now let us go back home again."

They returned.

———

According to a variant, the object of giving the loin-cloths to the wives is to make them work like men, and there is no idea of any charm for childbirth.

————

50

THE TWO WIVES, THE HYÆNA, AND THE DOVE.

This is about a Husband and his two Wives. One of the Women was well off, the other was not. One day the Chief Wife, the poor one, said "Well, I am going to travel in the forest," and her Husband replied "All right," so off she went. She travelled on and on, until the sun had fallen, and night had come, and then she said "May God give me a little hut," and immediately she saw a large house ahead of her. So she came close and entered it, but saw nothing inside, so she said "May God give me food," and He gave it to her. So she ate until she was satisfied, and then she said "May God give me a bed," and He did so, and she lay down.

As she was about to lie down (1), she heard a Dove coo-ing and saying "Make your soup and drink it," and the Woman said "Whatever kind of Bird is talking thus?" But she got up, and made her soup, and drank it.

In the night a Hyæna came, howling, and saying "May I come into the King's porch, may I come into the King's porch?" But the Woman shut the door, and the Hyæna went off.

In the middle of the night who should come but Dodo, and he was roaring, and saying "May I come to the King's porch?" And the Woman arose, and opened the door of the entrance-hall, and Dodo entered. When he had got in, she ran and entered her hut, and hid, but Dodo came on, saying "May I enter the King's palace?" So the Woman opened the door of the hut, and ran away and hid in the space beneath the bed (2). Then Dodo came into the hut, and climbed up on to the bed, and pulled off his tobe and trousers, and lay down. In the morning he threw down silver, and tobes, and pairs of trousers, and other goods, and left all of them for her, and went off. So when he had gone, the

Woman collected the things, and brought them home, and showed them to her Husband.

Then the Rival Wife said " Well, I also shall go to the forest," but the Husband said " No, no, what we have is enough for us all " (3). But she said " I *will* go though," and so he said " Very well," and off she went. She travelled on and on, until the sun had fallen, and night had come, and then she said " May God give me a hut," and immediately she saw a large house ahead of her. So she came close and entered it, but saw nothing inside, so she said " May God give me food," and He gave it to her. So she ate until she was satisfied, and then she said " May God give me a bed," and He did so, and she lay down.

As she was about to lie down, she heard a Dove coo-ing, and saying " Make your soup and drink it," and the Woman said " Whatever kind of Bird is talking thus ? " And she got up and took a stick, and hit the Dove, and killed it, and then she cooked and ate it.

In the night a Hyæna came, howling, and saying " May I come into the King's porch, may I come into the King's porch ? " But the Woman did not hear her, for she was asleep, and the Hyæna came and seized her, and ate her up (4).

Next morning another Dove heard the news, and she came and told the Husband, but he said " Oh well, I told her not to go, see, her blood is upon her own head." Then the Dove said " I see," and she flew off. So the Husband lived with the Chief Wife only.

In a variant (M.H. 34) the Second Dove found a finger of the Dead Woman, and she took it to the Husband's house and told him what had happened.

51

The Man and his Wives, and Dodo.

This is about a Man who had two Wives. Now whenever he used to go to the forest, he would leave his Dogs in the hut, and tie them up, and say that if either of the Wives loosed them he would beat her when he came home again.

One day when he had taken his flute (1) and had gone to the forest as usual, it happened that Dodo saw him from afar off as he was walking along. And when the Man saw Dodo he ran and climbed a tree, and took his flute and began to blow upon it. Immediately the Dogs heard it from where they were in the hut, and they began to whine. Then the Chief Wife said " Opp, whatever is making the Dogs whine like this? I will loose them." But the Rival Wife said " No, no, do not do so, the Head-of-the-House (2) has said that whoever looses them will be beaten on his return." But the Chief Wife said " I will let them go," so the other said " Oh, very well, do so if you like." So the Chief Wife loosed them, and no sooner had she done so than they raced off, and ran until they had reached the tree. Immediately Dodo fled, and the Dogs followed, and they caught him, and killed him on the spot.

When they had done this the Man returned home, and said " Who let the Dogs loose? " And the Rival Wife replied " It was she who did it, I myself said that she was not to do so." Then the Husband said " If she had not let them go, Dodo would have seized me." And he beat the Rival Wife, but he gave the Chief Wife a present.

———

A variant (L.T.H. ii, 3) is a mixture of this one, and stories 32 and 48. The Witch when she has taken the Youth into the forest changes herself into a Hyæna, and he goes through various transformations until he becomes a ring, and she does not recognize this as him (see F.-L. 46). He then changes into a Man, and climbs a tree, which she tries to root up. He then calls his Dogs and they rescue him, and lick up every drop of blood lest the spot should seize the youth.

52

THE WIFE WHO WOULD NOT WORK ALONE.

There was once a Man who had one Wife, and they lived thus for nine years. But one day the Wife said " O, Owner-of-the-House," and he said " Yes." " What kind of a Man are you ? " she asked. Then he said " Why do you ask me what kind of a Man I am, what have you to complain about ? " " It is this," she replied, " I have been alone with you nine years, am I never going to have a Rival Wife ? " Then he said " Oh no, I do not want to set up a Rival, lest you should be jealous." But she said " No, no, I shall not be jealous, I myself will find a Wife for you." So he said " All right, find one for me, will a Man refuse to marry ? "

So she went and got her Friend, a Widow, and brought her to the house, and she [the Widow] and the Husband wooed each other, and in the morning they were married (1), so the Bride lived with the Chief Wife and her Husband. As for the Husband, everything he got he would give it to her, and not to the Chief Wife. He left the Chief Wife's hut and always slept with the Bride (2).

This went on thus until one day the Chief Wife came, and said " Look here, O, Owner-of-the-House ! "

And he replied " Well." She said " Who brought you
this Bride, was it not I ? " And he said " It was you."
Then she said " Very well, I do not like her, so she
must leave the house, you must send her away." But
he replied " Oh no, I lived with you alone, and you
yourself said that you wanted a Rival, it was not I who
sought her, and so now I will not drive her out." Then
the Chief Wife said " Well, as far as I am concerned,
I cannot agree with her, you must send her away."
But he replied " No, it is you who must go," and he
drove her out of the house.

When she had been sent away, she said " Alas,
had I only known, I should not have done thus," and
she continued " He who rides the Horse ' Had I
known ' will feel sore " (3).

53

THE THOUGHTFUL AND THE THOUGHTLESS HUSBANDS.

A certain Man and his Friend started to go out
for a walk, and when they had gone, and were walking
along, they came upon a *diniya* tree, and they climbed
it—like honey is its fruit—and the Friend said " Let
us eat a little, and take some home." And the other
said " Very well." Now the fruits which the Friend
picked he put in his bag [but the other ate all of those
which he got], and after a time he said " Well, let us
go home." So the other said " All right, let us go,"
and they returned.

They went home, and in the night they were
sleeping with their Wives, and the Friend took some

fruits and gave them to his Wife, and she ate them all but a few. In the morning when she arose, she went to the house of her Husband's Friend's Wife, and she took some *diniya* fruits and gave them to her, and said "What, did not your Husband bring you any?" "Oh no," the other replied, "he did not bring me any."

That caused the Wife and Husband to begin quarrelling, for she said what had she done that her

Fig. 71.

Fig. 72.

Figs. 71, 72.—Steels for flint, carried in small leather purse. L. about 2 in.

Husband had not brought her any *diniya?* Then he said "Let me go and get you some." Now when he had gone and had climbed the tree, a Hyæna came and stood at the foot of the tree, and soon afterwards a Lion also came. Then the Man in the top of the tree began singing, and saying "O Hyæna, O Strong Hyæna, the Dancer" (1). Immediately the Hyæna began to dance, and she went off, and the Lion followed her. And when they had gone, the Man descended and ran

all the way home, and ever after that he would bring
his Wife some.

———

In another Story (L.T.H. ii, 57) a Boy is picking
dates for a Girl whom he has brought from another
city. She is standing underneath, and she hears the
Animals coming—for they all sleep there—and runs
away. The Boy plays his pipe, and the Animals all
dance away, leaving the Hedgehog on guard, but the
Hedgehog also dances off, and so the Boy escapes.

———

54

SOLOMON AND THE BIRDS.

A certain Woman, one of the Wives of the Prophet
(1) Solomon, went to another house, and saw that the
House-Wife had made a fine floor (2), and had made
her house look splendid. So she said " What did you
mix with the earth of your floor to make it look so
fine? " The other Woman replied " My Husband shot
a number of Wild Beasts, and I collected the blood and
put it in."

Now when his Wife had returned home, Solomon
spoke to her, but she remained silent. Then he said
" What has happened to you to make you angry? "
She replied " I went to call upon my Friend, and saw
that she had made a fine floor, her Husband had shot
Wild Beasts, and had given her the blood so that she
might mix it with the earth. Now, see here, all the
Birds come and hover over you like an umbrella (3),
you must take some and kill them, and give them to
me for my floor." So he said " Very well, to-morrow
some will be taken and given to you." " Good," she
replied, " May God bring us safely to to-morrow " (4).

Now next morning not one Bird came, but about breakfast time the King of Birds flapped his wings, and came to the Cock, who said to him "Have you heard what the Prophet Solomon said yesterday?" The King of the Birds said "What did he say?" "The Prophet Solomon said that he would kill us," replied the Cock. Then the King of the Birds said "Oh! Well, I am going home."

About ten o'clock the King of the Birds returned, and Solomon said "Have you been delayed in the town that you have not been here ever since dawn?" He replied "We have been arguing on three subjects at home." "What are the differences of opinion amongst the Birds?" asked Solomon. He said "They asked me 'Which is the longer, the night or the day?' and I replied 'From the morning, since the first call to prayers, until the evening, until it is almost time to go to sleep, all this is daytime, surely the day is longer than the night.' Then they asked me 'Who are the most numerous, Women or Men?' and I said Women, for a Man who is Led by his Wife is also a Woman'" (5). Then Solomon said "Go home." (6).

Now soon afterwards, his Wife went out and came to the house of the Owner-of-the-Fine-Floor, and the latter said "Oh dear, is it true that what I said to you in fun, you believed, and that you went and told it to the Prophet? I cut wood and beat it, and soaked it in water, and sprinkled the water on the floor. I was only making game of you."

In a Malayan story also (Skeat, page 64) King Solomon has an argument with the Birds, in which the Thrush, the Woodpecker, and the Heron show to advantage.

55

The King Who Coveted His Son's Wife.

Once there was a certain Maiden whose name was Kwallabbe, and she was very ugly. Now, her Mother [hated her for it and] turned her out of the house saying "Go to that city, you can find a home with someone there." So she went to the King's palace, and she was taken in and allowed to live there.

But whenever the King's Son came to eat his meals, he would say "Take her away"—for he said that she was very ugly, and that he did not like her. Then the Maiden returned to her Mother, and said "O Parent, they do not like me, they are trying to drive me out of the city." Then her Mother swallowed her, and brought her up beautiful, and said "Now, return to the city and stay there." So she went off, and returned to the King's palace, and while she was there the King's Son made love to her. So she went to her Mother and told her, and the Mother consented. So she married the King's Son.

After a time the King himself fell in love with the Maiden, and wanted her for his own, so he mobilized his Troops as if for war, and told his Son that he was to go with the Army. Now when the Son was about to start, the Maiden put a date-stone into the lock of hair (1) on his head, and the Troops moved off. Now after they had been marching for some time, [they arrived at a well], and it was now noon. Then the King said "Chiroma" (2), and [when he had come close, the King] said that he was to enter the well, and send up water for the Horses. So he said "Very good," and he went down, and sent up water until all the Horses had drunk their fill (3). Then the King

said " Now fill up the well with earth," and when this
had been done, [and his son had been entombed], the
King returned home. When he had arrived he summoned the Maiden, and said " Ah! see, your Husband
is dead." And she replied " It is so," and she refused
to touch any food; for about ten days she did not eat
anything.

Now the Son was in the well, and lo! the date-stone
in his hair began to grow, it shot up through the mouth
of the well, and grew up high. And the Son followed,
and followed, climbing the tree, until he emerged at the
top and it grew very high, and he remained in it (4).

One day his Wife's Slave passed, she used to go to
a Filani camp (5) to get milk, and she saw a Man like
Dodo. " O Girl, come here," said he, but she refused.
Then again he said " O Girl, come here," and she said
" Very well," and came close. When she had come, he
pulled the ring off his finger, and dropped it into the
milk (6), and said " Now, when you go home, do not
let anyone help you down with your calabash of milk
except my Wife," and the Girl said " Very well." So
when she returned, she said " Come and help me, Mistress," but the other refused. Then she said again
" But you must come," so she did so. And when she
had helped her to put it down, the Slave said to her
" Put your hand into the milk." So she dipped it
in, and took out the ring. Then she said " Who
gave you this?" And the Slave replied " You know it
then?" and she told her where her Husband was.

Then the Wife got a Horse, and summoned the
Drummers, and the Barbers, and they went off. When
she arrived she caused him to be washed, and when that
had been done he was shaved, and after that robes
were placed upon him, and then she said " Good, let

us go." So he mounted a Horse, and he went off, and
came upon his Father who was holding a council
meeting. Then the Son said "O People, what does
One do to an Enemy?" And they were silent. Then
again he spoke asking what One did to an Enemy.
Then he drew his sword and killed his Father, and
said "Praise be to God, the city has become mine."
Then the People said "Blessings upon you, and
fortune," and he replied "Thanks" (7).

So he lived in the palace and ruled over the city.

———

A variant (F.-L. 48), where the Girl after having
been swallowed emerges half gold and half silver, states
that the Mother was an Elephant, and that it would have
been unsafe for the Maiden to have remained in the
forest. That version certainly seems more satisfactory
than this, for here the Mother could have swallowed her
at first. Also why was this Mother living away from
the city? Another variant makes the Girl to be born
in a gourd, as is the Boy in a clay pot in Story 71.
In yet another (L.T.H. ii, 55) the Girl is named
Atafa, and, after her Mother and Father have
died, she swallows all the Animals and property, and
goes as a poor Maid into the City. The King's Son
despises her until he has found out that she is rich,
and then the King also wants her, as in this Story. The
Son is sent out with an Expedition (the King does not
go), and on reaching the well, each Man refuses to
enter it "because the Horses do not belong to his
Father," so the Son does. He is entombed, and the
date-tree grows up, and he appears, all white, and sits in
the branches. The rest of the story is as above.

———

An Annamite tale has some points of resemblance.
It is (S.F.T. 323) to the effect that a Woodcutter who
found some Fairies bathing, took the raiment of one
of them, and hid it, so the Owner had to become his
Wife (as in T.H.H. 4). A Son was born, but when he

was three years of age, the Mother found her clothes
and vanished, leaving, however, her comb stuck in his
collar. The Husband on his return, took his Son to the
fountain where they met some of his Wife's Servants
drawing water, and while speaking to them the
Husband dropped the comb into one of the jars. On
the Girl's return, the Wife recognized the comb, and
sent him an enchanted handkerchief by the means of
which he was able to go to her.

56

THE GIRL WHO MARRIED DODO'S SON.

A certain Man was on a journey, and he came to the
King of the city, and said " The Pagans are preparing
for war, but there is a river in the road which will prevent your passage." Then the King said " Indeed,
let me go and see." So he arose, and went to the
river side, and said " O River, let those which are in
this river hear, I have come to ask them to let me pass
that I may go and fight the Pagans." Then from out
of the water came voices " What will you give us if
you go to war ? " And he said " If I go and fight, and
return, and God has given me the victory, I will give
the Son of the King of the River a Daughter of my
own blood in marriage." Then they said " Agreed,"
and the River went over to one side, and left a passage
open. And when he had gone and fought, and captured
a large number of Slaves in the Enemy's city, and had
returned and crossed the river to go home, the water
returned and flowed on as before.

Now he lived at home, and traded off his Slaves
which he had taken, and said nothing further to the
River. So the River rose, and the water came almost

up to the city, until the People said " Verily the water
will destroy the city." Then the King arose, and
prostrated himself, and said to the River " Be patient,
the Girl is not yet marriageable, wait a little while
for her." And then the water fell again.

Then the King arose, and went into the palace, and
said " O Chief Wife," and she replied " Yes." " Will
you not give me your Daughter that I may give her
to the River-Dwellers ? " he continued. But she said
" I will not give you my Daughter." Then he arose and
went to the Youngest Wife, and said to her " I have
come to you with a petition, for the sake of God give
me your Daughter." " Very well," she said, " to
whom do both I and the Girl belong ? Are we not yours ?
Take her, and give her to them." So the King caused
the Girl to be brought, and kola-nuts and money, and
the marriage was proclaimed. Then he ordered ten
Men to take her to the River. So they took the Girl,
and made her prostrate herself, and said " Here, O you
River-Dwellers (1), see a Beautiful Bride whom we have
brought you." Then they went away, they returned
to the city, and left the Girl there, and when they had
gone, the River-Dwellers came out from the water,
seized the Girl's hand, and made her enter the water.
She was brought to the house, the house of Dodo, the
King of the River, and after a time the Children
of the River-Dwellers got to know her, and used to
play with her.

Now this Youngest Wife of the King of the city
had a Child in arms (2), and this Infant began to learn,
and in time she grew up. And the King's other
Children used to mock her, and say " We dislike you
because your Sister was thrown into the River." Then
the Girl said to her Mother " Is it true that I have a

Sister who was thrown into the River?" And the Mother replied "Yes, it is true that you had a Sister." Then the Girl said "Indeed! May God bring us together."

Now one day when she went to the market to buy something to eat, she procured a small gourd (3), and brought it to the place where the Worshippers in the Mosque used to wash (4), and she dug up the earth, and planted the gourd, and said "Now, Gourd, I want you to guide me to the place where my Sister is." So the gourd sprouted, and started creeping along, and went on until it had gone outside the city, and it grew and grew, until it had reached the river, and had entered and reached the Sister's house. Then it climbed the house, and blossomed, and fruited. Now next morning, the Girl said to her Mother " I am going to look for my Sister." " Do you know where she is ? " asked she. And the Girl replied " I shall follow this gourd, it will guide me." So in the morning as she was starting, her Mother said " Very well, go, if I could lose the Elder and yet bear it, surely I can put up with the loss of you, the Younger One."

So the Girl followed the gourd, and went on and on until she arrived at the bank of the river, and then she said " Really ! is that where my Sister is ? " Then she shut her eyes, and threw herself into the water. Now the Sister in her house heard the splash, and on going out she saw a Human Being, so she took her up in her arms, and carried her into the house. And when the Girl had recovered consciousness, she said " Where did you come from ? " The Sister replied " I am of the King's house." " Who is your Father ? " asked the Girl. " So-and-So is my Mother," replied the Other. Then the Girl said " O, Sister, I used to be mocked, People used to say that you had been killed in the river, that is why I have come to see you." Then the Sisters both burst out crying.

Just then the Husband, Dodo's Son, approached, and they heard him coming, and the Wife said to her Sister " Run, hide yourself lest my Husband see you." So the Girl arose, and got inside the space under the earthen seat (5), and her Sister had no sooner covered her with a cloth than he arrived, and entered the room. " Hullo," he exclaimed, " I smell a Mortal in my house." " It is nobody," she replied, " it is I." " Oh no," he said, " it is a Stranger." So he got up, and pulled away the cloth, and caught hold of the Girl, and said to his Wife " So we have a Girl-Visitor and you would not tell me, did you want to hide her from me ? " She said " Yes, it is my Sister who has come." So they lived together for five days, and the Girl made friends with Dodo's Son and played with him.

But one morning she said " I must leave and go home." And her Sister said " Very well, but wait until the Owner-of-the-House has returned, and I will tell him, then you shall go home." When Dodo's Son had returned, he said " O Girl, are you leaving to-morrow ? " And she said " Yes, I must go to-morrow lest my Mother mourn for me." " Very well," he replied, and then said to his Wife " To-morrow when morning has come, take her and put her inside the corn-binn that she may get two small baskets with lids, and take them." So next morning the Wife took her Sister to the corn-binn, and when she had taken out the small baskets, she said to her " Mind when you go, you give my regards to all at home." And she took her out of the water, and accompanied her a short distance on the way (6). At last she said " When you

have emerged from that forest you will see a low hill
ahead, and when you have got so far you must throw
down the basket which is in your right hand. When
you have traversed another forest, and have reached
another hill, you must break the basket in your left
hand." And then they parted, and the Sister returned
to her Husband in the water.

So the Girl went on as far as the hill which her
Sister had pointed out to her, and then she broke one
of the little baskets. Immediately Cattle, and Slaves,
and Horses emerged from it, and they took her up and
set her upon a Horse (7). Then when she had come to
the other hill, she broke the basket in her left hand,
and immediately Camels, and Donkeys, and Mules, and
Drummers, and Trumpeters, and Buglers emerged from
it, everything that could be thought of appeared. So
she set off again to go home. But she sent three Men
on ahead, saying " Tell the King not to run away
when he hears the noise of my Host (8), it is I who am
coming who have been to see my Sister." So the
Messengers came to the King, and told him the news,
and when she had arrived they all turned out to salute
her. She dismounted then, and went into the palace.

Now one of the other Daughters-of-the-House said
" I also will go and see my Sister." So she also
planted her gourd in the place where the Worshippers
used to wash, and the gourd grew and crept to the
river, entered the water, and climbed the Sister's house.
And when the Sister went outside the house, she said
" Hullo, I have got a gourd," and Dodo's Son said
" Good, keep it to yourself." And, he continued " I
must tell you something, on the day that anyone asks
you my name and you speak it, from then you will
never see me again " (9).

Well, the other Girl went to her Mother, and said
" I shall take the road to-morrow morning, I am going
to visit my Sister," and she was given permission.
So next morning she started off, and when she had
reached the river, she threw herself in. The Sister then
came out of her house, and lifted her up, and said to
her " And whence come you also?" " From the
King's house," she replied, and then the Sister took
her inside, and set her down. Just then the Son of the
King of the River arose, and approached the house,
and the Wife said " Get up and hide." But the other
Girl said " Certainly not, you want to hide me so that
I may not see your Husband " (10). When the Husband came into the hut, he saw the Visitor sitting down,
but he went out again without a word (11).

Soon the other Girl said that she must return on the
morrow, but the Sister said " Very well, but stay until
the Owner-of-the-House returns, and then he will bid
you adieu." So in the morning she said to him " The
other Girl is going home." He said " Very well, take
her to the corn-binn, and let her take two small
baskets." So she took her to the corn-binn, and told
her what to do, but when the other Girl had heard this,
she said " There are large baskets here, yet you tell
me to take small ones !" And she took one of the big
ones, and she was taken out of the corn-binn, arguing.
Then Dodo's Son said " Now go with her, and put
her on the road."

So the Sister went and put her on the road to her
home, and said " Now, see that hill over there, when
you have arrived there throw down this basket." So
the Sister returned to the water, and the other Girl went
on. But she broke the basket at once, and a lame
Horse, a Donkey and a Slave both blind, emerged, and

FIG. 73.   FIG. 74.

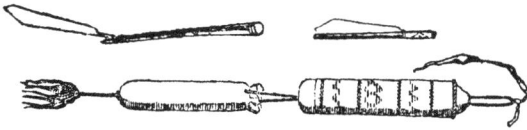

FIG. 75.

Figs. 73 and 74 show different patterns of razors, and Fig. 75 the case in which they are kept, an ancient stone axe-head being often used as a hone. The illustrations portray the attitude in shaving and hair-cutting.

a lame Goat. Then she set off home, she was very angry.

In a variant (L.T.H. ii, 62) the King gives his Daughter to the river itself. A Youth emerges, and takes her, and he turns out to be the Son of the King of the Dodos. He lives with her and his other Wife for some time, but then goes to his own city, telling the Girl to visit hers. Instead of this, she follows him, and has to escape from his Mother, in much the same way as do the Youth and the Spider in Story 95 (variant). Afterwards the Dodo-King dies, and the Youth succeeds him, once more going to the Dodo city, and this time he and his human Wife part for good.

A somewhat similar choice of baskets is given in a Japanese tale recorded by Lord Redesdale, in *Tales of Old Japan* (page 135), in which an Old Man kept a Sparrow, but one day when away, his Wife became angry with it, and, having cut its tongue, let it loose. Some time afterwards the Old Man met it, and it brought him to its house, and entertained him. When he went away, the Sparrow gave him two wicker baskets, one heavy and one light, and the Old Man chose the latter. On reaching home he opened his light basket, and " lo and behold ! it was full of gold and silver and precious things." Then the Old Woman went off also, but she had to ask for a present, and she chose the heavy basket. But when she opened it " all sorts of hobgoblins and elves sprang out of it, and began to torment her."

For another parallel see Story 93, variant.

57

THE MAN WHO MARRIED A MONKEY.

There was once a certain Man who married a female Monkey. He said that he had a farm, and he told her to go to it, but she said that her teeth were aching. So he said Oh, very well, that she could stay at home.

But when her Husband had gone, she climbed the barn (1) and stole some guinea-corn, and took it to the stones, and ground it. And while she was doing this she commencing singing, and saying that her tooth-ache was all a pretence, that her Husband was at the farm, and she was having a holiday. So she cooked food and ate until she was satisfied, then she took what was left, and hid it. But when she saw her Husband returning, she got on to the bed, and began crying, and saying that her teeth were very painful.

Now a certain Woman came, and told the Husband that his Wife was a fraud. And he asked himself what he would do. Then he decided to drive her out of the house, so he did so, and when he had sent her away he lived like a Bachelor (2).

A story on similar lines makes the Spider wed the Crown-Bird, but he, too, finds that his Wife will not perform any wifely duties, and so he drives her away.

58

THE MONKEY-WOMAN.

Once there was a Man who married a Widow, and lo! she could change herself into a Monkey. He had a tomato (1) farm, and when he had married her, he said " I am going to the forest to hunt, but see this farm, you must watch it lest the Monkeys come and plunder." And she replied " Very well."

Now, as soon as he had gone, she went off to the farm, and stopped in the centre of the farm, and pulled off her cloths, and laid them on top of an ant-hill. Then

she lay on the ground, and rolled about, and when she
had done so a Monkey-tail grew out of her buttocks,
and she became a Monkey out and out. Then she put
her hand to her mouth, and called " O Monkeys, O
Monkeys, O Monkeys," and Monkeys to the number
of about 500 came out of the forest, and she said to
them " [Now eat, but] not the blossoms, and not the
small ones." So they ate up all the full-grown
tomatoes, and then they went off, and she became a
Human Being again, and went home.

When the Hunter had returned, a Friend said to
him " Your Wife can change herself into a Monkey."
But the Other exclaimed " Oh ! You have begun to
make trouble have you ? You want to part us." " [You
think that] I do not want you to be happy, that I
wish you only evil ? " asked the Friend. And he continued " But since you think I am complaining without cause, tell her to grind corn for you because you
are going to watch [at another farm]." And the
Husband said " Very well," he agreed to that.

So [on the following day] the Wife ground corn
for him, and he went off and set up some posts
at the edge of the tomato farm, so that he could
sit on them (2), and he got a ladder, and mounted
it, and sat there. Soon afterwards, he saw her afar off
approaching the farm, she was coming in the shape of
a Human Being. But when she had reached the centre
of the farm where the ant-hill was—and he was watching her all the time—she pulled off her cloths and
threw them down, and she fell on to the ant-hill and
rolled about. So she became a Monkey, and she arose,
put her hand to her mouth, and called " O Monkeys,
O Monkeys, O Monkeys." Then he saw the Monkeys
coming out from the edge of the forest *rat tat tat, rat tat*

tat, and they ate up the tomatoes *kop*. When they had
gone, she became a Woman again, she took up her
cloths and folded them on (3), and went home.

So the Husband descended from the scaffold, and
followed her, and [when he arrived at his house] she
said " O Owner-of-the-House, welcome." But he replied " I want no welcome [from you], get your things
together, and get out, I am not able to live with a
Monkey ! " (4).

In a variant (F.-L. 47) the Man marries a Gazelle.
In another (L.T.H. 11) he soliloquises thus " I shall
never again marry a Woman whose People I do not
know."

59

The Despised Wife's Triumph.

There was once a King of a certain city who had
four Wives, of whom he loved three, but he did not
like the fourth at all. So he went and obtained birth-
potions for the three, and they came outside to grind
them upon the stones, and when they had done so they
went inside again, but the Unbeloved Wife had only
corn to grind there. Now God allowed them all to
conceive, the whole four of them, including her, and
at the proper time the King said " Let each return to
her Mother's house for the event " (1).

So the three Loved Ones left the city, and went off
to their homes, but the fourth did not know which was
her native town (2), and she went along the road aim-
lessly, and saying " God will provide me with a home
where I can be taken care of." So she went on and

on in the forest, until at last she saw afar off a little
hut. Now just then she heard a tornado rumbling in
the distance, and she ran towards the hut; but as she
ran it ran also, as she chased it, it was always ahead,
until she cried out in desperation "O God, wilt Thou
not make that hut stop so that I may enter it and
escape from the coming storm?" And immediately the
hut stopped where it was.

Now when she came up to go inside, she saw a
great Head* (3) lying in the doorway, and a Dog
crouching by its side. But [when she would have run
away], the Head grunted out "Um," and the Dog
interpreted. "That means, that you are to come in,"
he said. So she entered the hut, and no sooner had she
done so than down came the storm.

Soon the rain stopped, and then the Head grunted
"Um," and the Dog said to her "That means, 'Where
are you going?'" The woman answered "My Sister-
Wives have gone to the houses of their Parents to be
laid up, but I have no Relatives so I must find some
place where I can be attended to." Then the Head
again grunted "Um," and the Dog said "That means,
'Have you no Parents?'" And she replied "I have
none, I was carried away to the city when I was a
Tiny Mite, and I cannot remember the name of my
native-town." "Um," grunted the Head. "That
means, 'Would you like to stay here with us?'" explained the Dog. And she replied "Does a Human
Being refuse to live with his kind?" Once more the
Head grunted "Um," and the Dog said "That means,
'Be content, and stay with us.'"

About the tenth day afterwards, the pains of labour
gat hold upon her. Then the Head grunted "Um,"
and the Dog said "That means, 'What is making your

eyes look so strange?'" And she answered that she
had gnawing pains in her inside. Again the Head
grunted " Um," and the Dog said " That means, that
you must take this writing and dip it in a calabash of
water and drink " (4). So she did so, and drank the
ink and water. " Um," grunted the Head. " That
means, ' Go outside,' " explained the Dog. So she went
out, and found herself in another hut, and several Old
Women (5) came to help her, and she brought forth
her Child, a Son.

Now the King [her Husband] had said that whoever gave birth to a Son would have a Bull killed in
her honour at the King's palace on the day of her
return. And this Woman now had a Son! So they
washed the Child, and she saw that food had been
placed at her side, so she ate, though she did not know
whence it had come. Then she saw that warm water
had been placed in a vessel behind the hut, and so
she went and bathed herself (6).

She was there forty days, and then she went to the
Dog and said " Tell my Father (7), the Head, that
to-morrow my Rival Wives will be going home to the
palace." Then the Head grunted " Um," and the
Dog interpreted " That means, that to-morrow you
also shall go." Next morning the Head grunted
" Um," and the Dog said " That means, that you are
to come in here." So she entered, and saw that the
house was full of People, even her own Mother who
had borne her was there. One brought a present, and
another brought a present, all heaped up things for
her. Her Mother gave her a necklace of silver
dollars (8), strung on a purple cord, and she put it in
her basket. Then they escorted her to where the Head
was, and she knelt down, and said " O Father, I am

going home." "Um," it grunted, and the Dog said "That means, 'Bless you.'" "Um," it grunted again. "That means, 'Go in health and in peace,'" explained the Interpreter. So she started off, crying and weeping, and the People escorted her until they had brought her to the road which she knew, and then they stopped, and said "Now go on, and may you arrive safely."

So she went on, and overtook her Rivals at the river (9) where they were bathing. Now all three of them had given birth only to Daughters, and as she stepped into the river to go over the ford, the Chief Wife said "Are you not going to stop, and let us see what sex your Child is?" But she said "No." Then the Chief Wife ran after her, and pulled the Child from off her back (10), and when she saw that it was a Male, she put it on her back, and went off at a run, leaving her own Child on the bank of the stream. Then the Young Wife returned and took up the Chief Wife's Daughter, and went on home. The Chief Wife when she had reached home, said "Tell the King to come out and slaughter a Bull in my honour." But the Others went to their own houses quietly, the Young Wife entered in silence, she did not say a word.

Now the Boy grew up, and he began to go out to the forest (11), and one day he was seized with a sudden illness while in the bush and he died there. Then the other Boys returned, and said "Mohammadu has died in the forest," and the Towns-People mounted their Horses, and galloped off, and fetched him. They brought him to the palace, and were going to take him and bury him in the earth, when the Wise Men said "This Corpse is speaking, do not bury it." Then they summoned the four Wives to

come, and the Wise Men said " Go to your houses (12),
prepare food, and bring it."

So they went and made some, but the real
Mother had nothing but chaff to make food with,
and this she kneaded. Then each picked up her
calabash, and brought it to where the Wise Men
were. And the Wise Men asked " Which is the
Chief Wife? " and they said to her " Come here,

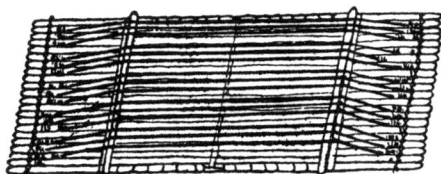

FIG. 76.

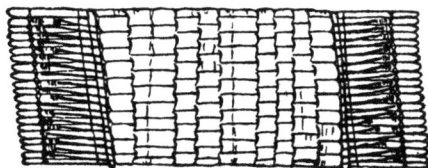

FIG. 77.

FIGS. 76, 77.—Front and back of reed auto-harp in general use.
L., 17¾ in.

and bring your dish." So she said " Good, if it is I
who have borne him he will rise up." So she went to
the Corpse and said " Arise, and eat this food," but he
did not move. Then Another came up, and said " If
it is I who have borne you, arise," but he did not.
The third Woman also came up, but he did not move.
Then his real Mother came up with the chaff—it was not
proper food—and said " Arise, and eat this chaff; it

was by treachery that you were snatched from me at the river-side." And immediately he rose up.

Then the King was overjoyed, and said that she was to be taken and placed in his own apartments. But she said " No. First cut off the heads of the Chief Wife, and of the other two, so that I may have a cooking-place " (13). And he consented.

So they had their heads cut off; but she lived happily (14).

———

Another Story (L.T.H. ii, 44) has some points of resemblance to this one, and to Story 64. A Merchant, when setting out on a journey, told his Slave to look after his four Daughters, and give them food. Three of them gave in to the Slave, and he gave them plenty, but the fourth, Auta, would not do so, and she got nothing. The Merchant had given each Daughter a looking-glass, and on his return he asked to see them. When the Girls looked, they saw that only Auta's was bright, so each borrowed hers and showed it to her Father. When Auta was going to him, the Slave took her glass and spoiled it, and the Father ordered that she should be taken to the forest and that her hands and feet should be cut off. The Slave did this, and left her, but she was rescued by another Merchant, who married her. Soon afterwards he and the Father went on a trip together, but he forgot something, and the Slave was sent back to tell the Chief Wife. He recognized the Girl, and said that he had been ordered to tell the Chief Wife to put the Girl and her newly-born Twins on a Camel, and drive them into the forest. This was done, and the Girl asked God for water, her hands and feet, and a house (see 50), and He gave them to her. Next morning when she awoke, she found that she was in the midst of a large city of which she was Queen, and soon afterwards who should arrive but her Father and her Husband. She told them about it, changed the Slave into a White-Breasted Crow, and lived happily.

———

60

THE GOOD KISHIA AND THE LUCKY BOY.

Once there was a certain Boy who lived with his Mother and her Rival Wife, the Kishia. And when he began to grow up, his Playmates, when they mounted their Horses and passed through the town, used to say "O Playmate, if your Mother is not displeased with you, let her buy you a Horse "(1). They were always saying this to him, and at last the Kishia said " Are you not going to buy your Son a Horse? " And the Mother replied " Would you like to do so, I have not a cowrie to spare." So the Kishia bought him a Horse, and the robes [proper for a Rider].

After that, whenever his Playmates mounted their Horses, he got his, and they used to go out riding together. This went on until the Boy reached marriage-able age, and the Kishia arranged a marriage for him (2). And when she had done this, she said to him " Go, wherever you wish to go, if you can go, go." So he said " I obey."

Now the King of the city summoned him, and said " While on your travels, if you go to the city with which we are now at war, bring back for me the King's spear." And the Boy said " I will."

So off he started with his Wife, and went straight to the city with which they were at war, and outside the walls they met the King's Daughter, and he said to her " Let us return to the city " (3). When they had entered, she took them to a lodging, a fine hut. Then he said to her " Now I have one favour to ask you, and that is that you will take me to where I can obtain a spear." " Opp, that is a simple matter," she replied, and she took him to a house where there were three huts, the first full of swords, the second full of spears, the third full of other weapons. Then she said " Here is the house of spears, choose any one that you like." So he said " Good," and he chose that of the King. Then he said " I have done so, will you return with me ? " And she answered " Um."

So they left the city, and after a time they came to a great river, and the river was full. But the other Girl could swim, for she was the Daughter of the King of the River (4), and she went and called, and canoes appeared. So they took up their bundles, and went to their own city, and the Boy went to his King and gave him the spear. Then the King divided the city into two, and gave half to the Boy to rule over, and he gave him Slaves, and Horses also. The Boy married the Girl from the other city also (5), and he and his Wives ruled the world.

———

In a variant (L.T.H. 25), the Youth was sent by a jealous Master to recover a spear with which he had wounded the hostile King during a war, leaving the spear in the wound. The King had died, and the Daughter ruled the city, so the Youth made love to her. He put scent instead of oil in his lamp, he gave his horse kola-nuts instead of grass to eat, and he tied him up with an expensive turban instead of a cheap rope. This so overcame the Lady that she gave him the spear, and went off with him, as in the above, but the Towns-People pursued them, and when stopped by the river they did not know what to do. Just then the Daughter of the King of the River came up, and said " Hullo, Servant-of the-Son-of the-King-of the-City-of-Us (6), what are you doing here ? " He replied " Look, do you see that crowd of Horsemen ? They are coming after me and this Woman. They want to catch me, and I do not know what to do ? " The Daughter of the King of the River exclaimed " Opp, is it because of that; is that all ? " And she took a piece of gravel, and threw it into the river, and immediately the waters divided, and he and the Woman crossed. As soon as they had gone over the waters returned, and joined together again; and so the fugitives made good their escape.

61

THE DETERMINED GIRL AND THE WICKED PARENTS.

This is about a Girl named Faddam. Now it happened that a certain Man wanted to marry her, and she loved him too, but her Parents did not like him, and her Parents' Relatives did not like him, and so they refused to give her to him. But one day, she scooped up the whole of the water of the town stream in a gourd (1), and climbed a tree, and thus everyone in the town was without water to drink. Soon People came to ask the Girl to give them water. "Who is asking?" she said. "It is your Mother," was the reply, and so she said "Oh! No, I shall not give *you* any."

This went on until People began to die, so the Parents were again sent to the Girl, and when they had come, they said "Give us water to drink lest the whole town die." "If I give you water to drink, will you give me Musa in marriage?" she asked, and they replied "Yes." Then she descended, and opened her gourd, and immediately the water flowed all over the town.

So she was married, and in due course she gave birth to a Child, a male. Now when she had brought forth her Son, she left him in the house, and her Parents came and suffocated the Child, and killed it. So when

the Girl returned she saw this, and told her Husband,
and he said " Very well, we shall be avenged." The
Parents were summoned to attend the funeral rites,
but the Husband dug a well, and hid the mouth with a
mat (2), and when the Parents had come, he made them
sit on the mat, and so they fell into the well, and were
killed.

_____

In a variant (M. 6), the well is first filled with
burning logs.

_____

62

THE WICKED GIRL AND HER PUNISHMENT.

There was once a certain Girl who loved a Youth,
but her Parents said that they would not give her to
him in marriage. He was always coming and begging
them to let him marry her, but they would say " We
shall not give her to you."

Now, one day the Girl came to him, and said " I
have come to you to ask you to give me your knife
so that I may go and kill my Mother, then we can
run away to some other town, and get married." But
he said " No, no, we must not do that." Again she
came and said " Give me your knife, that I may go and
kill my Mother." But again he replied " No, no, you
must not kill your Mother because of me," and he
continued " Go home and stay there. Those who can
give your Parents presents can give you some also " (1).

Five days passed, and then the Girl asked
" Will you give me your knife to cut pumpkins ? "
Now the Boy forgot, and he pulled out his knife (2) and
gave it to her, and immediately on receiving it, she

went and cut her Mother's throat. Then she ran to
the Youth, and said "Now, you see I have done it;
if we do not flee, you and I will be killed. Look at
the blood on your knife (3), I have cut my Mother's
throat with it." So they started off, the Youth took
a bow and arrows, sent the Girl in front of him, and
they escaped from the city.

They pressed on and on towards the forest; they
slept that night, and next morning they pushed on again
until, when they had reached the centre of the forest,
the Girl was seized with an internal pain, and she fell
down and died. Then the Youth drew out one of his
arrows and fitted it to the bow and stood and guarded
her body.

Soon the Beasts of the forest all assembled to eat
her, but he would not allow them to do so, but said
that nothing should touch her unless he should first
be killed. Then the Eagle came, and alighted in front
of the Youth, and said "Let us feast." But he said
"No, no, did I not promise that I should not leave her?
Shall I allow you to eat her body?" The Eagle replied
"Do not put your trust in Women, they are not
truthful." But the Youth said "I do not agree, I
trust this one." Then the Eagle said "Have you a
flask?" (4). And he said "I have." The Eagle said
"Give me it," and he took it, and flew off. But
soon he returned with water in the flask, and said
"Have you a knife?" And the Youth said "Yes."
Then the Eagle said "Separate her teeth," and he
plucked out two feathers from his wings, and stirred
them around in the water. So the Girl's mouth was
opened, the water was poured in, and immediately the
Girl rose up. Then the Eagle said to the Youth "See
these feathers, keep them, some day when you have

gone to another city, and have obtained something to eat, you will repay us for our feast which we have lost to-day."

So the Youth and the Girl went off again, and reached a city, and came to the house of an Old Woman, which they entered, and they remained there until the afternoon, they even slept there. Next morning they heard weeping, and they were told that the King's Mother had died. Then the Youth arose, and said " Let me go and see what can be done." So he started off and came to where the death had taken place, and when he had come, he went up to a Man and said " Can you obtain for me an interview with the King?" " The King's heart is broken," he replied " is anyone going to bother him now?" But another said " Here, do you know what his business is? Go and ask the King indeed." And the King when he had heard, said " Tell the Youth to come." So he was summoned, and he came, and said " If I bring your Mother back to life, what will you give me?" Then one of the Attendants said " Have you ever seen any-one who has died come back to life?" But the King said " Leave him alone, perhaps he has some magic "; and he continued, addressing the Youth, " I will give you ten Slaves." He said " See, this house also will I give you, and these Horses." So the Youth said " Very well, bring me water in a flask," and water was obtained and brought to him. Then he walked around to the back of the house, and stirred the Eagle's feathers in the water, and brought it back, and said " Now open the King's Mother's mouth." Imme-diately after the water had been poured down her throat, she rose up, and remained alive, so the Youth's presents were brought and given to him. Then he returned to his house, and remained in the town, and whenever anyone died, someone would come and summon him to give the Dead Person the charm so as to bring him back to life again.

Now after a time, one of the King's Slaves made the Girl fall in love with him, and he said "Look here, Girl, since we know each other so well, will you not give me your Husband's charm?" And she said "Very well." So when she went to bed and her Husband talked, she remained silent; when he asked her anything she did not reply. Then her Husband said "What is the matter with you?" And she replied "Well, we have been together for some time now, but you have got something which you are keeping secret from me; you are always hiding it." Then he said "Is it only that which has made you so quiet? Well, here it is; keep it for me." So he gave the Girl the Eagle's feathers. No sooner had she received them than she took a water-pot, and said that she was going to the river for water. But instead of doing so, she went and gave the feathers to the King's Slave, who took them to his house.

Soon afterwards, another death took place in the King's Family, and the Youth was summoned as usual, so he came and said to his Wife "Where is the thing which I gave you to keep for me?" And she replied "It is here somewhere, I put it just here." They looked but did not find it; they looked again but did not find it. But the King's Slave went, and said to the King "If I make him rise up again, how much will you give me?" The King replied "Everything that you want I will give you." So he said "Very well," and he made the Dead Man rise up. When he had done this, the

King's Slave asked that the Youth should be seized and given to him for a Slave, and the King said " Very well, go and seize him." So he went and caught him, and took his Wife for himself. The King's Slave bound the Youth, and put handcuffs on him, and took him to the forest, and made him clear the ground.

Some time afterwards, the Eagle came to where he was, and said " Where is that which you promised me ? I told you that the Woman was not faithful, but you said that she was. Now let me do you another good turn. To-night, hold your leg-irons up to your thighs (5), and go into the city and find me a Cat." So he went and found a Cat, and he returned and hid the Cat until daybreak. Then the Eagle came again, and said " The reason why we sought you, O Cat, is that we want you to get us a Mouse." So the Cat said ." Very well," and immediately she ran in where the Youth had been cutting wood, and caught a Mouse. Then the Eagle said " O Cat, and you, O Mouse, you know the smell of my feathers. Take the road, go into the city, and enter the house of the King's Slave, and if the Mouse sees any feathers, you, O Cat, take them, and bring them here."

So they went to the city, and entered the King's Slave's house. The Mouse looked everywhere, in the pots, in the quiver (6), but did not see them, and he went outside to the Cat, and said " I cannot see them." Then the Cat said " Return, go and look again "; and the Cat entered and cried out " Miyau." Then the Sleepers said " Thank God, she will catch that Mouse for us which has been preventing our sleeping." So they went to sleep, both the King's Slave and his Wife. Then the Mouse came and sniffed at the Slave's mouth, and saw where the feathers were,

so he said to the Cat " Here they are ; I see them."
" Where do you see them ? " asked the Cat. The
Mouse replied " In his mouth." Then she said " Very
well, go and bite him," so the Mouse went and bit him,
and he went " Poof," the feathers fell out, and the Cat
caught them, and took them to the Youth in the forest.
Next morning, the Eagle came again, and said " Where
are they ? " and the Youth replied " See them." Then
the Eagle said " Good, but let me have another
understanding. Some day you must pay me back for
my feast which I gave up."

Now it happened that next day another of the King's
Sons became ill, and died, and the King's Slave was
sent for and told to work his magic. But he said that
he had lost his charm. Then the King said " Summon
the other one to come. Here is a Horse, go quickly
and bring the one who is in the forest." He was sent
for quickly, and was brought, and when he had come,
the King said " See, we have summoned you. May
God cause your power to return to you." " How
can one who lives out in the forest obtain magic ? "
asked the Youth. But the King said " For God's
sake, help us." Then the Youth said " Very well, but
what will you give me ? " The King replied " Everything that is in the Slave's house I will give you."
Then the Youth prepared his charm, and raised up the
Dead Man, and the King said " Go and seize the
Slave." So the Youth went and caught the Slave and
his Wife ; he undid his own handcuffs, and put them on
the Slave, he took another pair and put them on the
Wife, and then he took them to the place where he
had been cutting wood, and said that they were to stack
it all in one place. Then he sent to the Eagle telling
him to come ; and when he had arrived, the Youth said

" Go, assemble all your Relatives, to-morrow we shall meet at the clearing."

Next morning the Eagles collected; all the Birds assembled, and all the Beasts of the forest also came. And when all had arrived, the Youth said " Now set fire to the pile." So they set fire to it; the fire consumed all the wood, and left a great mass of embers. Then he said to the Slave and his Wife " Get up and fall into the fire." But they refused, so he told his Attendants to get up and drag them in, and they threw them into the fire. Every time that they got out, they were thrown in again, and at last they were cooked. Then the Youth told the Attendants to pull the bodies out of the fire, and caused them to be put out in the open. Then he said " Eagle ! " And the Bird replied " Um ! " " Now see, here is your feast," the Youth said, and then he mounted his Horse, and returned to the city.

It is certainly true that Women are not to be trusted.

———

This and Story 29 are very widespread tales, for " in the Punjaub, among the Bretons, the Albanians, the modern Greeks and the Russians we find a *conte* in which a young man gets possession of a magical ring. The ring is stolen from him, and recovered by the aid of certain grateful beasts, whom the young man has benefited. His foe keeps the ring in his mouth, but the grateful mouse, insinuating his tail into the nose of the thief, makes him sneeze, and out comes the magical ring !" (A. Lang, *Myth, Ritual and Religion,* ii, page 315).

———

There are European stories in which a faithful husband defends his wife's body and succeeds in compelling her restoration to life. Afterwards she is unfaithful and procures his death by her lover; but he is restored to life and avenged on her. See Hapgood, *Epic Songs of Russia,* New York (1885), 217; Pitrè, vii,

Biblioteca, 5; Sébillot, iii, *Contes Pop. de la Haute Bretagne* (Paris, 1882), 32. In an Annamite story the wife is punished by being changed into a mosquito. Landes, *Contes et Légendes Annamites* (Saigon, 1886), 207. (H.)

63

THE TWO HALF-BROTHERS AND THE WICKED MOTHER.

This is about two Women, both Wives of the same Man. After a time their Husband died, and, as it

FIG. 78.—Violin (one string) and bow. L., 26½ in.

happened, he left them both with Child, so in due course the Women gave birth. Both brought forth Sons, and the Sons were exactly alike; they were as Twins—neither Mother could distinguish her Son.

After a time, when the Boys were growing up, the Mother of the rich Boy died (1), and the possessions

descended to her Son. Then the other Wife wondered
what she could do to kill the Son and get the property
(2).

So she went to a Magician, and when she had come,
she said " O Magician, what shall I do to kill the
Boy?" He replied "On your return, tell the Boy
to go to the forest with you; when you have gone,
tell him to climb a tree; and when he has climbed up,
seize him, and gouge out his eyes; then go home."
When she had returned, she said to the Boy " Come,
let us go to the forest." So they went, and when they
had gone, she said " Now, climb up." But when the
Boy had put his feet against the tree to climb, she
seized him, and gouged out his eyes, and returned to
her house alone (3).

Then the other Boy, his Half-Brother, said " Where
is my Brother?" And she replied " Oh, Goodness!
I have left him behind." So he was silent. Then she
prepared the evening meal for her own Son, but he
refused to eat, and as he refused to eat, she said
" What is the matter with you?" But the Boy refused
to talk. Soon afterwards the Boy went to search for his
Brother in the forest. And he went on, and on, calling
as he went, until at last he came upon his Brother in a
hole. So he pulled him out, and cried, and put mud
on his eyes, and gave him water to drink. And it
came to pass that God made the Boy see.

Now they lived there in the forest, and after a
time they built a town and became its Rulers (4). And
when the Mother heard the news that her Sons had
become rich, she said " Good," and she went to where
the Boys were, and saluted them, and they responded.
Then One, her own Son, said " What does One do to
his Enemy?" and the Counsellors replied " She

should be killed." Then the Son took a sword, and cut down his Mother.

In another story (L.T.H. ii, 31), a Girl is badly used, and is rescued from Hyænas by her Step-Mother after her real Mother has refused to aid her. She goes to another city, and marries the King, but returns on hearing that the Step-Mother is dead. She finds that the news is false, and she is overjoyed and gives her presents, she also makes gifts to her real Parents, but she will not stay in their city.

64

THE ORIGIN OF THE WHITE-BREASTED CROW.

A certain King was always saying to his Son that he was not his own Son, although the Son was exactly like him, and one day the King said "Let him be taken outside the town and killed, he is a Bastard." Now the Boy had for his Friend the Son of the Minister (1), and when the People of the city had gone to the forest, [he persuaded them to let the Son live, and] they cut off one of his hands, and showed it to the King, and said that they had killed him.

Soon afterwards a Female Leper came along, and found the Boy lying down, and she said "Who is this Son of Adam?" Then she returned home, and drew some water, and fetched it, and when she had washed the stump of the hand which had been cut off, she licked it, and it became as before. Then she sent him in front (2), and they went home. He grew in knowledge and in strength and, when he had become old enough to have a house of his own (3), she made one for him to live in, and he married the Daughter of the Ant. Then

he found some Traders, and got them to go to his
Father, and to say " See, he has married the Ant's
Daughter." But the Father sent to him, and said that
it was not the Ant's Daughter, but the Daughter of
the King of the Thicket whom he should have married.

Then he began to cry, and cry, until the Leper came
to him, and questioned him, and said " What has
happened to you ? " He replied " My Father says that
I must marry the Daughter of the King of the Thicket."
" Is that all that has happened to make you cry ? " she
asked, and then she took some money (4) and went to
the thicket to arrange the marriage, and she brought
back a Wife. Then he sent to his Father, and said
lo ! he had married the Daughter of the King of the
Thicket also. But the Father replied " It is not the
Daughter of the King of the Thicket whom he should
have married, but the Daughter of the King of the
Water."

Then the Boy began to cry, so the Leper said " Son-
of-the-Master-of-the-house-of-us (5), whatever troubles
you, tell me." When he had done so, she went into the
water and found the King of the Water, and said " I
have come to visit you, for I hear that you had some
Daughters, and I want one, I have a Son." Then he
called his Daughters together, and said " Choose the
one who seems best to you." So she chose one, and
they went home together, and she married them. So he
went and sent to his Father, and said that he had
married the Daughter of the King of the Water. But
the Father replied " It should not have been the
Daughter of the King of the Water, but the Daughter
of the King of the Heavens."

Then the Boy commenced crying again, and he kept
on crying until the Leper came, and said " What has he

done to you?" He replied "My Father says that I must marry the Daughter of the King of the Heavens." "Who will take me up there?" she exclaimed. But the Wild-Cat said "Catch hold of my tail, and I will take you to the Heavens." So she ascended, and found the King of the Heavens, and said "I have come to see you, for I have a Son, and I have heard that you have marriageable Daughters." Then he assembled them, and said "Come and choose." Now they were quite fifty in number, and she took the eldest, the Heiress of the House, and the King said "Count out your money and take her." So they came to the Leper's house, and the Boy and Girl were married. Then the Boy sent the news to his Father, but he replied that it should not have been the Daughter of the King of the Heavens, but the Daughter of the King of Agaddez."

Again he began crying, and the Leper came and questioned him, and then she went to the King of Agaddez, and said "I have a Son at home, give me your Daughter for him." But he said "I shall not give you the Girl until I have seen your Son." So she went out and brought the Son, and the King of Agaddez said "Very well, put them in a strong hut for a fortnight, and if during that time he does not eat any corn he shall be her Husband." So they entered the room, and the door was shut on them, and locked. Now every night the Boy's Mother (6) used to bring him food and drinking water, but the Girl did not know, for she used to enter softly, and rouse him, and when he had eaten she would take away the calabash.

They had reached the last day of their confinement (7) when the Girl said "I notice the smell of corn!" "Where could I get it?" he asked, "it is kola-nut."

[But she did not believe him, and] when evening came, she said " To-night I shall lie in front, and closer to the door." So when the Leper entered, she roused the Girl, thinking that it was her Son. Then the Girl got up, and plunged her hand into the soup, and she flicked her hand against the wall—she did not see the Leper—and said to the Boy " You are eating corn." " Where could I get any in this town ? " he asked, for he did not know that the Leper had roused her. She replied " To-morrow you shall die, you shall be killed." Then he said " Oh, all right, kill me, but where could I get any, O, Gimbia ? "

They went to sleep again, but the Leper [who had heard the conversation] went over to the other side of the hut, and roused her Son, and he ate the food. Then she returned to her house, and ground up some kola-nuts, and she took a lot of water (8), and brought it back, and caught hold of the Girl's hand, and poured kola-water on it, and she washed the Boy's hands. Then she went to the wall where the Girl had flicked the soup, and poured kola-water there also. When day broke the house was opened, for the Girl was calling out " He has eaten corn, open the door." But when the hut had been opened, much kola-water was found on the wall, and the People rejoiced. And when the Girl had seen it, she said that, as after all it was not corn but kola, he was to be her Husband. So he took her, and they went to their house, and he sent the news to his Father.

Now when the Father heard, he remained silent, but he made an alliance with the Pagans, and they came and surrounded the city. The Son was inside the house when he saw that the Pagans had surrounded the city, so he arose, and found the Ant's Daughter, and

said " See, my Father has come to make war on me."
" Had you not better go to the Daughter of the King
of the Thicket ? " she asked. So he went to the
Daughter of the King of the Thicket, and said " See,
my Father has come to make war on me, and I do not
know what I shall do." But she said " Will you not
go to the Daughter of the King of the Heavens ? "
So he went, and knelt (9), and said " What shall I
do now, see my Father has come to make war." " Is
it your Father who gave you being ? " she asked, and he
replied " Yes." Then she said " Go to the Daughter
of the King of Agaddez, will you not ? " So he arose,
and went (10). The Daughter of the King of Agaddez
was sitting on a chair, and he said " Gimbia, may your
life be prolonged," and he continued " See, my Father
has come to make war on me, he has allied himself with
the Pagans." Then she flicked the perspiration from
her brow, and said " Let them be annihilated, the useless Pagans " (11). " But not my Father and the Son
of the Minister " he exclaimed (12).

Immediately all the Pagans fell dead, and the Son
went and brought his Father and his Friend into the
city. Then he brought a tobe, a cap, and a turban,
and he saluted his Father, and gave him them ; and
he gave some to his Friend also, a tobe, a cap, and
everything. Then he took his Father to the door of
the council-chamber, and he drew his sword, and
questioned the People, saying " If a man hates you,
what is to be done with him ? " They replied " He
should be killed." So he took his sword, and cut off
the head of his Father, and the turban fell off, and rolled
itself around the neck (13). Then it rose up in the air,
and became a White-Breasted Crow, and called " Da !
da ! da !" (14).

In a similar story (F.-L. 36) a Malam supplies the Youth with ground-nuts, and the Girl finds one, and puts it in a tin in the pocket of her under-cloth, and wraps seven other cloths outside. During the night the Malam invokes the aid of a Cat—which makes the Girl sleep soundly—and a *darra*-stone is substituted for the ground-nut, so the Youth escapes.

65

The Brave Mother and the Cowardly Father.

A Certain Boy, the Only Son of his Mother, came home one day and died, and so the Father wandered about everywhere seeking charms to raise him up again. At last a certain Magician summoned him, saying " Come here, I have a charm," and the Magician said " Go to the market of the Filani Slaves who bring wood, and buy 100 bundles."

So the Father went, and bought 100 bundles of wood, and all were brought to one place, and made into a stack as big as a house. And People came, and set fire to the pile, and the fire burnt up, and died down, and nothing but the red-hot embers were left. Then the Boy's Father was told that if he took off his clothes, and threw himself into the fire, his Son would come to life again. So the Father said that he would throw himself into the fire, and he came up at a run; but when he felt the heat, he turned, and went round the fire [instead of through it]. Then he said " O Magician, may this be tried a second time? " And the Magician replied " It may be attempted twice." So the Father again came up at a run, but again he felt the heat, and went round the fire.

Then the Boy's Mother became angry, and said

"O Magician, may a Woman try it ?" And the Magician
said " She may " (1). So the Mother retired a little
way, and ran up with a rush, and when she had come
up, she jumped, and fell into the fire head first. Immediately the fire turned into a house of gold, but the
Boy's Father became a Jerboa. Then the Son came to
life, and the People said to him " Your Father has been
changed into a Jerboa," and they continued " If you
kill him, you will live with your Mother, if you do not
kill him your Mother will die." So the Son caught the
Jerboa, and killed him, and lived with his Mother.

FIG. 79.—Guitar. L., 22 in.

A variant (Harris, *Hausa Stories*, page 99) is to the
effect that a Boy had run off to the forest with a Girl,
but that Iblis had killed him there. The Parents followed, and Iblis told the Mother that she must go
through various dangers to bring her Son to life, bu
she refused. The Girl, however, volunteered, and
she plunged into the river of fire and swam through
it, she plunged into the river of water and swan
through it, she reached the rubber-tree, and entere
the hollow in it. She seized the Snake and put it out
side, and then she seized the Lizard (which give
leprosy) and brought it to Iblis, and said " Here it is

O Father." The Boy came to life, and had to decide which Iblis would put to death, his Sweetheart or his Mother.

66

THE FIGHTING RAM.

It happened once that some Filani left their district, and went off with their Cattle, but forgot a certain She-Goat which was with Young, and soon afterwards she lay down at the foot of a tree and gave birth to a Ram (1). The Ram wandered about and fed, and would go perhaps as far as Jagindi (2) for pasture, and return to his Mother in one day; he would go even as far as Keffi (3) for pasture, and return to his Mother in one day.

Now, one day, the Spider was passing, and saw the She-Goat, and he went and told the King, saying that he had seen something worth seeing—that could not be brought to the palace, but only to the Spider's house. Then the King said whatever went to the Spider's house was destroyed. So the Spider said to send him with some Men, ten Men, to go and bring him the Thing.

So they went, and found the She-Goat, the Parent, and they tied a rope to her. Then she began bleating and saying "Mé, mé-é-e. Son of Zaberrima, I am being taken away (4) to be killed, killed by the Townspeople." Now the Ram heard from where he was, far away, and said "I have overcome the Buffalo, I have beaten the Elephant, I will gore with my horns." And on his arrival—the Spider had not waited, he had only come to show where the She-Goat was—the Ram killed every one of the Men, and then he took his Mother, and led her back to the tree.

Now the Spider went, and told the King that those Men were Weaklings, and said to send him with a hundred Horsemen. So off they went and seized the She-Goat, and started to drag her along. Then she began bleating, and saying "*Mé, mé-é-é*, Son of Zaberrima, I am being taken away to be killed, killed by the Townspeople, come quickly." Now the Ram heard from where he was, far away, and said " I have destroyed Men with my horns, I have gored with my horns, I have overcome the Buffalo, I have beaten the Elephant." And then he came, and killed every one of the Horsemen.

Then the Spider went off again, and said to the King " Those men were not strong," and asked that he should be sent with two hundred Horsemen. So he was sent with them, and he went and showed them the She-Goat, and then he returned, and when he had gone they began dragging her along. Then the She-Goat began bleating, and saying " *Mé, mé-é-é*, Son of Zaberrima, I am being taken away to be killed, killed by the Townspeople, come quickly." Now the Ram heard from where he was, far away, and said " I have killed Horsemen, I have destroyed Men with my horns, I have gored with my horns, I have overcome the Buffalo, I have beaten the Elephant." Then he came, and on his arrival he gored all the Men, and killed them.

Once again the Spider went to the King, and it seemed as if all the Townspeople would be killed off (5), when a certain Man said " Let three Cats be bought," and he went and bought them himself. Then he asked that he should be sent with two Men, and he was sent with them, and he went and tied a rope to the She-Goat, and began dragging her off. As he dragged, she began bleating, and saying " *Mé, mé-é-é*, Son of Zaberrima, I am being taken away to be killed, killed by the Townspeople, come quickly." Now the Ram heard from where he was, far away, and said " I wear a collar of hair, I am the Son of Zaberrima, I have killed Horsemen, I have destroyed men with my horns, I have gored with my horns, I have overcome the Buffalo, I have beaten the Elephant." On his arrival—the Draught which he made had killed all the Men previously—the Man took a Cat, and threw it into the Wind, and the Wind caught it up and took it to the Ram, and the Ram stopped to eat it. Then again he came on, and again the Man took a Cat, and threw it into the Wind, and the Wind caught it up and took it to the Ram, and the Ram stopped to eat it. Then once more he came on, and once more the Man took a Cat, and threw it into the Wind, and the Wind caught it up and took it to the Ram, and the Ram stopped to eat it. And by this time the Men had dragged the She-Goat along, and had brought her to the King.

When the Ram had finished eating the Cats, he followed the tracks of his Mother, his Mother which had been tied up in the King's palace. And the Ram on his arrival pushed down the wall, and entered the palace, but they shot him with arrows, and he died, and his Mother was killed.

The People had meat.

————

In a variant (L.T.H. 156) the Hare is the Villain, the Mother is a Sheep. The Ram calls himself Zanzabariya and has Birds which are his servants and beat the Men with their wings, the wind helping. In this story some contestants are killed on both sides in the fights, and at last the Ram dies; there is no mention of any Cats. The Sheep is taken to the King's palace and mated with an old Ram, and "they are still having issue."

There is a story told by the Mbamba of Angola in which a cannibal husband is similarly delayed by his fugitive wife, who flings down first millet, then sesamum and lastly eleusine. Chatelain, *Folk Tales of Angola* (Boston, 1894), 99. (H.).

67

The Lucky Foundling.

There was once a Man of Auzen (1), and ever since he had been born he had never had a Child, and the Townspeople used to mock him. So he told his Wife that he was going to get a Son from a certain city, and she said " Let us go by all means," and he said " Very well." Now as they were travelling along, they came upon a Boy lying in the road, his mouth was full of ants (2) and dirt, perhaps something had killed him, they did not know. So they lifted him up, and bathed him, and took the ants out of his mouth. Then the Man of Auzen said " Good, let us go home, what we were seeking we have found " (3). So they returned.

Now when he had got home again, he said that the Boy was his, but his Fellow-Citizens said that the Boy was not his, that he had stolen him from some town; but he maintained that the Boy was his. Then they said " Very well, if he is really your Son, let us collect five Camels each, and give them to our Sons that they may take them to the forest and kill them." So the

Sons were given five Camels each, and they went and killed them, and returned.

Now, after this, some said that the Boy must be his Son, but others still maintained that he was not, and they said " If he is your Son let us collect our Horses, and give our Sons ten each that they may go and kill them." Then he exclaimed " Poof, that is nothing," and when the others had given their Sons ten each, he gave his Boy twenty, and put on gorgeous caparisons, and said " When you have gone, and have killed them, do not bother to bring back even the saddles." So the Boy said " Very well," and he mounted one of the Horses, and when the others had killed their Horses they brought back the saddles, but he did not bring even one, he left them all there.

Now after this, more People said that the Boy was his Son, but others still maintained that he was not, and they said " If the Boy is his, let him and our Sons go to the far city where there is a Beautiful Maiden, and seek her in marriage." Now this Maiden had no equal in beauty anywhere, even Kings came to woo her, but she refused them. Well, one day, about five of the Boys packed their bundles, and prepared to go off to woo the Maid. And as the Boy was about to start, his Father filled one pocket with silver, and another also, and he poured gold into his mouth, and silver also. So off they went to where the Maiden lived.

Each one tried, but wooed in vain; the first came and asked her and she refused; the next tried but she would not have him; the whole five of them tried to persuade her, but she would not listen to them; and there was only the Boy himself left. Then he came. Now before, the Maiden would not answer a word, but when he came she smiled, and when she smiled he said

" Praise be to God," and he poured out the silver from his mouth (4). Then she said " What, all silver, have you no gold ? " He opened another pocket and poured it out in front of her, and then she clasped him in her arms, and said that he would be her Husband.

Then the Boy returned home, and the People said " Of a truth the Boy is his Son." And the Boy told his Father about the Maiden, so a house was built for him, and the Maiden was brought. Then the Father gave Them twenty Slaves, and Horses, and Camels, and the Maiden the same.

This and the next are common, many variants exist, but with such slight differences that it seems unnecessary to give them.

68

THE WICKED FATHER AND THE KIND STRANGER.

A certain Man had a Son. Now he was very poor, and lived on Jerboas, and whenever he heard that there was a Jerboa which no one could catch, he would go and capture it straight off. One day he was out catching Jerboas, as usual, with his Son, and they came and dug out one ; but the Jerboa jumped up with a " buroop " and escaped. Then the Hunter said " Alas for me, I who can beat anyone at catching Jerboas have allowed one to escape ! I am disgraced !" Then [mad with rage], he hit his Son with a club, and the Son fell down with blood pouring from his nose, but the Father went away and left him lying there.

Soon afterwards, a certain Rich Man came along ; who had riches beyond avarice, but no Son. And he came close and lifted up the wounded Boy, and washed him with warm water, and he adopted him as his Son. The Rich Man brought a Horse and gave it to him, and he mounted it; he brought a tobe, and gave it to him, and trousers. Then he took him to his own city, and said to the King "See, I have been on a journey, and while on my travels I got a Son." The King said that he was lying, that it was not his Son. And he continued that if the Boy were his own Son let him give the Boy a Horse a day for ten days, and he, the King, would do the same with his Son, that they might race. And that when they had raced, they should unsheath their swords, and that each should kill his Horse for ten days running. That would mean ten Horses each. The Rich Man agreed, and when they had done thus, the King said " He certainly is your Son." Then the King brought his Daughter, and said " Give her to him, and let them marry." The Deputy-King also brought his Daughter, and said " Give her to him, and let them marry." Then the Boy was given a turban, and so became a Man.

Now it came to pass that the real Father, the one who had hit him with the club, heard the news of his Son, and so he came to him; and he wore a Jerboa skin in front, and a Jerboa skin behind. When he had come, he blessed the house, and asked the Rich Man to give him back his Son. But the Rich Man said " I ask you to leave me in peace, and, if you will do so, I will give you ten Slaves, ten Horses, ten Bulls, and ten Mules." He said " I will give you all these, but the fact that your Son *is* your Son you must conceal, for I have lied to the King in saying that I got a Son when on my travels. Take these gifts, and go to your own town. Whenever your Son wishes to see

you he shall come to you, for I will not take him from
you by force, and I will not sell him." But he said that
he would not agree, he, the Father, the wearer of the
Jerboa skins, and he went and let out the secret.

He went with his club to where a feast was being
held, and poked his Son, saying " Throw away that
turban, and come and eat Jerboa." Then the Rich Man
drew his sword, and put it into the Boy's hand, and
said " Now to-day I am disgraced before the whole city;
I have said that you were really my Son, and see, your
Father has come, and he says that he will take you
away." And he continued " As for me, I do not value
life now; take the sword, and kill either me or else your
Father." Then the boy cut down his real Father, and
they went back into the city (1), the Rich Man and the
Boy.

Now, for the sake of argument, do you think the
Boy did right or wrong?

69

THE WOMAN WHO COULD NOT KEEP A SECRET.

A certain Old Woman had never had a Child, but
one day a Boy came to her, and said that he liked her,
and would live with her, and that she could always
say that he was her Son. But he warned her never to
speak his name, which was " Owner-of-the-World,"
for from the day that she uttered it she would never
see him again.

Now when the other Boys of the town used to
mount their Horses, he also used to go riding, and they
called him " Son-of-the-Old-Woman." But another Old
Woman went to her, and questioned her, and said

" What is the name of your Son ? "   At first she re-
plied " I will not tell you his name," but the other
said for God's sake to tell her, so she did so, she said
" His name is ' Owner-of-the-World.' "   When the
Son was returning he was passing at a gallop, but the
other Old Woman called out " Hullo ! Owner-of-the-
World."   Then the Boy turned back and abused his
adopted Mother, and said that God would not bless her.
Then he began crying, and said that his name was
Owner-of-the-World, but that she would die in ashes.
He sang—

> " My name is Owner-of-the-World
>   I am going,
>   God may bring us together again,
>   I am going,
>   Good-bye until another day " (1).

While he was singing thus [he sank into the earth
so that] the sand in which he was standing was up to
his Horse's knees.   He continued to sing—

> " My name is Owner-of-the-World,
>   I am going,
>   God may bring us together again,
>   I am going,
>   Good-bye until another day."

And gradually the Horse was covered, and disappeared
into the earth.   The Boy still went on singing—

> " My name is Owner-of-the-World,
>   I am going,
>   God may bring us together again,
>   I am going,
>   Good-bye until another day."

and at last he also had disappeared.

So the Old Woman was left alone, she had no one to
care for her, and she died in the ashes (2).

In a variant (L.T.H. ii, 45), the Boy is not adopted, but is born in the Family, and no sooner is he born than he tells his Father and Mother that he must not be given a name nor must his head be shaved. They agree, and on the eighth day a Ram is killed, but the other ceremonies (see page 92) are omitted. After the departure of the Guests, he tells his Parents that his name is *Mamayad Duniya,* but that neither must mention it. He has four Wives, and becomes very rich, but one day the Mother tells a Friend his name, as in this story, and he sinks into the earth in sight of his Wives. They rush to save him, and disappear also, as do the Horse-holders. The Father kills the Mother and her Friend with a pestle, and then falls dead himself.

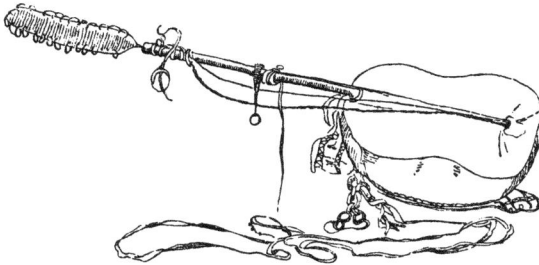

FIG. 80.—Long guitar with iron rattle. Total length, 53 in.

70

THE BOY WHO REFUSED TO WALK.

This story is about a Woman who had never given birth, and at last she said " O God, wilt Thou not give me even a Cripple or a Leper to bring forth ? " And lo ! God caused here to conceive, and she brought forth a Son, and called him Little Crab (1).

They lived on, and, even when the Boy had grown up, he refused to alight from his Mother's back and walk, and at last she said to herself " Whatever shall I do to the Boy to make him walk?" One day she went to a Magician, and, when she had arrived at his house, she said " O Magician, will you not give me a charm which will make the Boy walk about on the ground?" And he replied " I will, but first you must go and buy a Goat." When she had been, and had bought a Goat, he said " You must go into the depths of the forest," and he continued " When you have killed the Goat, say ' Boy, get down, so that I may go and get some wood to cook the meat for you,' and then the Boy will alight " (2). So she went into the midst of the forest, and killed the Goat, and said " Boy, get down, so that I may go and get some wood to cook the meat for you." Then the Boy alighted, and immediately the Mother ran away.

Soon after she had gone, the Hyæna came along, and exclaimed " O Boy, have you got some meat?" And he said " Yes," and he continued " but my meat is a reward for carrying me on the back." And he went on " If I give you this meat, and you eat it, will you carry me on your back?" " I will," replied the Hyæna; " Get up," and she ate up the meat. When the Hyæna had eaten the meat, she said " O Boy, get down, I wish to go away."* But the Boy replied " I refuse to do so unless you give me back the meat which you have eaten." Then she made as if she would bite him, but the Boy shifted to another spot, and she could not reach him, and so she had to go about carrying him.

When the Boy had been on her back for about ten days, the Hyæna went to the Magician, and said " O Magician, will you not give me a charm which will make the Boy get down?" And he replied " I will, you

XXIX.—Yams. XXX.—Sweetmeats!

Yams are somewhat rare in some parts of Northern Nigeria, but there are several varieties in others.
The sweetmeats may consist of any mess made of honey, or of squares of dried blood.

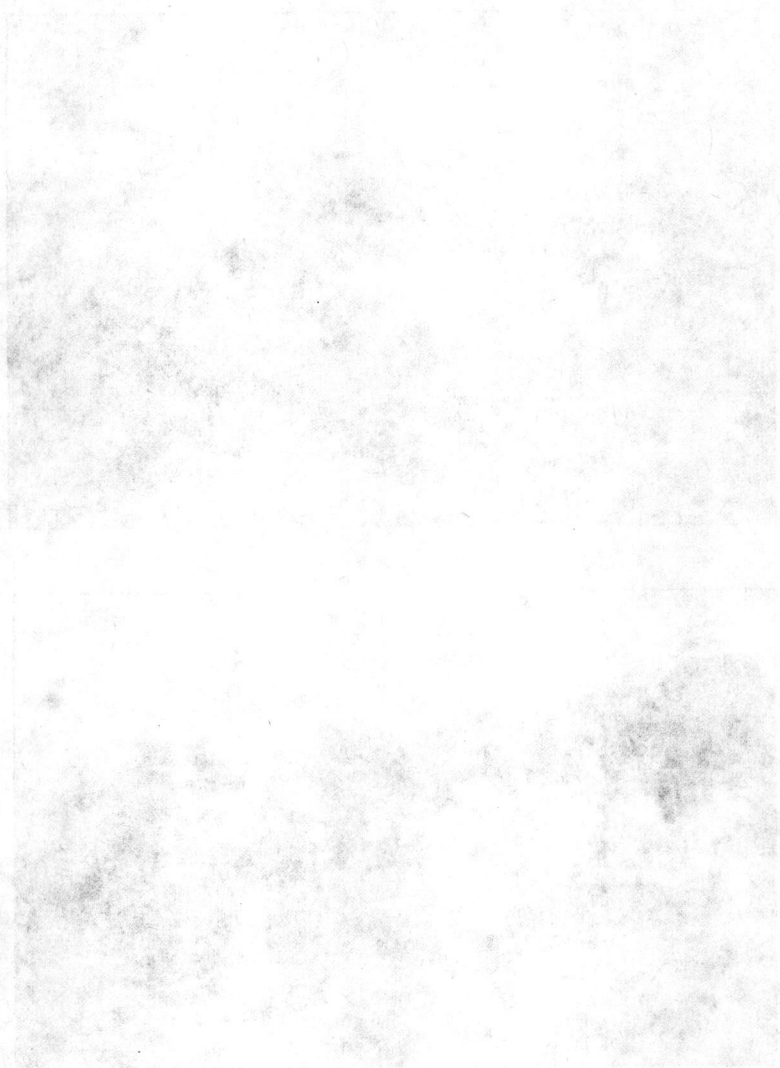

must go and buy a Goat, and take it to the forest, and kill it, and say ' O Boy, get down, so that I may go and get some wood.'' So the Hyæna said '' Very well,'' and she went to the forest, and killed the Goat. Then she said '' O Boy, get down so that I may go and get some wood for you,'' and he alighted; and immediately the Hyæna ran away. But after she had gone a little way, she returned to the place where the meat had been put, and climbed a tree, and she made a long hook (3), and drew up some of the meat, and ate it. Then she descended so as to get the remainder of the meat, but the Boy saw her, and he pulled the Hyæna towards him, but she escaped from his grasp, and ran away.

After a little while, the Spider came along, and when he saw the Boy and the meat, he said '' O Boy, will you not give me your meat?'' But the Boy replied '' My meat is a reward for carrying me on the back, if you will carry me on your back, you may eat it.'' '' Oh! It is a reward for carrying you on one's back!'' exclaimed the Spider. '' Indeed, carrying you on the back would not be difficult.'' Then the Boy said '' Very well, first take me on your back, and you may eat it.'' So the Spider lifted up the Boy, and put him on his back, and when he had done so, he ate up the meat. When he had finished it all, he said '' O Boy, get down,'' but the Boy refused. Then the Spider took the Boy to the Female-Spider's hut, and said to her '' Bring your stick, and beat this Boy.'' But when she had brought her stick, and had come up close to beat the Boy, he moved to one side, and she caught the Spider himself instead, and when she had hit him he fell down and died, and the Female-Spider ran away.

Then the Boy alighted from the Spider's body, and he went and threw himself into the water. Of old the

Boy was a Water-Dweller, so he merely returned to his home.

In a variant (L.T.H. ii, 22) the Hyæna has to fall down a well to escape—the Boy staying at the mouth to avoid being drowned—and after she has been in the water a month, he thinks that she must be dead, so he goes off. She is not, however, and she returns to her house, but the Boy hears of it, and gets in by a trick. The Hyæna dies of fright, and the Boy bursts open through laughing at her.

In a Sierra Leone story (Cronise and Ward, page 287) it is an Old Woman who gives the Spider a Sheep on condition that he carries her. The Spider lets her get on his back, and then finds that she can lengthen her limbs at will, and thus get such a grip that he cannot unseat her. However, by a trick, he manages to terrify her, and cause her to let go her hold, and then he escapes. Later on he returns to the place to find her dead, but the skull jumps upon his nose, and he has to carry it to the town, where it is removed by the Blacksmith.

71

THE WOMAN WHO BORE A CLAY POT.

There was once a certain Woman who had no Son, and she prayed to God saying " Let me have a Child, even though it be a clay pot." So God caused (1) her to conceive, and after nine months she brought forth a big clay pot which she took and placed among her crockery.

Now next morning, when the Mother had gone to the forest to look for firewood, the Son, who was in the pot, emerged, and also went to the forest to look for firewood. After a time he came upon the place where the Beasts of the forest had made a hedge, and he began cutting it. Then the Gazelle said " Hey, who is cutting this hedge? " for the Gazelle had been told off to watch the place until the other Beasts returned. The Boy said " Let me come in and you will see me," and, when he had entered it, he said " Here I am, I have come." " What is your name? " she asked. " The-Gift-of-God," he replied; and he continued " Will you not give me some water to drink? " So she brought him some, and he drank it, and then he said " Bring me some to bathe my head " (2). When he had been given it, he said " Get up, and let us wrestle." So he wrestled with the Gazelle, and threw her, and he plucked out her mane (3) and tied her up with it. Then he went and cut the wood, and took it home, and re-entered his clay pot.

In the late afternoon, the Beasts of the forest returned to their settlement, and when they saw what had happened, they said " O Gazelle, whatever have you been doing that you are tied up? " And she replied " A certain Boy came, and started cutting wood, and when I remonstrated we wrestled, and he bound me up." Then the Hyæna said " Oh, well, to-morrow 1 shall stay here, and keep guard."

Next morning the Boy came again and started to cut the wood, and the Hyæna said " Who are you? " He replied " It is I, who are you? " So the Hyæna said " Enter that I may see you." When the Boy had come into the cleared space [inside the hedge], he said " Give me water to drink." When she had given it to him, he said " Get me some that I may bathe my head," and when she had brought it, he said " Get up, and let us wrestle." Then the Hyæna thought " That

Boy has no sense, I am big and he is tiny." So she sprang upon him to seize him, but he caught her, and threw her on the ground, and he bound her, and left her, and went back to his clay pot. In the afternoon when the Beasts returned, they loosed the Hyæna, and said "Whatever have you been doing that you are bound thus?" And she replied "A certain Boy came and I wrestled with him, but he threw me on the ground, and bound me." Then the Elephant said "Oh! very well, to-morrow I myself shall stay and keep guard."

When the morning came the Boy arrived, and began cutting the trees *kop, kop, kop,* and the Elephant said "Who is that?" He replied "It is I," and he entered the clearing. Then he said to the Elephant "Give me water to drink," and, when she had given it to him, he said "Get me some that I may bathe my head," and when she had brought it, he said "Get up, and let us wrestle." And he threw the Elephant also, and bound her, and then he went home.

Now when the Beasts returned, they said "This is quite enough, since even the Elephant is conquered we must run away." So they began tying up their loads that afternoon in order that they might flee. But the Boy [who had guessed their intention], came by night to where they were, and got inside a jar of oil, and hid. When dawn came, the Beasts said "Now, let each take his load and escape, lest he come and catch us." So off they started, and they entered the depths of the forest, far, far away.

After a time the Hyæna began to lag behind, and she said to the others "You go on, I will catch you up later," and then she opened the jar to steal some oil. But the Boy dealt her a blow, and said "Lift it up, and go on." [She was so frightened that] she took it up again, and ran, and ran, until she had overtaken the others. [But she did not tell them, because by doing so she would have exposed her own evil intentions.]

So they went on, and came to the place which they were going to make habitable (4), and then they said " O Hyæna, come here and give us some oil." But she said " No no," for she was afraid of the Boy. They said " For Goodness' sake come and give it to us," but she still said " No." Then the Elephant grew angry, and seized the jar, and opened it, and at once the Boy dealt her a blow, *Pau*, and sprang out. As he did so, all the Animals ran away, and left their belongings behind, so he returned to the town and told the People, and they came and seized all the loads, and took them to his Mother.

After that he left the clay pot, and he never lived in it again.

In a Sierra Leone story (*Cunnie Rabbit*, page 55) a Girl wrestles with all the Animals who come to get fire, and, aided by the Mother who chants a spell, she beats all but the Snail, which has made the arena all slimy beforehand.

Mr. Crooke points out that the Rishi or Saint Agastya was produced, like a Fish, from a jar into which the seed of Adityas had fallen (Muir, *Original Sanskrit Texts*, part i, 1858, page 77).

72

THE WOMEN WHOSE OFFSPRING WERE A MOUSE AND A CAKE.

There was once a certain Man who had two Wives, one had given birth to a Mouse, and the other to a

Cake. The Cake was kept in a cooking-pot, the Mouse was put in a place of his own near the door.

Gradually they grew up, and at last they were taken to the gate of the town, and told to go out into the forest. When they had gone, the Mouse saw a lot of ripe *chiwo* (1) fruit above, and said that he would climb up, while the Cake collected the fruits for him on the ground. He also said that the Cake was to eat the black parts, and leave him the red, but the Cake ate the whole lot. When the Mouse descended, he said " O Cake, where is my fruit ? " And the Cake said " I have eaten it." Then the Mouse said " Now I am angry," and he said that he would nibble off a bit of the Cake, and eat it. The Cake said " Poof, nibble a bit then," so the Mouse did so, and ate it, but he left the rest.

Soon they started off again, and got some fire-wood, and the Mouse said to the Rest-of-the-Cake " Let us go and get some tie-tie." So they went and got some, and the Mouse said " Let me come and nibble a bit more," and the Rest-of-the-Cake said " Nibble a bit then." Then the Mouse ate up the Cake, and he took the firewood, and heaped it together, and tied it up, and went and put it down by his Mother's hut.

Now the Cake's Mother asked him where was her Offspring, and he said " The Cake is down by the river, bathing." But even when sunset came she had not seen the Cake, and she caught the Mouse, and pounded him up in the wooden mortar, and roasted him, and put him into the soup. Then she took one of the Mouse's legs, and put it on top of the dish of the Mouse's Mother (2). When the latter had been and had eaten her food, she came and said to the Cake's Mother " Where is my Off-spring ? " And the Other replied " What have you just eaten in your soup ? " Then they rushed at each other, and wrestled, and got nearer and nearer to the river.

Now the Spider saw them, and lit his fire, and no sooner had they come, still fighting, than he took one and put her on his fire, and then he took the other and put her on also. When they were cooked he ate them.

———

In F.-L. 21, the Dog starts on a journey with the Salt and the Cake. He kills the Salt by dissolving it in a river, but the Cake, by a trick, hands the Dog over to the Hyæna.

———

73

How the Beautiful Girl escaped the Dodo.

There was once a certain Girl, and in the whole city there could not be found her equal in beauty. Now her Parents would not allow her to go out of the house, for she was so pretty, and so before they went out they would give her *acha* and earth to soak (1), so that she would have to stay in.

But [one day when they had gone], her Friends came, and said that they wanted to take her to see the forest, and she said " I will come." When they had reached the middle of the forest, they said " Here, You, get down the well and hand us up water " (2). Yes, they told this Beautiful Girl to go down the well and hand them up water to drink—and the well was Dodo's well! So she said " Very well," [for she did not know this, although they did], and she went down the well, and handed up water to all, and they drank. Then she said " Now, help me out," but they all ran away [and left her there, for they were jealous of her].

Now about noon, Dodo came to drink water, and

he put down the bucket, but the Girl caught hold of it. When Dodo felt her holding the bucket, he called down "Whoever it is in the well, let go." Then the Girl replied "Let me get it for you." And when she had got it, he pulled the Girl out, and when he saw her, he said "Here is the water, take it, and carry it home for me (3), do not spill it." So she took it, and they went to Dodo's house.

Then Dodo said "Which would you like me to do, eat you or marry you?" And she said "Well, I should certainly prefer marriage." So he married her. And whenever he went to the forest, and killed a Human Being for his own food, he would kill for her some Wild Animal. He used to ambush People on the road, and kill them, and take their goods to her.

Now this went on until the Girl conceived, and she bore a Child half-Dodo, half-Man. Yes, she gave birth to this! And one day, Dodo, before going off to the forest, tied a bell to his Son's neck (4). When he had done this and had gone, the Girl mixed up some flour and water, and she squeezed it tight into the bell so that it would not sound (5), and she gathered up her belongings and ran away, and at last she reached her own home. Then she killed her Son, and when she had done this, she destroyed the belongings [which Dodo had given to her] (6).

———

In a variant (L.T.H. ii, 82) the Girl is pushed into the well, and Dodo, who lives at the bottom, seizes her. She is rescued by her Brother, who plants a gourd to show him the way, and on being chased by Dodo, she throws their Child into the river, and Dodo dives in after it, allowing her to escape.

———

74

The Precocious New-Baby settles His Father's Debts.

A certain Man went away to borrow some money. Now his Wife was with Child, and after three days the Woman gave birth, and when she had been delivered, the Son was taken, and laid upon a bed (1). Just then he from whom the Father had obtained a loan came to ask for repayment, and though he saluted the house

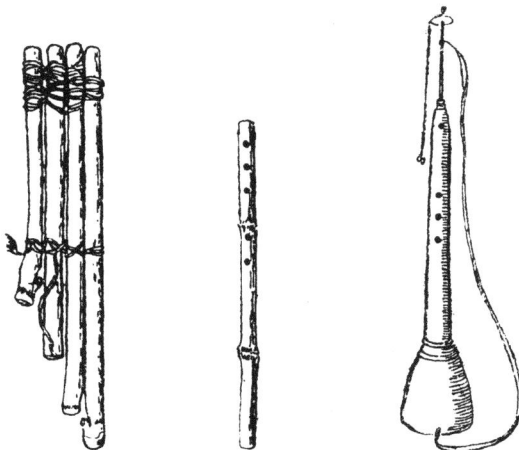

FIG. 81.   FIG. 82.   FIG. 83.

FIG. 81.—Syrinx. L., 17½ in.   FIG. 82.—Flute—general use. L., about 12 in.   FIG. 83.—Clarionet. L., 17. in.

he received no reply at first, for no one was at home. But the Little Boy who had just been born answered at last, and said " Let us go, for my Father is not here. Let us go to the court. I can recover a loan from another, and I will then pay you." So the Creditor took the Baby on his shoulder, and said " Very well, we will go to the Owners-of-the-Mighty-Mouths (2) that they may do us justice." Now the Baby, when he had come to where the mouths of the dye-pits were, stopped (3), and the Creditor said "Get up, and let us go on." But the Baby replied "You said that we should go to those whose mouths are mighty : are there any mouths which are greater than these?"

Then the Creditor said "Very well, let us proceed, and go to Those-Who-have-Red-Eyes" (4). When the Baby came to the pepper tree he stopped, and the Creditor said "Get up, and let us go on." But the Baby replied "Oh, no, you said that we should go to the Red-Eyed-Ones : are there any eyes that are more red than peppers?"

The Creditor said to the Baby "Get up again, and let us go to Those-Who-have-Large-Ears." Now when they had come to the *gwaza* plant (5) the Baby stopped, and the Creditor said "Get up, and let us go on." But the Baby said "Oh, no, are there any ears which are larger than the *gwaza*?"

Then the Creditor said "Let us go to the Elders that they may decide between us." So they came to the King, and the King said "Had I someone to shave me I should decide between you." So the Baby said "Bring water and I will do it for you," and water was brought. Now the Baby had five millet-heads, and he said "See this millet, pull the grain off for me."

When the Baby had taken the razor, he shaved the King, and then the King said "Baby," and the Baby replied "Yes." Then the King said "Put back the hair on to my head that I may judge between you." "Very well," the Baby replied, "but first put back the millet for me which you have plucked off, and then I will put back your hair on to your head." Then the King exclaimed "Heavens! What a Baby! I cannot

judge him! Here, Creditor, take him back to his
Father's house, and do not ask him again for your
debt." So the Creditor said "Very well, Baby, let us
return home, I cannot go to law with you."

So they returned, and the Creditor said to the
Father "I will leave you in peace with your gains for
your Son's sake."

———————

75
DODO'S DEBT.

Two women went to a stream to draw water, one
being with Child. When they had drawn the water,
the One-with-Child went into the bush, and the other
threw dust into her pot (1). Then she took her own
pot on her head and went off home, so when the other
returned there was no one to help her (2).

Just then, Dodo came out of the water, and the
Woman-with-Child said "There is no one here, you
must help me to get the load on to my head." So
Dodo came and helped her, and said to her "You are
with Child, if it be a Boy he shall be my Friend, if a
Girl she shall be my Wife," and the Woman agreed.

So she went home, and, about three days afterwards,
she gave birth. Then her Rival Wife went to Dodo,
and said "That Woman whom you helped has given
birth." "What sex is the Child?" he asked. She replied "It is a Girl." "O, very good," he said.

Now the Girl grew up, and one day a marriage was
arranged, for the Mother had never told Dodo. But on
the day of the wedding, the Rival Wife ran to Dodo,
and said "The Girl is to be taken to her Bridegroom's
house to-day" (3).

Then Dodo set off on the road, and came to the wedding; there was a great crowd there, and when he had come, he called out " See *Kadindi* has come." Then the Girl, who was sitting there, said " O Father, O Mother," and they replied " Um." " See, Dodo has come to demand payment of the debt," she continued. " Whose is this Horse? " asked the Father, and she replied " It is mine." Then he said " Seize it, and give it to Dodo in satisfaction of the debt." So she seized it, and gave it to Dodo, who took it, and swallowed it.

But again he said " See Kadindi has come to demand payment of the debt." Then the Girl said " Do you hear that, O Father? Do you hear that, O Mother? " Her Father said " Are not these Cattle yours? Give them to him to eat." So she gave him them, and he swallowed them.

But again he said " See Kadindi has come." So the Father said " Seize all your Guests," and she did so, and gave them to Dodo [and he swallowed them]. Again he said that he had come to demand payment of the debt, and her Father said " Give him these pots of food." She did so, but they were not enough, so she seized her Father and gave him to Dodo, but Dodo only said " See Kadindi has come." Then she cried out " O God, dost Thou hear? Dodo has come to demand payment of the debt." And lo ! a knife was thrown down to her from above, so she gave it to Dodo. But when he had put it in his mouth to swallow it, the knife ripped him open, from his mouth right down to his stomach, and Dodo fell dead.

Then the People came out, and also the Cattle, the Horses, the Guests, and the Father, all re-appeared. So the Bride was veiled and taken to her Husband.

In a variant (L.T.H. ii, 47) the Rival Wife hides and watches Dodo help the other. She tells Dodo of the birth of a Son, and he comes to congratulate the Mother. She hears in time, substitutes a Lizard, and shows it to him, and he swallows it. Later on, the Rival tells Dodo of the trick, and he waits for the Boy and catches him, but on being swallowed for the fourth time, the Boy emerges from Dodo's heart, and the Monster dies. The Boy then brings some of the flesh to the Rival Wife, telling her that it is venison, and she eats it, and is seized with such a thirst that she drinks the river dry, and it is only when the Boy pierces her with his spear that the water runs as before.

The incident of Men and Animals delivered from the stomach of a Monster by which they had been swallowed is very common in folk-tales. In Africa it is widely distributed. It is found among the Berbers in the north (Basset, *Nouveaux Contes Berbères,* 96, 106) and the Bushmen in the south (Bleck, *2nd Rep. concerning Bush Researches,* 8; Lloyd, *Account of Bushman Material,* 6) and among many intermediate tribes. Compare the story of Jonah and that of the rescue of Hesione by Herakles (H.). Perhaps the idea of Christ rescuing the souls from Hell is somewhat similar, for in the ancient print before referred to (in connection with spots, on page 162), the souls are coming out of Hell's mouth, which is like that of a monster, and, in fact, that is the usual mediæval idea.

76

How the Eagle outwitted the Townspeople.

There was a certain Man amongst the King's Followers who had seven Bulls (1), and he came to the People, and said " See my Bulls, he who buys them [need not pay any money, but] the day that the King's Mother dies they must be buried together, both the

Mother and the Purchaser who eats my Bulls." And a
certain Man agreed, saying " Give me the Bulls, on the
day that the King's Mother dies let me also be taken
away."

Well, he accepted the Bulls, and next morning he
slaughtered one, and, taking a piece of the meat he
climbed a tree, and crawled along, and placed it so that
the young Eaglets might eat it. [But when he tried to
sell the remainder in the market], the People refused to
buy it, for they said " It is the meat of Death," and
they would not eat it. So he ate the first Bull himself,
and when it was finished he slaughtered another one,
and chose a piece and took it to the young Eaglets in
the tree. But the Mother-Eagle, when she had returned,
said " He who is bringing this meat evidently wants to
kill my Young Ones." [So she decided to watch, for
she feared some trick] (2).

Well, when the Man had slaughtered another Bull,
he again brought a piece of meat to the Eaglets, but
this time the Mother-Eagle [was waiting, and] said
" Look here, what are you bringing this meat here for ?"
He replied " I bought seven Bulls, the condition being
that when the King's Mother dies we shall be buried
together. Now I have no one to help me eat them, that
is why I am helping you to look after your Young."
Then she said " I see, well go home now, on the day
that the King's Mother dies you come and tell me."
So he went home, [and at last he had slaughtered all
the Bulls] (3).

The very next morning the King's Mother died,
and immediately he went to the Mother-Eagle, and
said " She is dead." And the Eagle replied " Oh !
well, go back, when they have finished digging
the grave, and are about to bury the King's Mother,

and they have summoned you, say ' Let me have a moment more, I am really coming.' Then take some water in a gourd, and bathe your eyes and your feet, and stand up facing the East, and call on God three times, and you will see that God will help you. You must say ' O God, I am to die, but not because Thou wishest it, [but because the People are going to kill me].' "

The grave was dug, and they summoned the Man. Then he arose, and prayed, saying " God, he is God," and he again cried out " God, he is God," and again a third time. Then the Eagle replied " O " from up in the sky. " O God," the Man said " I am to die, but not because Thou wishest it, [but because the People are going to kill me]." Then the Eagle said " If you die, neither beer, nor water, nor anything else shall they obtain to drink." And when the People heard this, they exclaimed " It is God Who has spoken." And then they said to the Man " Go, shall the whole city perish because of one Man ? You are free."

In a variant (L.T.H. ii, 28) an Old Woman sells her Bull to the Chief Butcher on the condition that he will be killed at the feast of *Salla*. He feeds Birds on the meat, and the Eagle helps him in a way similar to the above, and the Old Woman is thrown into the ready-made grave instead. For other variants see F.-L. 4 and 5.

77

THE SPIDER PASSES ON A DEBT.

There was once a certain Woman who had a Daughter, and, when she was going to give her in marriage, the Daughter said that she had no basins, and no plates (1), [and that she would not be married without them]. So the Mother, who had a Bull, took it to the Slaughter-men and asked them to buy it, ten basins and ten plates was the price. But they said that they could not give that for it.

Now the Spider heard, and he came up, and said that he would buy the Bull, and that when the marriage was about to be performed he would bring ten plates and ten basins. So the Woman handed over the Bull to the Spider, and he took it home, and killed it.

When he had cooked it, he poured the broth into a pot, and took it, and placed it in the road, and he climbed a tree above, and hid there. Now the Goat [was passing, and he] was very thirsty, so he came up, and put his nose into the pot, and immediately the pot caught hold of his nose. Then the Spider slid down and said " Good." And he continued : —
" The Spider is the Buyer of the Old Woman's Bull
For ten large basins and ten large plates ;
The payment is upon you now, O, He-Goat."

And the He-Goat replied " Very well, I agree."

So he went to the river to drink water, and there a Crab seized his nose, and then he said—
" The He-Goat is the Drinker of the Spider's broth ;
The Spider is the Buyer of the Old Woman's Bull
For ten large basins and ten large plates ;
The payment is upon you, O Crab."

And the Crab replied " Very well, I agree.

Now when the Daughter came to the stream, she trod upon the Crab, and the Crab said : —
"The Daughter has stepped on the [poor little] Crab (2) ;
The Crab is the Catcher of the He-Goat's beard ;
The He-Goat is the Drinker of the Spider's broth ;

XXXI.—" Dainties." XXXII.—Milk.

The dainties may consist of dried fish, European tinned provisions, condiments, or any kind of vegetables, raw or prepared.

The milk trade is in the hands of the Filani, and sour milk is much preferred to fresh.

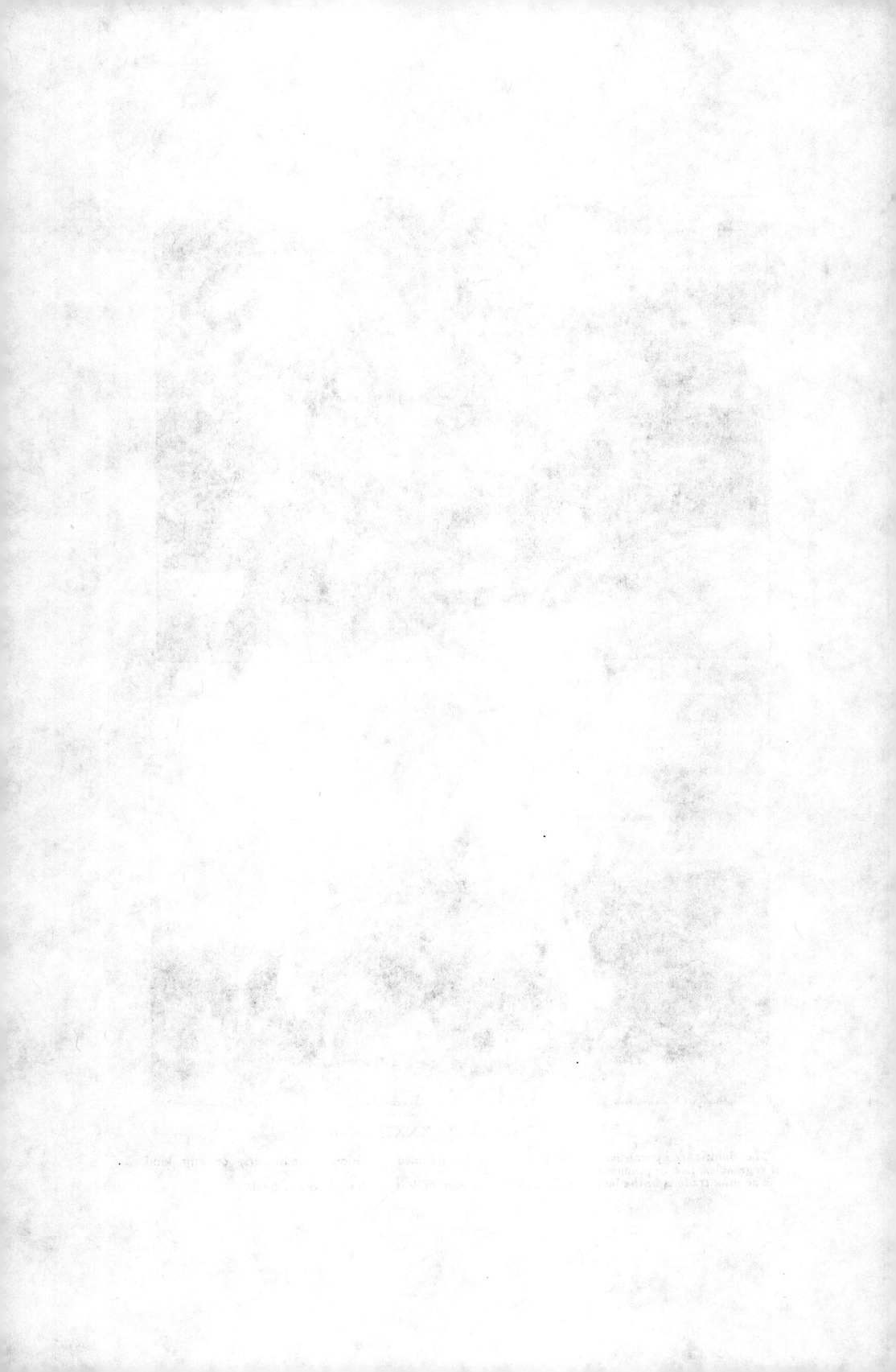

The Spider is the Buyer of the Old Woman's Bull
For ten large basins and ten large plates;
The payment is upon you, O Daughter."

And the Daughter said " Very well, I agree."

So the Daughter took the water which she had come
to get, and was going home, when the Slipperiness
caused her to fall, and she spilt the water. Then she
said—

" Slipperiness made the Daughter fall;
The Daughter is the Stepper on the [poor little] Crab;
The Crab is the Catcher of the He-Goat's beard;
The He-Goat is the Drinker of the Spider's broth;

FIG. 84.

FIG. 85.

FIGS. 84 and 85.—Brass trumpets. L., 50¾ in. and 62¾ in.

The Spider is the Buyer of the Old Woman's Bull
For ten large basins and ten large plates;
The payment is upon you, O Slipperiness."

And the Slipperiness said " Very well, I agree."

Now the Slipperiness stayed on the ground, and soon
afterwards a White-Ant came, and made a passage (3)
across the wet place. Then the Slipperiness sang—
" The White-Ant has built on the Slipperiness;
The Slipperiness made the Daughter fall;
The Daughter is the Stepper on the [poor little] Crab;
The Crab is the Catcher of the He-Goat's beard;
The He-Goat is the Drinker of the Spider's broth;
The Spider is the Buyer of the Old Woman's Bull

For ten large basins and ten large plates;
The payment is upon you, O White-Ant."

And the White-Ant said " Very well, I agree."

After a little while a certain Bird came and built [a
nest] upon the White-Ant's hill (4), and then the White-
Ant said—

" The Bird has alighted on the White-Ant's hill;
The White-Ant built on the Slipperiness;
The Slipperiness made the Daughter fall;
The Daughter is the Stepper on the [poor little] Crab;
The Crab is the Catcher of the He-Goat's beard;
The He-Goat is the Drinker of the Spider's broth;
The Spider is the Buyer of the Old Woman's Bull
For ten large basins and ten large plates;
The payment is upon you, O Bird."

And the Bird said " Very well, I agree."

Now the Bird stayed there, and one day a Boy who
was shooting came along, and when he saw the Bird
sitting on the Ant-hill he shot it.   Then the Bird said—
" The Boy is the Shooter of the [poor little] Bird;
The Bird alighted on the White-Ant's hill;
The White-Ant built on the Slipperiness;
The Slipperiness made the Daughter fall;
The Daughter is the Stepper on the [poor little] Crab;
The Crab is the Catcher of the He-Goat's beard;
The He-Goat is the Drinker of the Spider's broth;
The Spider is the Buyer of the Old Woman's Bull
For ten large basins and ten large plates;
The payment is upon you, O Boy."

And the Boy said " Very well, I agree."

So the Boy went home, and just as he had opened
his mouth to tell his Mother about it, she covered him
with blows.   Then the Boy said—

" The Mother is the Beater of the [poor little] Boy;

The Boy is the Shooter of the [poor little] Bird;
The Bird alighted on the White-Ant's hill;
The White-Ant built on the Slipperiness;
The Slipperiness made the Daughter fall;
The Daughter is the Stepper on the [poor little] Crab;
The Crab is the Catcher of the He-Goat's beard;
The He-Goat is the Drinker of the Spider's broth;
The Spider is the Buyer of the Old Woman's Bull
For ten large basins and ten large plates;
The payment is upon you, O Mother.''

And the Mother said " Very well, I agree."

Now it happened soon afterwards that a certain
Blacksmith burned one of the Mother's cloths, and then
she said—

" The Blacksmith is the Burner of the Mother's cloth;
The Mother is the Beater of the [poor little] Boy;
The Boy is the Shooter of the [poor little] Bird;
The Bird alighted on the White-Ant's hill;
The White-Ant built on the Slipperiness;
The Slipperiness made the Daughter fall;
The Daughter is the Stepper on the [poor little] Crab;
The Crab is the Catcher of the He-Goat's beard;
The He-Goat is the Drinker of the Spider's broth;
The Spider is the Buyer of the Old Woman's Bull
For ten large basins and ten large plates;
The payment is upon you, O Blacksmith.''

Then the Blacksmith said " Very well, I agree."

Immediately all the Blacksmiths started work, and
made ten basins and ten plates, and took them to the
Woman. The Woman took them, and gave them to
the Boy. The Boy took them, and gave them to the
Bird. The Bird took them, and gave them to the White-
Ant. The White-Ant took them and gave them to the
Slipperiness. The Slipperiness took them, and gave

them to the Daughter.   The Daughter took them, and
gave them to the Crab.   The Crab took them, and gave
them to the He-Goat.   The He-Goat took them, and
gave them to the Spider.   And the Spider took them,
and gave them to the Old Woman.

That is an example of the Spider's cunning.   He
himself ate the flesh of the Bull, but he made others
make the payment for him, he gave nothing in return
for what he had got.

———

In a variant the Spider owes an Old Woman money
as before.   He climbs a shea-butter tree but falls down,
so the tree has to take over the debt, and it then passes
on to the Girl who picks the nuts, a root which trips
her, a Goat which eats the leaves, a Slave who beats the
Goat, the King's Wife who beats the Slave, and then
to the King who quarrels with her.   But in this case,
the debt does not return to the Old Woman, for the
King pays it.

———

This story has some resemblance to " The House
that Jack built," and others of our nursery tales, but it
is quite possible that at one time it belonged to the kind
known as " All-around-the-Clock," *i.e.,* that the debt
having been brought back to the Mother, the story
would have ended, and she would have lost her Bull and
still have had to provide the basins and plates.   Thus
in a Malayan tale (Skeat, *op. cit.,* page 9) where
the Chevrotain has danced and has stepped on
the Otter's children, he excuses himself to King
Solomon by saying that the Woodpecker had
sounded the war-gong, and that he, being Chief
Dancer in the war-dance could not keep quiet, and
that he had   not noticed where he was stepping.
The Woodpecker said he had sounded his gong
(tapped the tree) because he had seen the Great Lizard
wearing his sword (his long tail); this was because the
Tortoise had donned his coat of mail; this was because
the King-Crab had been trailing his three-edged pike

(a spike at the end of his tail); this was because the Crayfish had shouldered his lance (antennæ); and this was because the Crayfish had seen the Otter coming down to devour the Young Crayfish.   So the Otter had no redress.

78

THE SPIDER PAYS HIS DEBTS.

The Spider had contracted a number of debts, he had borrowed from every Beast of the forest, and he took counsel with himself as to what he should do, for he had no money with which to pay.   So he gave out that, on the Friday, all the Creditors should come and receive payment.

When Friday had come, [while it was still] early in the morning, the Hen arrived to collect her debt.   And, when she had come, the Spider said "Good, I will pay you at once, but wait a minute or two while I prepare you some food."   So the Hen was waiting inside the hut, and soon the Wild-Cat came.   Then the Spider said "Good, the repayment (1) is in the hut, go and take it."   So the Wild-Cat went and entered the hut, and seized the Hen, and twisted her neck.

Just as he was about to go off, the Dog arrived, and the Spider said "Good, the re-payment is in the hut, go and take it."   So the Dog went and seized the Wild-Cat, and bit him, and killed him.   Just as he was about to go, the Hyæna arrived, and the Spider said "Good, the re-payment is in the hut, go and take it."   So the Hyæna ran and seized the Dog, and ate him up.   Just as she was about to leave, lo! the Leopard appeared, and the Spider said "Good, the re-payment is in the hut, go and take it."   So the Leopard sprang upon the

Hyæna, and killed her. Just as she was about to leave who should arrive but the Lion, and he came upon the Leopard.

So they began to fight, and while they were fighting, and fighting, the Spider took some pepper, and poured it into their eyes. When he had done this, he took up a big stick, and began to beat them, and he beat them until they were dead, both of them. Then the Spider collected the meat in his house, and said that he had extinguished his debts.

———

For an English parallel, see " The Crocodiles' Dinner Party."

————

79

THE YOUNGEST SON AND THE WISE EWE.

A certain Man was very rich, and amongst his possessions was one old Ewe. He had three Sons also, two he loved, the third he did not love. Now he was about to die, so he summoned his Eldest Son to the door of his hut, and said " When I am dead, say that you do not want any of my possessions except the old Ewe." But the Son replied " What, there are great riches here, what should I do with the old Ewe?" Then the Father said " Very well," and he summoned the Second, and said " When I am dead, say that you do not want any of my riches, but simply take this old Ewe." But he answered " I see that you are very rich, why should I be content with the old Ewe?" So the Father said " Very well," and he summoned his Youngest Son, Auta, whom he did not love, and said to him " Now, listen, when I am

dead, say that you do not want any of my possessions except this old Ewe." And Auta replied
" Father, even now when you are alive, riches
are of no account to me, they will matter even less when
you are no more," and he continued " The Ewe will
be enough for me." So the Father said " Good, and
remember that of whatever you have to eat, give some
to the Ewe first, then you may eat of it also." And
Auta replied " I will remember."

Now when the Father had ceased speaking, and had
re-entered his hut, he died, and there was wailing, and
wailing, and wailing. Then Auta took the Ewe, and
left the house, and the People said " Opp, there is one
who made a foolish promise, there are great riches, yet
he has given up his claims to them, and has taken only
the old Ewe."

So Auta travelled on, and on, and on with the Ewe,
and when he got water he gave her to drink before he
himself drank. At last they came to the hut of a
Weaver who was very poor, for he had nothing to
eat. When Auta had saluted the house, the Weaver said
" O Stranger, do you wish to rest here ? " And Auta
said " Yes." " Very well," said the other, " but I have
no food for myself, much less any to give you." Now
the Weaver had a Wife whom he loved, the House-
Mother (1), and she had a Daughter. There was also
a Second Wife whom he did not love, and she also
had a Daughter. And the Weaver said to his Beloved
Wife " O House-Mother, draw some water for the
Stranger to drink." But she replied " Poof, I have no
water in my hut, I have nothing to give the Stranger."
Then the Weaver said to his Unbeloved Wife " Hey,
you, draw some water for the Stranger to drink." The
Unbeloved Wife had a little guinea-corn in her binn,

about a handful, and she ground it, and put it into the
water, and took it to Auta.   He gave it to the Ewe first,
and they said " What ! drink it yourself indeed (2), the
Ewe will get her food separately."   But Auta said
" No, no, this will do for both of us."   So he gave it
first to the Ewe, and she drank some of it, and then he
drank also.

In the evening, when the sun had set, the House-
Mother said " Good gracious, is this Stranger going to
sleep here ? "   And the Husband said " Yes," and then
continued " Have you any more guinea-corn with which
to make gruel for him ? "   And she replied " I ?
All the corn I have left is one handful, and I
am going to make gruel for my Daughter, I shall not
give it to the Stranger."   Then he said to his Unbeloved
Wife " Is there a little guinea-corn in your hut enough
to make gruel for the Stranger ? "   And she said " All
I have is one handful, but I will make gruel, and give
it to him."   So she made gruel of the handful of corn,
and gave it to the Stranger, and when he had taken it,
he gave it to the Ewe to drink first, and then he drank
also.   And they rested until daybreak.

Now, that day the Ewe was going to talk to Auta,
so she said " Arise and let us go, accompany me as far
as the edge of the forest."   So they started off, and
the Host asked " Are you going to leave us ? "   But
they replied " Oh no, we are going only to the edge
of the forest, and will return."   Now when they had
reached the edge of the forest, the Ewe said " Stay
here."   But she went to and fro in the grass, and then
returned to the Boy, and said " Go, wherever you see
that I have been, you follow."   When he went, he came
upon about two hundred Horses, with their saddles and
bridles, and royal caparisons, and he returned to the

Ewe, and said " I have seen about two hundred Horses, with their saddles, and bridles, and royal caparisons." Then she said " Good, stay here," and again she went to and fro in the grass, and returned to the Boy, and said " Go, wherever you see that I have been, you follow." When he went he saw about two hundred Grooms, each one with a rug upon his arm, and when he had returned, and had told her, she said " Good, go, let each Groom hold a Horse." And when they had done this, she said " Now, let us return to the house at which we lodged."

When they arrived, the Weaver stared at the Horses surrounding his house, and said " Certainly that Stranger has not gone for good, his Horsemen have come." And, as he stared, he saw the Ewe in front, and she said " Yes, it is we, we have not left you." And then she continued " Take all these Horses (3) to the Unbeloved Wife."

When the Horses had been handed over, the Ewe said " Come, let us return to the edge of the forest," and, when they had reached it, she stopped, and said to Auta " Look in front." Then he looked, and saw Slaves and Concubines to the number of about three hundred, each carrying a sheaf of corn. Then again she said " Now let us return to the house at which we lodged," and she continued " Let all these Slaves, and Concubines, and sheaves of corn be taken to the house of the Unbeloved Wife."

Now when they had been handed over, the House-Wife said that Auta should marry her Daughter, but the Ewe said no, no, that Auta was to marry the Daughter of the Unbeloved Wife. So thus it was, she was given to him, and they were married, and her Father, the Weaver, and her Mother who was un-beloved, both had a share in the riches.

Well, they had been living there for some time—
the Ewe had had a house built for her—and Auta used
to mount a Horse covered with trappings, and his
Slaves used to follow him. But one day he said to
the Ewe that he wanted a Second Wife, and she replied
" Very well, but if you must marry, do not take a Bad
Woman," and he said " I will not." But one day he
had mounted a Horse, and was going for a ride, when
he saw a certain Bad Woman, so beautiful that there
was no one like her. Then he came and told the Ewe
that he had found a Woman to marry, and the Ewe
replied " Oh, very well, I have nothing more to say,"
she did not remind him [of her warning]. So he
married her, the Bad Woman, and brought her to his
house.

He lived there with the Bad Woman, and one day
he mounted his Horse to go for a ride, and when he
went, he left the Bad Woman at home with some of his
Runners (4). Then the Bad Woman said " Oh dear,
we have no meat to eat to-day, we must kill this old
Ewe." But one of the Runners said " No, no, the Ewe
was here before I came [and is not meant to be
killed] " (5). Then she said " If you do not kill that
Ewe I will have you sold." So he said " Very well,"
and he seized the Ewe, and cut its throat.

Now the Ewe was being skinned when the Boy
returned from his ride, and he asked " Where did you
get that meat ? " (6). Silence ! ! Then he said " Ah !
I have asked you a question, are you not going to tell
me ? " Then the Bad Woman said " Oh, it was I,
I had no meat, so I had the Ewe killed." Then he
said " I see," and he collected all the flesh, and wrapped
it in the fleece, and tied it up. Then he addressed himself to his first Wife, the [one whom he had taken as a]

Virgin, the Daughter of the Unbeloved Wife, and said
" Give me a pair of white trousers, a white tobe, a white
turban, and a knife." So he put on his white trousers,
his white tobe, and his white turban (7), and he took the

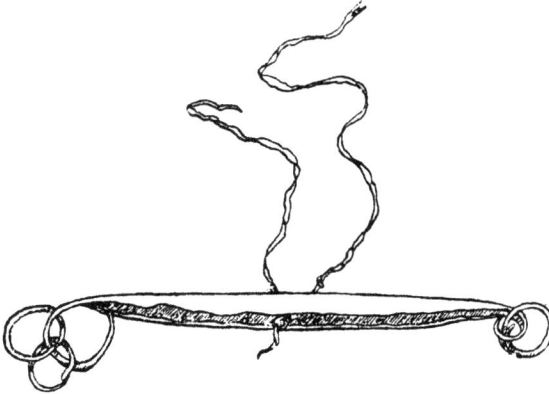

FIG. 86.

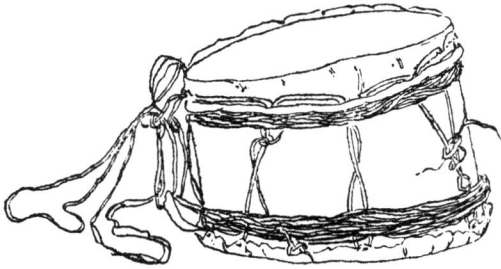

FIG. 87.

FIG. 86.—Iron rattle, tied to ankle when dancing. L. of body, 8 in.
FIG. 87.—Drum. The usual form is not so irregular as this. May be more
than 12 in. in diameter.

Ewe's flesh, and went off to the forest. There he
cleared a space, and placed the flesh of the Ewe in
front of him, and he took the knife and said " Since the
Ewe has died through my fault (8), I will stab myself,

and die also." Now as he took the knife to stab him-
self, the Flesh said " Stop," but, as he saw that the
Flesh did not arise, he said " No, no, I shall not stop,
I will stab myself," and again he took the knife to stab
himself. Then the Ewe arose, alive, and said " Verily,
I told you not to marry a Bad Woman."

Then he said to the Ewe " It is so, let us go home,"
and when he arrived he drove away the Bad Woman
(9), and said " One Wife is enough for me."

———

Another version of the death of the Father, and the
Youngest Son's promise, is found in T.H.H. 6, where
Salifu takes the Old Mare, and the Mare brings him
wealth, though in a different way.

———

Another Ewe story makes the Animal give the Boy
everything he wants on condition that he will give her
and her family water daily. The condition is kept for
a while, but one day the Boy refuses to get water, and
his riches are taken away from him again. This is a
variant of the Dove story, F.-L. 39.

———

The father who leaves apparently worthless objects,
which turn out to be magical, to his children is found
in Sicilian tales. *Vide* Gouzurbach; *Siciliansche
Märchen* (Leipzig, 1870), 192; Pitrè, iv, *Biblioteca,* 252.
Compare a Balearic tale, Archduke Ludwig Salvator,
Märchenans Mallorea (Urïrzburg, 1896), 50. (H.)

————

80

THE LUCKY YOUNGEST SON.

There was once a certain lucky Person, Ahmadu the
Rich Man, who had three Children, and three Wives,
each one having exactly one Son. At last he fell ill,

and knew that he was about to die, so he summoned his Eldest Son, and said " When I am dead, of all my riches do not take anything except my stick and my boot." But the Eldest Son replied " Father, is that the kind of Man you are? Of all your goods I am not to take anything except the stick and boot? Well, I shall not take only the stick and boot." Then the Father said " Very well, go and stay with your Mother." So he summoned the second of them, and said " Listen, Mohamma, when I am dead, do not take anything except the prayer-jug " (1). But Mohamma replied " Is that the sort my Father is? I shall not take the prayer-jug." Then Ahmadu summoned Auta also, and said " When I am dead, do not take anything except the stick and boot." And Auta replied " Father, I love you better than anything," and he continued " whatever you tell me to take, I will take only it." So Ahmadu said " Very well, take only the boot and the stick."

Now when Auta had taken them, and had left the hut, his Father died, and the Women of the house mourned. When they had ceased, they applied to the King for the division of the heritage, and when it had been divided up, the Eldest Son was given his share, and the Second was given his, but when Auta was given some of the property, he refused it, and said that the boot and stick would content him. Then his Mother came up, and began to abuse Auta, but when she had finished abusing him, he still said that he would not take anything, and when he had got tired of being abused he went off into the forest.

When he had reached the main road, he met with a certain Person who had collected some wood, and had lit it, and he said " O Youth, where are you going?"

" What has that to do with you? " asked Auta, and he
passed on. Soon he came upon a Hunter, who said
" O Youth, will you not give me your stick? " And
Auta took the stick, and gave it to him. Then the
Hunter saw a Bird in a tree, and he threw up the
stick at it, and the stick stuck in the branches. So he
took the Bird, and gave it to the Boy.

Then Auta went on, and came upon a certain Person
who had lit a fire, but had nothing to cook, and he said
" O Youth, will you not give me the Bird that I may
cook it? " When Auta had given it to him, he cooked
and ate it, and then he took some ashes, [and gave
them to Auta], and Auta wrapped them in his coat.

So he went on, and came upon a certain Woman,
who was making porridge, but had no ash to put in
it (2). So she said " O Youth, will you not give me the
ash? " And he gave it to her. Then she took a broken
piece of calabash [with some food in it] and gave it to
the Boy, and he went on.

Next he came upon some People digging on a
farm, and they said " O Youth, will you not give us
your porridge that we may eat? " And he took it, and
gave it to them, and they ate it, and then they took a
hoe and gave it to him.

So he went on, and came upon a Blacksmith who
had made a great fire with his bellows, but had no iron
for forging. So he said " O Youth, will you not give
me the hoe that I may make knives with it? " (3). And
Auta took it, and gave it to him, and the Blacksmith
made knives with it, and when he had made them, he
gave Auta one.

When the Boy had taken it, he started travelling
on again in the forest, and he went on, and came upon
a Weaver, who had made a white cloth.   Then the

Weaver said " O Youth, will you not give me your
knife that I may cut this white cloth ? " (4) When
Auta had given it to him, he cut the white cloth, and
then Auta said " Right, now pay me for my knife."
So the Weaver took all the white cloth and gave it to
the Boy.

Auta went on, and came to a place where a
Maiden had died. As for her People, they had no white
cloth in which to take her to the grave, and they said
" O Boy, will you not give us this white cloth in
which to take the corpse to the grave ? " So he took
it, and gave it to them, and they cut it up, and sewed
the strips together, and wrapped it around the Girl.
But when they were about to take her to the grave, the
Boy caught hold of the Corpse, and said " Pay me for
my white cloth." So they took the Corpse, and gave
it to him, and he lifted it on to his head (5).

He went on, and at last he emerged from the forest,
and went on, and came near to a large city. Now there
was a river at the gate of the city, and each day the
King's Wives would come there to get water. And
when he had come with the dead Girl, he dug two
holes, and put her feet in them, and stretched the body
upright, so that she stood up. Then he took the white
cloth, and wrapped it around her, right down to the
ground, and after that he went back in the shade, and
waited. When the King's Wives came to get water at
the place, he said " For God's sake will you not give
my Wife some water that she may drink ? I gave her
some, but she refused to drink because of her pride " (6).
Then one, the Chief Wife of the King, got some water
in her calabash, and came and said " Here you are "——
Silence, she did not accept it. Then another of the
King's Wives bounded forward, and seized the cala-

bash, and came, and said "Here!"—— Silence.
Then she hit the Corpse on the forehead, and the Corpse
fell down. Immediately the Boy ran out from the
shade, and began to cry, and he said that the King's
Wives had killed his Wife at the stream. The alarm
reached even to the King's palace, but the King said
that it was a lie, for his Wives would not quarrel.
However, he said "Go and see."

When the Messengers had come, they found the
Corpse lying down, so they went back, and said to the
King "Ah, it is true, your Wives have done murder."
Then he said "Very well, bring the Corpse here."
And, when it had been lifted up and brought to the
King, he said "Here, Boy, whence have you come
with this Woman?" But he said to the King "What
has that to do with you?" Then the Judge said "This
Boy may do mischief, settle with him, and let him go."
So the King brought two Wives of his own, and gave
them to him (7), and the Boy went out of the city
and entered the forest, and he went and lived in the
forest, and built a house there. But when he had
built the house, he drove away the two Wives whom
the King had given him, and said that he would live
alone.

One day a Frog said "Auta, may I come to your
house and live?" and he replied "Remain certainly."
Then a Monkey said "Auta, may I come to your house
and live?" and he replied "Remain certainly." Then
a Horse said "Auta, may I come to your house and
live?" and he replied "Remain certainly." A Camel
a Donkey, Stinging-Ants, Ordinary Ants, Large
Stinging-Travelling-Ants, a Mule, a Large Snake, a
Crown-Bird, and a White-Breasted Crow, all came and
lived with him.

Soon all conceived, at the same time, and a Bull came, and said that every one of them was to build a storehouse in the compound, there being thirty altogether. The Bull came, and built thirty receptacles inside the houses, and again he came and made thirty deep holes in the compound. Then the Bull filled all the storehouses with gold, that is what he gave birth to. The Mule came and brought forth silver, he filled all the thirty holes. The Camel filled the receptacles with cowries. The rest of the Family, the Small Ones, brought forth Slaves, they filled the house with Slaves.

Now, one day, the Spider came to the house to beg, and Auta took guinea-corn and gave it to him, and the Spider went to the King, and said " What will you give me for my news ? " The King replied " A kola-nut." " How many ears have you ? " asked the Spider. The King replied that he had two ears. " Add two more," said the Spider, " and you will hear news." And the King said that he had added them. So the Spider said " The Boy here in the forest, in the whole world there is not one who is so rich." " It is a lie," exclaimed the King. Then the Spider said " Very well, send me and the Councillors to go and see." So the King sent him and the Councillors, and they went off, and when they had been and had seen the wealth, they knew that the riches were greater than those of the King himself. So they returned and said " This Boy is very rich."

Now the King had a White Leper in his palace, and the advice of the White Leper was what the King listened to, so he said " Now White Leper, what shall we do that we may take this property ? " The White Leper replied " Take some soup, and put it in a bag (8), and take grains of guinea-corn, and put them in the bag." Now a great number were put inside the bag; and then black-*acha* grains were taken and put in the bag; elusine was taken and put in the bag; millet was taken and put in the bag; *acha* was taken and put in the bag; rice and beans were taken and put in the bag. When the bag had been filled and tied up, it was taken to the Boy's house, and he was told that by daylight he must have sorted out the grains separately. The Boy saw that he could not do this, and began to cry, he cried hard; but the Ant came, and the Stinging-Ant came, and they told him to be patient. So he took all his calabashes, and gave them to them, and one took a grain and put it here, one took a grain and put it there, and so by the time that day had broken, they had sorted them out separately, and when the Councillors came to take them, he lifted them up, and gave them to them. Then the King again called the White Leper, and said " Well, how shall we kill that Boy?"

Now there was a certain big lake which no one would enter, and there was a fan-palm (9) in the middle of the lake, so the White Leper said to the King " Tell the Boy to fetch two fruits of the palm-tree." So Auta was told to do so, and when he saw that he was unable to enter the water, he cried hard. But the Monkey and the Frog came to the Boy, and said " Dry your tears, because of such things we asked you of old if we could come to your house and live." Then the Monkey arose, and hopped to the edge of the lake, and from there he jumped, and alighted upon the fan-palm. But the Frog dived, and did not come up until he had reached the fan-palm, and he also climbed the tree (10). When the Monkey had plucked one, he jumped straight out [on to the bank], and the Frog pulled off his, and fell into the river, and did not rise until he was at the bank. So they brought the two fruits of the fan-palm, and the Boy went and put them aside, and when the Councillors came next morning to take the fruits, he took them, and gave them to them, and they brought them to the King.

Soon afterwards, the King said " Well, White Leper, what shall we do to get this Boy's riches? " He replied " It is now the dry season, there is no water, so you tell him to bring a leaf of the millet about daybreak." Then the King said " Very well " [and sent to Auta to tell him]. Then the Boy cried hard, until the White-Breasted Crow and the Crown-Bird came, and said " O Boy, what are you crying for? " " The King has said that I must bring him a millet leaf now, in the dry season," he replied. But they said " Come, dry your tears, and be easy." Then the Crow went north, the Crown-Bird went south, and they flew along, saying " *Da da da* " (11), [at least] the Crow did. She went on to a country where she found that the millet was high, the Crown-Bird came to a country where the millet had begun to put out eyes (12). The Crow found a country where the millet was ready to be threshed, so she arrested her flight and took a bundle. As for the Crown-Bird, she found a place where the leaves were peeling off, so she also tied up a bundle. The Crow carried hers, the Crown-Bird carried hers, and they brought them to the Boy, so when day broke he took them to the King.

Now the Snake saw that the Boy had been very near losing his life, and said " O Youth," and Auta replied " Um." The Snake said " The King has a Daughter of whom he is very fond." And it continued " Let me enter into her stomach, and even if all the Magicians

in the world be assembled to attend to the Girl she
will not get well. But you, when you go, you will heal
her. I it is who will give you medicine with which to
heal her." "When you go to the King," it continued,
"you must say that your medicine is difficult to obtain,
and the King will say 'What can be difficult to me?'
You must say 'It will certainly be hard for you,' but
he will reply 'O Youth, whatever the difficulty, I will
get it.' Then you must say 'Very well, I want a
White Leper's liver brought me immediately.'" The
Snake went on "When you have been brought the
White Leper's liver, put it with some water in a pot,
and give it to this Girl that she may drink, and she will
be healed at once." So the Boy said "Very well."

Now the Girl was playing with the other Girls of
the city, her Fellows, when the Snake reached her, and
it crawled inside her stomach. Then the Girl said to her
Playmates that she had a stomach-ache, and that she was
going home, so the other Girls said "Let us go, the
King's Daughter is not well." When she had reached
her home, she lay down, and her stomach began swelling, and swelling, until it was as big as a storehouse.
Then the King arose, and began crying, and crying,
and crying, and falling down, and doing all kinds of
things. The White Leper of whom the King was fond
came, and gave his advice, all the Magicians in the
city were summoned, every one gave her medicine. But
it was no good, the Girl did not get better. They went
to Faki Fatatika (13) and summoned the Magicians
of the town, and they came and worked their spells, but
the Girl got no better (14).

At last the Rich Boy came with one old rag on, he
did not wear a good tobe, and he came to the King
and said "May your life be prolonged." Then the

White Leper arose, and hit him, and said "The King's Daughter is ill, have you, a Wearer-of-Rags come to bother him ?" (15). "I have come to give her medicine," he replied. Then the White Leper said "The Magicians have not been able to cure her, can you, a Wearer-of-Rags, know what medicine to prescribe ? " Then the King heard, and said "No no, leave him alone, everyone has the gifts that God has given him." And he continued " Go with the White Leper to where the

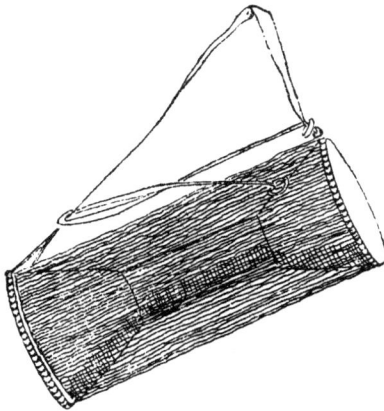

FIG. 88.—Drum. The note can be altered by pressing the string with the arm. L., 18¼ in.

Girl is." When he had gone, and had returned to the King, Auta said " Now, O King, I know an antidote, but my antidote is hard to obtain." " Tell me what it is," replied the King; " however difficult it may be, the medicine will be obtained and brought." Then Auta said " I wish you to get me the liver of a White Leper at once. Now here is a White Leper with you, will one go searching in the city to look for one? " And immediately the Councillors rained blows upon the White Leper there, in the hall, until they had killed

him. Then his body was seized, and torn open, and
the liver was pulled out, and given to the Boy,
who told them to get some water for him and to
put it in a pot. When water had been poured into a
new pot, it was brought to him, and he put the liver
in it, and shook it up, and then he said " Give it to the
Girl to drink." Now when it had been given to the Girl,
and she had drunk, she became violently ill,* and the
Snake came out, and went away* (16); no one saw it.

Then the Girl arose, and asked to be given porridge
to eat, she said to give her flour and water to drink,
and she was given some, she was also given kola-
nuts, and she ate them. Immediately the King took
the Boy aside, he brought five Horses and gave
them to him, he brought five tobes and gave them
to him, he brought twenty pairs of trousers, and dark
blue tobes and gave them to him. Then he separated
off one-half of the city and offered it to him, but Auta
said " No, as far as I am concerned, I do not wish to
live in the city, I am going home."

So he took his Horses and the other presents
which the King had given to him, and he went
to the forest, and he overtook the Snake, as he
was going home. The Snake said " O Boy, the
treachery is done with, there remains only mine
to you " (17), and it continued " Now, look here,
I am going to live in an Ant-hill." Then Auta
said " If you live in an Ant-hill, how can I repay
you ? " The Snake replied " Every Sunday you must
give me a piece of meat." And the Boy said " Agreed,
I understand." So when Sunday came, the Boy arose
from his bed, and went out, and got a piece of meat
in the house, and he took it, and carried it to the Ant-
hill, and then he returned home.

Every Sunday Auta did this for him, until one day he went out of his hut in the morning, but did not see the piece of meat in the house, for as it happened, the Frog had come, and had taken it in the early morning. Now as he had not obtained a piece of meat, the Snake arose, and came to Auta, and said to the Boy " To-day is Sunday, but I have not seen my piece of meat." " I am now looking for it," he replied; " must you come and ask me for it ? " And he continued " Formerly I had a store of them in the house, but to-day when I got up I did not see any, there are no more pieces." Then the Snake said " Indeed ! Is there disloyalty in your own house ? " And Auta replied that he did not know. " Will you give the Thieves over to me that I may come and seize them ? " asked the Snake. And the Boy said " Very well," for he thought that all were acting fairly towards him. " Very well," he said, " but who is the one to be punished amongst them ? " The Snake replied " Right, I am going home, I shall know the Thief when he comes." But when the Snake had gone a little way, it returned and hid behind the door of Auta's house.

Now the Rich Boy could not rest without going and reasoning with the Snake, so he went out of the door of the house, and the Snake (which was by the door of the house) bit him, and when the Snake had bitten him, Auta went back into the house, and lay down, for his leg was painful. Then the Frog came up, and said " What has befallen you, O Rich One ? " And Auta replied " Something bit me by the door of the house." Then the Frog said " Whatever it be, I will go and see." So he went out, hopping, and came to the door of the house, and the Snake bit him, so he also went and

lay down. The Frog died, he also, the Rich Boy,
died.

That is the end of this.   The Frog brought this
upon Auta.   Because he took the meat, he brought
disaster upon him.

———

In a variant   (L.T.H. 129) the story goes on the
same lines as far as the trick with the Corpse, but the
Youth takes a Girl offered him and marries her.   He
has a Daughter by her, and sings to the Baby, telling it
that he had obtained the Mother by the means of a
Corpse.   The ending is the same as that of F.-L. 12.

———

With the White-Leper incident in this story may be
compared one from the Malay Peninsula (*Fables and
Folk-Tales from an Eastern Forest,* W. Skeat, page 3).
The Great King of all the Tigers was sick, and the
Tiger-Crown-Prince suggested that he should eat the
flesh of every Beast until he got the right one.   All the
Beasts were summoned, and all came except the Chevrotain, and the Tiger-King ate of them.   Last of all came
the Chevrotain, whose excuse was that he had had a
dream in which the proper medicine had been indicated.
When the Tiger-King had asked what it was, the
Chevrotain replied that he must devour that which was
nearest to him.   Immediately the Tiger-Crown-Prince
was seized and eaten, the King-Tiger got well, and the
Chevrotain became Crown-Prince.

A Sierra Leone story (*Cunnie Rabbit,* page 249)
bears a greater resemblance to the Hausa one.   Here
the King is envious of the Boy's riches, and, acting on
the advice of a Messenger, sets the Boy to pick fruit
from a tree covered with Poisonous Ants, but the White-
Ants do it for him.   Next the Boy is ordered to pick
out a certain Cow from a herd, and the Butterfly shows
him which is the right one by settling upon her head.
The third test is to make the Boy sit on a chair on a
mat which hides the mouth of a hole filled with knives
and broken bottles, but he pokes the mat before sitting
down, and the plot is exposed.   Lastly the King is

going to throw him into the river, but by a trick the Messenger is drowned instead, and so the Boy is molested no further.

The contract with a Snake appears in an Indian tale, and Snakes are supposed to live in ant-hills (Crooke, *op. cit.*, pp. 135 and 276).

The youth, who, starting with the capital of an article of negligible value, by repeated commercial transactions like those of the youth in this story, arrives at riches, or brings himself into collision with a wealthy and powerful man and is condemned to be drowned, but extricates himself, contrives to substitute his opponent as victim and succeeds to his possessions, is a favourite in European and African folk-tales. Among the variants recorded in Africa are tales current among the Kabyles (Rivière, *Contes Pop. Kabyles,* Paris, 1882, 79, 95), Ewhe (i, *Rev. d'Ethnographie et Sociologie,* Paris, 1910, 71, where other references are given), Anyanja (iii, *Folk-lore,* 92; xv, 344), Herrero (Bleek, *Reynard the Fox,* 90) and Zulus (Calloway, *Nursery Tales,* London, 1868, 37). Variants are even found as far to the east as among the Katchins of Burma (iv, *Anthropos,* 121, 135). The corpse often figures in the story. (H.)

81

THE DIVISION OF THE INHERITANCE.

There was a certain Man who had three Children, two Daughters and a Son; the name of the Son was Karrambanna, one of the Daughters was called Kumbu(r)rin Dammo, and the other Maihakuri (1).

Now their Father died, and left twenty thousand cowries and one cowry, and, when the property was about to be divided, the King (2) said " What can be done with one cowry? Let it be given to Karrambanna as he is the eldest." But Kumbu(r)rin Dammo said that she would not agree, she said " Let it be divided into three so that no one can get the better of the others." So the King said " Very well, but who can divide a cowry into three equal parts?"

Then a certain Old Man said " There is one who can divide the inheritance equally, his name is Atteyu, his whole body is nothing but liver." So they went and summoned Atteyu, and the King said to him " Here are twenty thousand cowries and one cowry, there is no one who can divide them equally, that is what caused us to summon you." " Opp," he replied, " that is easy," and he asked How many Children had he?" And they said " Three." Then he said " Give them 5,000 each," and of the 20,001 cowries there remained 5,001. He said " Give them 1,000 each "—so there were 2,001 left. " Of the 2,001 give them 500 each," he continued —and there remained 501. Then he said " Give them 100 each "—and 201 were left. " Of the 201," he continued, " give them 50 each "—and there were still 51. Then he said " Of the 51 give them 10 each "— so 21 remained. " Of the 21," he continued, " give them 5 each "—and 6 were left. " Now of the 6 remaining give them 2 each, and so no one will get the better of the others." Then he said " I have divided the inheritance for you."

82

THE CITY OF WOMEN.

There was once a Bachelor, who had no Wife, and he went and worked on his farm, but after he had gone home, a Tortoise came, and said " O Farm of the Bachelor, rise up in disorder," [and the farm became as if it had never been worked].

Now when the Bachelor returned, and saw this, he said " Oh dear ! Who has done this to me ? " And he continued " Well, I will wait in hiding, and see who is spoiling my farm." So when he had finished work, he hid himself at the edge of the bush, and waited. When the Tortoise arrived, he said " O Farm of the Bachelor, rise up in disorder," and the farm became as it was before. Then the Bachelor came up, and took a hoe, and beat the Tortoise on the back until he cried out " O Bachelor, let me off, let me off, and I will give you a Wife." [And when the Bachelor had desisted], the Tortoise said " Now, go, Bachelor, and make a bundle of stalks " (1), and, when this had been done, the Bachelor said " Here it is, I have made it." Then the Tortoise said " Good, now get inside, and I will carry you," and the Bachelor said " Very well."

So the Tortoise carried him to a certain city where there were only Women, there was not even one Man, and when he had brought him to this city where there were no Men, he said " Listen to the weeping " (2), and he undid the bundle. Now when the Lower-Class Women saw the Bachelor, they said " Oh, this One is too good for us, let us take him to the Queen." And when the Queen saw him, she gave him a tobe, a pair of trousers, and a turban, and she bought him a Horse, all the good things suitable for a King she gave him, [and she married him].

One day she said " I am going off to the war," and she continued " See this little basket with a lid, you must not open it. Everything in this palace is yours except this little basket, and if you open it you will have a great shock " (3). So she started off, and went to the war, leaving him at home. Now when she had gone, he said " Well, everything in this palace is mine, so I will open this little basket." But no sooner had he done so, than he found himself back in the middle of his farm, with nothing but a leather loin-covering, and a hoe, he could see the palace no longer. Then he began to cry, and he said " Where shall I get another Tortoise to take me back ? "

So he went to the edge of the bush, and found a young Tortoise, and he took him up, and said " Now, when I have farmed, you must say ' O Farm of the Bachelor, rise up in disorder,' when I come to pick up the hoe to beat you, you must say ' Let me off, let me off, and I will take you to the city of Women.' " When they had done this, the Bachelor said " Good, now tell me to make a bundle of stalks," and the Little Tortoise said " Do so." When he had made it, he got inside, and said " Little Tortoise, carry me," and the Tortoise said " Very well." So when he had got inside, the Little Tortoise managed to lift him up, but he began to groan, for he was not strong, and he said " Alas ! Alas ! "

Soon he met a Hyæna, and the Hyæna said " O Little Tortoise, what are you carrying ? " and the Little Tortoise replied " Oh, the Bachelor said that I must carry him." . Then the Hyæna said " Throw down the Base-born One of his Parents,* and let me eat him." So the Little Tortoise threw down the bundle, and the Hyæna came up and tore it open, and took out the Bachelor, and ate him.

———

An Annamite story (S.F.T. 200) relates how a Daughter of a Jinn was married to a Mandarin who had sought her in the abodes of the Immortals. " His happiness continued until the day when it was his Lady's turn to be in attendance upon the Queen of the Immortals. Ere she left him she warned him against opening the back door of the palace where they dwelt, otherwise he would be compelled to return home, and his present abode would be forbidden to him from that moment. He disobeyed her. On opening the door he beheld once more the outside world."

The typical tale is that of the *Third Kalandar in the Arabian Nights* (Burton's Translation, i, page 139). The earliest mention of the City (or rather the Isle, as it is usually represented) of Women is in *Pomponius Mela,* iii, 9, where an island is mentioned off the West Coast of Africa, inhabited only by women. The Hausa, inhabiting an inland district, naturally speak of a city, not an island.

83

The Town where None might go to Sleep.

A certain Woman had two Daughters, one was married to a Man who lived in a town where no one was allowed to go to sleep, the other to one in a town where no one might spit.*

One day she cooked a dish of sweetmeats to take to the Daughter who lived in the town where no one was allowed to go to sleep. As soon as it was ready she started off, and when she had arrived, all the Household said to her " Welcome, welcome." Food was prepared for her, for the Son-in-Law said " See, my Mother-in-Law has come." But the Daughter said " O Parent, no one may sleep here, do not eat too much lest sleepiness should overcome you." But the Mother said " I knew long before you were born that sleep was not permitted here." "Oh, very well then," replied the Daughter, "I'll say no more." And the Mother ate every bit of the food that was brought to her.

That night, although she lay down, she managed to keep awake, and in the morning the Daughter took up her jar to go to the stream for water (1), and said to her Mother "See here, I have put the breakfast on to boil, please keep up the fire while I am away." But when the Daughter had gone, although her Mother managed to replenish the fire for a time, drowsiness overcame her in the end, and she lay down and fell fast asleep. Just then a Neighbour came to get fire (2), and, when she saw the sleeping Woman, she exclaimed "Alas, So and So's Mother-in-Law is dead."

Then the Drummers (3) were sent for, and soon the whole town had assembled at the house, and a grave had been dug (4). The drums were saying

"*Birrim, birrim* (5), get a corpse-mat (6),
Death's in the Son-in-Law's house."

But the Daughter heard from where she was, and she cried out

"Stay, oh, stay, don't get a corpse-mat,
We are accustomed (7) to sleep."

And when she had come, she roused her Mother, and said "Wake up, wake up." Then the Mother awoke with a start, and the People were terrified, [but they soon saw that it was nothing to be afraid of], and the whole town began to learn how to sleep.

Now the Mother returned to her own home, but one day she cooked more sweetmeats, and decided to visit her other Daughter, the one living in the town where no one might spit.* When she had arrived, the Household said "Welcome, welcome," and the Son-in-

Law said " My Mother-in-Law has come." So he killed a Fowl, and sent her a dish of rice. But the Daughter said to her Mother " Do not eat too much, you know that in this town no one is allowed to spit." The Mother replied " Thanks for the information ! I knew that before ever you were born." So the Daughter said " Very well," and took no more notice; and the Mother ate until she was full.

Now when night came, she wanted to spit badly, but she did not know where she could do so [without being found out]. At last she went to the place where

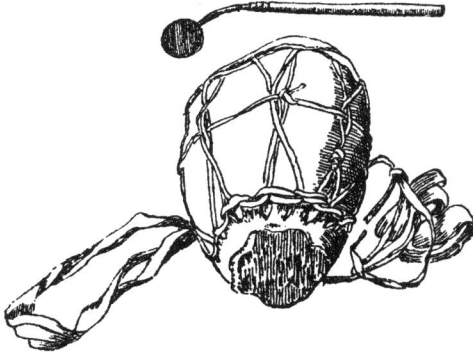

FIG. 89.—Drum, of uncommon shape, and stick. H., 10¼ in.

the Horses were tied up (8), and she spat, and covered it up with some of the cut grass there. But the earth was not used to this, and the part spat on rose up and began to complain, saying

" *Umm, umm,* I am not used to this,
 Umm umm, I am not used to this."

Soon all the People came, and said " Who has spat here ? " Then they said " Bring out the Magic Gourds, the small one and the large, and let everyone come here, and step over them; and the gourds will catch hold of the one who has spat." So all the People of the town stepped over them, but no one was seized, [and they were surprised]. Then someone said " See here, there is a Stranger amongst us, let her come and step over the gourds." Immediately she had come, and had lifted up a leg to step over, the gourds seized her, and everyone said " It is she who has spat, it is she who has spat." And the gourds began singing these words

"The things which clasp and hold on,
    The Mother-in-Law has got them."

She could not sit down, for they held on to her body.

Now, the Spider, the interfering Person, met her, and said " O Mother-in-Law, how lucky you are to have gourds which sing such a beautiful song, I should like to have them." So she replied " Very well, spit on the ground, and say that it was not you who did it." And when he had done so, he said " There, but it is not I who have done it, if it is I, O You Magic Gourds seize me." And immediately the gourds loosed the Woman and seized him. Then they began singing

"The things which clasp and hold on,
    The Spider of Spiders has got them,"

and the Spider felt exceedingly pleased, and began to dance.

But soon he got tired, and said " O Mother-in-Law, Thou Thing to be avoided (9), come and take your gourds." But she refused to do so. Then the Spider climbed a tree, and when he had got high up he threw himself down on his buttocks, so as to smash the gourds. But they did not agree to this, and moved to one side, and so the Spider's back was broken, and he died. Then the magic gourds returned to where they had come from (10), and all the Townspeople began to spit, for they saw that there was no harm in it.

In a Banks' Islands myth, Quat, who began the work of creation, sailed to the foot of the sky to buy darkness from Night, and Night darkened his eyebrows, and showed him how People fall asleep of an evening. On Quat's return, the sun began sinking in the west, and his People were much afraid, and when their eyes began to blink they feared that they were about to die. But he reassured them, and at daybreak they awoke to find themselves still alive (Frobenius, *op. cit.,* page 300).

84

THE MENDER OF MEN.

All the Maidens of the town had assembled, and had gone to the forest to pick certain herbs, and, while they were doing this, it began to rain, from the east it came, and they ran, and got inside the hollow of a Baobab tree (1), and the Devil closed it up. When the rain had ceased, the Devil said that each must give him her necklace and cloth before he would release her, and all gave them to him except one Girl who refused to do so. So she had to remain, but the others went off home.

Now the tree had a small hole in the top, and they went and told the Maiden's Mother, so she started off, and came to see the place where her Daughter was. Then she returned home, and prepared food, and she went back to the tree in the evening, and said " Daughter, Daughter, stretch out your hand, and take this food." So she stretched out her hand through the hole, and she got it, and ate it, and then the Mother went home again.

As it happened, a Hyæna had heard all this, and later on he (2) returned, and said "Daughter, Daughter, stretch out your hand, and take this food." But she replied "That is not my Mother's voice," [and she would not]. So the Hyæna went to a Blacksmith (3) and said "Alter my voice for me, [so that it will resemble that of a Human Being]," and the other said "If I do improve your voice for you, even before you have arrived at the foot of the tree you will have eaten whatever you have found," and he continued "but I'll do it for you," [and he did so]. But as the Hyæna was returning, he saw a Centipede, and he said "Does one ignore what he finds in the morning?" (4). And he took the Centipede, and ate it. Then he went to the tree, and said "Daughter, Daughter, stretch out your hand, and take this food." But she replied "That is not my Mother's voice."

So the Hyæna became angry, and he returned to the Blacksmith, and was about to eat him, but the other said "Stop, stop, stop, you must not eat me," and he continued "Why do you want to eat me?" Then the Hyæna replied "Because you did not alter my voice properly." Then the Smith said "Stop, I will do it properly." So he altered the Hyæna's voice, and then the Hyæna returned to where the Maiden was, and said "Daughter, Daughter, stretch out your hand, and take this food." This time she stretched out her hand, and, when she had done so, the Hyæna seized it, and pulled the Maiden out of the tree, and ate her, leaving only the bones. Then he went away.

Now the Maiden's Mother brought food in the evening, and, when she had come, she saw her

Daughter's bones, and she burst out crying there. Then she went home, and got a basket, and she returned, and collected the bones, and took the road to the city where Men were mended.

She travelled on and on, and after a time she came to a place where food was cooking itself, and she said " O Food, show me the road to the city where Men are mended." Then the Food said " Stay here and eat me," but she replied " I have no appetite, I do not wish to eat you." So the Food said " When you have gone so far, take the road on the right hand, and leave that on the left."

After a time she came upon meat which was grilling itself, and she said " O Meat, show me the road to the city where Men are mended." Then the Meat said " Stay here and eat me," but she replied " I have no appetite, I do not wish to eat you." So the Meat said " When you have gone so far, take the road on the right hand, and leave that on the left."

So she started again, and as she was travelling, she came upon *fura* which was mixing itself in a pot, and she said " O Fura, show me the road to the city where Men are mended." Then the Fura said " Stay here and eat me," but she replied " I have no appetite, I do not wish to eat you." So the Fura said " When you have gone so far, take the road on the right hand, and leave that on the left."

She travelled on again, and at last there she was in the city where Men were Mended. Then the People said " What has brought you here?" And she replied " The Hyæna has eaten my Child." " Where are the bones?" they asked. And she put down her basket, and said " See, here they are." So they said " Very well, to-morrow your Daughter will be mended."

When morning broke, they said to her " Go out

and tend the Cattle," so she unloosed the Cattle (5) and took them off to feed. Now these Cattle had no food except the fruits of the *Adduwa* tree (6), and when she had picked off the fruits above, and had thrown them down, she picked out the ripe ones, and gave them to the Cattle, but she herself chose the green ones to eat. She fed them thus until the evening, and then they returned home, and as they reached the enclosure (7), the biggest Bull began bellowing—

"This Woman a good heart has,
Mend her Daughter well."

So the Daughter was mended well, and the Mother returned to her hut, for the People said to her "Sleep here, and to-morrow you will go home." So next day the Daughter was brought and restored to her Mother, and they went home.

Now the Mother had a Rival Wife, who also had a Daughter, but a very ugly one, and, when the Mother had returned home, the Rival said that she too would kill her Daughter, and go to the city where Men were mended.

So she took her Daughter, and put her in a mortar, and began to pound her up. Then the Daughter cried out "O Mother, are you going to kill me?" But she went on pounding, and at last she took out the bones, and she brought a basket, and put the bones into it, and then she took the road to the city where Men were mended.

She travelled on and on, and after a time she came to a place where food was cooking itself, and she said "O Food, show me the road to the city where Men are mended." Then the Food said "Stay here and eat me," but she replied "Opp, do you need to invite me to eat you?" So she stayed and ate up the food.

After a time she came upon meat which was grilling itself, and she said " O Meat, show me the road to the city where Men are mended." Then the Meat said " Stay here and eat me," and she replied " Opp, do you need to invite me to eat you ? " So she stayed and ate up the meat.

She started again, and as she was travelling, she came upon *fura* which was mixing itself in a pot, and she said " O Fura, show me the road to the city where Men are mended." Then the Fura said " Stay here and eat me," and she replied " Opp, do you need to invite me to eat you ? " So she stayed and ate up the *fura*.

So on she travelled again, and at last there she was in the city where Men were mended. Then the People said " What has brought you here ? " And she replied " The Hyæna has eaten my Child." " Where are the bones ? " they asked. And she put down her basket, and said " See, here they are." So they said " Very well, to-morrow your Daughter will be mended."

When morning broke, they said to her " Go out and tend the Cattle," so she unloosed the Cattle and took them off to feed. Now when she had picked off the fruits of the *Adduwa* tree, and had thrown them down, she picked out the green ones, and gave them to the Cattle, she herself chose the ripe ones to eat. She fed them thus until the evening, and then they returned home, and as they reached the enclosure, the biggest Bull began bellowing : —

" This Woman a bad heart has,
Mend her Daughter ill."

So she tied up the Cattle, and went to her hut, for the People said to her " Sleep here, and to-morrow you

will go home." In the morning, the Daughter was
created with one leg, one buttock, one hand, the whole
consisted of only one side, half a nose was there, the
other half was missing. And when the Mother came,
and said that she was going home, the Daughter was
brought out to her, and they went off along the road.

When they had emerged from the forest, the Mother
said " I am not your Mother," and she started off at a
run, and went and hid in some grass. But the Daughter
followed the footprints, and went on and on [until she
had found her], and said " Arise, let us go on." Then
the Mother said " Go away, you are not my Child."
But the other said " Ah, it is you who are my Mother."

Soon afterwards, the Mother again started off at a
run, and went and hid behind a tree. But the Daughter
followed the footprints, and went on and on [until she
had found her], and said " Arise, let us go on." Then
the Mother said " Go away, you are not my Child."
But the other said " Ah, it is you who are my Mother."

After a time the Mother again started off at a run,
and went and hid in a cave. But the daughter followed
the footprints, and went on and on [until she had found
her], and said " Arise, let us go on." Then the Mother
said " Go away, you are not my Child." But the other
said " Ah, it is you who are my Mother."

Once more the Mother started off at a run, and
entered their own town, and went into her hut, and shut
the door. But the Daughter came to the door, and
called out " O Mother, I have come." But the other
remained silent. " O Mother, I have come," said the
Daughter again, and she opened the door, and went to
her Mother. So they lived together, and the Rival
Wife had to put up with the fact that the other's
Daughter was beautiful while her own was hideous.

In a variant (M.H. 50), the Girls were caused to fall down from the roof of the hut, and, though their bones were broken, they were not killed. The second Girl, however, was not made into a Half-Girl.

Compare the English story of " The Three Little Pigs " in Jacoby's *English Fairy Tales* (1890), pages 68 and 233.

85

THE PORCUPINE BECOMES A STEP-FATHER.

There was once a certain Old Woman, and whenever she gave a cough, it turned into a Child, so she had given birth to a whole city, and when she had borne them all, she died. Now they also, the Children, all died, and went to the next world (1), and they roused her, and said " Where is our Father? " Then she said " Don't you trouble yourselves, I'll find your Father for you," and she continued " To-morrow your Father will come." So they slept, and when God's day had broken (2), they came, and said " O Mother, where is our Father? " And she replied " Your Father has not yet come."

It was always thus, until one day the Porcupine heard the news, and next morning he went and said to the Old Woman " When these Children come again, say to them ' See, your Father has come.' " So next morning when the Children came, she said " See, your Father is in the hut," and then the Porcupine came out, and said " Let each one come and take hold of one quill each, and if you see that they are the same number as you, you will know that I am your Father." So they all came, and each took hold of one quill, and the quills were exactly the same number as they were. Then they said " O Father, when you die what inheritance are you going to leave us?" (3).   And he replied that there was an inheritance that he would leave to them.   Then he told them that on the day that he died, they must come and pull out the quills which they had taken hold of, and that when they had done so, each must bury his in the grave.

So they lived on there until the Father died, and then each Child came, and plucked out a quill, but only half of them buried theirs, the other half put them in their huts.   Now as for those who had buried theirs, after seven days the quills turned into Cattle, and they came out of the grave.   But as for those who said that they would not bury theirs, the quills said that they would not remain without any hiding-place, so each arose, and stuck itself into a Child's body, and each of these Children died.

Nor will they ever rise again, for they ignored their Father's words; but the others were happy.

86

How Auta killed Dodo.

A certain Dodo came to the town, and began calling out " In this town who is able to fight with me?"   And the whole of the People hid, and at night they even lay in the grain-binns (1).

Now a certain boy called Auta [Little Mite] heard about this, and he came and stopped at the house of an Old Woman in the town.   And when night came, and Dodo was calling out " Who is my equal in this town ? " Auta said " I am." But the Old Woman said "Are you mad, Boy? Come into the house quickly, Dodo is coming." But Auta said " You go to sleep in peace." Then he picked up seven stones, and put them in the fire, and Dodo was calling out, and Auta answering back, until at last Dodo came up close to the door !

Then Dodo said "Where is he who is equal to me ? " And Auta replied " See me." Then Dodo stooped down, so that he might enter the porch to seize Auta, but Auta took one of the stones and threw it into his mouth, and when Dodo had swallowed it, he went outside again and stood up.

Then again Dodo said " Who is equal to me ? " And Auta replied " I am equal to you." So Dodo again tried to enter the porch, but Auta took another stone, and threw it, and Dodo swallowed it, and went outside again. And Dodo kept on coming, and Auta kept on throwing stones until the seven were finished. Then Dodo went outside again, and stayed until the dawn, when he died. [But Auta went out during the night and cut off Dodo's tail, and hid it in the house.]

Now in the morning, the Women came out of their houses to go to the stream, but, as they were going, they saw Dodo lying where he had died. Then they put their hands to their mouths and gave the alarm, calling out " *U, U, U.*"

Then the King told the Drummers to beat the assembly, and said to his Soldiers " Go to where Dodo is, and see if he be alive or not, to him who has killed him I will give ten Slaves." But as each one came near, his Horse saw Dodo, and at once bolted, until at last the *Sa(r)rikin Karma* (2), the Swordsman, came, and when he had examined Dodo, he saw that he was lifeless, so he went and said to the Townsmen " Come, look, he is dead." So then they all arose, and their Horses also, and went to where Dodo was.

Then the King sought all over the city, but could not find his Slayer, until one Man said " I heard a certain Boy answering Dodo back from the Old Woman's house." So the King said " Is that so? Go to the house, and see, and if the Boy is there bring him." So they went and brought Auta, and he brought Dodo's tail, and showed it to the King. Then the King chose ten Slaves and gave them to him, he brought his Daughter and married her to him, and he chose a house and gave it to him.

That is all.

———

A variant of this is the more common, perhaps. It states that there was once a certain Rich Man who had a Daughter named Barra, and a Son named Auta. The Father died, and the Mother also died. But as they were about to die, they said " See here, Barra, you must not let him be unhappy, whatever he wants you to do, do it."

The Brother and Sister lived there, and one day Auta began crying " *Kuhum*," and she said " What is it, Auta?" He replied that he wanted to assemble all the Slaves, and to sell some, give others away, and kill the rest. Then she said " Auta, what you want to do is not right." But he replied " Mother and Father said that you must not make me unhappy." So she said " Very well, do it." So he assembled all the Slaves, he sold some, he gave others away, and he killed the rest, so that of all the Slaves there were none left, and there had been a hundred!

Then again he cried " *Kuhum*," and she said " What is it, Auta, the Brother of Barra?" He replied " I want to collect all our possessions, and burn them, the clothes, the cowries, the salt, the pounding implements, and the corn." Then she said " Auta, Brother of Barra, what you want to do is not right."

But he replied " Mother and Father said that you must not make me unhappy." So she said " Very well, do it." So he burned up all their possessions, and the house, so they had nothing to eat.

Then she said " Well, as far as I, Barra, am concerned, I had better take you up and go to another city lest you bring some other misfortune upon us, and kill us both." So she took him, and put him on her back, and went to another city, to the King's palace. Now the harvest was ripe, the corn was being brought

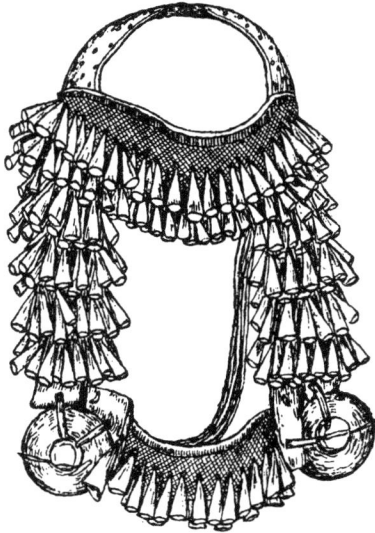

FIG. 90.—Bridle of leather, cloth, and brass.

from the farm, and the whole city assembled to go to the King's farm to get the corn (3). The King had two little Sons, and Barra said " Now, Auta, you wait here and play with the King's Sons, for I am going to where the corn is being collected " [and she went off].

After they had been together for a time, Auta said to the King's Sons " Come and let us play *Kirribi, kirribi, rup karupki* " (4), and, he continued, " I'll lift up one of you, and throw him down on the ground, and then he can lift me up and throw me down also."

So he lifted up one of them, and dashed him on the ground, and he died, and Auta threw him by the door of his Mother's hut. Then he lifted up the other, and dashed him on the ground, and he died too, and Auta threw him by the door of his Mother's hut.

Now, as it happened, Barra was saying to herself " Let me make haste and outstrip the Harvesters, and get in front of them all, perhaps Auta has done me another evil turn." So she outstripped them, and came, and found that Auta had killed both of the King's Sons, and was sitting down and playing in the dirt. No sooner had she arrived, than she snatched him up, put him on her back, and ran. As she was running away, the King returned and found that his two Sons had been killed, so everyone mounted his Horse, and said " Pursue Barra, her Brother has killed the King's Sons." They would have been captured had not a White-Breasted Crow caught them up and flown off with them, and Auta repaid her kindness by wounding her with a sharp stick.

The tale is then practically the same as the one above, but in addition to taking Dodo's tail, Auta placed his boots on the body. Next day the boots were taken to the King, who said that he whom the boots fitted had done the deed. So the whole city came and tried on the boots, but they did not fit. Then a certain Man said " Ah! there is a Boy at the Old Woman's house." Then another said " If all the Strong Men have failed to kill Dodo, could a Boy have done it ? " But the King said " Summon him, however, one never knows." And when the Boy had come he put on the boots, and they fitted exactly (5), and then he produced Dodo's tail.

87

How the Zankallala killed Dodo.

This is a story of the Zankallala (1), and Dodo, the Swallower-of-Men. Now one day, Dodo was chasing a certain Boy on the bank of the river, and the Boy was running away, until at last he came upon the

Zankallala, and the Zankallala said " Where are you going?" He replied " I am running away from Dodo." The other said " Stay here, Dodo will not do anything to you."

All of a sudden, a silk-cotton tree grew up above the Zankallala, and the Birds in the tree began singing his praises, saying :—

> " The Lion is afraid of the Zankallala,
> The Hyæna is afraid of the Zankallala,
> Dodo is afraid of the Zankallala."

And as they were singing and saying this, Dodo came up, and heard, and said to the Zankallala " Where is my property?" " What property have you given me?" asked the Zankallala. Then Dodo replied "Very well, if you will not give me my prey, you yourself shall furnish my meal." So he seized the Zankallala, and swallowed him, but the Zankallala emerged from his stomach, and jumped up, and told the Birds to sing his praises. Then Dodo again seized him, and swallowed him, but he emerged from the middle of his back, and told the Birds to sing his praises. Then once more Dodo swallowed him, but he emerged from his head, and Dodo fell down, and died.

Then the Zankallala said to the Boy " Now you can go in safety, you have seen that one is more powerful than another, you have escaped because you met me."

———

Two variants of this story have been published already (F.-L. 44 and *Man* 5), the Girl or Boy being promised help by Warriors and others against the Snake or Witch before they are saved finally by the Centipede or the Hedgehog, as the case may be—or, as in this story, by the Zankallala.

———

A tale from Altair, on the other side of the world, is given by Dr. Haddon (*op. cit.*, page 166): " Once

upon a time a man named Nadai, living on the Island
of Boigu, went into the bush to collect the eggs of the
Mound-Bird. . . . He found a large mound, and dug
into it until he came to what he thought was an egg.
He tried to pull it up, but it stuck fast; then he tried
to get another, but neither would that come away. It
so happened that a Dorgai [Bogey] named Metakorab
was sleeping under the mound, and she was wearing
several large white cowry shells, and it was these that
Nadai was pulling at, mistaking them for eggs. Nadai
at last caught hold of the shell, which was tied on to
the Dorgai's chin, and giving a tremendous pull he
dragged the Dorgai out of the ground. He was so
terrified at her appearance, that he fled back to the
village and called out to the inhabitants to arm themselves and kill the Dorgai, who was sure to follow after
him.

" By-and-by a fly came, and behind it came the
Dorgai; but the men no sooner saw her terrible face
than they threw down their weapons and ran away in
a fright. Then Nadai went on to the next village, but
the same thing happened again. So he went on all
round the island, but it always happened as before.
At last Nadai came to a village called Kerpai, on the
north side of the island, and he begged the people to
stand firm and attack the Dorgai. They armed themselves, but when the fly came, and after it the Dorgai,
they all took to their heels as the others had done
before, with the exception of one man named Bu. He
remained in the bachelor's quarters, and armed himself with a bow, and with arrows that are used for
shooting wild pigs. When the Dorgai arrived, Bu
shot her and killed her.

" Both are now in the sky [forming the constellation
of Dorgai]; the Dorgai going first, being continually
followed by Bu."

88

THE WRESTLERS AND THE DEVIL.

There lived once a Youth, Awudu, who was nick-
named the Strong One. His Father had 150 head of

Cattle, and he slaughtered them all, and made bags of the hides, and then he went off on a trading trip to sell them, and Awudu went out into the world to try his strength.

As he was travelling along, he met another Youth, called Hambari (1), and he also was noted for his strength; he had just arrived at a well, and had opened his mouth and had drunk the water, when Awudu came upon him, and they travelled on together. Now they went on, and came to a running river, and Hambari beat the water with his hand, and the water divided into two. Then Awudu said "Hullo, Hambari, you certainly are strong."

As they were travelling they met Dashira (2) who also was a powerful Man. And he said to them "Are you going out to try your strength?" And they said "Yes." He said that he would go also, and so there were now three of them.

As they were travelling, they met Tankoko (3) who also was a powerful Man. And he said to them "Where are you going?" They replied "We are going out into the world to try our strength." And he said that he would accompany them, so there were now four of them.

Well, they went into the forest, and slept that night at the foot of a Monkey-bread tree, all four of them. Next morning they said "Ah! the day has broken, let us go hunting, but let us leave Hambari to keep guard over our possessions." So they went off, the other three, to hunt.

Now, as it happened, there was a Devil in the foot of the tree (4), and the Devil came out, and said "Hullo Hambari, it is reported that you are strong, get up and wrestle with me." So they got up and started wrestling, the Devil and Hambari, and the Devil threw Hambari on the ground, and bound him, [and then he went back]. So when the others returned, Awudu said " Opp, what has happened to you Hambari ? " And he replied " I wrestled with the Devil, and he threw me, and bound me." So they [unbound him and] said " Oh, well, to-morrow let us leave Dashira on guard."

Next morning the others went off hunting, Awudu and Tankoko, and the Devil came out again, and said " Hullo Dashira, it is reported that you are strong, get up and wrestle with me." And when they had wrestled for a time, the Devil threw him, and bound him, [and then he went back again]. So when Awudu and Tankoko returned, Awudu said " Opp, Dashira, what has happened to you ? " And he replied " I wrestled with the Devil, and he threw me, and bound me." Then Awudu said " Very well, Tankoko, to-morrow it will be your turn to look after the place."

So next morning Awudu went off alone to hunt, and, when he had gone, the Devil appeared, and said " Hullo Tankoko, it is reported that you are strong, get up and wrestle with me." And when they had wrestled for a time, the Devil threw him, and bound him, [and then he went back again]. So when Awudu returned, he said " Opp, Tankoko, what has happened to you ? " And he replied " I wrestled with the Devil, and he threw me, and bound me." Then Awudu said " Very well, to-morrow I shall not go hunting, let the Devil come and meet me."

So next morning the Devil appeared, and said " Hullo Awudu," and the other answered " Um." Then the Devil said " You have come out in the world to try your strength, you four, yet I alone am equal to you all." And he continued " You see I have

TAKAI. XXXIII.—THE CHALLENGE. XXXIV.—THE ASSEMBLY.

This is a war dance. It may be performed by men only, who hit each other's sticks as they pass round in opposite concentric circles, or by both sexes, the women clapping hands instead of using sticks.

already beaten three, you are the only one left." Then
Awudu arose, and they started to wrestle, Awudu and
the Devil began wrestling. And they wrestled, and
wrestled, neither one being able to beat the other,
and they rose up to the sky, grunting all the time.
Then Hambari, Dashira and Tankoko ran away. But
Awudu and the Devil kept on grunting, and they have
never stopped even unto this day, that is the reason
of the rumbling of the thunder (5).

In a variant (L.T.H. 17) the food of the three Hunters was stolen by a Dog, and when they beat it, " The-
One-inside-the-Tree " came out and wrestled with them
in turn. The third Hunter threw his Adversary, and
then he and the other two killed him.

In another (L.T.H. ii, 32) Dodo takes the place of
Iblis, and eats the Hunter's food, until he is killed by
the youngest (6).

89

THE TWO GIRLS AND THE DEMONS.

This is about a Beloved Daughter and one who was
not loved. The Parents' farm was far away in the
forest, and they called the Unbeloved One and took her
to the farm, and said " You are never to come home
again," they told her that she was to stay there, and
keep the Monkeys away (1). So she lived there, and
watched for the Monkeys, and at night she would enter
her hut alone and sleep.

One day some Demons (2) came, and assembled at
the door of the hut, and when they got up next morning
to go, they brought her presents, and left them at the
door of the hut, and went off. These she sent to her

Father at home, and said that her Father must come and take the presents from her hut. So the Father came, and took the presents, and they all went to the town, and she returned to live at home (3).

Now when the Mother (4) of the Beloved Daughter saw the presents she said " Where did she get them ? " So they said " She got them at the farm." And then she said that the Beloved Daughter should go also. By the time that the Beloved Daughter had arrived, it was night, and she entered her hut, and, while she was lying down, the Demons arrived. Then she went outside the hut, and mixed with them, and immediately they pulled off the flesh from her body, and ate it, and disappeared (5).

She died.

90

THE THREE YOUTHS AND THE THREE DEMONS.

Three Youths used to go to a certain town to get Women to bring back to their own town to sleep, they were always doing this. Now, as it happened, there were Devils on the road, and three of the Female-Demons said " Let us take counsel that we may kill these Youths."

So they adorned themselves, and when the three Youths set out from their own town to bring Women, lo ! they met the three Female-Demons, and said " Well, look here ! We came to look for Women, and see we have got them." Then the Women said " Let us sit here awhile, and talk, and after that we will return with you." So they sat down, and were talking, and were leaning against the Women's thighs, when the eldest of the Youths stretched out his leg, and touched a foot of one of the Women—and lo! it was a hoof, like that of a Horse!

Then he felt afraid, his body trembled, and his heart sank, and he called the youngest of the three, and said let him send him home, for he had forgotten something. But when they had gone aside, he said to him " When you have gone home, do not return, these Women are Devils." So when the youngest of them had gone, he stayed at home. Then the eldest Youth called the next, and said " I sent Auta to bring me something, and he has not returned, go quickly, and call him." But when they had gone aside, he said " When you have gone home, do not return, these Women are Devils." So he followed Auta. And then, except for the eldest himself, there was no one left but the three Female-Demons.

Soon he said that he was perspiring too much, and he pulled off his tobe, and rolled it up tightly. Then again, he said that the perspiration was bothering him, and he pulled off his trousers, and rolled them up tightly, and took the tobe, and put it inside his trousers, and put them on the ground close to him (1). Suddenly he jumped up, snatched up the bundle, and hung it on his shoulder, and bounded off at a run. And the Female-Devils followed him.

When he had reached the fence of his house, he jumped, intending to fall inside, but they caught his foot, and so his head was swinging to and fro in the compound, for they kept hold of his foot. Then he said " Opp, it is not my foot that you have seized, but a post " (2). And they let it go, and he fell, and ran inside the house.

So the Female-Demons went away.

This story is to some extent a variant of No. 10,
but the ending resembles that of a variant of No. 23 in
which the Hyæna sends her cubs away one by one to
get water for the Goat, who has frightened her, telling
them secretly not to return. When all have gone, she
goes also " to see what has become of them."

————

91

THE UNGRATEFUL MEN.

Once there was a certain Woman who went to
where a Witch was getting herbs for her broth. Now
this Woman had nine mouths, [but no one knew], and
she went and got leaves of the locust tree and boiled
them, and when she had made the broth she took it
to her Husband, and after that, she took some to her
Husband's Father, and to his Mother, and to her Rival
Wife.

Now the Husband uncovered the food, but no sooner
had he done so, than the food cried out " Cover me,
cover me, if you do not cover me up at once you will
die." Then the Husband's Father uncovered his food,
to eat, but it also called out " Cover me, cover me, if
you do not cover me up at once you will die," so he
covered it up. Then the Husband went and got his
Mother's calabash of food (1), and he heaped that of
his Mother and his Father with his own, and he went
and threw it upon his Wife's head, and immediately her
nine mouths could be seen. Then she rushed upon the
People, and became an out-and-out Witch; before that
she had not been a real one.

Well, the whole town was depopulated, everyone
ran away but a Blind-man and a Lame-man (2). The
Blind-man said to the Lame-man " Ahem, that Woman

is a Brute, her Husband told her not to get the leaves
of the locust tree but she did so." And, as it happened,
the Woman was standing close to them. Then the
Lame-man said " Hey, Blind-man, I have no feet,
you carry me, for I have eyes, and if I see her I will
tell you, and we can run away." So the Blind-man said
" Agreed," and he took the Lame-man on his back.

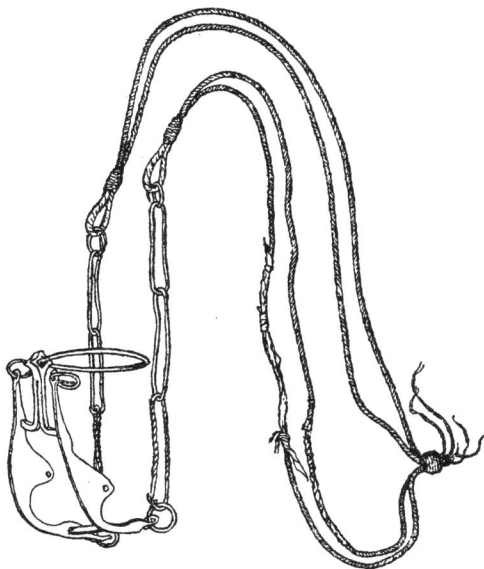

FIG. 91.—Bit and reins used with fig. 90.

But as he did so, he saw the Witch, and she came up
to them, and said " O Blind-man, touch my mouth, and
feel it." Then the Lame-man said " It is she," but the
Blind-man said " Let me feel," and he put out his
hand, and immediately she pulled it off. Then the
Blind-man shook off the Lame-man, and went away at a
run, and he went and hid in a thorn-bush (3). And

the Lame-man crawled off, and he got inside a hollow Monkey-bread tree.

Now after a time the Lame-man found that he had got feet again, and his legs were lengthened, and he could walk a little. And he called out " O Blind-man, I can walk." Then the Blind-man said " O Lame-man, I have got back my eyes," for he could see a little. Then the Blind-man emerged from the thorn-bush, and the Lame-man came out of the hollow Monkey-bread tree, and when they met, they said let each return so that he could be quite healed. So the Blind-man returned to the thorn-bush, and the Lame-man again got inside the hollow Monkey-bread tree. But when they had done so, the Lame-man's legs became crooked again, and the Blind-man's eyes once more grew dim, so the Lame-man died in the hollow Monkey-bread tree, and the Blind-man died in the thorn-bush.

God had given them some alleviation of their distress, but they were not thankful, they only said that they would not be content until they were quite cured (4).

———

Compare Grimm's story of the Goldsmith who, not being satisfied with the present which the Pixies had given him, even though they had also removed a hump which he had had on his back, tried to get more, and found that his present had become worthless, and that his hump had reappeared.

————

92

THE MAN AND HIS WIVES WHO WERE WITCHES.

There was a certain Man who had married three Wives, and all of them had the art of magic. One's magic was not that of eating Men, but that of the other two was of that kind.

Now they used to go to the forest, and have magic dances with their Drummer, and as they danced he would sing, and say " O House-Mother, can you not do the witchcraft dance ? " And she would reply that the witchcraft dance was too hard, wait until she had given her Husband as an offering. Then the Drummer would say " O Second Wife, can you not do the witch-craft dance ? " And she also would reply that the witchcraft dance was too hard, wait until she had given her Husband as an offering. Then the Drummer would say " O Youngest Wife, can you not do the witchcraft dance ? " But she would reply that the witchcraft dance was too hard, wait until she had given her cloth as an offering.

Now the Drummer went and called the Husband, and said that he was going to roll him up in a mat (1), and that he must stay quiet, and hear what his Wives would say. So the Husband remained in the mat, and the Drummer came, and took up his drum, and began drumming, the beat of the witchcraft dance. When the two Wives said that they would seize their Husband to give him as an offering to the witchcraft dance, the Husband jumped up and ran towards them. And as he ran, he seized one Wife and killed her, and he came and seized the second, and took her to the top of a tree, and tied her there, but he left the other, the one who said that she would give her cloth to the dance.

They lived together, for the black magic was gone.

––––––––

In a variant (L.T.H. ii, 97) the Good Wife warns the Husband, and he pretends to go off on a journey,

but really stays with his Friend, the Drummer. He is
rolled up in a mat, and hears one Wife say that if God
will give her money, she will give it to the Drummer,
but the others say that they will give him the liver or
heart of a Man.   The Husband returns to his house
after seven days, and drives out the two Witches, and
lives with the other Wife (2).

93

How the Ill-treated Maiden became Rich.

A certain Man had two Wives, and each gave birth,
and brought forth a Daughter. But the Mother of
one of them died, so the Father said to the other Wife
" See now, this One's Mother is dead," and he
continued " You must look after both your own and
her's." " Very well," she replied, " I will do so."

They lived on, and the Maiden grew up, and the
Wife was always beating her Step-Daughter. One
day the Father scolded her for it, and she said " Oh !
so you would quarrel with me because of her? I will
take her to a place where she will be eaten " (1).

Now there was a certain river called the River
Bagajun, and whosoever went there was eaten by a
Witch (2), and one day the Step-Mother declared that
the Maiden had soiled* a skin [used as a mat for the
floor], and that she must go to the River Bagajun to
wash it. So the Maiden started off, and was travelling
along in the forest, when she saw a river of sour milk
flowing along, and the river said " Here, Maiden,
come and take some of me to drink." But she replied
" No, no, what is the use?" and she passed on. Then
she came to a river of honey flowing along, and the

river said " Here, Maiden, come and take some of me to drink." But she replied " No, no, what is the use ? " and she passed on. Next she came upon some Fowls which were cooking themselves, and, as she came up, they said " Here, Maiden, look here, we are cooking ourselves ; you must come and take one to eat." But she replied " No, no, what is the use ? " and she passed on.

Soon afterwards she came to the River Bagajun, and she stood close up against a tree, and watched a certain Woman who was washing herself in the river. All over her body were mouths, and the mouths were saying :—

> " Here you have given me,
> Here you have not given me."

After a little while the Maiden emerged into the open space on the bank (3), and immediately the Woman [who was the Witch] beat her body with both hands, and the mouths became one like that of an ordinary Person. Then she said " Welcome, Maiden," and she continued " What has brought you to the River Bagajun to-day ? " " Because I soiled this skin, and I was told to come and wash it," replied the Maiden. Then the Witch said " Indeed ! Then come here and rub me." So the Maiden went to her, and while she was rubbing her back, lo ! the back opened—but the Maiden remained silent. Then the Witch asked " What is it ? " And the Maiden replied " Your back has opened." " What do you see inside ? " demanded the Witch. " A little basket with a lid," was the reply. Then the Witch said " Take it, you may go home, I give it to you." And she continued " After you have gone, if, when you say ' Shall it be broken here ? ' you hear

[a voice saying] 'Break, let us divide,' do not break
it [but go on].''

So the Maiden departed, and, while she was
travelling, she said " Shall I break it here ? " And
she heard " Break, let us divide," so she passed on.
After she had walked on a good distance, she again
said " Shall I break it here ? "—silence ! " Shall I
break it here ? "—silence. So she broke it ; and
immediately all kinds of riches appeared, Cattle, Slaves,
Camels, Goats, and Horses, and she sent on word to
her Father saying that he was not to be afraid, and
run away, it was only she who was returning from
the River Bagajun (4).

When she had arrived, and her Mother's Rival
Wife had seen the possessions, she was seized with
anger, and she said to her own Daughter " You also
soil a skin, and go to the River Bagajun." [So she
did so, and started off, and] she went on, and on, until
she came to the river of sour milk, and the river said
" Here, Maiden, take some to drink." Then the
Maiden replied " You are full of impudence, must I
wait for you to ask me to take some ? " So she took
some, and drank until she had filled her stomach, and
then she passed on. Then she came to the river of
honey, and the river said " Here, Maiden, come and
take some of me to drink." Then the Maiden replied
" You are full of impudence, must I wait for you to ask
me to take some ? " So she took some, and drank
until she had filled her stomach, and then she passed
on. Next she came upon the Fowls which were cooking
themselves, and as she came up, they said " Here,
Maiden, come and take one and eat it ? " So she took
one and passed on.

Soon afterwards she arrived at the River Bagajun,

and saw the Old Woman in it, washing, her mouths were saying :—

> " Here you have given me,
> Here you have not given me."

Suddenly the Girl jumped out with a boop, [and ran into the open], and the Old Woman hit her body, and the mouths became one again. " Did you see me ? " she asked. And the Maiden replied " Great Scot ! I should think I did see you, with about a thousand mouths." " What has brought you to the River Bagajun ? " asked the Witch. " Oh ! I came to wash a skin," was the reply. " Come here and rub me," said the Witch. But the Maiden replied " Nonsense, I have come to wash a skin." " Come nevertheless," said the Witch. So the Maiden said " Very well," and when she had come, and had rubbed, the back burst open. " There, it is through your own silliness," exclaimed the Maiden, " I said I should not rub you." " What do you see ? " asked the Witch. " What could I see except a little basket ? " was the reply. Then the Witch said " Take it, I give it to you," and she continued " After you have departed, and are going along, if, when you say ' Shall I break ? ' you hear ' Break, let us divide,' pass on." But the Maiden replied " Nonsense, If I hear ' Break, let us divide,' I will break it."

As soon as she had departed, she said " Shall I break ? " And she heard " Break, let us divide," so she broke the basket. Immediately Lepers appeared to the number of about a thousand, and Lame-men about a thousand, and Cripples and Blind-men ; and she sent them on in front to go to the town. But her Father heard the news, and he said that she was not to come into the town, but that she must live out in the forest with her unclean Family.

In a variant (M.H. 19) the Maidens eat food with the Old Woman, and stay with her for several days. She is evidently a Witch, for she performs wonders with her provisions, dry bones turning into meat, and so on. It corresponds in many respects to Grimm's tale of the two daughters visiting Madam Holle.

In a Sierra Leone story (*Cunnie Rabbit,* page 265), the Step-daughter dirties a rice-stick, and is sent to the Devil's river to wash it. The Devil knows, and, changing himself into first a hoe, and then a Man—a " pusson (who) get one yi' middle heen head "—meets her on the way, and, although the Girl is surprised, she is polite, and does not show her astonishment. At last she arrives at the place, and finds the Devil, who has taken human form and invites her to pull the lice out of his bald head (5). This Devil had so many eyes that he could see if she played any trick, but she did not, and so the Devil washed the rice-stick for her, and told her to choose four eggs from a heap. She took four small ones, and was told to break them one by one *en route* to her home. She did so, and, of course, got all she wanted. But her Step-Sister, who came afterwards, was rude to the Devil, chose four large eggs, and, on breaking them, was stung by Bees, crushed by Snakes, flogged by Men, and lastly burnt up with her Mother. The good Girl, however, managed to raise her own Mother from the grave. Here we see that the Devil was able to have eyes all over his body, or only one in the middle of his head, as he pleased.

94

DAN-KUCHINGAYA AND THE WITCH.

Once there were certain Boys, three of them, one named Dan-Kuchingaya (1), and his two Brothers, and they were courting Maidens. Now, these Maidens were the Daughters of a Witch, but the Boys did not know this (2), and they went to the Maidens' house.

When they had arrived, food was prepared for them, and they went outside to walk about [while it was being cooked]. Now it happened that they came upon the Witch, combing the plaits of one of her Daughters,

FIG. 92.   FIG. 93.

FIG. 92.—Saddle in general use, of wood, iron and leather, covered with skins. FIG. 93.—Stirrup and leather.

and looking for lice (3), and the Boys came up and said "Peace be upon you." Then the Mother loosed her Daughter's head, and when she had done so, the Boys came and sat down. And when evening came, food was brought to the Boys, and they ate it.

Now that night, the Witch was unable to sleep, and

she took a knife and began sharpening it. But Dan-Kuchingaya [heard her, and] pulled off her Daughters' breasts, and put them on to his Brothers [and himself] while the Witch was sharpening the knife. When she had sharpened it, she came to cut the Boys' throats, but Dan-Kuchingaya coughed, and said " Um." Then she exclaimed " Oh ! Boy, what do you want ? " He replied " I want an egg, to do something with it " (4). So the Witch went and brought it to him, and then went and lay down. Then Dan-Kuchingaya went and pulled off the under-cloths of the Witch's Daughters, and put them on his Brothers [and himself] ; and he pulled off his Brothers' loin-cloths and his own, and tied them on to the Witch's Daughters (5).

No sooner had he done this, and lain down again, than the Witch came, and began feeling about [in the dark], and when she found a loin-cloth she killed the wearer. So she killed all her Daughters [without knowing it], and, after she had done so, she returned, and lay down by herself. Then Dan-Kuchingaya dug a hole in the floor of the hut, and made a tunnel right to his town, and he roused his Brothers, and they went off, only he alone, Dan-Kuchingaya, stayed in the Witch's house.

When morning broke, the Witch came, and said " Get up, you Children, day has broken." Then Dan-Kuchingaya emerged, and said " I am Dan-Kuchingaya, I will show you what I have done." So she went and found her Daughters, and saw that she had killed them all, and she said " Mark me, I will be avenged on you for what you have done to me." Then the Boy went home and told his Brothers, and said " If you see a Woman come soliciting, do not go with her."

Now the Witch arose, and became a Bad Woman, and came to the Boys' town on market-day, and it happened that Dan-Kuchingaya's Elder Brother saw her—she had put forty needles in her hand [but he did not know this]—and when he saw her, he wanted to go with her, and she said " Very well." But Dan-Kuchingaya came up, and saw her, and he called his Elder Brother aside, and said " Do not go with that Woman." But the Elder Brother abused the Boy, so he said " Oh, very well, go." So the Elder Brother called the Woman aside, and they began to talk together, when, all of a sudden, she plucked out his eyes, and disappeared. Then Dan-Kuchingaya said " Ah! I told you not to go with her," and he continued " Now I must go and get back your eyes for you." And the Elder Brother said " Good."

So Dan-Kuchingaya transformed himself, and became a beautiful Filani Maid, and he carried some milk for sale, but he did not begin to offer it until he had reached the door of the Witch's house (6). And, as it happened, the Witch said " Bring it here." So he took it to her, and she bought it. Then he asked her, saying " Do you know of a charm to recover eyes ? " And he continued " Dan-Kuchingaya, a Wicked Boy, has been and has plucked out the eyes of my Cattle." " Is that so ? " the Witch replied, " Well, go, and get the eyes of a Black Goat (7), and when you have procured them, I will give you a certain ointment to put with the eyes, and you will see that the eyes of your Cattle will be restored." So he said " Good [but give me the ointment now." And she gave it to him] (8).

So Dan-Kuchingaya left her, and when he had got a good distance away, he changed himself into a Youth again, and said "I am Dan-Kuchingaya, it is on account of the eyes of my Elder Brother which you plucked out, that I came and questioned you." Then she said "Go and get some pepper, and put it in." But he replied "Oh! I know all about that" and he went off. So they bought a Black Goat, and killed it, and Dan-Kuchingaya put the eyes into his Elder Brother's sockets, and it came to pass that his eyes were restored.

A variant (L.T.H. ii, 38) makes *Dan Kuchin-da-Gayya* a Younger Sister, and the story proceeds upon the same lines as The Girl who Married a Snake (F.-L. 44), except that the Snakes are Dodos. The escape, however, is like the one here—by changing the clothes —as in the story of Hop-o'-my-Thumb.

Compare the Breton story of La Perle, Sébillot, i, *Contes Pop. de la Haute Bretagne,* 131. It is also told among the Shuswap of North America, ii, *Jesup North Pacific Expedition* (Mem. American Museum of Nat. History, Leiden and New York, 1900-1908), 757. French trappers have perhaps been the medium of transmission. (H.)

95

THE BOY, THE WITCH, AND THE WONDERFUL HORSE.

There was once a certain Hunter, he was always hunting; and he had a Son who was also a Hunter. Now, one day, the Son went into the depths of the forest, and there he saw a shed, and said to himself "I am going to see who lives in that shed," so he climbed up into a tree. And when he had climbed up, and was sitting there, suddenly a Woman came out of

TAKAI. XXXV.—THE BATTLE IN PROGRESS. XXXVI.—THE FINAL MELÉE.

All the dancers become greatly excited, and the mimic fight sometimes becomes so realistic that they have to be restrained. *Vide* Illustrations XXXIII. and XXXIV.

the shed, and, when she had come out, she got a great
jar, and put it on to boil, and, when it began boiling,
she brought a sackful of *acha* [and poured it in], and
began stirring, and stirring it. Then she took it off the
fire, and beat her body, and suddenly over the whole
of her body appeared mouths, and she took the food,
and began feeding the mouths, and they ate. Each
mouth would say " O Mother, are you not going to
give me any ? " Soon all the food was finished, even
the dregs, and she beat her body again, and her mouths
once more became only one. Then she took the jar,
and carried it into the shed, and soon afterwards she
came out again with a mat, which she spread at the
foot of the very tree in which the Boy was, and she
lay down.

Now the Boy was sitting up above her, and he broke
off a branch, and threw it down on her, and she said
" O God, ever since that tree has been here its branches
have never fallen, whatever has happened to them ? "
Then she cast up her eyes, and saw the Boy, and said
to him " Descend," so he did so, and then she said
" O Boy, did you see me ? " And he replied " I did
not see you, Mother," and he started to go off. But
she said " Come back," and, when he had done so, she
said " O Boy, you saw me." But he said " No, I
did not see you, O Mother," and then she said " You
may go." When the Boy got to the gate of the city,
he blew horns and trumpets, and said " To-day I saw
a Woman with many mouths, one would say ' You
have given me some,' another would say ' You have
not given me any.' "

Now the Woman heard from where she was, and
when she had heard, she bit her fingers [hands], and
said that the Boy had put her to shame in the city.

So she made preparations where she was, and turned herself into a Woman beautiful in all truth. And when she had done this, she came to the door of the King's palace. The King said that he wanted to marry her, but she took a little basket with a lid, and placed it by the King's door, and said that whoever hit and opened it, he would be her Husband. Then the King threw at the basket and hit it, but it did not open, so he made room for the Heir to try, and the Heir hit it, but it did not open. So the Councillors were given the chance to try, and they hit it, but it did not open.

Now the Boy, the Hunter, was away in the forest, and a Friend left [the spot where the throwing was taking place] to go home, and, as he was going, he met the Boy, who had returned from the forest, so he said " Come and let us throw at the basket." The Boy said " Whose ? " And the other replied " It belongs to a certain Woman, a most beautiful one." Then he asked " Has the King not thrown ? " and the other said " He has." " When he threw did he not win her ? " asked the Boy. [Then the other replied " No "], and the Boy said that if the King had tried, and had not succeeded, how was he going to do so ? But the Friend said " Let us go, how do you know that you cannot ? "

So they went, and when they had come to the place the Boy took a tiny stone, and threw it, and, when he had done so, the basket opened ! Then she said that now she had got a Husband. So they were married, and they left the place, and went to the Boy's house. He left the hut in which formerly he used to sleep, and he lived with the Woman. He refused to go near his First Wife, he preferred the new one. But his Father told the first one to say nothing, and so they lived thus.

Now, one day, the New Wife said that she must go to her own city, and at night they began talking. At last she said " Do you go hunting with charms? " And he said " Um," and he began telling her [what they were]. But his Father swore at him, and then he kept silence. So in the morning he arose, and was going to girth the saddle on his Horse, but the Woman said " Are you going to ride, and kill me in the forest with the Horse? " So he left the Horse, but he took up his sword. Then she said " Are you going so that you can cut me down in the forest? " So the Boy returned, and left his sword, but he took up his water-gourds. Then she said " Are you going to make some charm against me in the forest? " So he left all his weapons in the hut, and was going off thus, when his Father scolded him, and said " Get all your things from your hut, and take them," so he got them. Then his Father said " Your Horse says that he is going to follow you in the forest," so he said " Very well, I will saddle him." So he put on the saddle, and mounted, and he sent her in front of him, and they started off.

After a time, she said to the Boy " Do you know this part? " and he replied " Certainly I do know it, for we hunt in all directions." At last they reached her shed, and she said " Do you know that shed? " And he said that he knew it. Then she asked " What did you see in it? " And he replied that he had seen a Woman, a Many-mouthed one. Then she exclaimed " Oh hoh! " So they went on, and on, and on, for six days they travelled, and then she asked " Do you know this part? " And he said that he did not. On and on again they went, until they had been going for ten days, and then they arrived at the city.

When they had got to the house, she prepared her magic, she got food, and took it to the Boy, and he ate it. And in the night she sharpened her teeth, for she was going to enter the Boy's hut, and eat him. But the Horse spoke, and the Boy asked " Who is there ? " And she replied " It is only I." Then he said " What has brought you ? " and she answered " I was wondering if the fire was out." Then the Boy said " Oh no, go away." So she went out, and re-entered her own hut (1).

For three days the Boy was in the city, and there was nobody else there but them. Then the Boy said to his Horse " To-morrow morning do not eat any grass." So when morning came, the Horse did not eat any. Then the Woman asked " What is the matter with your Horse ? " And he replied " He has pains in his inside." Then she asked " What is the cure for that ? " And he replied " Here is a basket in which water can be drawn (2), if he has water from it he will be cured." So she took the basket and went off to the river, and when she had gone, the Boy put the saddle on his Horse, and mounted, and started galloping away.

Now the Woman tried, and tried, but whenever she took it out, the water would not remain in the basket, until at last she made a charm, and the water remained there. Then she returned to the house, but she did not see the Boy, so she threw down the water (3), and took to the road, and followed the Boy. Soon she saw him afar off, and she called out " Alli, (4) you Youth possessed by fear, you have left your loin-cloth, you have left your turban " (5). Then the Boy turned his head, and said " I have left them as a present." But she replied " That present is given because of fear."

So she ran on [and overtook the Boy], and was about to seize one of the hoofs of the Horse, when lo! the Horse's tail became a razor, and cut her hand. Then she stopped and began licking the blood.

But soon she started off again, and followed, and called out " Alli, you Youth possessed by fear, you have left your loin-cloth, you have left your turban." Then again the Boy turned his head, and said " I have left them as a present." But she replied " That present is given because of fear." So she ran on [and overtook them], and wounded one of the Horse's legs. Then the Boy was very much frightened, and said " O Horse, would you fail me? Take me home, it is not close." And the Horse replied " Even had I only one leg I would take you home safely," and he continued that he would carry him for the Boy's own sake, not his. Soon the Woman came on again, and followed, and followed, and called out " Alli, you Youth possessed by fear, you have left your loin-cloth, you have left your turban." Then again the Boy turned his head, and said " I have left them as a present." But she replied " That present is given because of fear." So she ran on [and overtook them], and wounded another of the Horse's legs. Then the Boy said " O Horse, O Loved One, would you fail me? Take me home, it is not close." And the Horse replied " Even had I only one leg I would take you home safely," and he continued that he would carry him for the Boy's own sake, not his.

At last they arrived at the gate of their city, and just then the Woman managed to wound another of the Horse's legs and he fell down dead. Now the Father knew what was going on, and he opened the hut where the Dogs were kept, and they followed behind him, and they chased the Woman, she got away only just in time. Then the Father said " That is enough for now, there will be more to do to-morrow." So the Boy dismounted from his Horse, and took the path to his home, and he bought white cloth, and the Horse was wrapped in it, and buried.

After about two days, the Woman turned herself into a mass of flowers, and the Women of the town went and began picking them. Then the Boy's Friend came to him [and asked him to go also], but he replied " It is that Woman." Then the Friend said " Poof, are you afraid of *her*?" So the Boy said " All right, let us go." So they went, but the Boy would not go to the place where the flowers were, and when he had returned home he said " I tell you that it is that Woman." And in the morning, when the People had gone to look for the flowers there were none. Then the Boy said to his Friend " You see, I told you so."

About two days later, she transformed herself into a Horse, and said that she would kill the Boy, [so she wandered about loose in the streets of the town]. Now the Youths of the town went and caught the Horse (6), and mounted it, and made it gallop, and the Boy's Friend came to him, and suggested that they also should go and catch the Horse, and ride it. But the Boy refused, saying " It is that Woman." Then the Friend said " Poof, are you frightened of your own Wife?" So the Boy replied " Very well, let us go." So they went to where the Horse was, and the Friend caught it, and rode it, he galloped, he rode away, and then returned. So then the Boy also mounted it, and, when he had done so, and was galloping, she turned herself into a Wind, and was going to carry the Boy up in the air, but he caught hold of a branch of a tree, and, when she saw that he had done so, she went off. Then the Boy descended from the tree, and went to his Friend, and said to him "You see, I told you that it was that Woman," and the other said "Yes, it was so," and they went home.

FIG. 94.

FIG. 95.

FIG. 94.—Brass stirrup. L., 10¾ in. FIG. 95.—Head ornaments (for horse) of leather, coloured flannel, and cotton.

Again the Woman came, and changed herself into a Sword [and went to the market], there was no other like it in the whole city, and the Youths came and tried it. Then the Boy's Friend came to him, and suggested that they also should go, and see the Sword. But the Boy said " It is that Woman." Then the Friend said " Poof, are you afraid of your own Wife ?" So the Boy replied " Very well, let us go." They started off, but, as they went, he called his Dogs, and no sooner had he arrived than he cut at the Sword with his own, saying let him test its edge with that of his own. So he cut it in two, and lo ! the Woman appeared, and the Dogs chased her, and ate her flesh (7). Wherever even a single drop of blood dropped on the grass he told the Dogs to take it, and so all the Dogs followed, and licked up the blood.

———

In a variant (M.H. 20) the Youth buys a Horse with the breasts of his own Mother which he has cut off, and he sets out to see where the world ends, the Spider accompanying him, riding on a leaf. At last the Travellers arrive at the end of the world, where " there is no land, not a tree, nothing but wind, water, and darkness." The Youth will not touch the food at first, but the Spider says that there is no harm in it, so he eats it. In the night the Cock warns them three times that the Witch is coming, and so she has to desist. In the morning she asks her Visitors if they have seen her do anything which was not quite the thing, and they reply in the affirmative. She manages to capture the Cock and kill it (though at first it contrives to escape and to hide in the grass), and she gives it to them to eat. Three times she comes in the next night also, and the Spider, who is watching by the door, beats her on the head with an iron club on each occasion, breaking her head, so she retires to lick the blood which is flowing on to her body. Next morning, they say " Good-bye," and go off. She follows, and catches the Horse's tail, but her hands are cut by razors which have been tied there, " again she comes like the wind," and catches them at a river of hot water, but again her hands are cut. They pass through rivers of fire and of cold water with a similar result, and at last they reach *terra firma,* the Witch turns back, and they arrive home in safety.

———

In a Sierra Leone story (*Cunnie Rabbit,* page 184) a Girl is wooed by a Half-Devil and is taken to his home, her Young Brother following them against the Half-Devil's wish. In the night the Devil sharpens his knife, and creeps up to kill the Girl, but the Brother speaks, and asks for more clothes; next time he coughs, and asks the Devil to get him some water in a fishing-net, and the Devil goes off to do this " Because he wan' hurry yeat de ooman, he stupid; he no wait t'ink he no able get wattah wid fis'-net." While the Devil is away, the Brother and Sister go off, of course, and escape.

————

96

THE BOY WHO CHEATED DEATH.

There was once a very Rich Man, there was no other in the whole city so rich, and he had a Son. The King of the city also had a Son, and the latter said that he wanted the Rich Man's Son to be his Friend. But as for any real friendship [there was none, for] the King's Son did not really like the Rich Man's Son very much, and he, the Rich Man's Son, did not really like the King's Son very much. The King's Son was friendly to him on account of his Father's riches; and the Rich Man's Son was friendly to the other because he was the Son of the King of the city.

Now there was a certain town where Death lived, with her Children, and whosoever went there never returned. And one day the King's Son said to the

Rich Man's Son " Look here, you are very proud of yourself because your Father is rich." And he continued " [If you are as fine a Man as you think), go to Death's house, eat her food, and bring me the remains."

Then the Rich Man's Son told his Father, and said " Listen to what the King's Son said to me when we were at the games (1), in front of the Women, before all the People (2). He said that my Father is rich, let me go and eat Death's food, and bring him the remains." Then the Father said " Well, look here, I will give you twelve Slaves to take with you, and while she is killing them, you can get away, and escape." But the Son replied " No, no, I am not afraid, let my Horse be saddled, and I will go." So his Horse was saddled, and off he started.

He went on, and on, and on, and after a time he came upon a certain Man who was carving out stools (3), and the latter said " O Rich Man's Son, where are you going?" " I am going to Death's house," he replied. " Then let me give you a stool," the Man said, " it will be useful to you." So he took it, and started again.

He travelled on, and on, and on, until he came upon a Blacksmith, who said " O Rich Man's Son, where are you going?" " I am going to Death's house," was the reply. " Then let me give you this hammer," the Blacksmith said, " It will be useful to you." So he took it, and started again.

He travelled on, and on, and on, until he came upon a Woman who was collecting firewood, and she said " O Rich Man's Son, where are you going?" " I am going to Death's house," was the reply. " Then let me give you a bundle of wood," she said, " it will be useful to you." So he took it, and he put all of them behind him on his Horse.

Soon afterwards he arrived, and came upon the Children of Death, who were farming, and they said " O Rich Man's Son, welcome, welcome." " Where is Death ? " he asked. " She is at home," they replied, so he came up, and saluted. Then Death came out, and said " Ah ! Rich Man's Son, welcome," and she said to her Children " Cook rice for the Rich Man's Son, prepare a meal for him." When they had cooked it, and had got it quite ready, she said " Good, give it to him to eat, I am going to the stream to find my Husband."

Now when the Children had given the Rich Man's Son the food, and he had eaten, and was filled, he threw the remains into his haversack, and then he [remounted his Horse, and] spurred it, and galloped off. And when Death returned, and asked the Children where the Rich Man's Son was, they said " Oh ! he has gone." But she exclaimed " It cannot be true ! Does he who comes to my house ever return ? "

Then she pursued him, she ran on, and on, but just as she had come up close, and was about to seize the Horse's tail, he let the stool fall, and immediately it became a great tree, and it closed the road. So she returned to her house, and got an axe, and came again, and started chopping. She chopped, and chopped, and, while she was doing so, the Rich Man's Son was getting further away.

When she had chopped through the tree, she threw down the axe, and ran on, following the Rich Man's Son, but just as she had come up close, and was about to seize the Horse's tail, he let the hammer fall, and closed the road. Then Death said " Bother it, I must go and get the hoe, and dig under the hammer, and loosen it and throw it aside.''

By the time that Death had loosened it, the Rich Man's Son was a long way ahead, so she ran after him again, but just as she was about to seize the Horse's tail, the Rich Man's Son let the bundle of wood fall, and it closed the road. Then Death exclaimed '' Bother it, I must return to the place where I left the axe.''

By the time she had chopped it through (4), the Rich Man's Son had reached the gate of his own city, but she ran on, and almost caught him. Then [when he had escaped] she stopped, and called out '' O Rich Man's Son, you are very lucky; you will not die until God Himself kills you, for you have come to my house, and have returned alive.''

When the Rich Man's Son had entered the city, he went to the King's Son, and said '' Here is Death's food which I have saved for you.'' But the King's Son replied '' That is a lie ! You must have played a trick upon her; if you are not afraid, go to the house of the Rago ''(5). At the Rago's house, for him who arrived one day would be killed the Guest who had come the day before, and the New Arrival would be slaughtered for the morrow's Visitor.

So the Rich Man's Son went and told his Father, and said '' Listen to what the King's Son said to me. He dared me to go to the house of the Rago.'' Then the Father said '' Well, look here, I will give you twelve Slaves to take with you, and while the Rago is eating them, you can get away, and escape.'' But the Son replied '' No, no, I am not afraid, let my Horse be saddled, and I will go.''

When he had arrived at the Rago's house, he

saluted, and the Rago said "Ah! Rich Man's Son, welcome." So the Rich Man's Son dismounted, and there was killed for him the Stranger who had come the previous day, and by the time he had been killed, and soup had been made, the Rich Man's Son and his Horse had gone inside the Rago's house. Now when the meal had been served and eaten, the Rago's Wife opened the door at the back of the house, and the Rich Man's Son galloped off, but the Rago was in the entrance-hall (6), and did not know that they had escaped.

Just then another Stranger arrived, and saluted, and when he had done so, the Rago said "Welcome, welcome," and, when he had welcomed the New-Comer, he entered the house, and said "Where is the Rich Man's Son?" He wanted to kill him for the Stranger. Then the Wives said "Oh, none of us have seen him, he must have run away." But the Rago exclaimed "It cannot be true. I shall follow him," and he ran after him, calling out "O Rich Man's Son stop." Then the Rich Man's Son replied "Oh! no, I will not stop; why do you not run and catch me if you can?" So the Rago followed him, and ran on, and on, and on, but the Rich Man's Son escaped. When he had got right away, and had reached the door of his house, the Rago said "O Rich Man's Son, you are indeed lucky, you will not die until God kills you."

Now when the Rich Man's Son had returned, he went to the King's Son, and said "I have been to the house of the Rago." But the King's Son replied "It is a lie, to-morrow you must mount your favourite Horse, I also shall mount my favourite Horse, and we will gallop before the door of the council chamber, my Father's door (7).

So next morning, the Rich Man's Son said to his Father " Listen to what the King's Son said to me, he said that I must mount my favourite Horse, and that he would mount his favourite Horse, and that we must gallop before the door of the council chamber, his Father's door." So the King's Son rode a Horse worth ten Slaves, the Rich Man's Son rode one worth twenty, and when they had come to the open space at the entrance of the council chamber (8), the King's Son said " O Rich Man's Son, you gallop first." But the Rich Man's Son replied " No, no, you must go first, this is your Father's door " (9). So the King's Son galloped off, and when he had come back, he said " There you are, now you go." Then the Rich Man's Son said that he would, but as he was returning to where the King's Son was waiting, his Horse neighed, and, when it had finished neighing, the King's Son and his Horse had disappeared, the neighing had carried them off, there was no one who knew where they had gone, he and his Horse.

Then the Rich Man's Son went to his Father, and said " See, I galloped with the King's Son, but he has disappeared, I have not seen him since."

So the King mourned the loss of his Son.

———

In a Sierra Leone story (Cronise and Ward, page 292) a Girl and her Dog go with the Ghosts to their country—which was far away on the other side of a big, big valley—and the Ghosts disappear one by one, until she is left alone with the one whom she has followed, and his house is furthest away. The Ghosts come and try to kill her, but she is saved by her Dog—which can see " dem die pusson "—on condition that she never calls him " Dog " again. All goes well for a time after their return, but one day she uses the word in a fit of anger, and falls dead.

97

THE KING WITH THE CANNIBAL TASTES.

There was once a certain King, and, while his evening meal was being prepared, a Hawk, which was

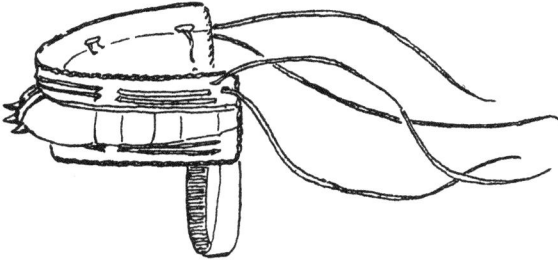

FIG. 96.

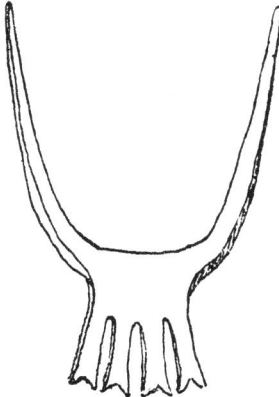

FIG. 97.

FIG. 98.

FIGS. 96, 97.—Spurs.   FIG. 98.—Iron bell tied to horse's mane.
H., 1¼ in.

carrying a piece of human flesh, flew over the palace, and, while she was flying, the flesh slipped from her grasp, and fell into the soup, and no one saw it. So when the food had been cooked, it was taken off the

fire, and brought to the King, and the soup also was
brought. So the piece of human flesh was put before
him, and he ate it.

Now when he had eaten the food, he thought that
he had never tasted anything so nice before—it was
the piece of human flesh which he thought so good, but
he did not know—and he asked for more. So he had
a Goat killed, but he did not get a flavour like that
of the other, then he had a Bull killed, but again he
missed the delicious taste of the flesh. And though
he sent and had brought to him meat of every Beast
of the forest, when he ate it, he did not get the flavour
he wanted.

At last he had a Slave seized, and he killed him,
and ate him, and then he recognized the taste, so he
kept on seizing the People of his household, and killing
them, until they were all finished (1). And then the
other People in the city ran away, and left him alone,
and so, when the longing overcame him, he would pick
off a piece from his own body, and eat it. At last he
was nothing but bones, and when he ran, you could
hear the bones rattling, and making a sound like
gwarrang, gwarrang.

One day he went along the road to the resting-
place of the Traders, and he lay in wait to rush upon
them, and on their arrival he [let them pass, and then]
followed one at a run to catch him, and bring him
back to eat. So he went and killed him, but when he
wished to carry back the corpse, he fell down, he was
too weak to carry it, and he died.

That is all.

————

In a variant (L.T.H. ii, 49) the King discovers what
the flesh was by seizing the Slave who comes to light

his fire, and, as this happens always, the Wives find it out and run away. His Married Daughter comes to visit him, and nearly loses her life, but manages to escape in time.

In a Malayan tale (Skeat, *op. cit.*, 59), an Attendant takes the carcase of a Goat to the river to wash it before roasting for the Prince. A Vulture flies down and carries off the heart, and as the Attendant is afraid to take the flesh back thus, he kills a Boy who is passing, and substitutes his heart for that of the Goat. The Prince so much enjoys the new meat that, when he has found out what it is, he has a Boy killed daily, and he gradually grows tusks.

98

THE MANY-HEADED CANNIBALS.

This is a story about the *Girringas*, the Many-headed Cannibals. There was one Girringa who had two heads, and he went to a far city to get a Wife, and while they were returning, he and his Wife, they met with another Girringa who had three heads, and when he saw them he sang : —

  " Welcome Girringa."
And the other replied, also singing,
  " Um, hum, Girringa."
And then they sang again,
  " Welcome Girringa."
  " Um, hum, Girringa."
" Where have you come from ? " asked the one with three heads.
" I come from Kano," sang the other.
" What did you go for ? " asked the new-comer.
" To find a Wife," replied the other.

" Where is the Woman ? " asked the Three-headed One.

" See her behind me," was the reply.

" What is she crying for ? " asked the other.

" She is crying at the sight of your heads," said the Husband.

" Wait until she sees the King," replied the other.

So they parted, and [the Wife and her Two-headed Husband] went on towards the city, and lo ! they met with a Four-headed Being, who sang :—

　　　　" Welcome Girringa."

And the other replied, also singing,

　　　　" Um, hum, Girringa."

And then they sang again,

　　　　" Welcome Girringa."

　　　　" Um, hum, Girringa."

" Where have you come from ? " asked the one with four heads.

" I come from Kano," sang the other.

" What did you go for ? " asked the new-comer.

" To find a Wife," replied the other.

" Where is the Woman ? " asked the Four-headed One.

" See her behind me," was the reply.

" What is she crying for ? " asked the other.

" She is crying at the sight of your heads," said the Husband.

" Wait until she sees the King," replied the other.

So they parted, and [the Wife and her Two-headed Husband] went on towards the city, and lo ! they met with a Five-headed Being, who sang :—

　　　　" Welcome Girringa."

And the other replied, also singing,

　　　　" Um, hum, Girringa."

And then they sang again,
"Welcome Girringa."
"Um, hum, Girringa."
"Where have you come from?" asked the one with five heads.
"I come from Kano," sang the other.
"What did you go for?" asked the new-comer.
"To find a Wife," replied the other.
"Where is the Woman?" asked the Five-headed One.
"See her behind me," was the reply.
"What is she crying for?" asked the other.
"She is crying at the sight of your heads," said the Husband.
"Wait until she sees the King," replied the other.
So they parted, and at last [the Wife and her Two-headed Husband] arrived at the city, and they went to the palace, and then she saw the King of the Girringas who had ten heads! And the King sang :—
"Welcome Girringa."
And the other replied, also singing,
"Um, hum, Girringa."
And then they sang again,
"Welcome Girringa."
"Um, hum, Girringa."
"Where have you come from?" asked the King.
"I come from Kano," sang the other.
"What did you go for?" asked the King.
"To find a Wife," replied the other.
"Where is the Woman?" asked the King.
"See her behind me," was the reply.
"What is she crying for?" asked the other.
"She is crying at the sight of your heads," said the Husband.

Then she was taken to her Husband's house, but she refused to go in, and cried, and cried. Then they argued, and argued, with her, and at last she entered the house. Goats were killed in her honour, three of them, and she hid some of the flesh to eat, and she ate her fill (1).

Well, she lived there for some time, and they fed her up until she had got very fat (2). And on the very day that they meant to kill and eat her, they gave her a pot to get water with which they were going to wash her [although she did not know what it was for] (3). So she went off to the river, but when she had got there, she began to feel afraid, for they had never before allowed her to go outside the house. So she [determined to escape, and] turned herself into a tree-stump.

Now as she delayed, and did not return, one of the Girringas went and followed her tracks, but he could not find her, so he returned and told them that she had run away. Then they said "Oh well, we must put up with it," and so they went about their business. But at night she became a Woman again, and she ran away to her own city.

———

This is possibly a variant of F.-L. 45 (and see 94), one of the Men being sent out to marry a Girl with the intention of bringing her back for the Family to devour.

———

99

WHY THE YOUNG GIANT LOST HIS STRENGTH.

There was a certain Youth, a Giant, as high as from Jemaan Daroro to Kano, or to Bauchi (1); amongst all the others there was not his like. Now a Magician had given him a charm, and had said that he must never know a Woman. [And while he remained single] if a Giant came, no matter whence, when he arrived, then the Youth killed him when they boxed.

Now there was a certain Girl, a Virgin, who was as tall as Sokoto is distant from here (2); Men used to leave places like Damarghera and go to see the Girl because of her beauty. Supposing the King of Damarghera (3) said that he wanted her, she would say that she did not like him. Supposing the King of Zungo (4) (Malam Yerro) came to her, she would say that she did not like him.

But one day she heard the news of this Young Giant, and she said that she would go to him. So she started off, and commenced the journey, and after two months' travelling, she came to the Youth. When he saw her, he said that he wanted to marry her, so he took her, and led her to his house, and married her. Now for the next day a great tournament had been arranged, so the Youth went out, and showed off. And another Giant came from somewhere else, and he also showed off. Then they approached each other, and got to close quarters, and the Stranger caught the Youth's hand, and he watched his armpit (5), and when he punched him, he killed him (6).

Now, when the Young Giant's People saw this, they came and said " Girl, see, him to whom you came has been killed in the tournament." Then the Girl said " What is the remedy for this? " They replied that there was a remedy, and when a grave had been dug, they said that if the Girl came and entered this grave, and was buried inside, the Youth would arise again. So she agreed, and was buried in the grave, and the Young Giant arose, and the Girl who had been buried in the grave arose with him. Immediately the grave became a great palace, and inside this palace of the things in all the world there was not anything wanting, so they settled down, and were married (7).

100

THE BOY AND THE ONE-SIDED GIANTESS.

There was once a certain Boy, a King's Son, who said that he was going out into the world. So he started off, and travelled on, and on, in the forest. Soon he came to a big lake, and he went round, and round the brink, but he could not see any footprints. Then he took out a handful of water, and drank it (1), and he took another handful, and gave it to his Dog. Then he said that he would see that very day what kind of Animal used to drink water there (2), so he climbed a tree, and his Dog lay down at its foot. The width of the water was like from here to the barracks (3).

After a time, in the afternoon, he saw a certain Woman, a Giantess, with one arm, one leg, and one eye, coming to the shore of the lake, and she drank up the water *pap*, and it was finished. Then she began crying, saying that her thirst was not quenched. The water was finished really because the Boy had taken a handful for himself and had given his Dog one!

But she calmed herself, and walked towards the house (4), and she went and brought out a whole barnful of corn, about two hundred bundles, and she pounded them up, and made a porridge of the corn. Then she went and caught two big Bulls, and came and slaughtered them, and made soup with them.

Now the Boy arose from where he was, and came
to her house, and when he arrived, he saw a tree close
to the door, so he climbed it, and left his Dog at the
foot. Just then the Woman brought out her soup,
and she went and brought out her porridge, and then
she entered her hut again to get her proper cloth to
wear when eating food (5). While she was there, the
Boy pushed his spear into the porridge, and drew it
back, and picked off [a little piece of food that had
stuck to it]. This he divided into two, one piece he
put into his mouth, the other he threw down to his
Dog on the ground.

Just then the Woman emerged again from her hut,
and came and sat down to eat the food, and she began
to eat the porridge first. When she had finished, she
began to cry, and to say that Something had stolen her
porridge from her that day (6). Even until midnight
she was crying, but then she calmed herself, and went
inside.

Then the Boy climbed down, and called his Dog,
and escaped at a run, he did not pause until he had
reached his own town. And when he had arrived, he
said " O my Father, I have seen what is in the world."

In a variant (L.T.H. ii, 7) a Hunter comes upon the
houses of two Witches. He creeps up, and takes a
little food from the pot of one of the Witches, and
gives it to his three Dogs, and the Witch, called
Pando Pando, complains to the other, *Kumbo Kumbo,*
that she has not had enough. Kumbo Kumbo suggests
that there must be a Man in the house, but they can
find none, and later on, he and his Dogs escape.
Pando Pando resolves to be avenged, however, and the
story then continues as does number 48. She takes him
to the forest, and tries to kill him, but he gets up a tree,
and calls his Dogs, and they kill both of the Witches.

There are some drops of blood left, and he calls out " May I descend? " The drops of blood reply " If you do we will kill you." So he waits until the Dogs have eaten every bit, and have licked up all the blood.

In European. tales also, drops of blood can speak, *vide* page 18, where reference is made to one of Grimm's stories.

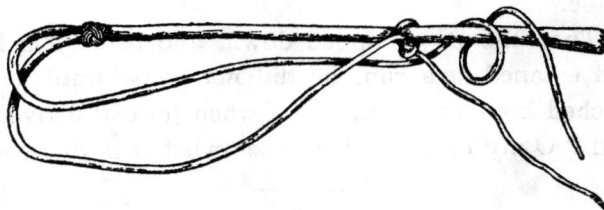

Fig. 99.—Whip of hippopotamus hide.   L., extended, 48 in.

FIG. 100.

FIG. 101.

FIGS. 100, 101.—Dane-guns or bunduks, imported from England. Patterns in cowries (embedded in rubber) on butts as charms. The barrel and stock of the lower one are bound with grass, rubber and leather. L., 5 ft. 7 in.

PART III.

Notes.

I.—ON THE TALES.

N.B.—There is no note for *, it simply means that a word has been purposely mistranslated.

I.

[1] Literally drunk water.

[2] On a charge of theft, but the punishment for serious forms of this crime was the cutting off of a hand or foot (left hand first), not impalement, this (or cutting off the parts) being more usual in sexual offences. In the case of an ordinary theft, where the thief was equal in status to the person robbed, the punishment might be that of tying a long piece of wood to one side of the thief's head so that it projected before or behind. Mutilation and other barbarous punishments have been abolished in the districts under British control, but in

some of the large capitals, specially appointed native courts have the power of passing sentence of death, and of carrying it out after the sanction of the Resident has been obtained.

There was no fixed scale of punishments, a powerful chief could order what he liked, but usually the *lex talionis* prevailed except when the chief himself had been injured. Sometimes the offending slave or animal would be handed over. In one story (L.T.H., ii, 86) a man gives up his wife so that she may be put to death, because he himself has killed a woman. But this is probably not a Hausa rule, it seems to have been borrowed from the Berbers, though there is a trace of it in Story 80, see LXXX, 7. In Hausaland, as elsewhere, the early court helped the successful party to enforce the judgment (62).

In one story, an old woman who was called in to wash the dead body of a young virgin, touched a certain part of the corpse and made an untruthful remark about the virtue of the deceased. Immediately the old woman's hand stuck fast, and it was not until she had been flogged with the proper number of lashes for slander that her hand was released. This seems somewhat analogous to the touching of the body of a dead man by persons suspected of having killed him.

II.

[1] Not Sunday, but our Saturday, the Seventh Day (*Ran Assabat*). I am not sure if all the pagan Hausas had a holy day, but it is quite possible, for members of one community do not work on Sunday, but sacrifice to their Gods on that day (*Man*, 1910, art. 40), and in the Gold Coast " no fishing ever takes place on a Tuesday, the day being sacred to the fetish

of the sea, and devoted to the repairing of nets "
(N.W.S. 15). If the holy day had been a Mohammedan innovation, it would have been Friday, and
not Saturday, as is shown in the other tales.

III.

[1] The daughter of a rival wife, who was evidently
dead, as we hear nothing of her, and the step-mother
is in charge of the girl.

[2] There is no indication as to what kind of fish
it was. Perhaps the manatee is meant, for it is
found in the Niger. But talking fish are common in
folk-lore, and a dead fish laughs in Somadeva, *Katha-
Sarit Sagara* (Ed. Tawney, i, 24 (C)).

[3] In some places the masculine pronouns are
used, in others the feminine, and to avoid confusion
I have called the fish " it," but there is no neuter in
Hausa.

[4] The *Salla,* at the end of Ramadan. Horse-races
and dances are held at these times and people dress up
in new clothes and all their finery, see illustration,
page 16. Two of the dances are described in T.H.H.
pages 262-264.

[5] There were proper preliminaries to be arranged
first, and the chief would have to approach her father
at home, in the usual way. There is a saying that a
bride should never be chosen on a feast day, because
she will be excited and painted, and over-dressed, so
it will be impossible to tell what she is really like.

[6] Really they must have found him at the dances,
for the wife was still there, and she heard them talking.

[7] The new one, the bride.

[8] They did not wish to be seen. Perhaps it would
have been dangerous for any person who saw them.

[9] It is possible that there was some tabu on her doing household work, such as that on speaking which we find in European tales. Compare Story 30.

[10]   Rather a mild punishment for such mutilation. In most of the stories the rival wives are killed for much less than this.

IV.

[1] A strange expression, corresponding in some respects, perhaps, to our " Lend me your ears." A more usual reply is " Increase the number of your ears and you will hear some news," implying that two are not enough for the wonders to be described. This is more intelligible, and is something like our " He listened with all his ears."

[2] As long as the bull pulled against it, the rope could not be undone. The narrator gives no reason why the peg itself was not pulled out, by far the more simple proceeding.

[3] Wives, concubines, and others would all be jealous of the new arrival, especially as she was considered too much above them and too delicate to help in the ordinary work (grinding and pounding corn, fetching water, cooking food &c., evidently the latter in this case). The idea of protecting one's wife from work seems more in accordance with the European than with the native temperament; the true solution is probably to be found in *tabu,* to which a Kaffir tale seems to give a clue. The variant suggests a different reason, however.

[4] In North-west Uganda, if " your enemy is already afflicted with loathsome specific disease, you may take a branch of the castor-oil tree, and with it beat the place where he has been sitting; the result will

be that the disease will become chronic and refuse to get well." (Kitching, *On the Backwaters of the Nile*, page 238.)

V.

[1] Evidently a tabu. Mr. Crooke tells me that in India a man often refuses to live in the town where his wife's family resides, and thinks that this may be a survival of marriage by capture. Dr. Seligmann tells me that he has noticed the same thing amongst the Beja of the Red Sea Province of Kordofan. It has been observed amongst the Matse, an Ewhe tribe in German territory on the Slave Coast. Here, when a woman lives in her husband's house, he may not eat in the house of her parents, and they may not eat in his. A breach of this rule is shameful; many people say that it would prevent the wife from bearing children. (Frazer, *op. cit.*, vol. ii, page 581. See also XXIV (6).)

[2] So that he could feel his way back in the dark.

[3] I do not know why it should be a mare, unless she would be more likely to sympathize with the wife's parents!! Mares are kept for breeding purposes, and are dangerous to ride because the horses are entire.

VI.

[1] The cakes are made of flour soaked in honey, water and pepper.

VII.

[1] There is usually some hiding place for non-combatants where food is stored and other preparations are made for the outbreak of war. All over the country in the old days of the slave-raiders (and even now in the districts of the unsubdued tribes) no town knew when it might have to fight for its very existence.

[2] The Commander-in-Chief, usually called the "War-Father," a man is meant. I am told that the *Uban Ya(i)ki* in each district is always chosen from among the members of a certain family unless they happen to be incompetent or in disfavour with the chief. The office, therefore, is to a certain extent hereditary.

[3] Apparently quantity and not quality is the native's idea of happiness, as in the case of Job.

[4] The word *surukuta* means "shame," "avoidance," or "relationship of mother-in-law and son-in-law."

[5] I saw very little leprosy amongst the Hausas, and I did not question them on the subject, but it is often attributed to the bite of certain species of lizards. The Kagoro say that it has nothing to do with a fish diet, but Canon Robinson (*Hausaland,* page 150) found that there was such an idea in Kano, and he ascribes the disease to the rotten fish eaten in the inland districts, for there was less leprosy nearer the coast, although there was a more plentiful supply of fish, because the fish was fresh. The Hausas will eat fish so rotten that no European could come near them during a meal, and it would not be surprising if such food were the cause of many diseases.

VIII.

[1] Locusts are caught in nets, and when fried are considered a great delicacy; or they may be boiled in oil and well salted, and they then taste rather like an insipid prawn. They cause great damage in Hausaland. It is related that Mohammed once read these words upon the wings of one of these insects: "We are the army of God; we lay 99 eggs, and if we laid

100 we should devour the whole earth.'' The Prophet was aghast, and prayed to God to destroy the locusts, and an angel appeared, telling him that a part of his prayer had been granted. The best charm even now is said to be a piece of paper on which is written this prayer, stuck on a stick in the plantation threatened.

[2] This does not mean that she did so at once. The child would probably not be carried on the back for some time after birth, but in a calabash on the head. See T.H.H., page 306.

[3] Meaning that some were killed and the others ran away. I have left it thus just to show the apparent contradictions which increase the difficulty of translation.

[4] Chronological order wrong, the lion said it before he went, of course.

[5] Apparently there was nothing in the wife using the lion's name to make him commit suicide, it was simply the fact that he had been discovered, so he evidently had the same objection to being seen as have witches. The ending of the first variant shows that this story was invented to account for the lion's living apart from man.

[6] See remarks on *Alkawali* in Chapter IV. The lioness was killed to atone for the death of the boy's mother, and now the youth has to commit suicide to make things even again.

[7] Iddah, or better Idda, is on the Niger River, almost opposite Egori, the first town in Northern Nigeria.

IX.

[1] A form of address.

[2] Probably no crime on the poor man's part, and so preferable to suicide.

X.

[1] Owing to tornadoes, a shallow stream with high banks may become a river in an hour or so, and when the bed is of sand, the channels may be altered almost as quickly.

XI.

[1] These titles do not refer to the powers of good and evil, much less to God and Satan. King or chief is merely a title (see introduction), and corresponds somewhat to our captain.

[2] So as to keep the father in.

XII.

[1] No reference to the powers of good and evil. See Note XI [1].

[2] Instead of the speech continuing after the interruption, it goes off in a new direction.

[3] But he still remained the King of Good, of course!

XIII.

[1] Really no worse than the belief of the old slavers that God would give them good store of slaves. See N.W.S., page 6.

[2] Apparently it was too dark by then for her to distinguish the ram.

XIV.

[1] See LVI (1).

[2] She pretended to be insulted because Dodo could tell that the smell of human flesh was stronger than usual.

[3] The creation of beings by means of spittle or excrement to answer for an escaping hero is not un-

XXXVII. and XXXVIII.—BOXING, OR *DAMBE*.

Blows may be dealt either with the bandaged left fist, or with either foot. The drum is often
necessary in order to encourage the boxers to serious efforts.

common in folk-tales, *vide* Hartland, *The Legend of Perseus,* ii, 60.

[4] *Zirka* is perhaps a corruption of *zikri* " to pray," or may be from *dirka,* " a post." The word *bude* means " open." I have kept the Hausa form as it is usual in such cases. *Gumgum* is a corrupted word and

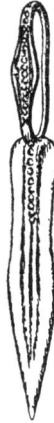

FIG. 102.   FIG. 103.   FIG. 104.

FIG. 102.—Arm-knife. L., 12½ in. FIG. 103.—Knife or Dagger. Red sheath has strips of green and yellow leather. L., 14⅜ in. FIG. 104.— Naked Iron Knife (? of Munshi manufacture). L., 11 in.

means " shut." *Zarga,* in the variant, probably means " move."

XV.

[1] Ground-nuts are grown mainly in the north of the country, and some kinds are valuable to Europeans commercially because of their oil, while most make a

very good soup.   There are several varieties, *e.g.,* *aya* which gives the oil for watches, *gedda* which gives oil for lamps, and *gujia,* used mainly for food. The plants grow low on the ground, and have yellow flowers.

[2] Apparently he took other nuts with him to sow —or else Mrs. Spider must have been rather easy to deceive.

[3] Possibly if the wife had worked the farm she would have had a right to sell a part of the produce and to keep the proceeds for herself.

[4] Rubber (principally landolphia) is found in many parts of Northern Nigeria, but the natives are gradually killing off the supply by digging up the roots.   What they sell is often so much adulterated that it is almost worthless.

[5] A long neck is supposed to be a sign of great beauty, the breasts indicate the age to some extent. The Hausa seldom pays much attention to the face of his beloved, it is her body which attracts him. To call more attention to her charms the narrator here says " See her neck, see her breasts !" Compare F.-L. 9.

[6] The Spider had evidently taken the shape of a man.

[7] Grease is rubbed into the *bulala,* the cat of hide, to make it soft and pliant, but it is not necessary to do this in the case of a switch.

XVI.

[1] The Arabic salutation, in great favour in Hausaland.

XVII.

[1] It is hard to render this in English, we might say "a bean or two," although meaning a sufficient

quantity, but the Hausas often use the singular for the plural, so "cook a bean" means "cook a dish of beans."

[2] Really the water-tank (earthenware) of the house, too big to be carried to the river.

[3] Only one is mentioned in the Hausa text, though it is obvious that all must be meant. The fact that the bodies of the Gazelles could not go into one bag would not trouble the narrator, but there is more than one bag, for there are several donkeys. This is another instance of the plural being included in the singular.

XVIII.

[1] *Uwarmu* ("our mother") is the name given to any woman who provides food, or otherwise takes care of or protects others, who become her "children." Compare the *uwar tuo* in the remarks on *Bori,* and see Story 45, where the poor boy becomes his rival's ruler and "father." It is usually, though not necessarily, a title of respect (*cf.* the Scotch "wifie").

[2] This shows that the variant making the hare the hero is the true version.

[3] A very favourite ending to a story, but showing the attention to certain details.

XIX.

[1] The native carries hoes, axes, &c., thus, nothing is carried in the hand but a weapon in ordinary circumstances.

[2] The slave did not hear this, of course.

[3] The best.

[4] Not rifle-men, the guns being long muzzle-loading weapons of modern make, from Birmingham,

which are usually known as " Dane-guns." See figs. 100 and 101.

[5] Unnecessarily elaborate means, see Chapter II.

[6] The native beer (usually called *pito* by us, Hausa name *gia*) is very heady if drunk while out in the sun. It is often called " water " in fun (cf., our " Adam's ale "), but probably here the slave was pretending to think that both gourds really did contain water.

[7] Mr. Hartland sends me the following note :—
The principal incident of this tale is to be distinguished from that of The Letter of Death, whether it accomplishes its object as in the case of Uriah the Hittite, or is superseded by a forged letter as in the case of Hamlet the Dane. The incident above is found in many European tales, having an edifying purpose, in which the hero escapes from having turned aside to attend a religious service (see De Puymaigre, *Vieux Auteurs Castillans,* ii, 84; Schischmanoff, *Légendes Relig. Bulgares,* 97; Bérenger-Féraud, *Superstitions et Survivances,* ii, 264, apparently from the *Roman Martyrology;* the Fables of Cattwg the Wise in *Iolo MSS.,* 166 *sqq.*). Among the Siamese, potters are said to be excluded from bearing witness in a Court of Justice on account of a similar story (*Journ. of the Indian Archipelago,* i, 407). In the Hausa tale, the magic contest which follows seems to have no real connection with the former. It is a common incident in folk-tales, of which the best-known example is found in the story of the Second Calendar in the *Arabian Nights.*

XX.

[1] The meaning is that the wild-cat intended to accompany the cock and kill the other fowls (and so

cause two deaths), but when he heard that the cock was living with the dog, he knew that he himself would be killed if he attempted it—that would be the third death.

[2] According to. Major Edgar, the cock (in the variant) missed entirely the sarcasm of the wild-cat's remark, and, being without any sense of humour, took it quite literally to mean that the cat was coming with him to the funeral, and so would have the pleasure of meeting his friend, the dog.

XXI.

[1] I do not think that this has any reference to the preparation of a charm, it is simply to save the wild-cat the trouble of flavouring his victim. An infusion of the root of the *bazere* is often drunk as a charm.

XXII.

[1] The house is a compound containing a number of huts, each wife would have a separate one. This is a deadly insult, signifying that the occupier is worthless.

[2] But the rooster still remained the principal person (cf. the relationship of a Governor and the G.O.C. troops in a colony) because the original quarrel was on his account.

[3] See description in XLV [4].

[4] In this case the word *goro* (kola-nut) is used, it is much the same as *alkawali* in this sense. See Chapter II.

XXIII.

[1] A male guest would not be expected to do the ordinary work of the house, for the Hausas are very

hospitable, but the women might help in the preparation of food.

[2] This is generally done where there are two performers. The conjurer at Jemaan Daroro (T.H.H., page 207) would sing a line (impromptu), and the youth would reply " It is true, God knows it," or something to that effect. Where the performer is only one of a number the whole company may take up the chorus.

[3] The kid was sharp enough to see its mother's plan, and acted accordingly.

[4] As it was intended that she should.

[5] Possibly the variant explains why the hyæna lives in the forest, while these two animals are domesticated.

XXIV.

[1] Probably a gourd from which spoons are made. See LVI [1].

[2] But this is really affectation on the Spider's part, for most of the people use the four fingers of the right hand, the fingers being held stiff. They remind one of European babies eating bread and butter.

[3] Evidently a kind of *alkawali.*

[4] Perhaps the following story accounts for the guinea-fowl's stupidity. It is said (M.H. 40) that when things were first made to fly " all the birds said ' If God wills, we shall rise.' But the guinea-fowl said ' Whether God wills or not I will fly,' and she rose in the air, but fell down. Then God said to her ' I retract my blessing from you, O guinea-fowl, you will travel on your legs.' " The bird can fly, of course, but most often it seeks safety by running if there is cover available.

[5] And that he was to be pursued for having killed one of their number. Drums are always used to give the alarm. The francolin is called "bush-fowl" in British West Africa.

[6] In this story the Spider seems to have no hesitation in eating in the house of his Parents-in-Law, in the variant he does not go there. In a Kagoro tale (*R.A.I. Journal*, 1912, vol. xlii, page 190) probably borrowed from the Hausa, the Hare seems to object to eating even in the town of his Parents-in-Law.

XXV.

[1] The lot is drawn by holding out pieces of grass of unequal lengths as with us. In a variant (M.H. 77) where the hare is the hero, cowrie shells are used as dice for the purpose—they are loaded sometimes.

XXVI.

[1] A large tree with many branches, bearing a sweet edible fruit.

[2] Although the monkey was still in the tree, apparently! But a little difficulty like this is not worth the consideration of the narrator.

[3] An aperient is made from the fruit of the *Kimba,* so the monkey's speech was hardly polite!

[4] He is the *Malamin daji,* see Chapter II.

[5] This would seem to indicate that in the ancient native trials (as in ours to-day) the prisoner appeared to be free so that no prejudice would be raised against him. But such, I believe, was not the case.

XXVII.

[1] See XXXI [1].

[2] Potash is often smoked with tobacco, and

ground-nut oil, cow-butter, or shea-butter may be added in order to produce more smoke. After all, soda was once drunk with tea!

[3] The youths go out with the cattle, the girls sell the milk, the women stay at home in the camp and look after the calves, and the older men visit their neighbours, or help to guard the cattle if required.

[4] Not much sense of proportion in this.

[5] He is nearly always the chief of the market also.

XXVIII.

[1] The correct reply, the intonation making it a sound of pleasure, and not merely a rude grunt.

[2] A woman always kneels when handing food to a man.

[3] This can be used like whitewash, and the calabashes are coated outside, a decoration particularly appropriate at wedding feasts I believe. Here a mark of favour. The white powder is sometimes obtained from the bones of cattle, burnt and ground. Several of the calabashes in the illustration, page 368, are whitewashed in part.

[4] Little round grass mats which act as covers or lids, see fig. 69.

[5] The farms are the only clearings in many parts where the population is not too plentiful.

[6] He was so hungry that he would have been unable to resist eating the whole, for he thought it contained food.

[7] So that she could take her own away again.

[8] A proverb, meaning that whatever you do for a man who is fated to be unlucky he will not profit by it. See an expansion of the proverb in the next story.

XXIX.

[1] The Hausa trader is known all over North-West Africa, both as a traveller and a bargainer.

[2] He got more because of his profit.

[3] The most valuable.

[4] Long soft boots, see fig. 24. The sides fall together when off the legs, as do the breasts of old

FIG. 105.—Wooden club, bound with leather, in general use. L., 32½ in.

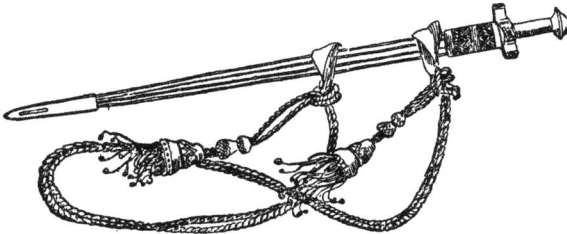

FIG. 106.—Sword in general use. Sling of purple and green cotton. L., 37½ in.

women. Sometimes they are compared to razor-strops. It is needless to say that the Hausa women's breasts are very long.

[5] It does not mean that the old woman was obtained in direct exchange for the three cloths, for this would have been an excellent result. It means that at the end of his trip (see Story 27) she was all he had to show.

[6] *Ga fura, ga fura,* a very common cry in the markets during the heat of the day. See XXXI [1].

[7] The man walks behind his wife to be ready to

help her with her load, and also to guard against her being surprised and robbed.

[8] A hundred slaves would probably be less valuable than 1,000 horses, so the progression is not clear. Rather a high price for one old woman.

[9] *Mafari* usually means "origin," but here seems to bear the meaning ascribed, though perhaps germ or nucleus would do.

[10] The fact that they could not have overtaken him when his horse was the faster and he had had a start does not occur to the narrator.

[11] I do not think that there is any idea of a City of Refuge in this, it is probably merely because to have gone further would have meant fighting.

[12] The elder brother is nearly always indebted to the younger in the stories, and is benefited even though he does not deserve it.

[13] This points to the conclusion that kindness to animals precedes a good turn done by them.

[14] The native dogs are scavengers, and wander about at night.

[15] They build nests in the roof, have white bellies, and are smaller than the ordinary variety. They would always be in the house, and would see what was going on.

[16] Why he should have been awakened the narrator could not explain, for it was not necessary since the ring had been secured. This has evidently been introduced from a variant. See Story 62.

[17] Where anyone wanting it could obtain it himself for nothing; but the lucky man would persuade him to buy instead.

[18] Another example of the virtue of laziness, the fourth wife "had never done anything but lie down."

XXX.

[1] In many towns strangers are the chief's special care, and lodgings in special huts are set aside by him for that purpose. See T.H.H., pages 245, 246.

[2] I could not obtain any explanation of this, the reason is not apparent. It might possibly have been meant as a compliment to the girl to persuade her to talk (such "working-bees" are quite common, see F.-L. 6), but it is more likely that she was to be put to shame as in Story 3.

[3] A complimentary form of address. For an equivalent in England compare the Roman Catholic priests and superiors of convents.

[4) Accented to resemble the sounds of the pestles in the wooden mortars. The women were evidently three to a mortar, and each making one beat in turn, as there are six sounds which represent two rounds of beating. Sometimes two women pound together, more often there is only one. Something like this can be seen in England in the case of road repairers using very heavy hammers. *Cf.* LXXXVI, 4. See fig. 41.

[5] The literal translation of the proverb runs: " If a boy lives with a bad master he will invent tricks." Here it means that the girl was not going to allow any rivals, especially as the elder wives were her superiors.

[6] At one time dogs were eaten by the pagan Hausas, and this story seems to be connected with the dying out of the practice under Islam.

XXXI.

[1] Flour and water, known as *fura,* is the regular uncooked meal. Travellers take dry flour in bags and

mix it with water *en route,* and evidently enjoy the paste thus formed, though it looks very uninviting to a European. A little sour milk makes the drink a very dainty beverage. See Story XXVII [1]. It is sold in the markets, XXIX [6].

[2] *Tulu* is a large and long earthen vessel kept in the hut, the ordinary pots taken to the stream are much smaller and more round. The latter are also used for cooking.

[3] There does not seem to be much point in this story, greed is rather rewarded than punished, for few people would mind being driven out of a town if they thereby obtained four slaves.

XXXII.

[1] Not bullock, there is no such mutilation amongst these people so far as animals are concerned.

[2] Not matches, of course—for these are a European introduction, and not known even yet in some districts—but a burning ember, or a fire-stick. A flint and steel (see figs. 71 and 72) are used in many districts.

[3] Generally recognized, I believe, as the perquisite of the person acting as butcher, if he be part-owner, in return for his trouble. At any rate the skin always went to such a one when goats were killed by one of my caravan.

[4] It can hardly be imagined that the Hausas consider it right to allow flies, &c., to share in the feast, and yet judging by the crawling masses of stinking meat in the markets one might be led to think so, but the story evidently is intended to emphasize hospitality.

XXXIII.

[1] See note (2) on fire in preceding story.

[2] The Hausas talk of the fire " being killed," and

of its " dying." There is, at any rate now, no objection to its going out except that of the trouble of lighting it again. See T.H.H., page 193.

[3] Always removable in the case of small round mud huts, they are made separately. See T.H.H., page 140, and the illustrations in this book, page 80.

[4] Should be about 4.30 a.m.

[5] The real words used on such occasions are not fit for translation, but they reflect on the parents of the person abused, and so sting more than if applicable only to the person himself. Unless the Hausas indulged in ancestor-worship, the reason is hard to imagine, considering the loose morality of the people. Perhaps it is a case of " The greater the truth the greater the libel "—or slander rather.

[6] It used to be a good thing to be a chief's son. Can we wonder that our rule is unpopular with the old nobility ?

[7] Usually such a thing does not bother the narrator, and in this case it may have been merely that the Spider was too lazy to carry the Elephant, not that he could not do so. One can usually carry more than one can eat at one meal.

XXXIV.

[1] A mark of greater respect, mats being cheaper in Jemaan Daroro (where this story was told), and not so soft as skins. A distinguished visitor might have several mats and a skin on top as well. Another reason is given by the Spider.

XXXV.

[1] A very handy doctrine for servants and others.

XXXVI.

[1] The shea-butter tree. The oil obtained from its seeds is an important article of diet in Africa, but in Europe it is more useful as an ingredient in candles and soap.

[2] There being no conveniences in the native houses (except in a few cases for the chiefs) all must go out of their huts as soon as they awake. Therefore dawn is usually synonymous with "The town is astir," and this is another name for it.

XXXVII.

[1] The animal evidently belonged to the one who had killed it, and not necessarily to the one who had caught it, as is usual in the district (see T.H.H., page 291), though sometimes there might be an agreement to pool the bag.

[2] Thinking, like Ananias, to make the Something believe that that was all she had. *Kura* (hyæna) is feminine, *Zomo* (hare) masculine.

XXXVIII.

[1] These insects build little hills, which are different to those of the ordinary white-ant, for they are much smaller, and not black but red. If they are knocked over, husks of corn can often be seen in the little tunnels which run from the hill into the ground. See story F.-L. 45.

[2] Absolutely the height of bliss to the native mind, of course. Lizards are always plentiful in the houses.

[3] What is the moral in this? That the husband should do nothing and the wife everything? It would seem so.

XXXIX.

[1] This evidently refers to the facts that the frog is seldom seen in the heat of the sun, and apparently does nothing towards keeping himself, while the fowl is always busy with something.

XL.

[1] It is perhaps worth noting—though I do not say that this story suggests anything of the kind—that a cure for snake-bite is inoculation with the poison obtained from another snake, and, according to Canon Robinson, this treatment is practised not only in Hausaland, but all along the coast. He says that there are 343 different kinds of snakes in Hausaland. The Hausas rub onions on their feet to keep snakes away, and drink an onion broth if bitten. Onions are used also against ticks and tsetse-flies.

XLI.

[1] The corn is planted in April, after the rainy season has commenced. The ground is first cleared of weeds, &c., and then long more or less parallel hollows are made with hoes, the earth from these forming ridges. Probably millet is sown in the furrows, and it will ripen in three or four months' time, but the guinea-corn (planted in the ridges) will not be ripe until after the commencement of the dry season (November). The latter sometimes reaches a height of nearly twenty feet !

[2] Not at all an uncommon proceeding, and quite the reverse of our saying to turn our swords into ploughshares. But if peace and not war is desired, the hoes are often given as part of the tribute, wedding gifts, &c., and in this latter case there may be some notion of symbolism as well as of utility.

[3] The animal workmen can delay quite as well as their human mates.

[4] This is why he has no house now and must live in a web, I was informed afterwards, but as it was not the narrator who told me this, but a servant, I have not inserted it in the story.

XLII.

[1] Moses.

[2] The literal translation is " she was feeling shame of him," and it may mean that avoidance was necessary and (also the non-mentioning of the name) because she regarded Musa as her " spiritual husband."

XLIII.

[1] Soft new sprouts of the *diniya* tree (which has a fruit resembling a plum) are squeezed and put into water with certain seeds; the whole is then dried, fried, and pounded up with salt, and this is Denkin Deridi. A very good liqueur can be made with the fruit, resembling sloe-gin in taste.

[2] Robinson's " Hausa Dictionary " gives " sweet potato " for *gwaza,* but it is a very bitter root, the leaves being something like those of the water-lily in shape, but standing up straight perhaps 3 ft. from the ground. See LXXIV. It is an article of diet much despised by the Hausas, and used by them only in the case of the scarcity of other foods.

[3] A plant with evil-smelling fruit which is dried and pounded up before being cooked.

[4] Windows are unknown in the ordinary round huts, so the text simply says " there was no door," but that would not be sufficient for a translation.

[5] Sometimes the women squat in the water and get others to rub their backs with some native substitute for soap. Possibly the old woman was a witch, for such beings like to be rubbed. See Story 93.

[6] See note on nicknames in Chapter VII, 1, and [12] below.

[7] The Hausa is *Dan Yaro,* the literal translation of which may be little boy, or son of a boy, but either would sound contemptuous in English though not so in Hausa.

[8] When fried in butter with plenty of pepper and salt, these roots remind one of stale and rather tasteless asparagus, but they are a welcome change.

[9] The Hausa method of cooking it is this, according to the narrator. A pot of water is placed on the three stones, and above this (forming a lid) is a calabash full of bread-fruit, the steam entering through a small hole in the bottom of the calabash.

[10] She, naturally, would not call it by the name that the others had used.

[11] See LIX [13].

[12] Does this mean that *dadawam basso* is the best of all dishes? It is possible, for judging by what they eat, one would think that the more evil the smell the greater the delicacy of the food!

XLIV.

[1] Agaddez is the southern capital of Air or Asben. There is a curious legend regarding the origin of these people which may account for the magic powers of the hero of this story. It is said that a certain demon or jinn stole King (Prophet) Solomon's ring, and by its means managed to get into the women's apartments. Solomon had a thousand wives, and the demon man-

aged to make one hundred of them conceive before he left. But the King heard of it, and drove these women out of his palace into the wilderness, and there they brought forth their children, the Asbenawa.

[2] Buy is the literal translation, but probably the cowries were a phallic emblem, and sending them conveyed an invitation; it would certainly seem to be so from what follows. Perhaps this was a preliminary to marriage, the girls of certain Arab tribes were required to obtain a dowry by prostitution before being wedded, and there may have been something similar in the case of the Hausas.

[3] I could hear of no reason why he or she should have been beaten, perhaps the explanation is to be found in [1]. Possibly, however, the father beat his daughter simply in revenge, for the youth was evidently the son of the King of the city, and did not belong to Asben. It has been suggested that the beating here and in Story 42 was intended to act as an aphrodisiac.

[4] Pairs of trousers are a form of currency, as are the other articles.

[5] We ought not to be very much surprised at this, for " the art of medicine," says Lord Redesdale in *Tales of Old Japan* (page 219), " would appear to be at the present time in China much in the state in which it existed in Europe in the sixteenth century, when the excretions and secretions of all manner of animals, saurians, and venomous snakes and insects, and even live bugs, were administered to patients. ' Some patients,' says Matthiolus [in 1574], ' use the ashes of scorpions, burnt alive, for retention caused by either renal or vesical calculi. But I have myself thoroughly experienced the utility of an oil I make

myself, whereof scorpions form a very large portion of the ingredients. If only the region of the heart and all the pulses of the body be anointed with it, it will free the patients from the effects of all kinds of poisons taken by the mouth, corrosive ones excepted.' Decoctions of Egyptian mummies were much commended, and often prescribed with due academical solemnity;

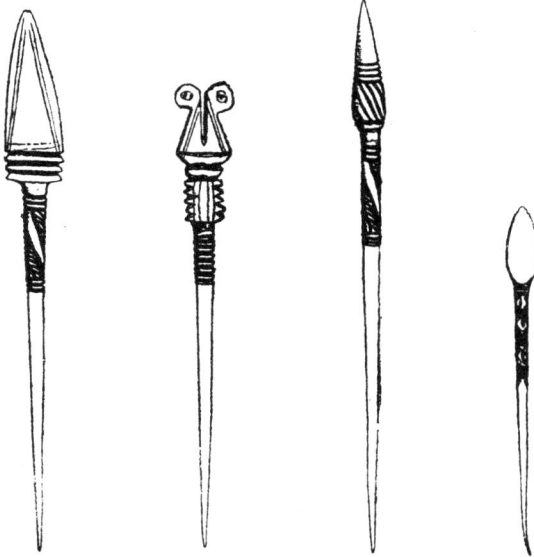

FIG. 107.   FIG. 108.   FIG. 109.   FIG. 110.

FIGS. 107-109.—Bone Hairpins.   Design in red and black.   L., about 6¼ in.   FIG. 110.—Brass Hairpin.   Engraved design.   L., 7⅛ in.

and the bones of the human skull pulverized and administered with oil, were used as a specific in cases of renal calculus."

[6] All Malams and students beg, and usually to some purpose. They are hard to get rid of, and their voices are loud and harsh, so they are particularly unpleasant visitors to an invalid.

XLV.

[1] The same contempt for the " suburban person " is felt by the city dweller in Hausaland as elsewhere. Compare the well-known proverb '*Shi ke nan birni,*' *en ji Bakauyi.* " This is the city, so says the villager." A *kauyi* may consist of only one compound, or of several.

[2] The *tsaiwa* is a blind of coloured string, hung in a doorway, like our " Japanese blinds " of reeds and beads. It is usually made of a grass called *rumewa,* so this was a very special one. Another kind of blind made of reeds or canes tied loosely together, one above the other, is called *munafiki* (treachery) because those inside the hut can s ˜ what is going on outside (*e.g.,* watch the master of the house) while they themselves are hidden.

[3] The doorways of the inner huts are often too low to allow an adult to pass in with a bowl of water on her head, for she would have to keep erect, and this is evidently the case here.

[4] This may be an exaggerated description of the size of the nuts, or the narrator may be comparing them to a certain shrub of that name.

[5] Were they all bewitched ? Potash is smoked with tobacco in many parts, but not by itself.

[6] The house (*gidda*) consists of several huts (*da(i)ki*) surrounded by one or more mud walls (*bango*), hedges (*shinge*), or fences (*dampammi*), arranged in circles, and having only one outlet for each, the exit being a hut or enclosure-hall (*zaure*) with two doors opposite one another. The outside hut is generally used for horses, or for strangers, but there might be slaves there also, and if the horses were valu-

able they would probably not be in the outside *zaure,* but in an inner one. The dogs usually sleep in their respective owners' huts, or wander about the town making night hideous. For an account of Hausa house-building see T.H:H., pages 138 to 143.

[7] Here the story-teller got mixed, for he altered the arrangement, but I have left it as he told it me. It helps to illustrate the difficulty one experiences in obtaining the correct rendering of a tale.

[8] See page 104.

XLVI.

[1] This probably means that a woman who marries out of her tribe may bring ruin on her own people (like the native mistress of Cortez in Mexico).

XLVII.

[1] It is possible that the variant shows Moham- medan influence.

XLVIII.

[1] These pits are valuable and are usually if not always in the centre of the town (in Jemaan Daroro in the market) so that they can be guarded. The smell is sometimes offensive. The owners of the dye-pits pay a special tax, the *Kurdin Korofi.* The chief dye is obtained from the *baba,* or indigo tree, by the fer- mentation of its leaves in water.

[2] No slight reward in a country where wives are practically property, and must be paid for in the ordinary way.

[3] A variant makes the task the opening of the basket instead of knocking it over as above, and the narrator has evidently mixed up the two. So as to keep

the continuity, and yet not disturb the story, I have introduced the words " knock it over and." This shows one of the difficulties of story-collecting.

XLIX.

[1] Worn only by men, women have a short petticoat instead. Both are tied by a string, part of which may hang down behind, and is called the *wutsia* (tail).

[2] Thought more of than a daughter. Charms for child-birth are in great request. In India, says Mr. Crooke, Mohammedan women who long for children often wear their husband's trousers as a magical means of getting them.

[3] The natives have a good idea of rhythm, and drums are generally used to spur them on and make them keep time. Very often the foreman will sing a few words, and the others will repeat it as a chorus.

[4] Being tied very tightly between the legs, it would be much more uncomfortable than the garment which she was accustomed to wear.

[5] This must be an original Hausa story, for it is not thought fitting to make a wife hoe. " Farm-work is not becoming for a wife, you know; she is free, you may not put her to hoe grass " (*Specimens of Hausa Literature*, page 6). Still, the rule is honoured as often in the breach as in the performance, as also are the directions which follow.

L.

[1] See remarks on chronological order in Chapter II.

[2] These beds are made of mud, and have fire-

places, *tsaria,* underneath to keep the sleeper warm in the Harmattan season, and it was in one of these that she hid.

[3] This does not mean that the chief wife must share her possessions with her rival, for she, at any rate, keeps all that has been given to her, but that the rival was already rich, and so had no need for more. The chief wife had been the poor one.

[4] Hyænas will seize sleeping adults, though usually afraid of them when awake. They have been known to enter grass huts at night and carry off infants.

LI.

[1] Probably made from a guinea-corn stalk, very common in harvest time. *Vide* T.H.H., page 250.

[2] A wife must not mention her husband's name even to a co-wife.

LII.

[1] There are no elaborate ceremonies with a widow as with a maid.

[2] This is wrong, as each wife is entitled to her turn.

[3] " Had I known " means remorse.

LIII.

[1] The form of address is *Ya Kura, Kure bangaya.* The last word may come from *banga,* " a procession," or *bangara,* a drum, but " dancer " is probably correct.

LIV.

[1] Higher than King. Solomon is said to have known the bird-language. *Vide Koran,* xxvii, 40.

[2] The women always beat the floor, either stamping it down with their feet, or hammering it with smooth pieces of wood. There are certain songs sung during the performance to ensure that the women keep time, and to cheer them on to more exertion.

[3] To shield him from the sun, apparently.

[4] Meaning " I am impatient for the morrow."

[5] Usually the point of the story would come in a third question and answer since three subjects are mentioned. The second is missing here, for the narrator had forgotten it, but Mr. Evatt sends me the following : The King of the Birds asked Solomon which men preferred, (*a*) riches, (*b*) children, or (*c*) a wise and contented disposition—and the form of the tale which he heard is evidently somewhat different to mine, for to fit into Story 44 it would be the bird's answer which is related. Solomon said " Once upon a time three men were asked which they would rather have, and the first man said ' I will have riches,' and they were given unto him. And the second man said ' I will have children,' and they were given unto him. And the third man said ' I will have a wise and contented mind,' and it was given unto him.

" Now the men who had been given riches and children found a house, and lived together, but the contented man went far away, and lived alone. And one day, the child of the man who desired children entered into the rich man's store and scattered his money about, so that much of it was lost. And the rich man came home, and found his money gone, and he beat the child, who ran away.

" Then the rich man went to the man who had children, and said to him ' Your child has scattered my money, you have your children [which are, in a sense, property] but I have no children, my possessions are my children.' And the man who had children replied ' Go and live far away so that you cannot beat my children, who, being children, will be continually scattering your money.' And the contented man continued to live far away, owning nothing.

" Now the story of these three men was told to Mohammed, the Messenger of God [who, in that case would have lived before Solomon's time], and Mohammed said ' I would fain see this man who wishes for nothing but a wise and contented mind,' and he was brought to him. And Mohammed asked ' Do you want nought but contentment ? ' and he replied ' Nothing.' Then Mohammed said ' You surpass those men who wanted riches and children, and I will make you a present. I will give you riches, and children, and slaves, and kingship in addition to the wise and contented mind which you have already received.'

" And it was done."

[6] It must have been somewhat *infra dig.* for the once-wise Solomon to have been lectured by a bird ! The idea of the great king living in a mud hut and being concerned about the colour of the floor of that of his wife is rather amusing. But it is also instructive as an instance of people being unable to imagine any condition better than a glorified edition of their own.

LV.

[1] Men may wear a lock of hair (a scalp lock) but usually they are close shaved. In some cases, the lock shows that the wearer is a hunter.

[2] One of the high ranks, generally held by a prince. Possibly duke would be an equivalent, but the title is not hereditary.

[3] A mode of execution. See T.H.H., page 66.

[4] He and the tree were evidently connected together, for he could not move from the spot.

[5] The Cow-Filani live in grass shelters in the bush with their cattle. They do not build proper huts, their shelters resemble the mia-mias of the Australian aborigines, or the bell-tents of our army. A temporary camp is called *ruga*.

[6] Which was in a calabash on her head, of course.

[7] The Hausa says only " *Um hum,*" but the intonation is everything.

LVI.

[1] White people with very long hair.

[2] The Hausa says " at the back," of course.

[3] The *du(m)ma* is a creeping and climbing plant which bears a fruit (*gora*) which can be cut and used as calabashes. A smaller sized gourd is used as a water-bottle (fig. 49). If a long neck be present it is cut in two lengthwise, thus making a pair of spoons, or ladles (fig. 63). If not cut in two, this gourd has a hole pierced at each end, and is then used as an enema, the operator blowing down the hole in the large end, the patient lying on his stomach.

[4] As being more holy and fertile; evidently a Mohammedan touch.

[5] This is larger than a *tsaria,* a space under the earthen beds. See L [2].

[6] A mark of respect as with us. See T.H.H., page 51.

[7] Only very high ladies in Hausaland have such an honour, in most cases the husband rides while the wife carries his baggage on her head.

[8] Otherwise he would have thought that it was a

hostile army coming to destroy the city, and so he would have fled, for strangers who come in force are *prima facie* hostile.

[9] Seems quite superfluous in this story as nothing happens. Possibly a part is missing, though I think not, as there is the usual ending here, except that the father ought to have ordered the bad daughter to stay in the bush.

[10] Lest I win him from you—a tabu.

[11] He did not like such behaviour in a stranger.

LVII.

[1] The opening is at the top, see note on house.

[2] See remarks on marriage in Chapter V.

LVIII.

[1] Very small yellow or red tomatoes, not much bigger than large grapes.

[2] See LXXXIX, i.

[3] Only the under petticoat is tied on, nothing is pinned or buttoned, the cloths are simply wound on and folded over, and there they stop. A woman carries the baby on her back simply by folding her body-cloth around it and herself!

[4] Possibly totemism is indicated here, *vide* Chapter VI.

LIX.

[1] A survival of matrilineal descent, the parents of the wives formerly taking the children. The same thing happens in the case of some of the Beja tribes, so Dr. Seligmann tells me.

[2] This was often the case with natives taken when children from their towns by slave-raiders.

[3] The word in the Hausa is not "head," but another part of the anatomy. Considering the context, it is just possible that there is some phallic significance, but this is so very doubtful that I think no harm will be done by the translation given here.

[4] See remarks on charms in Chapter VII.

[5] The midwives; there is no male *accoucheur*, I believe.

[6] Often, if not always, done outside in a sheltered spot, the newly-made mother being helped usually by other women. I heard one being washed, and the operation was evidently a painful one. It is possible that the after-birth is then brought away, but I do not know for certain, I did not see what was happening, and I am told that the washing is not done until afterwards.

[7] See XVIII, 1.

[8] Maria Theresa dollars are greatly prized, especially in Bornu, and it is not uncommon to see them elsewhere used as ornaments. Value from 1s. 6d. to 3s. See N.W.S., page 29.

[9] Evidently the stream near which the town was built, they would naturally wish to look their best on their return.

[10] It is needless to say that this is where they are carried except when newly-born—then in a calabash on the head if the woman be travelling.

[11] Probably to hunt, or to take part in other manly exercises. Possibly he used to farm, as the "farming age" is as much a recognized stage in development as is the "house age," or fitness for marriage.

[12] Each had a separate hut, of course, for herself and her children.

[13] A cooking-place is made of three stones. See T.H.H., page 316.

[14] These last two sentences are rendered graphically in Hausa by six words only : He said " Agreed." Severed. She remained.

LX.

[1] One of the things expected of well-born youths is that they should ride, so this one naturally felt some disgrace.

 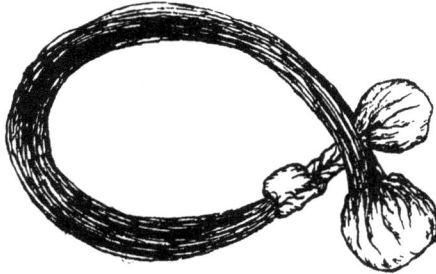

FIG. III.   FIG. 112.

FIG. III.—Green glass bracelet, made from European bottle.
FIG. 112.—Wristlet of horsehair, with leather knobs. L. (open), 10½ in.

[2] She bore all the expense which ought to have been met by the real parent.

[3] This means that he was pretending that they had come from the city.

[4] Sa(r)rikin Rafi is king of the stream, a spirit. Sa(r)rikin Rua is king of the water, an official in charge of the ford or ferry. Evidently the former is meant here, because the canoes appear from nowhere, and in the other version the girl throws a stone and divides the waters.

[5] It is just possible that this story may have some connection with the fact that it was a custom of the Sudan for the conquering chief to demand a girl from the royal family of the conquered tribe as a wife, a gentle means of cementing the union of the peoples.

[6] The literal translation.

LXI.

[1] Every town is built near a stream or lake of some kind. This is magic, of course.

[2] The ordinary beast or man trap is a hole, the mouth of which is covered with sticks and grass, but there may be sharp stakes or ropes inside it. For other kinds, see T.H.H., pages 58, 124, and 292.

LXII.

[1] Meaning that a bridegroom rich enough to satisfy the demands of the parents would be able to keep her in much greater luxury than he, the youth, could afford.

[2] A sheath-knife like a dagger, hung usually by a sling, but often furnished with a leather armlet, to enable it to be worn on the arm. See figs. 102-104.

[3] Even the Hausas know how to "forge" real evidence, for the bloody knife would have told against the youth himself of course. Or it may have been that the owner of the knife would be held responsible in any case, for in other parts, I am told, if a native injures himself with a borrowed weapon, the real owner is held liable.

[4] A small gourd with a neck, and in shape like a carafe, slung over the shoulder by a string (fig. 49).

[5] The only mode of progression. If the legs are

not sore and the irons not too heavy, the prisoner can travel at a fair rate.

[6] Hung up at hand in every house in unsettled districts, in fact in most houses all over Nigeria.

LXIII.

[1] No previous mention of any difference, but in these Hausa tales one mother is usually rich, the other poor and so jealous. This is a curious way of saying " the richer wife died." It is not explained either, how the mothers became able to distinguish their sons, but such details are often omitted.

[2] The real mother would have had a share in the property which the father left to the son, but evidently she had had private property of her own also, else both wives would have been equally well off. Probably in the case of the death of the orphaned son, his property would have passed to his half-brother—in which case the women would have taken a share as mother of the successor—or else the step-mother would have been entitled as such to a share.

[3] I do not think that the tree had any magical part in the performance, it seems that the boy was told to climb simply because he would then be in the most suitable position for the operation.

[4] The town would be called *Giddan Mutum Biyu* (House of Two Men) at first, in all probability. See remarks on " Development " in Chapter V.

LXIV.

[1] The order of precedence of the officials varies in different towns. See Robinson's Dictionary. Heiress, mentioned later, is only a title.

[2] Evidently to protect him, the male usually walks behind.

[3] The Hausa expression is " he reached house," *i.e.,* marriageable age, probably about 16 years.

[4] Marriage is, of course, but a modified form of purchase. See remarks in Chapter III.

[5] Means something like Young Master. Possibly she was not allowed to mention his name, for he had become her eldest son by adoption.

[6] By adoption, but anyone who supplies food may be called by this name.

[7] The *Fita furra,* see Chapter V. It may be noted that the erection of the *gausami* (page 77) resembles to some extent the pole-rite of some of the wild tribes of India (Hopkins, *The Religions of India,* pages 378 and 534). Hopkins believes that the phallic practices of the Hindus were borrowed from the Greeks (*op. cit.,* 471), and if so, could not the Hausas have obtained theirs from the same source *via* Egypt?

[8] In which they were soaked. The walls would appear as if kola-nut chewings had been spat upon them.

[9] He must have felt in sore straits to have done this, for the opposite is usually the case. He was even more humble to the next.

[10] He married five girls, but he had only four wives at the end, apparently, so this may be a pagan tale influenced by Islam.

[11] Evidently an act of magic, the pagans being thrown down as was the perspiration.

[12] The *Sa(r)rikin Agaddez* seems to have retired or died (as kings conveniently do in tales), and to have made room for the boy and his bride to inherit the land, for the narrator told me that the fight took place at

XXXIX. AND XL.—WRESTLING, OR *KUKUA*.

The wrestler gets his head as low as possible, and spars or a chance to catch hold of the other's body, often pulling his opponent's arm as a feint or to upset his balance.

Agaddez. It is possible, however, that the youth had returned to his own (the leper's) town with his bride; certainly the other wives had gone there.

[13] This accounts for the white breast.

[14] " O Son ! O Son ! O Son ! "

LXV.

[1] Sometimes magic rites cannot be performed by females.

LXVI.

[1] I do not know if this is intentional; the narrator said it was as he had heard it, so Europeans are not the only ones who confuse these animals.

[2] Jagindi, a town twelve miles west of Jemaan-Daroro. The name means " Red Behind," probably a nickname of the founder.

[3] Keffi is the chief town of the Nassarawa province, about 70 miles north of the Benue, and 50 miles south-west of Jemaan Daroro. *Keffi* (or more correctly *Kaffi*) means " stockade."

[4] *Literally* " War is taking me away," and this usually means enslaving, but here the obvious meaning is as given.

[5] Towards the end of the Filani rule, the chiefs became so corrupt and avaricious that they would sell even their own people into slavery, and risk the lives of any number for the sake of a small personal gain. It would be too dangerous to say that this story was intended as a skit upon this state of things, though it certainly does for one.

LXVII.

[1] Or Absen, or Asben, it is all the same to the Hausa. See XLIV, 1.

[2] One of the native tortures is to fill the victim's mouth and other parts with honey, &c., and lay a trail to an ant-heap. This, however, would not appear to be the case here (nor have I heard of the Hausas using this particular form of cruelty), for ants naturally crawl upon anything on the ground.

[3] See remarks on adoption in Chapter V, and on sacrifice in Chapter VI.

[4] Silver speech with a vengeance.

LXVIII.

[1] The conversation was evidently in private, the three seem to have gone away from the feast. In fact all this is stated in a variant (L.T.H. 29). As the son killed his father, the townspeople would think that the latter had been lying, and so the kind stranger's character would be re-established.

LXIX.

[1] The song begins *Tatabarra wanni kambarra, sunana Maidunia,* &c. Tantabarra or *tatabarra* is a pigeon; I know no word kambarra, but *Kamberi* is a man of Hausa parentage born and brought up in an alien state. The narrator had no idea what the meaning was, nor had anyone else whom I questioned, the only thing I can suggest is that the words have become changed in the song and that the translation should be " She obtained (*Ta tabba, i.e.,* touched) a Hausa Son " (*Kamberi*), but I have omitted this part.

[2] Childless. If a woman has children she is said to die " in the open." The expression " to sleep in the ashes " applies to a woman who, having had a child or children, so illtreats them as to make them leave her when old enough. The neighbours' children mock

her, and after death she is taken far into the bush, and buried in a grave so shallow that the hyænas can find her.

LXX.

[1] The insect, not the shell-fish.

With regard to this story and the next one, Mr. Hartland remarks that the literal fulfilment of a wish is a frequent subject of tale and superstition. Among *märchen* of Supernatural Birth it is often the incident on which the tale is founded, and the child that is born is often enclosed in a husk or envelope. Thus in a story from the Greek Archipelago a poor woman wishes for a Son, even though he were a Donkey; and a Son is born in the form of a Donkey. He afterwards casts his skin and remains human (W. R. Paton, *Folk-Lore* xii, 320). In a Gipsy tale from Southern Hungary a childless Woman wishes for offspring, even though it were only a Hazel-nut. She gives birth to a Hazel-nut and a Worm, and throws them away. The nut takes root and grows into a bush, from which a Maiden appears, and is caught and wedded by a King (von Volislocki, *Volkssichtungen der Siebenbürge und Südungar-zigeuner,* 343). The Husk, however, often exists independently of the Wish incident. In a Chain tale from Annam a Girl having drunk of a magical spring gives birth to a Son round as a cocoa-nut and covered with a cocoa-nut envelope (A. Landes, *Contes Tjames,* 9). In another story from the Greek Islands a poor Woman gives birth to a pumpkin, out of which eventually a Boy comes (Paton, *Folk-Lore* x, 500).

[2] The son was still on her back, else she need not have returned to him; or, at any rate, she need not have taken him on her back again. In a variant it is

explained that the mother and the magician arranged all this without the boy understanding, by " making words with their hands," *vide* Chapter IV.

[3] From a small tree, at the junction of several branches, which when prepared has something of the shape of an umbrella frame. It is then turned upside down, and tie-tie is attached to it to suspend it. See T.H.H., page 135.

LXXI.

[1] The literal translation is " gave her stomach." There is apparently something miraculous in the conception since the child was no ordinary one.

[2] The verb used here, *shafa,* usually applies more to ceremonial washings, but it would hardly be safe to say definitely that anything of the kind was meant here, though it is quite probable.

[3] Evidently some mixture of animals here.

[4] By clearing the ground and levelling it, &c.

LXXII.

[1] *Chiwo.* A climbing tree or shrub, very tough at the fork, with soft fruit. A native rope is made from it. There is a proverb " O Chiwo, you are hard at the (nose) fork, you ripen, but do not fall," *i.e.,* a stingy man does not give readily. This is a *kirari.*

[2] The meat is placed in a little heap, on top of the porridge.

LXXIII.

[1] *Acha (Pennisetum typhoideum)* is a very small " dirty white " grain, and would be very hard to distinguish from earth. Probably the grain would float, though, and thus be separated. It grows to a height

of about 18 inches, and gives two or three crops per annum.

[2] Apparently the water was very low, and the girl, standing up in the well, could reach the outstretched arms of those above. There is often a rope and a bucket, but evidently there was neither in this case until Dodo had brought them. The bucket would be a calabash or a skin unless the owner had bought a foreign article. Sometimes a long pole is erected and weighted at the

 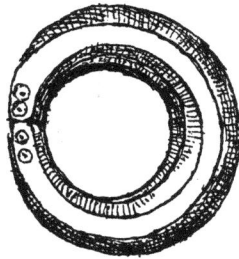

FIG. 113.   FIG. 114.

FIG. 113.—Bracelet of tin or silver. FIG. 114.—Ring of the same metal.

short end, while to the long arm is attached a bucket for purposes of irrigation.

[3] Carrying water is, of course, " women's work," and no self-respecting male, whether man or Dodo, would do it when there was a member of the weaker sex available.

[4] So that Dodo could always know where his son was. Bells are tied to horses and cattle as well as to sheep. *Vide* fig. 98.

[5] The narrator did not know why she could not have simply taken the bell off instead of having to stuff

it up. Perhaps it would have sounded of itself if so treated—like the giant's harp in our tales.

[6] See remarks on Infanticide, in Chapter V. Why should Dodo's gifts have been taken away only to be destroyed? Their weight would make her less able to run. It is possible that there is some idea of sympathetic magic in this, and that he could have exerted some influence over her by their means had she left them behind.

LXXIV.

[1] And the mother apparently went away, and left him.

[2] Means those whose utterances have weight. This story is a play upon words, as *ba(i)ki*, "mouth," is used (as with us) in both senses, *ku(n)ne* means "ear" or "leaf," and *ido* has many equivalents besides that of "eye."

[3] The baby could hardly stop when the creditor was carrying him. It evidently means that the baby made him stop, and then got down.

[4] Probably directly through much reading, or else indirectly by over study and insufficient nourishment, and so means learned men.

[5] It has very large flat leaves like a water-lily. See XLIII, 2.

LXXV.

[1] So that she should be scolded for bringing back dirty water, or at any rate have to drink it herself since the wives would be in different huts.

[2] It is almost impossible for a person to get a heavy load up on to his head without assistance, even though he may be able to carry it easily when once

there. One way is to get it up gradually into the fork of a tree, and then to place oneself underneath, but a pot of water could hardly be treated in this way. Sometimes when a trader makes a temporary halt he backs himself against a tree, catching one end of the load in a fork, and steadying the other end with a long staff. See illustration, page 256. Often there are recognized places where this is done.

[3] See remarks on marriage, in Chapter V.

LXXVI.

[1] Only Bulls are brought to a town. The cows are kept in the *rugas* by the Cow-Filani. Even in the districts where the natives do not milk the cows, they keep them to bear calves, and so they do not come to the meat-market.

[2] *Mikia* here, and in Story 62, I have translated as eagle, as it is thus called in the dictionary. Canon Robinson also gives it as "a species of buzzard with white breast = *Neophron percnopterus* (?)." Another writer gives *meke* (another form of the same word, probably) as "the black and white fishing vulture (*Gypohierax angolensis*)."

[3] Where cattle are used to draw carts or for riding, there would not be the same anxiety to sell them, but such transport is restricted to certain districts, and is not used (except by us) in the greater part of Hausaland. Thus to keep them alive would mean a loss of time and of money spent in their upkeep.

LXXVII.

[1] Becoming very common in Hausaland, and fit and proper articles of the trousseau. Sometimes plates are let into the mud walls as decorations.

[2] I have inserted the words to better resemble the rhythm. The words are sung in Hausa, the syllables being drawn out to the length required.

[3] The white-ants build up covered passages (above the ground level) to protect themselves when travelling to and fro or up trees. They are really termites, and are a prey to all kinds of ants and of birds, hence the necessity for this protection. One species (? a soldier) can give a very painful sting.

[4] They are often to be seen sitting upon these hills, but I have never seen a nest there. Possibly the narrator was wrong in using the word " build " (*ginni*), especially as he alters it to " alight " in the song.

LXXVIII.

[1] Repayment in kind is quite usual, of course.

LXXIX.

[1] Or chief wife, the first one. She has authority over the others.

[2] One can imagine the disgust and anger of the starving people at seeing a sheep fed with food which they could ill spare, and which was too good for an animal. But it is a frequent occurrence in Folk-lore.

[3] Horses are one form of currency, also their saddles, &c.

[4] Slaves who run alongside the chief's horse, grooms, and others.

[5] It seems that no one knew of the ewe's wonderful powers except Auta, the weaver, and perhaps the first wife. But it may have been that the second wife knew of the ewe's warning, and for that reason had a spite against her.

[6] It may seem strange that even a chief—as Auta

(still called " the Boy ") now was—could not get meat whenever he liked, but out of the cattle districts even Europeans to-day cannot obtain fresh meat from the natives, they must depend on fowls, and perhaps fish also in some places.

[7] Possibly these clothes took the place of the white shroud used for a corpse—for Auta was going to commit suicide. Or they may have been merely the signs of mourning for the ewe.

[8] The literal translation is "without my knowledge," but, as in Story 76, *sa(n)ni* means more than this, it has something of the Biblical sense of permission—" And one of them [the sparrows] shall not fall on the ground without your Father."

[9] A very mild punishment. It may be that Auta remembered that he himself was the cause of his trouble, but I doubt if many native chiefs would be willing to make allowances on that account !

LXXX.

[1] A small earthenware jug taken by a man going to the Mosque, which holds water to wash with, see fig. 43. It is not clear why this has been substituted for the stick and the boot; probably the person who told the narrator the story was careless, and mixed up a variant, so the mistake became crystallized.

[2] Many natives use ash (of guinea-corn or *acha*) instead of salt when the latter is unobtainable.

[3] The same piece of iron ore may take many shapes during its life-history (*cf.* Story 41).

[4] Made in long strips about 4 inches in width.

[5] The proper way to carry it.

[6] A woman usually gets water for a man, not *vice versa.*

[7] And, apparently, there was then no need to punish the wives who had been declared guilty of the murder. Auta's property (the girl) had been damaged, but the injury had been more than made good to him, so he could not complain, and it was not likely that the king was going to lose more wives than he could help. See I, 2.

[8] Bolster-shaped with a slit in centre, and slung on donkeys so that the slit is above the middle of the back.

[9] Giginnia, the dileb palm. The fruit is much prized, resembling to a slight extent a very large apricot in colour and shape. The leaves are used for making hats, mats, and baskets. There is a proverb " Only at a distance (from the trunk) can the shade of the fan-palm be enjoyed," because there are no branches except at the top, and this is applied to a man who neglects his own family but helps outsiders.

[10] In a variant (T.H.H. 6), he waits at the bottom of the tree, and a crow throws down the fruits, or rather kola-nuts.

[11] See Story 64, end.

[12] " Eyes " (*ido*) where we should say " ears."

[13] A town between Zaria and Kano.

[14] Or else it was that the learned men were summoned, and gave her medicine; the words are the same in Hausa. The belief in sickness caused by a snake or other animal swallowed by or generated in the patient is world-wide, says Mr. Hartland. The commonest alternative to a snake is perhaps a newt (*cf.* Douglas Hyde, *Beside the Fire*, 47; *Folk-lore*, X, 251; XV, 460) or a lizard (Hill-Tout, *J.A.I.*, xxxv, 156). The usual remedy is to cause the parasite intolerable thirst and to entice it to crawl out of the patient's mouth in order to obtain

drink. The process is graphically described in Dr. Hyde's Irish tale.

[15] The word of a poor man has not much weight in Hausaland.

[16] This seems very much like a tapeworm.

[17] The narrator could not tell me why this phrase was inserted. It may have been to account for the fact that snakes bite men; or else it signifies that Auta owed a debt of gratitude to the snake.

LXXXI.

[1] The usual meanings of these words are Impudence, Proud (or Swollen) Lizard, and The Patient One, but as there may be some other meaning implied in the second one, the Hausa names are given instead of the translations.

[2] Probably the King, as he would get something for his trouble. Now a Malam usually does it, and takes a fixed percentage as a fee.

LXXXII.

[1] Used for carrying soft articles, might also be wrapped around a corpse and bound tightly.

[2] Because of the lack of men, so the narrator told me.

[3] A " little basket (with a lid) " is always the " magic bottle " of the Hausa. See figs. 68 and 70.

LXXXIII.

[1] It must be hardly necessary to state that there are no water pipes in this country, and that the women have to go to the streams and wells for water.

[2] See XXXII, 2.

[3] As much noise as possible is necessary in funeral

rites, and the drums are also used as signalling instruments to call the mourners.

[4] No time can be lost in hot countries. See remarks in Chapter V, and T.H.H., Chapter XIV.

[5] The *birrim* corresponds to our *boom*, but the sound is a double one; another rendering is *Birrip*. The sentence should be accented to resemble the beats of a drum.

[6] Corpses are wrapped in mats. See " Death and Burial " in Chapter V.

[7] The literal translation would be " sleep is our inheritance " and the meaning would be, perhaps, " entitled to sleep," but the above probably conveys the idea sufficiently well.

[8] Sometimes the horses are kept in the entrance-halls, sometimes in special huts inside the compound, but they are often simply tied by one leg to a peg in the ground. If there is plenty of room, the horse is tied by a hind leg, if but little then by a fore leg. See XLV, 6.

[9] The literal translation is " thing of shame," but there is no shame in the fact of her being a mother-in-law, the words merely refer to the avoidance by her daughter's husband. See remarks in Chapter V, and T.H.H., pages 197 and 233.

[10] " Returned home " is the translation, and evidently this means that they left the town, otherwise the danger would still have been present.

LXXXIV.

[1] *Kuka*, also called the Monkey-bread tree, supposed to be inhabited by spirits. See remarks on *Bori*, and Story 88.

[2] The hyæna is masculine in this story, I do not know why.

[3] The blacksmith is regarded by some of the tribes around Jemaan Daroro as having greater powers than the ordinary individual (T.H.H. 136), but the Hausa has no such belief now, I think, though this seems to point to such a superstition in their case, also at one time.

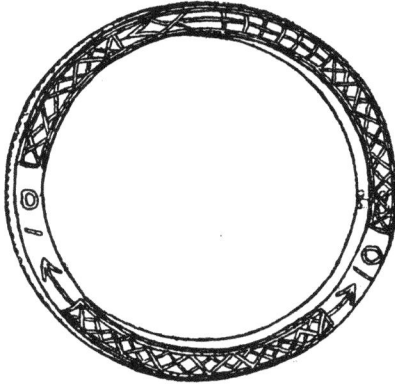

FIG. 115.   FIG. 116.

FIG. 115.—Wooden armlet, inset pattern of brass.   D., 4⅞ in.
FIG. 116.—Wooden comb.   H., 7¹¹⁄₁₆ in.

[4] Possibly this also indicates some superstition—the Hindu, I am told, will never let his first customer in the morning go away without anything, and a similar fancy has been met with in England. In Keta, on the Gold Coast, the early morning is the best time to ask or to give a thing, *vide Alone in West Africa,* page 287.

[5] Tied by the leg during the night.

[6] Thorny tree from which gum can be obtained. Robinson gives the name as *Balanites Ægyptiaca.*

[7] A zareba is formed of branches of thorn and other trees to keep off the hyænas and other animals, and also to keep the cattle from being lost or stolen.

LXXXV.

[1] The word used here is the Arabic *kiama* which really means " resurrection."

[2] Literally, the city of God was astir. See XXXVI, 1.

[3] Apparently they would have preferred a father of the usual kind. See remarks on "The Next World" in Chapter VI, and on " Inheritance " in Chapter V.

LXXXVI.

[1] Some consist of separate huts, built in the compound, with removable grass roofs. Others are much smaller vessels, placed in the dwelling huts. It is the latter kind which is referred to here.

[2] *Sa(r)rikin Karma,* one of the chief's principal slaves, many of whom used to hold high office.

[3] The whole adult population would help in this Hausa Harvest Home.

[4] This represents the sound of the pestles in the mortars (*cf.* XXX, 4), a possible translation is " Pound, pound, bang the pestles."

[5] Judging by the Hausa idea of a fit, the account of the trying on of the boots must have been borrowed from foreign sources. See figs. 24 and 25. It is worth noting that in a Boloki story given by Weeks (*Among Congo Cannibals,* page 203), Libanza, the hero (who went forth with his sister into the world) turned blacksmith, and killed " The Swallower of People " by throwing molten iron into his mouth.

Possibly Auta was the first blacksmith to arrive amongst the pagan Hausas!

LXXXVII.

[1] The narrator told me that the *zankallala* was a kind of locust, but the description given on page 130 is the more satisfactory, perhaps.

LXXXVIII.

[1] Hambari means " kicker," the narrator informed me. I do not know the word.

[2] A name of the Magazawa, or pagan Hausawa.

[3] Probably a wrestler, from " *tankwaria,*" bending.

[4] This tree is supposed to be inhabited by spirits. The Bori dancers have a particular veneration for it, as already noted. The word used here is the Arabic *Iblis*.

[5] But not of the sharp claps.

[6] Wrestling is regarded as being important. In one Magazawa community a *gausami* (pole) is set up in the village, and wrestling contests are held in the vicinity. As long as the pole stands, so long will the youths of the village be strong; if it falls down it is not erected until the next generation is ready to wrestle (*vide Man*, 1910, Art. 40). This pole is symbolical of the virility of the clan or village, in all probability, *vide* LXIV, 7.

LXXXIX.

[1] Always a nuisance; the watcher has to keep calling most of the day, and when the dog-faced Baboons come in numbers the watcher may lose his life if he tries to drive them away. He sits upon a platform raised (on poles) sufficiently high for him to

see over the fields. For birds, strings are tied on sticks above the corn, and the watchers (usually boys) pull these to and fro and call.

[2] *Aljannu* means " jinns," " demons." Here they are apparently good spirits rather than evil.

[3] For, having made a profit out of her, the father was now graciously pleased to take her into favour.

[4] Always different mothers in the tales, the chief wife and the rival wife, and they are always at daggers drawn.

[5] The demons were incensed at her coming amongst them uninvited. See remarks on " Tabu " in Chapter VI.

XC.

[1] The long tobe and the loose trousers (like those of the Arabs, see illustration, page 32) would have impeded him very much.

[2] The fence (*danga*) is made of grass-mats, twigs, or canes, supported by posts which usually stick out at the top. See illustration, page 112.

XCI.

[1] She would not be eating outside with the men, of course, but inside the hut. The food when cooked would be placed in calabashes, and covered with a round mat (see illustration, page 368).

[2] Blindness is very common in Hausaland, so is lameness, the feet often being eaten away by leprosy, or through the destruction of the toes by the " jiggers."

[3] The juice of the euphorbia is one of the causes of blindness, so why a thorn-bush should heal the complaint is not quite apparent, for all prickly trees would be dangerous. Possibly the idea is much the

same as that of the Kagoro, who imagine that the water in which a spear has been dipped will cure a wound inflicted by that spear (see T.H.H., page 194). Or it is a case of " the hair of the dog that bit you."

[4] One of the few stories which has a moral.

XCII.

[1] Like a load, see illustration, page 288.

[2] Merely driving a witch out of the house does not appear to us to be a very severe punishment, but it may be considered adequate by the Hausa husband.

XCIII.

[1] Presumably she said the last sentence to herself.

[2] This does not agree at all with the description following, for even the rude girl was well treated.

[3] There would be an artificial clearing, if no natural one existed, where the washing was done, and the drinking-water was drawn. A flat sandy open space would be chosen when possible.

[4] See LVI, 8. The father was evidently the king of the city.

[5] The authors (Cronise and Ward) remark " A common sight among the natives is a little child busily engaged in picking the lice from the woolly head of some older person. Sometimes the child's place is taken by the pet monkey. If the monkey fails to find the object of his search, he loses his temper, and expresses his feelings in strong language, and in boxing the person's head." See also page 176. Monkeys are very useful in keeping dogs free from ticks and fleas.

XCIV.

[1] *Ku chi gaya*=" You will have revenge."

[2] The two brothers did not, but Dan-Kuchingaya knew it.

[3] See remarks in T.H.H., page 243, and the parallel to the last story.

[4] In order to gain time. The great object of the intended victim is to delay the operations of the witch or devil (see parallel to next story) so as to allow him to escape about daybreak.

[5] The native certainly can sleep very soundly, but this is flattering his powers in that way to some extent. The differences between the men's and women's garments are explained in XLIX, 1.

[6] Lest he should be sold out before he saw her. In the usual course the wares are "cried" by the sellers as they go along.

[7] A black goat has magic properties. See remarks on *Bori,* in Chapter VI.

[8] This is evident from the context. There seems to be an idea that the wound could be healed only by the one who caused it.

XCV.

[1] Why was she not sleeping with him, she was his wife? For explanation, see page 112.

[2] Some baskets are lined with cow-dung, clay, &c., and will hold honey and even water (see T.H.H., page 287), but this was evidently not one of that kind.

[3] Meaning that she did not wait to let it down carefully so as to save the water. This would have taken time as there was no one to help her.

[4] The first time his name is mentioned—can a witch do this without fear? It would seem so, but I am informed that this is not the case.

[5] Apparently referring to the haste in which he had departed.

[6] For there was no owner to claim it.

[7] The woman appeared in two halves and was bleeding. The dogs ate the flesh, but apparently even a single drop of the blood would have been dangerous, and might perhaps have developed into a witch.

XCVI.

[1] Probably in the market square, or in some place where dancing, &c., is indulged in.

[2] So that if he refused to go he would be branded as a coward.

[3] Made from a solid block. The Hausa stools are round with short legs, very small ones being carried by women on their waists. See fig. 42, p. 159.

[4] About the last thing a native would think of would be to remove the obstacle, he would go round it, and this is the reason why most of the West African roads wind in and out. Death clears the way perhaps to show that she is no ordinary mortal, but probably it is merely to suit the story.

[5] *Rago* means " ram," and also " Terrible One." A mixture of both is intended here, for this *rago* is *Kuri,* the god with the ram's (or he-goat's) head.

[6] This should have been the only entrance or exit at night.

[7] The council meetings are usually held in the entrance-hall of the chief's house. This seems a very mild test after the two dangerous ones.

[8] There would be a clear space in which courtiers, visitors. &c., could congregate while waiting for an audience, and where processions could be formed up.

[9] Probably there is some etiquette in this apart from the fact that the king's son was of higher rank.

XCVII.

[1] If cannibalism really existed in the district in which this story originated, it was due, apparently, to no religious reasons, but simply to a taste for the flesh. See T.H.H., pages 180-184.

XCVIII.

[1] Perhaps at one time the wife could not share in the feast at all, even now she must keep apart, inside the house.

[2] This story also shows that cannibalism is attributed to a taste for the flesh.

[3] Some South American tribes actually bred from captive women so as to secure constant supplies of flesh. They were permitted to eat such offspring, because, as kinship went by the female side, the father was not akin to his child by the alien woman. (A. Lang, *op. cit.*, page 70.)

XCIX.

[1] Kano is about 180 miles away, in a straight line, and Bauchi 100, but a few miles more or less makes no difference in a story of course.

[2] Perhaps 350 miles.

[3] In what is now French territory to the north, once tributary to Asben.

[4] Near Daura on the northern boundary of the Kano province.

[5] See the attitude in illustration, page 496.

[6] Absolute continence is frequently found to be a

condition of the continuance of wonderful powers. The importance of it in magic rites is found in many parts.

[7] This is merely carelessness on the part of the narrator, it does not mean that a second marriage was necessary.

C.

[1] The two hands are generally used, held tightly together, but one of my servants used to throw the water into his mouth with each hand alternately. The distinct methods of drinking remind one of the story of Gideon.

[2] The water is said to be a stream, but he has encircled it, and the woman drinks it all up, so I have rendered *rafi* by " lake." Had it been a stream, he might have searched for human footprints so as to know where there was a ford. A lake is so rare that he would be certain to search there for the spoor of animals.

[3] About a mile, with a river between, when I was there, but since 1909 the Resident's quarters have been moved to the other side, and the distance is now not more than a couple of hundred yards, I am told.

[4] No previous mention of this, but such sudden introductions are typical, as is also the dropping out of one or more of the characters.

[5] The narrator said that women always loosen their body cloths, and remove the outer one. There does not seem to be any reason for this except the wish that it may not be soiled. Another man says that the women merely loosen their cloths so as to give themselves greater comfort. I have not seen a woman eating.

[6] The narrator offered no explanation of the

reason why she could not see the youth, nor even the dog which was close beside her.

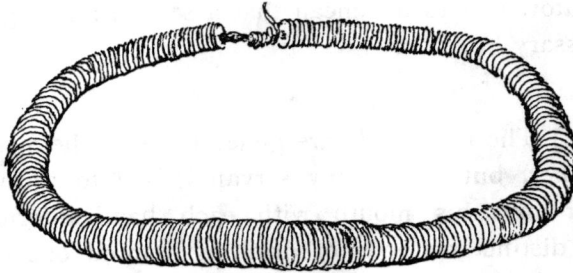

FIG. 117.—Cut shell girdle, worn by women.

II.—ON TRIBAL MARKS.*

No. 2.   An arrow on each side of the neck is very common.

No. 3.   The first figure was outside of each eye, and the second (a conventionalized lizard) on each side of the neck.   The latter is said to be a charm to attract prostitutes, and is called *kwanche da masoye* (sleeping with the one desired).   There was also a lizard on each upper arm and rows of small cuts, *kaffo,* on the back.   Both of his parents came from Girku (Zaria) according to him.

No. 4.   (Abdominal pattern only.)   Parents from Zamfara and Zaria respectively.

---

* For a fuller account and measurements of head, &c., see *R. A. I. Journal,* Jan.-June, 1911.   I ought, perhaps, to apologize for the drawings of the heads and bodies, but, on a previous occasion, when I had them drawn by an artist, the result was that many of the designs were incorrectly rendered, so I have done them myself this time.   After all, the outlines are not important.

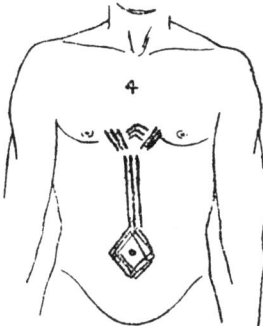

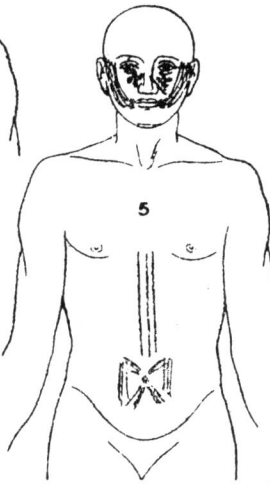

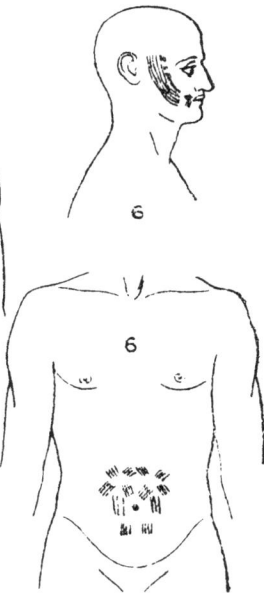

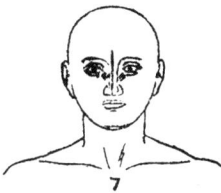

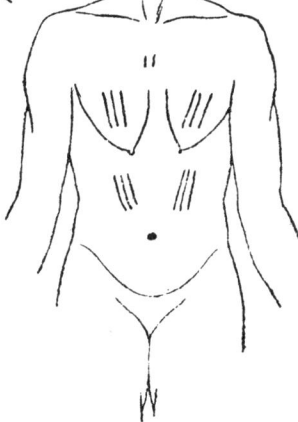

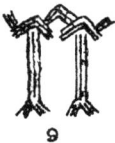

No. 5. The lines *yam ba(i)ki** on each side of the mouth are common, though the number is more often three or nine, but the catherine-wheel (*dan taki,* "cowpot," said to denote ownership of cattle) on each cheek is very unusual. The abdominal patterns are called *yan chikki* (young ones of the stomach). Parents from Kano.

No. 6. Both parents from Kano.

No. 7. The long line down the forehead seems to indicate Filani blood somewhere, though the bearer denied it. The mark is not so deeply cut as with the Ijo in Southern Nigeria, and is, I was told, optional. Parents from Bauchi and Kano respectively.

No. 9. These patterns, *kalango,* were outside the eyes; the one above (right side of head) was done early—and badly—the other shows the true form. Both parents from Kano. The wearer was a slave in all probability, as a free man would have *zubbe.*

No. 10. Mayiro (a corruption of Miriamu), a woman, had this pattern behind each eye. It is very common and is called *akanza.* Parents from Zaria and Bauchi respectively.

No. 11. Kumatu, a woman, had what were said to be *abwiya* (friendship) marks, and may have been a charm to preserve friendship. Parents from Zaria and Gobir respectively.

Nos. 12 and 13 are somewhat unusual abdominal patterns. Parents from Kano and Zaria respectively.

No. 14. These *yan chikki* show the commonest pattern, except that four lines instead of three are used once on each side. Both parents from Kano.

---

* *Yan* or *Yam* (*n* changes to *m* before *b*) the plural of *da* and *dia* means "children of," "young ones of," &c., hence "children of the mouth."

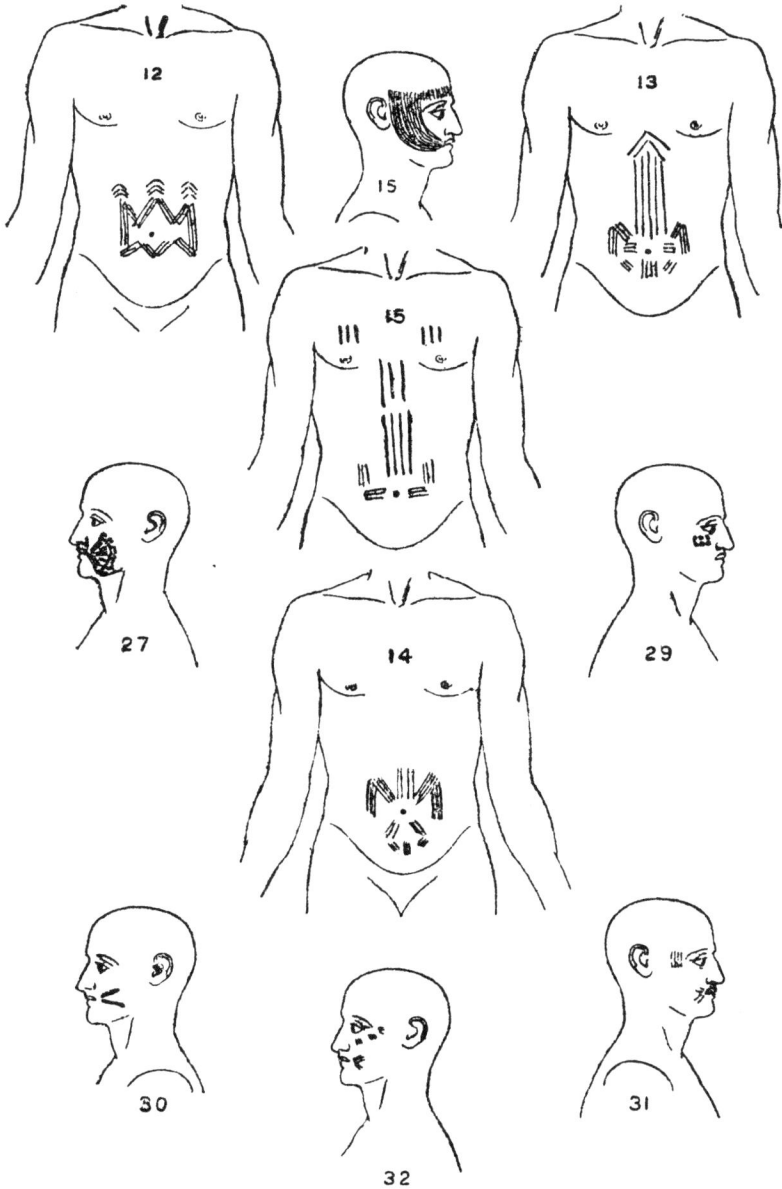

No. 15. Fourteen lines on each cheek and eight on forehead. Said to be marks of Zanfara. Both parents from Bakura.

No. 27 shows a very elaborate pattern of *yam ba(i)ki*. Both parents from Uti (Kano).

No. 29. The six small squares underneath and outside each eye are known as *tsuguna ka chi doiya* ("squat and eat yams"), and—as their name implies—are a charm to obtain plenty of food. Both parents from towns in Kano.

No. 30. These two lines are farther back from the mouth, and much broader than the usual *yam ba(i)ki*. Both parents from Daura.

No. 31. There was also a short cut down the forehead, which, the wearer said, was to prevent headache. The eye marks he called *daure,* and said that they had been done on reaching puberty. Both parents from Dutsi (Kano).

No. 32. Both parents from Girku (Zaria).

No. 40. An unusual pattern. Parents from Tofa and Yelwa (Kano) respectively.

No. 41. There once were similar marks also on the right side of the body in all probability, but they were too faint to be distinguished. Abdu said that the marks on the face were those of Gobir, but that his parents came from Katsina and Sokoto respectively.

No. 43. Both parents from Zaria.

No. 44 had what he called *babba goro* on the left side of the body below the waist, but no marks on his face. These, he said, were to relieve stomachache. Both parents from Zakua (Kano).

No. 45 had no tribal marks, but nine cuts under the left nipple to relieve pain because it swelled. Both parents from Zaria—probably Gobir.

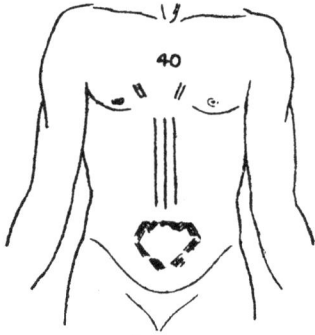

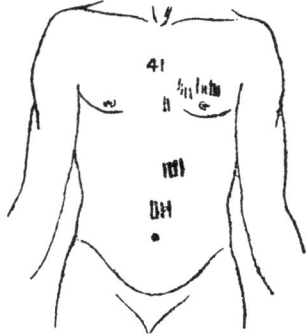
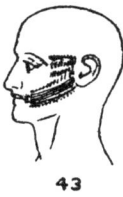
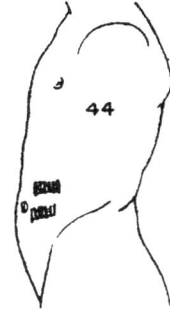
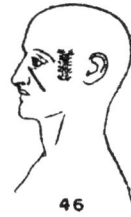

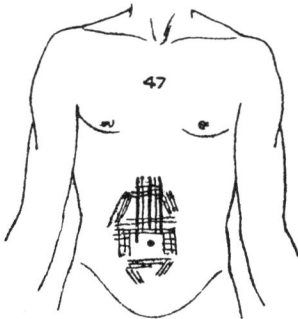
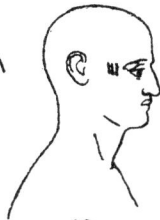
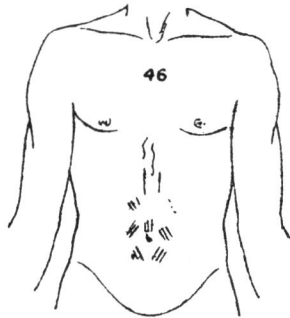

No. 46.	Both parents from Kano.

No. 47 had faint *yam ba(i)ki* and two plainer marks like No. 30 on each side of mouth, and there was a strange pattern around the navel also, and I think that the bearer had tried to obliterate his old marks by adding those of another clan.	Parents from Kano and Zaria respectively.

No. 48.	Both parents from Kano.

No. 51.	The wearer said that both his parents were Hausas from Kora (Kano), but that he had been caught and enslaved by Ningi people, and that they had made these marks, obliterating his own.

No. 53.	Both parents from Bauchi.

No. 55.	There were no marks on the face except a *dan taki* on each cheek like No. 5.	The four rows of cuts on his abdomen were to prevent internal bleeding, so he said.	Both parents from Bauchi.

No. 56 had a pattern of *yam ba(i)ki* which he called *lemu*.

No. 57.	Both parents from Kano.

No. 58.	These the wearer said were Buzu (? Asben) marks, his grandfather being of that tribe.	Both parents from Geso (Kano).

No. 62.	Both parents from Kura (Kano).

No. 64.	Gude (wife of No. 65), had a very ornamental mouth, with even more cuts than No. 27, and there were lines beneath the lower lip, a *bille* and six rows of four above the nose.	The chest and abdomen were also decorated, the pattern here showing as far as the clothes would permit.	Both parents from Anchari (Kano).

No. 65.	Both parents from Zaria.

Nos. 66 and 67.	Both parents from Bella (Bauchi) in the first case, from Gaya (Kano) in the second.

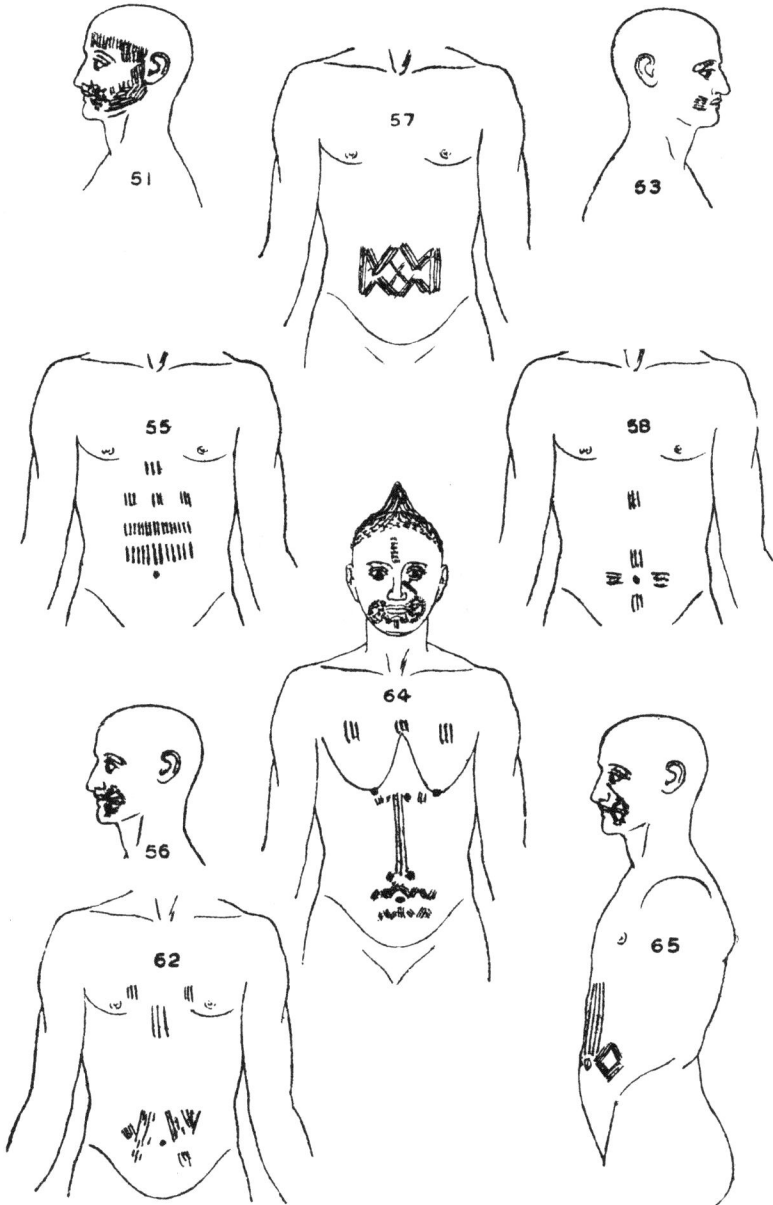

No. 69. The four lines on each side resemble the *kumbu* of No. 53, but are slightly lower than the mouth. Both parents from Bauchi.

No. 70. Both parents from Kano.

No. 72. The pattern on the abdomen was surmounted by cuts to give relief from (?) stomachache. Both parents from Igabi (Zaria).

No. 74 had what he called *haka(r)rika(r)rin kifi* ("ribs of fish") in place of a *bille* to the right side of the nose for the purpose of attracting women. There was also a *tsuguna ka chi doiyo* like No. 29. Both parents from Ringi (Kano).

No. 75. Parents from Tofa and Rimin Gado (Kano) respectively.

No. 76. A double *kalango* on each side (see different pattern in No. 9 and a single one in No. 46). Both parents from Zaria.

No. 77. The chest and abdomen showed a pattern which is partly a conventionalized lizard, apparently, and is called *zanen bangaro* (? the marks of a butcher). The cut above the left ear is very unusual. Both parents from Kano.

No. 78. Parents from Kano and Kantamma (Kano) respectively.

No. 80. The wearer said that these were the marks of the Wangarawa. Both parents from Goram (Bauchi).

No. 81. Both parents from Kano.

No. 84. Both parents from Kano.

No. 85 had a cut down the nose, made, so he said, by Nigawa, who caught and enslaved him. Also a double *bille* on the left side, and an *akanza* (see another shape in No. 10) outside each eye. Parents from Takai and Falale respectively.

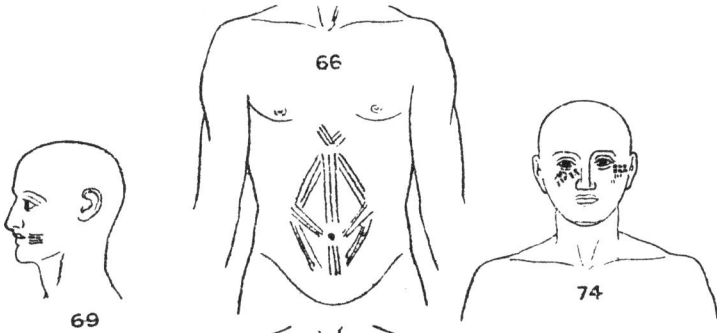

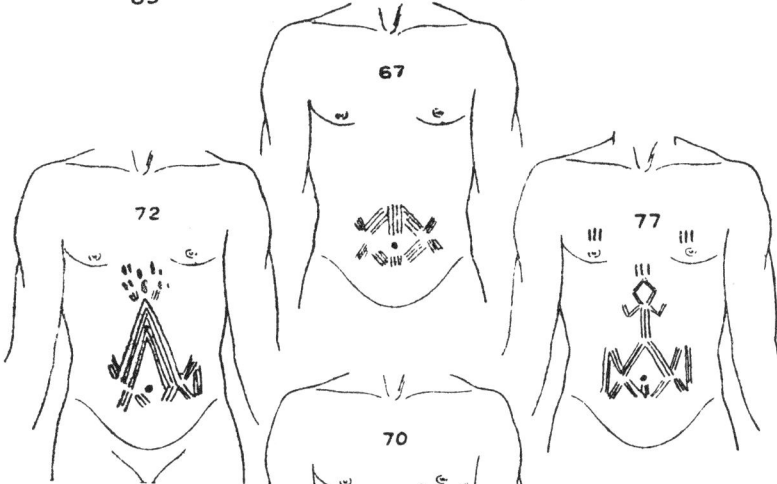

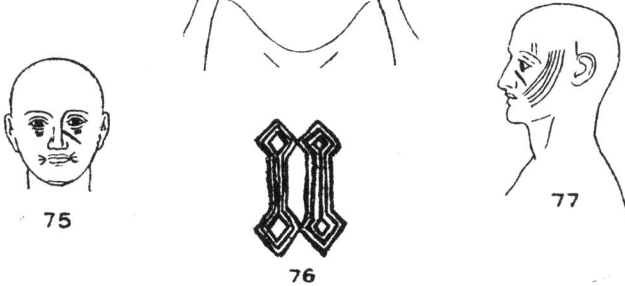

No. 86. Both parents from Bauchi.

No. 89 had a conventionalized lizard's head above his nose, and a double *bille* on the left side. Both parents from Kano.

No. 90. These were said to be the marks of the Kutumbawa. Both parents from Kano.

No. 91. Both parents from Kano.

No. 92. Both parents from Kano.

No. 93. Both parents from Kano.

No. 97. Auta (woman), had *yar gira* (eyebrows) above each eye, which, she said, were for ornament. Both parents from Gani (Kano).

No. 98. Hassana (woman), had *yam ba(i)ki* like No. 56, but in threes (one four) instead of in fours. Both parents from Kano.

No. 99. The irregular cuts between nipples were either badly done tribal marks or, as he said, to prevent pain. Both parents from Bebeji.

No. 100. Parents from Kano and Gwalchi (Bauchi) respectively.

No. 101. Both parents from Kano.

No. 102. Both parents from Kano.

No. 107. Pupils of eyes bluish, and irritating from *amoderre* (? a kind of blight). In another case the eyes were light blue, said to be due to cactus (*Kerenna*) juice, which causes blindness. Both parents from Kano.

No. 109. Had a long cut down the nose like No. 7, and the square pattern probably represents a book. Both parents from Kano.

No. 110 had another kind of *haka(r)rika(r)rin kifi* (see No. 74). Both parents from Bauchi.

No. 112. The three inside lines were made, he said, to cure sore eyes. Parents from Kano.

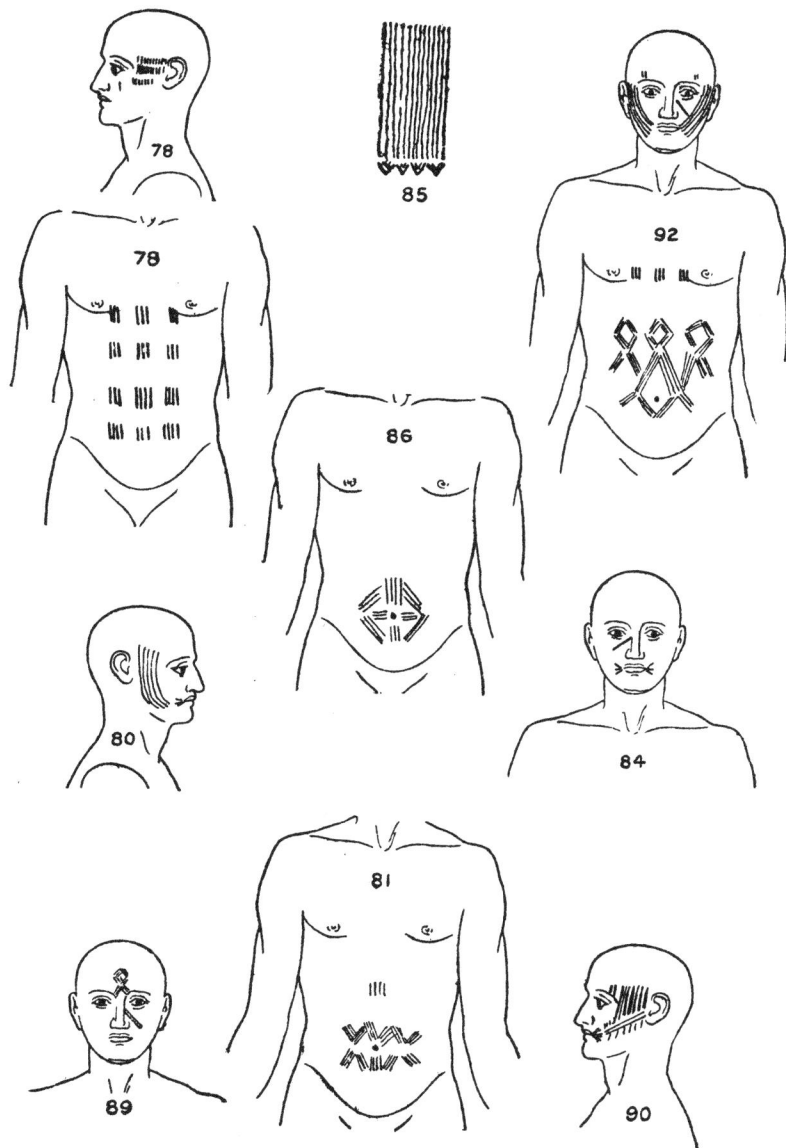

No. 113.   Both parents from Kano.

No. 114 had a very badly executed pattern on his cheeks.   Both parents from Kura (Kano).

No. 156.   Both parents from Kano.

No. 158.   Both parents from Zaria.   The lower, central figure is probably a simplification of the lizard in No. 3.

The final nine figures have been taken from Dr. Kumm's *From Hausaland to Egypt*.   He says that they represent the marks of the people of Kano (1, 2, 3, *cf*. 48, 84 and 107, above), Sokoto and elsewhere (4), Daura (5, *cf*. 30, above), Zaria (4 and 6), Rago (7), Katsina (5, *cf*. 155, above), and Gobir (9, *cf*. 41, above).

III.—On Bori.

I HAVE been trying during the last two years to get someone to take a photograph of this "dance" for me, but to no purpose, as the performance is absolutely forbidden now.   I had, therefore, to be content with the snapshots forming the frontispiece, and since it is quite possible that bori may never be seen again in Northern Nigeria, I give this extra note even at the risk of repeating myself in part.

The master of ceremonies is called the *Uban Mufane;* he takes charge of the offerings of the spectators, but they are afterwards divided amongst the musicians (a violinist, and a man who drums on an overturned calabash), and the dancers.   A mat is usually spread in front of him, so that those onlookers who wish to give money will know where to throw it—though it is not refused should it fall elsewhere.   Often a particular dancer will have kola-nuts poured into his or her

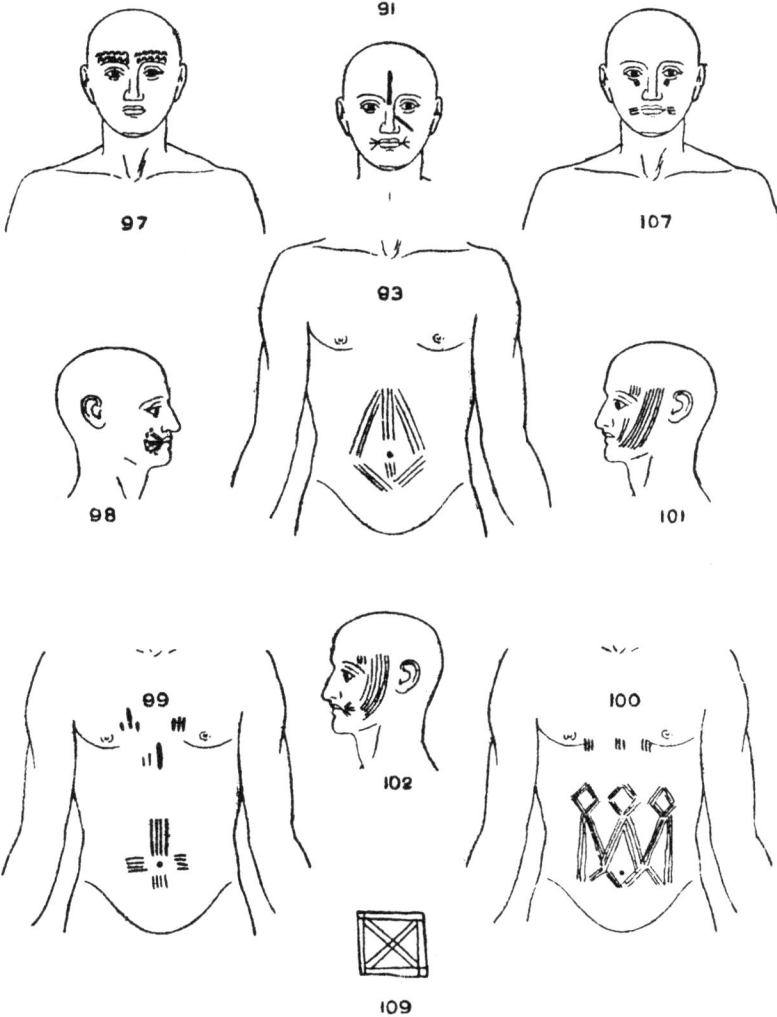

mouth, as is shown in the frontispiece. Soon after the
musicians have commenced, some of the dancers begin
to go round and round in a circle with shuffling steps,
the hips swaying from side to side, and in a few
minutes the strains of the violin and the scents used by
the dancers take effect. The eyes become fixed and
staring, the dancer becomes hysterical, grunts or
squeals, makes convulsive movements and sudden
rushes, crawls about, or mimics the actions of the
person or animal whose part he is playing, and then
jumps into the air, and comes down flat on the buttocks,
with the legs stretched out in front horizontally, or with
one crossed over the other.   The dancer may remain
rigid in that position for some time, often until each
arm has been lifted up, and pressed back three times
by one of the other performers.

This may be the end of that particular dancer's part,
but often he will continue to act up to his name, his
words and actions being supposed to be due to the spirit
by which he is possessed, and if it is not clear which
spirit it is, the chief *mai-bori* present will explain, or
the performer himself may do so.   Finally, in most
cases, the dancer will sneeze, this evidently being for
the purpose of expelling the spirit.   Sometimes, not
content with the dashing on the ground, the dancers will
claw their chests, tear their hair, or beat various parts
of their bodies, and even climb trees and throw themselves down, but all deny that they feel any pain while
possessed, whatever they do.   Sneezing expels the
spirit, as has been said, but it is some days before the
effect of the seizure wears off, even if no serious injury
has been done, the appropriate diet meantime being
kola-nuts and water.

Owing to the inquiries of Mr. Evatt, and the author

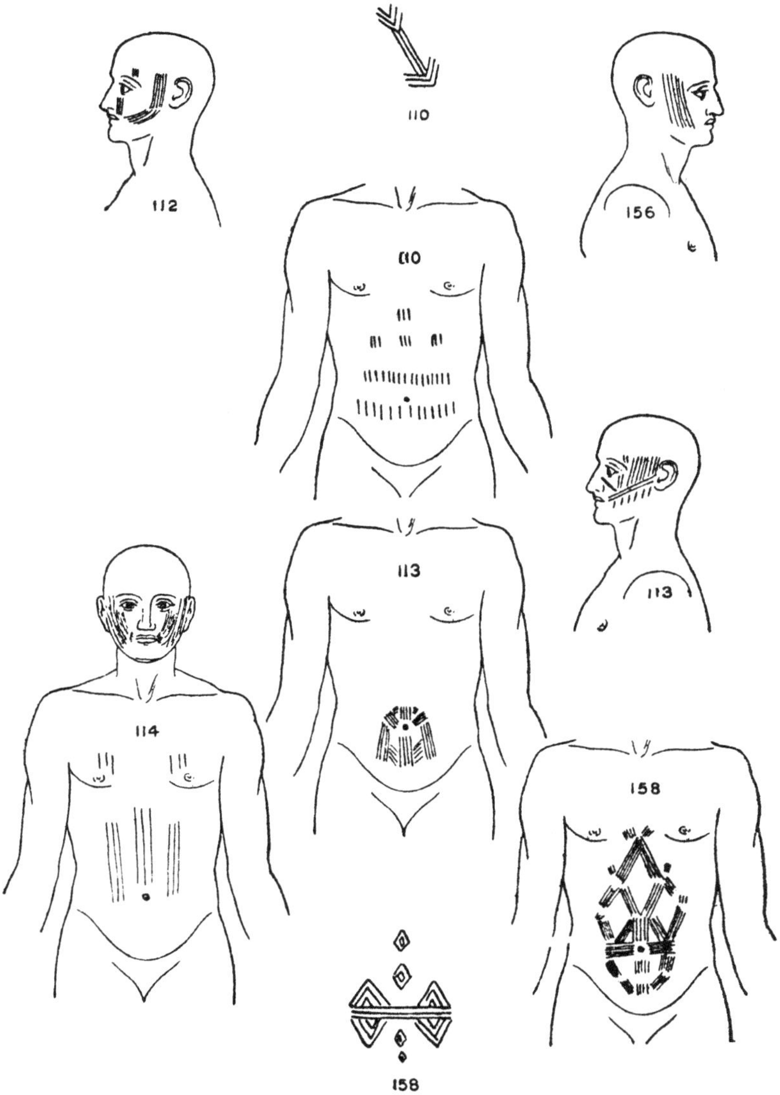

110
112
156
110
113
113
114
158
158

of *Hausa Sayings,* I am enabled to make the caste of characters much longer than the one I gave before*, and it is possible that this is exhaustive, but it seems likely to me that every trade and profession is represented, and there may be no limit to the length of the list.

(1) **Ba-Absini**—Person from Asben, despised by the Hausas, *vide* Note xliv, 1. Played by both sexes. The dancer hops on each foot alternately, at the same time raising and dropping his spear. He wears a black tobe, trousers, and turban.

(2) **Alfanda**—Lion. The *tsere* is a black fowl which has a heavy plume—representing the mane.

(3) **Malam Alhaji**—Learned man and pilgrim. Pretends to be old and shaky, and to be counting beads with his right hand while reading a book in his left. He walks bent double, and with a crutch, coughing weakly all the time. He is present at all the marriages within the *Bori* sect. His *tsere* is anything white—the malam's proper dress being of that colour.

(4) **Almajiri**—Disciple. He copies a malam to some extent. His *tsere* is a small iron bow.

(5) **Anakwanche**—Lying down. The person may pretend to be helpless. His *tsere* is two brown chickens.

(6) **Andi**—? His *tsere* is a monkey-skin.

(7) **Aradu**—Thunder. The person is possessed during a storm, and either imagines himself to be the cause of it, or else that the spirit of the storm has entered into him.

(8) **Nana Ayesha**—The wife of the Sa(r)rikin Rafi. The dancer rushes about waving a sheet over her (or his) head, and, when tired, bends down and rubs or scratches her legs. The *tsere* is a blue cloth.

(9) **Sa(r)rikin Bakka**—Chief of the Bow, *i.e.,* Principal Huntsman. He moves about as if stalking game.

(10) **Sa(r)rikin Barde**—Prince, leader of cavalry. He (or she) is always in front of the other dancers. He moves round in a circle, stamping the outer foot, and resting a staff first upon his right thigh, and as the pace quickens, trailing it on the ground. Suddenly he sits down with a bump, covers up his head, and pretends to sneeze. The dancer, even if he be a male, wears a woman's cloth, tucked under the arms in the ordinary way. The *tsere* is a red cloth or cock, red being the royal colour.

---

* *The Tailed Head-hunters of Nigeria,* pages 254-257.

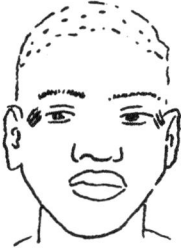

1

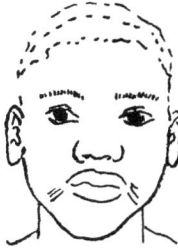

2

3

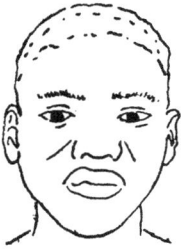

4

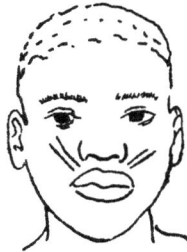

5

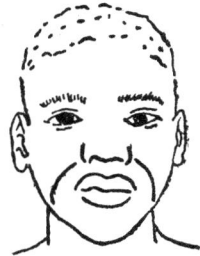

6

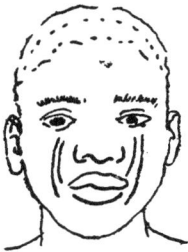

7

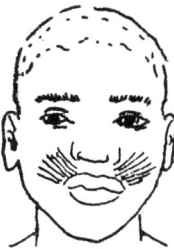

8

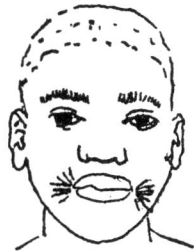

9

(11) **Son Bawa**—The Desirer of a Slave. He or she walks about weeping and saying " I am looking for a slave," and calling upon other *Bori* spirits to help in the quest.

(12) **Bebe**—Deaf Mute. He or she sits alone, with tears streaming down the cheeks, or runs around, mouthing, in either case making no sound.

(13) **Birri**—Monkey. The player climbs trees and apes this animal generally.

(14) **Buwaye**—Strong one. The same as Dan Galladima, *q.v.*

(15) **Mai Jan Chikki**—The drawer along of the stomach. He crawls with his belly on the ground, and imitates the movements of a snake.

(16) **Dogon Daji**—Tall one of the forest, *i.e.*, guinea-corn, and so *gia* (guinea-corn beer) and drunkenness. The *tsere* is *gia*.

(17) **Kworro na Daji**—Insect of the forest. The *tsere* is a small chicken.

(18) **Ba-Dakua**—? Also said to be a wife of *Sa(r)rikin Rafi*. The *tsere* is a speckled hen.

(19) **Daudu**—David, or *Dan Sa*, Son of a Bull. Said to be the same as Dan Galladima.

(20) **Mai Ga(r)rin Daura**—?

(21) **Dogua**—A double spirit (see page 118). The wife of *Malam Alhaji*, but acted by both sexes. Indoors, it is known as the wearer of the white cloth, and for this character the dancer lies at full length on his side (either one), and rocks himself backwards and forwards, while one person behind and another in front flap a cloth which is laid over him. The outside part of the spirit is known as the wearer of the black cloth, and for this the dancer lies on his face, a man sitting on his head and stretching out his legs so that they grip the dancer's sides, and the latter puts his arms around the body of the man sitting upon him. Another man then sits by the dancer's feet, and he and the one at the head flap the cloth.

(22) **Sa(r)rikin Filani**—Filani Chief. He goes around with a staff, counting imaginary herds of cattle, and then presents himself to the *Dan Galladima*. His *tsere* is a string of small cowries, the shells being a favourite ornament of these people.

(23) **Sa(r)rikin Fushi**—King of Wrath, *i.e.*, a bee. He is said to be a younger brother of *Babban Mazza*. The *tsere* is honey.

(24) **Dan Galladima**—Son of a Prince. The dancer puts on

a large cloth, which comes over his head. He walks along slowly, head bent, and then, crossing his feet, he sits down. He is then approached and saluted by everyone. He is the highest judge of the sect, appeals being brought to him from the court of the *Wanzami*. If he agrees with the decision of the latter, he remains seated, if not, he jumps up and falls down three times, and then he gives his decision. The *tsere* consists of the full attire of a prince, *viz.*, a blue tobe and trousers, white turban, shoes, and scent.

(25) **Zeggin Dan Galladima**—Equerry of the Dan Galladima. He or she precedes him, helps him to sit down, and then fans him.

(26) **Garaje**—? The same as Mai Gworje? The dancer stamps about, taking four steps forward at a time in any direction. He (or she) holds his head high, but eventually crosses his feet and falls backwards.

(27) **Dogon Gidda**—? Tall one of the house? The *tsere* is fresh milk.

(28) **Ba-Gobiri**—Man of Gobir. The *tsere* is a weapon, the Gobirawa being renowned warriors.

(29) **Mayannen Gobir**—He with the comrades from Gobir. The *tsere* is a pair of irons.

(30) **Ba Gu(d)du**—Not running, *i.e.*, brave man. The *tsere* is a white kola-nut and a woman's white headkerchief, white being the colour of death, which this spirit does not fear.

(31) **Gwari**—A Gwari (pagan). The dancer wanders about, stooping and leaning on a staff, and carrying a load of rubbish in a bag or bowl on his back, after the manner of the members of the Gwari tribe.

(32) **Mai Gworje**—He with the bell. The *tsere* is a small stick.

(33) **Ibrahima**—Abraham. The *tsere* is a white-bellied kid.

(34) **Inna**—Stuttering. The actor pretends that he is afflicted with an impediment in his speech.

(35) **Janjare or Janzirri**—? From Khanziri, a hog. The same as Nakada. Sometimes, if not forcibly prevented, the person possessed, naked, except for a monkey-skin, will rush about devouring or rubbing his body with all kinds of filth, and pushing an onion or tomato into the mouth is the only cure. On other occasions he hops round a few times, then puts a stick between his legs for a hobby-horse, and prances. Finally, he simulates copulation, falls to the ground, and pretends to sneeze. The *tsere* is a monkey-skin and a bell, the latter to rouse it.

(36) **Kaikai**—Itch. The actor is continually scratching his body.

(37) **Kandi**—? A female spirit which is said to be responsible for the raising of the magic hoe (see page 167). The *tsere* is a small hoe.

(38) **Kaura**—See page 112. The dancer moves around about ten times, stamping the right foot, and then falls backwards. The *tsere* is a yellow cloth or a sheep with dark markings round the eyes.

(39) **Kure**—Hyæna— or ? god (see page 111). The dancer (either sex) goes on all fours, growling and champing his jaws, and pretending to be looking for goats. Sometimes a man holds a girdle tied around the dancer's waist, and the latter pretends to try to escape. The *tsere* is a piece of meat.

(40) **Kuruma**—Deafness. The actor pretends that he cannot hear.

(41) **Kuturu**—Leper. The actor either sits like a leprous beggar, and, hiding his legs, pretends that they have been amputated at the knee-joint, or he walks as if his limbs were distorted, making faces and noises. He contracts his fingers, and, holding a cap in them, begs for money, and drives away flies from his imaginary sores.

(42) **Kyembo**—? The *tsere* is a large bead.

(43) **Lambu**—? Possibly the same as *Sa(r)rikin Bakka*. The dancer, carrying a miniature bow and arrows, and sometimes wearing the skin of a Burutu bird as a head-dress, goes through the movements of sighting, stalking, and killing game.

(44) **Madambache**—The boxer. He pretends to box. The *tsere* consists of a boxer's equipment, as is shown in illustration No. 38.

(45) **Be-Maguje**—See page 111. The dancer wears a loin-cloth, a quiver, and a bag in which are tobacco and a flint and steel. He carries an axe on his shoulder, a bow in his hand, and smokes a long pipe. He walks along, mimicking a pagan, and presently lights his pipe with a spark from the flint (the Hausas now use imported matches). He then calls out " Chewaki, Tororo (two common pagan names) bring beer," and on a person bringing him some, he drinks greedily, letting the beer run down his chin. He then gives back the calabash of beer, relights his pipe, and moves off.

(46) **Masaki**—Weaver. The dancer (either sex) wears a woman's cloth folded tightly under the arm-pits. He passes a wisp of grass from one hand to the other (as if throwing the shuttle), and rubs it along his thigh (like a strand of cotton). Finally, he covers up his head and sneezes.

(47) **Bakka Mashi**—Black spear. The *tsere* is a black stick.

(48) **Maye**—? A wizard.

(49) **Babban Mazza**—Great one amongst men. The *tsere* is a cock, preferably one with red feathers.

(50) **Dan Mayiro**—Child of Meramu.

(51) **Meramu**—Miriam. The *tsere* is a string of scented cowries and a small red cloth.

(52) **Dan Musa**—Son of Moses. Possibly the same as *Mai Jan Chikki*. The dancer, covered with a black cloth, imitates the movements of the *samami*, a large snake with a red neck. Has this any reference to the contest before Pharaoh? The magicians are supposed by some to have come from West Africa (N.W.S., page 16).

(53) **Nakada**—Nodder. The same as Janjare, *q.v.*

(54) **Dan Nana**—Child of Ayesha. The dancer pretends to be a small boy suffering from stomach-ache, and he groans, sits down, and holds and rubs his body.

(55) **Sa(r)rikin Paggam**—?

(56) **Sa(r)rikin Rafi**—Chief of the river, *i.e.*, of the fishermen, canoe-men, &c. He pretends to be spearing fish all the time, or he stares, beats his breast, and walks round in a circle, bringing one foot up to the other, and leading off again with the same foot. The *tsere* is a *hanurua* nut (species of kola) and a small chicken.

(57) **Mai Bakkin Rai**—He with the black soul. The *tsere* is anything black.

(58) **Mai Jan Rua**—He who has red water. He behaves as if he had fever, and is covered with a black cloth which is flapped to and fro to fan him. Under this treatment his stomach gradually swells, and eventually he vomits, and then recovers.

(59) **Na Rua Rua**—? Possibly a modification of the preceding one. The dancer at first stands, then kneels, nodding his head all the time. Finally he bends over until his head touches the ground, and he turns it to and fro, groaning as if suffering from stomach-ache.

(60) **Sambo**—?

(61) **Dan Sa(r)riki**—Son of a Chief. He is the principal actor, but he does not dance, but seats himself and cries because his father has not given him a present. The other *masu-bori* salute him, stand when he stands, and generally pay him the marks of respect due to a prince.

(62) **Tsuguna**—Squatting. The actor sits like a dog.

(63) **Wanzami**—Barber. The judge of the *Bori* sect, the members of which obey his sentences. He puts four to six razors into his mouth and turns them round, and then strops them on

his fore-arm. Finally he places the razors on the ground, and cleans his teeth with sand and tobacco flowers. The *tsere* is a razor.

(64) **Za(i)ki**—Lion. The dancer runs around with a bone in his mouth, and calls out " God is to be feared, man is to be feared " (see page 28). Another man holds a girdle made fast to the dancer's waist. The *tsere* is a bone or a piece of meat.

(65) **Zubu**—? The dancer moves around in figures of 8 until he drops.

Those are all that I have been able to collect so far, but I have no doubt that there are many others, and it is to be hoped that a record will be made of them while particulars are still to be obtained.

XLI.—THE BORI JUMP.

L'Envoi.

AND now I must say *Au Revoir*. The Hausa is a very interesting person, good-natured, honest, brave, and in many respects admirable. He has his faults, of course, and his ideas of morality are not ours, but, on the whole, his good qualities easily outweigh the bad ones. My aim has been to give a true picture of him, hiding nothing, and exaggerating nothing. I believe that my opinion of him is accurate, but can a European living for most of his time in a European country ever be absolutely certain that he has got thoroughly to the back of the black man's mind? I have had to leave the solution of other problems to the spider (page 96), and perhaps the safest course is to refer this question also to

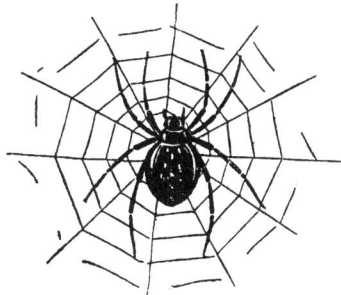

THE KING OF CUNNING AND OF FOLK-LORE.

Index to Parts I. and III.

For Product Safety Concerns and Information please contact our EU
representative GPSR@taylorandfrancis.com
Taylor & Francis Verlag GmbH, Kaufingerstraße 24, 80331 München, Germany

www.ingramcontent.com/pod-product-compliance
Lightning Source LLC
Chambersburg PA
CBHW070614270326
41926CB00011B/1686